THE GLASS INDUSTRY IN SANDWICH
VOLUME 3

First Edition

THE GLASS INDUSTRY IN SANDWICH

VOLUME 3

RAYMOND E. BARLOW
JOAN E. KAISER

PHOTOGRAPHS BY
FORWARD'S COLOR PRODUCTIONS, INC.
LEN LORETTE
HUGO G. POISSON

EDITED BY LLOYD C. NICKERSON

BARLOW-KAISER PUBLISHING COMPANY, INC.

OTHER BOOKS BY RAYMOND E. BARLOW AND JOAN E. KAISER

The Glass Industry in Sandwich Volume 4
A Guide to Sandwich Glass Vases, Colognes and Stoppers
A Guide to Sandwich Glass Witch Balls, Containers and Toys
A Guide to Sandwich Glass Candlesticks, Late Blown and Threaded
Barlow-Kaiser Sandwich Glass Price Guide

FORTHCOMING BOOKS BY RAYMOND E. BARLOW AND JOAN E. KAISER

The Glass Industry in Sandwich Volume 1
The Glass Industry in Sandwich Volume 2
The guides to Volumes 1 and 2 will contain:
    Whale oil and burning fluid lamps, with accessories
    Kerosene lamps and accessories
    Cup plates
    Lacy glass
    Blown molded glass
    Free-blown glass
    Pressed pattern tableware
    Salts
    Household items
    Cut, etched and engraved glass

THE GLASS INDUSTRY IN SANDWICH, Volume 3
First Edition

Copyright © 1987 by Raymond E. Barlow and Joan E. Kaiser

All correspondence and inquiries should be directed to
Barlow–Kaiser Publishing Company, Inc.
P. O. Box 265
Windham, NH 03087

in conjunction with

Schiffer Publishing, Ltd.
1469 Morstein Road
West Chester, Pennsylvania 19380

This book may be purchased from the publisher.

Try your bookstore first.

First Printing

Library of Congress Catalog Number   86-63065
International Standard Book Number   0-88740-081-7

ACKNOWLEDGMENTS

A SPECIAL "THANK YOU" TO

The Bennington Museum, Bennington, Vermont.

The Corning Museum of Glass, Corning, New York.

Ford Archives and Tannahill Research Library, Henry Ford Museum, The Edison Institute, Dearborn, Michigan.

The Rakow Library, The Corning Museum of Glass, Corning, New York.

Sandwich Glass Museum, Sandwich Historical Society, Sandwich, Massachusetts.

The Toledo Museum of Art, Toledo, Ohio.

Town of Sandwich, Massachusetts, Archives and Historical Center.

Edward (Ned) Drew Nickerson, for recording in picture and word the history of the North Sandwich (Bourne) industrial area.

Mildred (Mrs. Edward D.) Nickerson, for preserving the Nickerson papers, for making them accessible to historians, for many happy hours spent with the authors, and for caring.

AND

Bourne Town Archives
Colony House Museum, Keene, New Hampshire
The Historical Society of Western Pennsylvania, Pittsburgh, Pennsylvania
Trayser Memorial Museum, Barnstable, Massachusetts
Ima Adono
Carolyn Alspach
Mr. and Mrs. John Andrews
Grace M. Barlow
Richard Carter Barret
Helena Beal
Richard A. Bourne
Janice Caron
Louis Cataldo
Elizabeth R. Choate
Frances Ciarfella
Fletcher Clark, Attorney at Law
Mary Stetson Clark
Quentin L. Coons
Miriam Vodon Crocker

Elizabeth Cummings
Albert Doolittle
Robert H. Ellis
Mr. and Mrs. Thomas C. Ellis
Mr. and Mrs. William J. Ellis
Marjorie Faulkner
Mrs. Edmond Ford
Austin C. Foster
Mr. and Mrs. William E. Foster
William F. Foster
Mrs. Ralph Freeman
Helen French
Alice Gibbs
Barbara Gill
Elsie Guinta
Benjamin S. Harrison
The Hollander Family
Mrs. Seth Holway
Channing Hoxie
Mrs. Nils R. Johaneson

Carol Foster Jones
Frederick A. Kaiser
Doris Z. Kershaw
Stanley Knight
Dorothy Kraft
Mr. and Mrs. Robert R. Kreykenbohm
Jesse C. Leatherwood
Marie Leonard
Priscilla Lovell
Russell A. Lovell, Jr.
Ernest William Lutz
Walter Gifford Lutz
Mr. and Mrs. William Francis Lutz
Frances MacCaffrey
Mr. and Mrs. Joseph MacCaffrey
Annie Mahon
James Measell
Mr. and Mrs. Robert Mercier
Charles E. Meyer
Mr. and Mrs. Edward B. Meyer
George Michael
Mary Lutz Money
Mrs. John Montgomery
Dierdre Morris
Carol Morrow
Miriam E. Mucha
Barbara Najarian

R. Barbara Nickerson
Mr. and Mrs. Herbert W. Oedel
Mr. and Mrs. William Pelley
Creighton B. Perry
Elizabeth Foster Pierce
Hugo Poisson
Dorothy Pratt
Everard S. Pratt, Jr.
Susan C. Pratt
Harry W. Rapp, Jr.
Judith Rebello
Pamela Russell
Mr. and Mrs. Walter Samaritter
Mary Leonard Shaw
Mr. and Mrs. Robert Slade
Eleanor Spurr
Geoffrey Spurr
Jerome Spurr
Russell Spurr
John J. Stinson
Sylvia Lutz Stringos
Mr. and Mrs. William A. Thompson
Marion Vuilleumier
Mr. and Mrs. Frank Wennerstrom
Mrs. Alan S. Wilhite
Francis (Bill) Wynn

FOREWORD

Richard Carter Barret
Former Director, 1951–1974
The Bennington Museum
Bennington, Vermont

It is a tacit tribute to the important position earned by the Massachusetts town of Sandwich, on Cape Cod, that Ray Barlow and Joan Kaiser entitled this work simply *The Glass Industry in Sandwich*. Indeed, the name *Sandwich* is now more often used as a generic word by glass collectors and dealers, rather than as a geographical location where glass was made by many factories over a period of many years.

Surely it is food for thought to wonder why in every antique show and many antique dealers' shops, one hears the generic use of Sandwich: "Is this a piece of Sandwich?"; "You can always tell it's Sandwich because . . . ". Food for thought, perhaps, but not food for growth of knowledge nor even food for the roots of growth.

The origins of glass have always been shrouded in myth and mystery, fed by misrepresentation and folklore. Facts, fragments and definitive interpretations are scarce, although the more important the production, the more important the published information. In the introduction to her pioneer book, *Sandwich Glass, The History of the Boston and Sandwich Glass Company*, Ruth Webb Lee was well aware of this and laments the existence of the condition in 1939 when her book was first published. She wisely closes her introduction with the happy awareness that the number of research workers and investigators doing serious work is fortunately increasing. Perhaps it was the future team of Barlow-Kaiser that Ruth Webb Lee had in mind.

A brief explanation of why the last volume of the Barlow-Kaiser four-volume set was the first to be published will indicate the basic philosophy and working honesty that typify this work by Mr. Barlow and Mrs. Kaiser. It is to be hoped that people adding this present Volume 3 to their library already own Volume 4, which has been already published. Much of the documentation of some never-before-printed information about the glass industry at Sandwich was discovered by the Barlow-Kaiser team, and involved close relationship with many of the surviving relatives of individuals actually involved, in one way or another, with the glass production. The Barlow-Kaiser team was not accidentally given access to this information,

but actually did an incredible amount of research to locate the family members. They were so successful in obtaining the trust of the descendants that they jointly agreed to do the unheard of favor to people who had become their friends, by deciding to publish the last volume first, so that the many descendants would enjoy seeing the material they supplied incorporated into an actual book. Thus, the last became first, an almost impossible organizational feat.

So now that Volume 3 has been completed, it becomes the natural foundation for all the information contained in Volume 4. Together, these two volumes represent only half of the prodigious amount of research completed by the Barlow-Kaiser team.

The research, which has taken well over a decade, was and is being done as accurately as is humanly possible. No detail was too small to be overlooked, nor too complicated or expensive to verify. This encyclopedic collection of facts and illustrations will indeed become the "Bible of Sandwich Glass".

How often does one encounter the etymological development of meanings of words in a book on glass, or any other group of antiques. How often today do collectors of glass or pottery wonder about such a thing. Barlow and Kaiser wondered about the names of many items made in Sandwich. To illustrate the accuracy used in researching this Volume, Webster's Dictionary, Edition of 1847 was consulted for the then meaning of the common word *vase*, which was described as: "a vessel for domestic use or for use in Temples; as a vase for sacrifice, an urn. An ancient vessel dug out of the ground or from rubbish and kept as a curiosity." However, by 1864 the editors of Webster's added: "especially a vessel of antique or elegant pattern used for ornamental purposes". But ten years later, in the Boston and Sandwich Glass Company's catalogue of 1874, *vases* were used as holders for flowers as well as ornamental pieces designed not to hold flowers, but nowhere was the term *flower holder* used. Furthermore, there is no mention in any glass company's records of the word *vase* to be found with the word *celery*. When an upright container was used to hold celery, it was called either a *celery stand* or simply a *celery*. *Vase*, however, was used as an adjective describing

vii

a type of kerosene lamp; a *vase lamp* having a large glass bowl surrounding a metal container in the base which held a large quantity of kerosene.

Often, in the profession of museum curator, I have been requested to identify pieces of glass and pottery, with emphasis being given to their value (always) and places of origin. I was often forced to say "I don't know" in such a manner as not to make me appear ignorant, but rather possessed of so much knowledge of the subject that positive pin-pointing was impossible. This was especially true about items made of glass. I always attempted, as I still do, to explain that the more knowledge one learns, the more difficult it becomes to be positive about a lot of things. But fortunately, negative information is frequently as important as positive information. To be able to say "I know this did not come from Sandwich (or Bennington, if pottery), is at least a step in the identification process. After a major source is eliminated, the secondary sources may be examined, sometimes with positive success.

This volume is full of cautions; full of "be careful that" and "if this is missing it could have been made at" or even "Don't forget that Mount Washington Glass Company also used wafers on some things". To me, the cautionary comments are as important as any other information.

As far as value is concerned, how about this caution: "The value of covered pieces is in the cover". So, "If you find a cover, buy it, as the lower unit will eventually surface." In the chapter on covered containers there is much to be learned. Covered egg cups were not made anywhere! They were either covered pomade jars, covered salts, covered horseradishes, or if the cover has a cut-out for a spoon, covered mustard jars. Excellent line drawings indicate the differences in the bases, as egg cups were indeed made in quantity, but never with covers. The covers came from other containers, both base and cover usually made in color, as the contents were not especially artistic. All of these items were made in pressed patterns that were popular tableware designs, many of which were being made at many other glass factories including the other two on Cape Cod; i.e., Cape Cod Glass *Works* (1858–1864) and its successor, Cape Cod Glass *Company* (1864–1869).

The source of some of the glass items made in Sandwich cannot be distinguished from similar pieces made elsewhere in the United States and even in England and on the Continent. On the other hand, the source of many items can be directly traced to Sandwich. It was Alexander Pope who wrote "A little learning is a dangerous thing."

Of particular interest is the caution to be familiar with all the patterns and forms used for the base unit of a covered piece. The Sandwich-made covered hen dish bottom unit has a swag design not at all unlike a French piece, and without its cover, looks like an oval dish. The hen top from Sandwich has a hollow tail with the opening underneath the cover, while those from the Pittsburgh area are open at the back of the tail, and perhaps others made elsewhere have this same opening also.

The two Cape Cod Glass factories (CCG *Works* and CCG *Company*) were much larger and had far more important production than historians have previously recorded. In 1860, the Boston and Sandwich Glass Com-

pany was producing 100,000 pounds of finished products each week, with over 500 men and boys employed. With more modern equipment, the Cape Cod Glass Works during the same period was producing 75,000 pounds of finished items with the employment of a maximum of 200 hands, a considerable savings in labor costs. Both factories had been founded by Deming Jarves and both factories were making the same designs in pressed pattern glass.

It is no wonder that it is difficult, and sometimes impossible, to make a positive identification of the origin of a piece of glass. In addition to the same patterns being made by more than one glass factory, many pieces of glass have no pattern, only shape, form, color and quality of workmanship and materials to serve as identification for today's collector. The authors of this volume list statistics compiled at the time which show that in 1822 there were 22 glass factories in the United States; in 1860, 112 glass factories and in 1880 the surprising total of 206 glass factories. Imagine being able to positively identify even one single piece of production from each of 206 factories!

Deming Jarves' influence on the entire glass industry was tremendous, especially at Sandwich. It is impossible to list briefly all the pies in which he had his fingers. By virtue of his skillful manipulation of his various companies, he actually did a great deal of good to the economy of the Town of Sandwich. When the Board of Directors of the Boston and Sandwich Glass Company finally asked for and received his resignation, he promptly organized and built the Cape Cod Glass Works in Sandwich and continued to use his own sources for his needed materials. By searching through local newspapers from all the small surrounding towns, covering decades of details, the Barlow-Kaiser team has put together an almost unprecedented saga of one man's efforts, successes and ultimate failure to obtain his original, personal goals.

The history of this transition period could make a magnificent documentary film of the glass industry in Sandwich. The bibliography of sources, both published and unpublished, is testimony to the exactitude of the authors' attention to devious detail.

As important as is the text portion of this volume, the captions to the extraordinarily clear and comprehensive photographs are equally informative. One often hears variations of the thought that one picture is worth a thousand words. This noteworthy volume of *The Glass Industry in Sandwich* should use the ratio that each picture used is worth one hundred thousand words. Rarely have such clear, well-lighted photographs been used so abundantly with no regard to costs. (There is nothing harder to light than glass, because of its transparency and its hard, shiny surfaces which reflect all light sources located anywhere.) The photographs obviously took much time to obtain, as the credits for them indicate many pieces used are from institutional as well as private collections. There are over 400 colored plates plus numerous black and white photographs and line drawings. The color has a fidelity that is rarely seen in volumes offered to the public.

In producing a publication of this magnitude, it is impossible to please everyone. There has been no truly definitive work previously published on all the myriad facets of the glass industry in Sandwich. As was explained in Volume 4, both of the authors' own personal collections were obliged to be considerably diminished because they then contained pieces of good glass which were not produced at Sandwich, the authenticity of which resulted from their own research findings, including fragments they dug up at factory sites. I am certain that Volume 3 will upset a number of collections and collectors, because of the facts that the Barlow-Kaiser team has therein published for the first time. My wife and I experienced this unhappy loss of pieces of Bennington pottery in our own collection when I did extensive research for my books on that subject.

Many large and complicated problems are considered to be "a can of worms" nobody wants to be responsible to open. And some problems are often referred to as being "the tip of the iceberg" because of the much larger problem underlying the smaller, visible tip.

Ray Barlow and Joan Kaiser, in their monumental work *The Glass Industry in Sandwich* have uncovered the iceberg for us to study. Thoroughly researched, documented and arranged, the text, the photographs and the line draw-

ings are actually more like a museum exhibition within the covers of a book. I was fascinated with the information on each page, both the familiar and much that was new to me. I marvel at how the Barlow-Kaiser team (or any two people) could have gathered together such detailed material from so many obscure and heretofore unknown sources. Not only is this book an obvious labor of love, but also one of great dedication requiring much acumen and both physical and mental activity and stamina.

It has been difficult to write an adequate foreword to this book. It is a volume which needs to be owned, read, reread, studied and restudied. Each volume in the four-volume set surely will become the definitive work in its field. The four volumes will surely become the foundation for any library on American glass, regardless of town or state of origin. All of us should appreciate especially that Raymond Barlow and Joan Kaiser have the determination that nothing will stop them from finishing this uncommonly great work. We should appreciate also the many sacrifices they have already made to share their knowledge with us all.

Richard Carter Barret
Bennington, Vermont

CONTENTS

INTRODUCTION TO VOLUME 3

For hundreds of years, man has made some of his utensils from sand. He learned that heat changed the sand into liquid, which could be shaped, allowed to cool, and retain its form forever. There was no usable glass sand in Sandwich, Massachusetts, nor were there men interested in the shaping of their utensils from sand. Yet the glass industry became an intricate part of the everyday lives of everyone who lived there. In the early 1820's, a man named Deming Jarves walked among them, quietly bought up their coastline and forests, and drastically changed their lives. Jarves was a skilled businessman from Boston who was possessed by a dream — a glass factory built to his standards that would financially enrich the Jarves family for generations.

In the spring of 1825, he built an eight-pot furnace out on the marsh and called it the Sandwich Glass Manufactory. Sand was brought in from considerable distance, and, almost before the people of Sandwich became aware, magnificent glass was being made, glass that would soon establish the small town as a leader in the art.

In the beginning, skilled workers were brought in from other glass factories. These artisans soon taught the young men of Sandwich how to become masters in the making of glass.

Jarves reorganized his company after one year. He had found a market for his product but was financially limited. Bostonians who knew of his great skill and relentless drive quite willingly provided financial backing. This allowed the company, now incorporated as the Boston and Sandwich Glass Company, to grow at a rapid rate and compete with the best glass that the industry had to offer. Jarves functioned as the company's agent, as he had done formerly during his years with the New England Glass Company.

The labor force was diverse in its skills. Some came from the agricultural communities that surrounded the factory, many from other towns and other countries. Many were housed in a factory village that was quickly becoming known for its tall smoking chimneys. The Industrial Revolution had come to Sandwich.

Soon after manufacturing began, improved methods of pressing glass were developed and productivity increased substantially. The Boston and Sandwich Glass Company became the leader in the pressed glass segment of the industry. For the first time, European glass houses took their lead from a glass house in the United States. Through the 1830's, the Sandwich factory pressed great quantities of Lacy glass, improved their formulas, and increased their variety of colors. They led the country in the development of products made of glass that had formerly been made of pewter, tin, and wood.

By 1840, the company employed three hundred workers and had control of over ninety buildings, many of them apartment houses where employees and their families lived. The area had become so large that it was a town within a town, and soon became known as Jarvesville.

In 1845, a vein of sand was discovered in the town of Cheshire, in the western part of Massachusetts. The Boston and Sandwich Glass Company began to use this sand, which greatly improved the quality of its glass. By 1849, it became necessary to double the capacity of the company. The factory yard soon covered seven acres of land. Five hundred hands were employed, and 100,000 pounds of glass was being shipped weekly to countries in both hemispheres. Four furnaces were in operation by 1851.

Although sales agents had been employed by the company in various cities since the earliest days of production, larger salesrooms became an intrinsic part of the business. The agents who manned these showrooms took orders that were transferred back to the factory to be filled. So successful was this method of selling that very seldom in the history of the company was it necessary to have traveling salesmen.

Wherever Agent Deming Jarves saw a need, he stepped in and took command. When the company needed brick, he purchased a brickyard. When it needed lumber, he purchased a sawmill. When it needed molds, he owned a foundry. When it needed space in Boston, he built the buildings. Jarves was a born leader. Ironically it would be this same quality that would eventually end his tenure as agent of the Boston and Sandwich Glass Company.

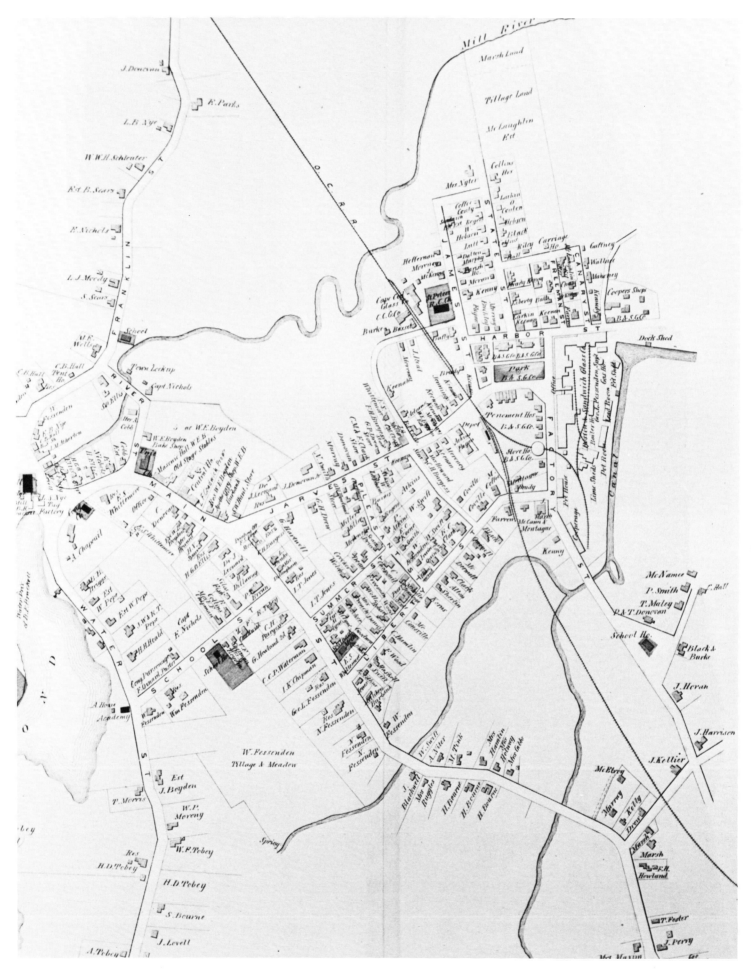

Property map of Sandwich in 1880. The Town of Sandwich underwent major street changes during Deming Jarves' years of influence. After his death in 1869, the Town stabilized and little change took place until 1935, when the Bourne and Sagamore bridges were completed across the Cape Cod Canal.

CHAPTER 1

BOSTON AND SANDWICH GLASS COMPANY

1858–1882

THE TRANSITION PERIOD
1858–1859

The spring of 1858 came to Sandwich with Deming Jarves, the company's founder, deeply embroiled in controversy with the Board of Directors. The controversy was not the result of production problems, nor did it involve employee discontent, which might be expected during a period of economic depression. Strangely, it dealt with the company store at 51 Federal Street in Boston.

Deming Jarves had built two buildings in Boston, one at 45 and one at 51 Federal Street. One of the buildings was occupied jointly by the Boston and Sandwich Glass Company and G. D. Jarves and Cormerais, which was a separate and independent retail store set up by Deming Jarves and his partner, Henry Cormerais (see Appendix). The Jarves and Cormerais store sold imported as well as domestic glass, table cutlery and plated ware.[1] From time to time this joint venture had caused problems in Jarves' relationship with the Boston and Sandwich Glass Company. As owner of the retail store, Jarves bought domestic glass from his own Mount Washington Glass Works in South Boston to be resold in the store he owned jointly with Cormerais. At the same time, he was the agent in charge of receiving orders and selling glass for the Boston and Sandwich Glass Company, glass which was produced on order at the factory in Sandwich. Under these circumstances, it is understandable how a lucrative glass order intended for the Boston and Sandwich Glass Company could have been "inadvertently" sent to the Mount Washington Glass Works.

According to the glass company records now at the Tannahill Research Library at the Henry Ford Museum, Boston and Sandwich Glass Company Director Richard S. Fay, during the first week in June 1858, openly accused Jarves of misdirecting orders yearly in the amount of $50,000 since 1854. He also accused Henry Cormerais as being as deeply involved as Jarves. At a meeting of the Board of Directors on June 9, 1858, a letter was read from Cormerais stating that he took exception to the accusation of being involved in any such improprieties. He also asked the Board to discuss his reputation with Nathaniel Francis,

one of the Directors. "He has known me from infancy. I am unwilling that he should believe that I have lived by fraud rather than by the sweat of my brow."

The letter from Cormerais lacked any specific denials of the accusation, and Jarves was also unwilling to give any. Relying on a maneuver that he had used on other occasions when he felt threatened, he placed his letter of resignation before the Board of Directors on June 9, 1858, giving them the opportunity to accept it if they felt any wrongdoing had taken place. By the end of the day, the Board had unanimously voted to accept his resignation. They immediately called for a committee to meet with attorneys to arrange for the separation of the Boston and Sandwich Glass Company from G. D. Jarves and Cormerais. The Boston and Sandwich Glass Company was to move out of the building at 51 Federal Street and establish a suitable store elsewhere in Boston.

This incident was only one of the many examples of poor management practices which ultimately led to the failure of the Boston and Sandwich Glass Company. It took *four years* for the Board of Directors to discover that $50,000 worth of orders had been "skimmed" from the company each year during the past four. And the fact that Deming Jarves was able to blatantly use the Boston and Sandwich Glass Company to further his personal ambitions stands as one of the most corrosive examples of the failure of the Board to function as a governing body.

The newspapers of Boston and Cape Cod notified the glass world that the company had accepted Jarves' resignation as factory and sales agent, a most important position in the company which he had held for thirty-two years. Following his father's action, John W. Jarves submitted his letter of resignation as head of the laboratory, a position he had held since early 1854. John stated that he would be willing to terminate his services on July 1, 1858. The Board considered this letter at their June 21 meeting, and accepted it. Thus began a major shake-up in both company policy and personnel, repercussions of which were felt at every level. Also as a result of the June 21 meeting, John's father-in-law, Paymaster Charles C. P. Waterman, was dismissed.

Boston and Sandwich Glass Company factory as illustrated on stationery used in the 1850's. The fenced area in the foreground is St. John's Park. The horses are traveling along Factory Street. The roof of the round railroad engine house is visible on the right. The factory buildings are accurately illustrated.

The ousting of both Jarves and Waterman generated strong feelings in the area. Although there had been times when the town of Sandwich resented Jarves' power and Jarves' money, the suddenly insecure townspeople rallied to support him and denounced the governing body that failed to appreciate his efforts. Almost one year later, the editor of the *Barnstable Patriot*, who had been Jarves' friend since the advent of the horse railroad, wrote about the facts and opinions that were prevalent during the summer of 1858.

Having heard, at times, some slight innuendoes respecting the dismissal of this tried servant (Waterman) of the Boston and Sandwich Glass Company, we take pleasure, in this connection, to do him the justice to publish some facts. Mr. Waterman had been, as we have said, in the service of the company from the start. In June 1858 a new order of things was commenced, but on the 11th of June, Mr. Waterman received a copy of a vote of the Company "that all the present employees of the Company be notified and requested to continue their present duties under the direction of the President and Treasurer." The President added — "In the meantime (the Board of Directors) is in hopes that you will continue your efforts to serve the company with fidelity and energy." Thus assured, Mr. Waterman kept on his station. Before the end of the month, however, he received notice of the following vote, in a communication dated June 29: "Voted that the duties now performed by Mr. Waterman be transferred to one of the clerks now in the Counting Room, under the direction of the Superintendent, and that the services of Mr. Waterman be dispensed with on and after July 1." Thirty-two years is thus dismissed *with one day's notice.* The clerk of the Company, in communicating this vote adds — "the following extract is from the report of the Committee who recommended the change which makes your discharge necessary. Speaking of the duties performed by you the report says: 'All monies pass through his hands, and he pays out all. He has been in the employ of the Company from the beginning. His payrolls are without errors, and his character for honesty and integrity is without a stain.'

It gives me great satisfaction," the clerk continues, "to be the medium of communicating to you a testimonial so highly honorable to yourself, and which, permit me to add, I think so well deserved."

And here let us say, that the County of Barnstable, and especially the town of Sandwich, owes a debt of gratitude to Mr. Jarves that can never be repaid. How much he has done to give employment to laborers and mechanics, how much money he has disbursed in our County, how much he has added to its taxable property, in times past, it would be hard to calculate. And now he has done another noble work in erecting this new manufactory and opening a new field of labor, a new source of employment. The few malignant enemies of Mr. Jarves will live to see the truth of what we here state, and live to regret their unjust and ungrateful course of action towards him. How he carried the Boston and Sandwich through the panic of 1857–8 few of those who benefited by his sacrifices will ever know. How he sustained the credit of the company and upheld the integrity of its stock, and at what loss he did it, they may not exactly see, but in time to come, even now, the property saved, their credit protected, their stock upheld in fact, in its intrinsic worth, though cried down in its market sale by interested managers, will fully prove on whose broad shoulders they reclined in the storm. The fact that Mr. Jarves advanced in cash to the company more than $73,000 in the great panic of 1857–8 and kept a cash balance at his bank, averaging $20,000 for over three months of the hardest times, daily subject to his check, and he not the treasurer of the company, indicates that kind of assistance he afforded. Mr. Jarves is yet a stockholder of about five hundred shares of the Boston and Sandwich Glass Company, which shows that his interests are still largely involved in the success of that corporation.

At that point in time, the Board of Directors had no idea that the dismissal of Deming Jarves would bring a level of chaos to the company that would test the skills of the finest businessmen of Boston. They immediately learned that Jarves intended to build a second glass factory in Sandwich and become an active competitor. His son,

John W. Jarves, took steps to become a partner in the new glass works. Key employees who were loyal to Jarves and were skilled in management and glassmaking resigned or were released from their duties at the Boston and Sandwich Glass Company. A feud with the Cape Cod Railroad Company over the lack of freight cars when needed, the overpricing of tonnage, and the railroad's practice of shipping raw materials in the same car with pigs had begun in the early 1850's. This continuing argument had not been settled at the time of Jarves' resignation.

But these were minor compared to the tremendous problems the Board had to face as it attempted to release the firm hold that Deming Jarves had on the Boston and Sandwich Glass Company.

His influence extended far beyond the management of the Federal Street office. As agent, Jarves was responsible for the purchase of all the raw materials needed for making glass. He was the only contact the supply companies ever had with the company. On many occasions, Deming Jarves' private funds were used to bolster the company during cash shortages.

Within the week, Treasurer Samuel R. M. Holbrook was authorized to buy supplies, such as coal and any other raw materials the factory required. It was necessary to set aside $75,000 for this purpose, above the cost of payroll. The constant supply of lumber coming into the factory yard from Jarves' sawmills had to be stopped. Bricks, used for repair at the factory, had been made at the Sandwich brickyard owned previously by Deming and now by John Jarves. It was also necessary to find a new source for the making of molds and other castings. Some molds had been supplied by a Boston mold maker, whose office was located at 51 Federal Street. Other molds had been cast at the North Sandwich foundry owned by Deming (see Chapter 7 in this book). A fire in 1857 had seriously curtailed its production, and the time was surely propitious to transfer the company's account to another foundry.

The transition period was an extremely difficult one. The anxiety of the Board was further intensified when it learned that Jarves owned many of the houses and tenements that had been thought to be factory owned. The rent on these houses had been collected by withholding money from the workers' pay. A request by Jarves to have this procedure continued created an uproar within the Board when it realized that the ownership of all factory-related properties would have to be studied.

Jarves had acquired dictatorial power over almost every aspect of the business.

- He had used his own money at will for company expenditures.
- He had done all the hiring and firing.

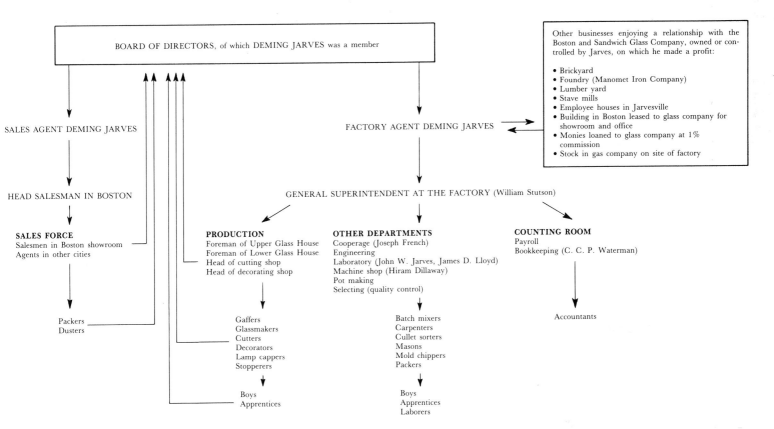

Although employees at every level reported to their immediate superiors, everyone answered to Deming Jarves. An unpopular decision made by a department head resulted in a worker taking the unresolved problem to Jarves. This weakened the authority of department heads. Even the lowliest laborer had the right to communicate by letter to the Board of Directors, of which Jarves was a member. On February 25, 1854, the Board agreed to notify employees that no one could employ or dismiss another employee or make any purchases or any contracts for the company without instructions from Jarves. This gave Jarves absolute control over the purchase of everything needed at the factory, so most purchases were handled in a way that gave Jarves a personal profit.

- Over the years, he had controlled the sale of glass by buying Boston and Sandwich Glass Company products privately at a discount and selling them through G. D. Jarves and Cormerais.
- He decided which of the orders that came into 51 Federal Street were to be forwarded to the Boston and Sandwich Glass Company . . . and which ones were to be forwarded to his other glass factories.
- He controlled subsidiary industries that supplied the Boston and Sandwich Glass Company with materials that had nothing to do directly with the making of glass, such as bricks, lumber, barrels and nails.

In today's business world it is highly unlikely that such control by one man would ever be tolerated. Available records reveal, however, that the Board of Directors simply lacked interest in the running of the factory and allowed Jarves, by default, to usurp the powers traditionally assumed by a Board.

About this time also—to compound the problems—the license for the company-owned steamer *Acorn* expired. This was the ship used by the company to transport glass to Boston. The propeller-driven vessel had first been registered in the name of Samuel H. Fessenden for the Boston and Sandwich Glass Company in 1854. Several days later, the registration was transferred to Deming Jarves, acting as agent for the company. Now it became necessary for Board member Richard S. Fay to place his name on the registration. In the process, the whole issue of transportation of supplies and glassware had to be examined closely. On August 30, 1858, the transportation committee came to terms with the railroad, and reasonable rates were established to transport raw materials into and the finished products out of the factory yard.

As if such crises were not enough, the normal changes that take place within a business had to be attended to. H. H. Thayer, owner of a planing mill and lumber yard on the Jarves property that was to become the site of the Cape Cod Glass Works, sold his business to the firm of Howland, Hatch and Company. A new contract for barrel staves and headers had to be negotiated, and was awarded to G. W. L. Hatch of that company.

For some years the Boston and Sandwich Glass Company had laid gas pipes in the streets to supply certain houses and stores with illuminating gas that exceeded the amount used at the factory. Those who held high positions within the company did not pay for this service. John Jarves was one of those people because several rooms in his house on Jarves Street were used by the company for private meetings. John was notified by the superintendent that he was expected to pay for the gas he had already consumed and would be expected to pay for the service if he wanted to be continually supplied in the future.

One can almost feel the shock experienced by the Board of Directors when they realized that Jarves had extended his authority to a point where he could spend company funds, or invest his own money and then take it back out. He could build Jarvesville houses, put the deeds in his own name, but have his rents collected through the Boston and Sandwich Glass Company counting room. He could own other businesses and monopolize orders so that no com-

petitive bidding took place. He was able to build a gas company on glass factory property and monopolize the stock.

So when the Board realized the position that they had allowed themselves to be put into, they over-reacted. It took them a year to come to grips with their problems. So paranoid were Board members by this time that they took the authority that had been held by Jarves and fragmented this authority into more than a dozen positions, with no one person powerful enough to bring about a smoothly-running facility.

On June 29 Theodore Kern was made production head of the factory, with an annual salary of $1,200. Until this time, he had been a gaffer—the head of a shop. He was directed to order quality raw materials for the production of glass. William Stutson, Deming Jarves' brother-in-law, in addition to his duties as general superintendent, was made superintendent of the pot room, lead room, sand room, ashery, and was put in charge of receiving coal. Henry Vose Spurr (see Chapter 2, Volume 4) was to head the selecting department at the lower glass house, also known as the X house. Francis Kern was to head the cut-

Theodore Kern, promoted to production head of the factory.

ting room, puntying room, and "the room occupied by females". George Lafayette Fessenden's salary was increased $100 as compensation for being put in charge of the payroll and two clerks in the counting room. Responsibility in the counting room would be shared equally by Fessenden and Charles Southack. Charles Chapouil was to be head of packing and head of selecting at the upper glass house. These changes were deliberately implemented so that never again would a single individual become so powerful that his leaving could jeopardize the very foundation of the company.

It took several months to bring about all such changes. The most important position, which had been held by Jarves, was agent of the company. It was one of the last positions to be filled. Early in August, according to the *Sandwich Advocate and Nautical Intelligencer*, Sewall Henry Fessenden, brother of George L. Fessenden, was appointed to fill this critical job.

Sewall Henry Fessenden was born in Sandwich on June 30, 1821. His parents were Sewall Fessenden and Hannah Morse Smith of Boston, who moved to Sandwich shortly after their marriage on October 23, 1814. Sewall Henry

began working at the factory when he was thirteen years old. He eventually transferred to the Boston office and worked his way up to head salesman under Jarves. His background of twenty-four years in both manufacturing and sales made him an excellent replacement for Jarves. However, unlike Jarves, his power would be limited. He was to be in charge of all sales, and act as the emissary between the Directors in Boston and the works at Sandwich.

Despite internal strife, the Boston and Sandwich Glass Company strove to maintain a strong public image. An article in the *Barnstable Patriot* of July 20, 1858, described their cut glass as "truly artistic". They reported that Joseph Marsh could supply all kinds of glass from the factory to anyone on the Cape who wished to employ him as their agent.

The company had gone through a long, devastating period during which trade had been dull and demand for glass weak. Not since 1844 had the market dropped so drastically. But it weathered the financial panic of 1857, and, by the fall of 1858, orders began to arrive. The stockholders made the decision to reduce the capital stock from

William Stutson, Deming Jarves' brother-in-law.

Charles H. Chapouil, appointed head of packing, and head of selecting at the Upper Glass House. He eventually became head bookkeeper. *Courtesy, Sandwich Glass Museum, Sandwich Historical Society*

$500,000 to $400,000, thus wiping out $100,000 of debts and enabling the company to begin paying a dividend as the market strengthened.

The workers slowly returned to their jobs as orders began to arrive. The *Barnstable Patriot* of October 12, 1858, said that one hundred pages of orders had been received for kerosene lamps of different sizes and styles, and it would be necessary to return to full production to fill the orders. Meanwhile, another change was made as Hiram Dillaway was directed to head the machine shop and to have complete charge of the engine room.

Christmas orders came into the Boston office, still at 51 Federal Street, in sufficient quantity to guarantee that the glass works would be operating at capacity through the end of the year.

One should keep in mind that the factory had been in almost continual operation since its inception in 1825. All of the equipment used in the production of glass had begun to show its age. The boilers alone had been in service for twenty years or more. Three new ones were ordered after an explosion on January 6, 1859, caused the death of fireman John Kennedy. Isaac K. Chipman, the coroner, placed in his report that Kennedy's death was caused by defective materials in the twenty-five foot long boiler, resulting in a crack in the metal. Better judgment, he reasoned, should have been used. A later inquiry showed that a sample of water, taken from well No. 3 under the old cutting shop and used to fill the boilers, was contaminated with salt water. Salt water, when exposed to extreme heat, can cause deterioration of metal, resulting in the accident. The well was pumped out and sealed, and steps were taken to assure that it could not happen again.

It must have seemed to the Board of Directors that there was no way to rid themselves completely of their founder! In January 1859, they still had not settled the argument over the store at Federal Street. A final decision from Jarves to the company agreed that they could vacate the store at their convenience if they left the furniture and fixtures. So the Boston and Sandwich Glass Company was one step closer to breaking their lease with G. D. Jarves and Cormerais.

But the Jarves name continued to haunt them. Records show that on February 10, an argument raged over who owned the stock in the gas company. Jarves had made it out in his own name and, when he was approached to transfer it to the glass company, he refused until he consulted with his attorney. For the next ten days the Board tried unsuccessfully to sort out the facts. Minutes of their meetings reveal that they were more than a little upset over this newest dilemma, as well as the continuing controversy over ownership of some Jarvesville houses. For example, William Smith, the gilder, purchased one of these houses, but it was not clear to whom he owed the money.

In February the Massachusetts Legislature honored the Board's request for the reduction of capital stock, which would remain at $400,000 until 1878.

But it was not yet over. The final blow came when the company's New York inventory was sold at an unauthorized auction. No one then in charge or on the Board had apparently approved of the sale.

A lengthy Board meeting was held on March 15, 1859, during which future policies of the company were discussed at length. A new direction was beginning to emerge. The Jarves method of doing business no longer prevailed. Unpaid consignments of glass were not to be sent to distant cities and foreign ports. Instead, elegant showrooms for the Boston and Sandwich Glass Company were being readied by agents Jacob J. Nichols in New York City and R. A. Swain in San Francisco. In Boston, a suitable building was finally located at 26 Federal Street where greatly expanded displays were installed. Key personnel such as bookkeepers, sales agents, and salesmen, were given sizable salary increases along with increased responsibility.

The steamer *Acorn* was offered for sale. It was thought that she would have to be sent to New York for this purpose, but in April she was purchased by a group of men for $12,500, to be placed on a route between Boston and Provincetown, Massachusetts. Repaired by the new owners and reregistered in Provincetown, she began a new life as the largest vessel ever used by Provincetown's travelling public.

In the meantime, Deming Jarves and his son John were well into their Cape Cod Glass Works construction program. It seems incredible, but research reveals that at no time in any of the meetings of the Board of Directors was the coming of a second glass works to Sandwich mentioned, even though it was announced in the *Barnstable Patriot* of May 24 that Reverend Joseph Marsh was to be Jarves' superintendent.

The weakness of the Board of Directors once again is shown in the minutes of their meetings. Deming and John Jarves were ready to open a brand new factory in Sandwich, right in the center of Jarvesville! There was no doubt that Jarves would attempt to hire away the most skilled help employed by the Boston and Sandwich Glass Company. As a consequence, shop groups that had learned to work together would be broken up. Supervisory personnel would resign. Pattern makers and machinists would have to be replaced, as well as laboratory workers to fill the void left by chemists James Lloyd and John Jarves. Critical to the labor force of any glass factory were the young boys who served as apprentices, already in limited supply in a town the size of Sandwich. Yet no attempt was made to prepare for these losses! It would seem that a governing body interested in the growth and prosperity of its company would have spent many hours in conference finding ways to minimize the effect of Deming Jarves' new Cape Cod Glass Works. Strangely, there is no evidence that such an effort was ever made.

Upon completing its separation from Jarves by determining at Barnstable County Registry of Deeds the ownership of several properties, the Boston and Sandwich Glass Company no longer existed in the shadow of Deming Jarves. It had taken a full year to find its new direction—changing sales methods to reach more of the retail trade, broadening authority over a larger number of management personnel and defining their purpose. With the coming of a new working season in the fall of 1859, the company was ready to test its new approach.

THE YEARS OF MAXIMUM PRODUCTION 1859–1866

The company's new policies and attitude paid off. The fall of 1859 saw large orders roll in, making it imperative that all four furnaces be in good working order. They were repaired and modernized to the extent possible. The *Yarmouth Register* of September 23, 1859, reported that every workman was busily employed and the prospects for steady work at good wages would continue as a matter of company policy.

In October, it was found that General Agent Sewall Fessenden had been selling glass privately. The agent was understandably told forcefully that this practice could not continue. The company had experienced enough of this when Jarves had been at the helm, so no employee would be allowed to deal in glass outside the company.

January 1860 saw a slightly slower work schedule, with the factory operating three furnaces. But the business was turning a good profit and employed about five hundred men, boys, and girls. Its reputation for quality spread world-wide, and its new and expanded showrooms and enlarged sales force were paying off handsomely.

On February 27, 1860, the Board took up the question of an increase in salary for Hiram Dillaway, who asked to be assured of $1000 a year. Dillaway's request was denied, as were requests over the next several months by William Stutson, Francis Kern and San Francisco agent R. A. Swain. Swain had his credit line increased to $10,000, and an additional $8000 in credit was allowed for goods in transit. The San Francisco area was developing rapidly, and the glass company turned a profit from this growth. The records show that the Board of Directors in power after Jarves left, although weak in some areas, used extremely good judgment in the way they handled the production facility and the men in their employ. They held the company together until the financial panic of 1857 had run its course, then dramatically set the company in motion to stimulate its growth as world conditions improved. On March 27, 1860, the Boston and Sandwich Glass Company announced to its stockholders that it planned to pay two dividends: 5 percent on April 1 and another 5 percent in October.

On April 30, the Board authorized Agent Sewall Fessenden to paint and put in order all the company's tenant houses in Sandwich. The townspeople said that Jarvesville now had a bright and cheerful look.

On May 28, 1860, the company took legal action against Bernard Eger and Company of Paris. They showed overdue accounts of $3670.20. Power of Attorney was given to one John Monroe of Paris to collect. Although this may seem trivial, it is important because it proves that the company truly had world-wide business affiliations. Way bills to India showed large orders, and Frosted Madonna time lamps were sent to Brazil. Glass from Sandwich took many long journeys to world markets.

Through the summer the factory had been running two of its four ten-pot furnaces. On August 27, the agent was authorized to start a third. If orders continued at the present rate, it was anticipated that the factory would be at full production by Fall. On October 9, the *Barnstable Patriot* informed Cape Cod readers that the Boston and Sandwich Glass Company was manufacturing lamp plinths, a new and beautiful article. "The demand for them has given an impetus to glass manufacture." *Plinths* were lamp bases made of glass which were attached to glass fonts by the use of a brass connector, rather than by use of the glass wafer. This new style in lamp design was introduced along with kerosene as fuel. Kerosene required differently shaped and eventually larger fonts, as well as burners specifically designed for kerosene.

So 1860 saw an increased market for lamps that benefitted both Deming Jarves' new Cape Cod Glass Works and the old Boston and Sandwich Glass Company. Each had as many order as it could handle and had difficulty finding enough hoops, staves, and headings to make casks in which to ship the glass. The Boston and Sandwich Glass Company agent was ordered to procure them wherever he found the price to be favorable.

With the security of brisk business and the promise of good times ahead, Agent Sewall Fessenden was ready to marry and start a family. On October 10, 1860, at the age of thirty-nine, he married Louisa Green Bursley.

The year ended with all hands working steadily. The town of Sandwich had much to be grateful for as 1861 was ushered in. Business continued to be brisk and prosperity brought an understandable happiness to the people at Sandwich. The town grew rapidly, and became the manufacturing and trade center of the Cape. New businesses and stores went up on Main Street. Houses were converted to businesses. But no one in his wildest imagination could predict that 1861 would bring disaster.

The rumblings of Civil War were noted in the local newspapers and in the political rhetoric of the time. But even if war should come, it was a general belief that it would have little or no effect on isolated Sandwich. Southern forces fired on Fort Sumter, South Carolina, on April 12, 1861, plummeting the nation into all-out war. Certainly no one connected with the glass company had any idea that the result would be chaos for the industry. As President Abraham Lincoln called for 75,000 volunteers to join the Union Army, the Boston and Sandwich Glass Company was making plans to construct a new leer. Glassworkers volunteered for the Union cause and the Sandwich Guards were formed.

Formal organization of the Sandwich Guards took place on the evening of May 6, at the Town Hall. Officially, they were Company "D" of the Third Regiment of Infantry, Second Brigade, First Division of the Massachusetts Volunteer Militia. They were enrolled for an initial period of three months, under the command of Captain, later to become Major, Charles Chipman. Many glass company employees were listed in the muster roll of Company "D"—Charles Brady was First Lieutenant, Henry A. Kern was Second Lieutenant, decorator Alfred E. Smith was Third Lieutenant, and Edward A. Brady, James Cox, Christopher B. Dalton, Timothy G. Dean, Warren P. Dean, George Dennis, and John McLaney were among the volunteers. They were escorted to the depot by the Sandwich Cornet Band, and, according to the *Barnstable Patriot*, were provided with a sumptuous dinner in Boston

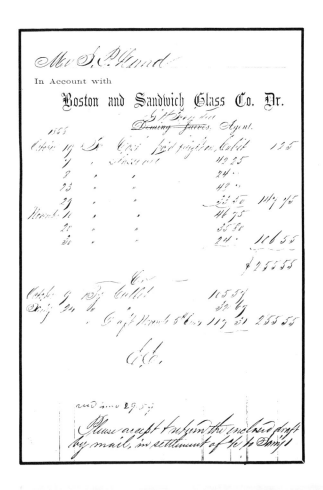

J. P. Lund was a glass retailer located in North Fairhaven, Massachusetts. This is a statement of his account with the Boston and Sandwich Glass Company from October 1858, to January 24, 1859. On October 9, Lund was credited $105.54 for cullet he sold to the glass company. He was credited $32.67 for cullet on January 24. The company paid three cents a pound for cullet.

Boston and Sandwich Glass Company draft issued to Lund on November 5, 1858, and referred to in the statement of his account. It is signed by Sewall H. Fessenden.

Invoice dated July 30, 1859, for twenty dozen lamps purchased by J. P. Lund, now from New Bedford, Massachusetts.

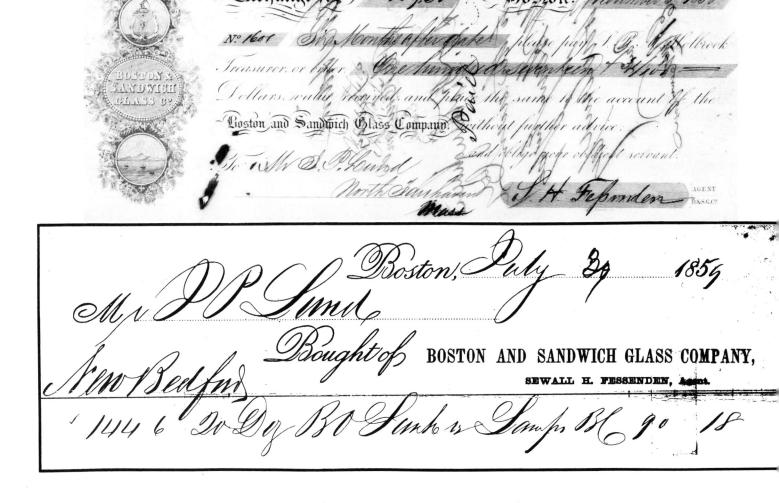

by glass company agent Sewall H. Fessenden before they left for Fort Monroe.

As these men stepped out of their positions around the furnaces, and cutting rooms, and left skilled positions in machine shops and blacksmith shops, the Boston and Sandwich Glass Company found itself unable to function. This was true at the Cape Cod works as well. The loss of one skilled hand in a shop group severely interfered with the overall production of that group, dropping their daily output drastically. One furnace was closed out, and remaining employees were combined into new work teams. The efficiency of the new groups was greatly reduced compared to that of the old groups whose members had learned to work effectively together. As the skill of a new team improved, only to have another member leave for war, the productivity of the group was again critically diminished.

By June 24, 1861, seventy-three days after the firing on Fort Sumter, the Boston and Sandwich Glass Company found itself with only one of its four furnaces functioning. Production from that furnace was running well below a profitable level. A 10 percent reduction in wages was called for starting July 1. Affected were key management people such as Agent Sewall Fessenden, bookkeeper Elisha James, salesmen Henry F. Spurr, Charles W. Spurr and E. McQuestion, treasurer S. R. M. Holbrook, paymaster George L. Fessenden, superintendent William Stutson and the heads of the various departments at the factory. This was not because orders were not readily available, but because of the war effort's depletion of manpower. As the three months enrollment of the Sandwich Guards expired and all Massachusetts companies were reorganized into battalions, it became clear that the Civil War would last for some time.

Although production was low, management worked diligently to improve the factory in other ways. The new leer was constructed, fifty-eight feet long and wide enough so that dollies with pans thirty-two inches wide could be moved along iron rails. This wider leer provided for a larger amount of glass to be annealed at a more efficient rate. The old leer was repaired, the hay storage room was enlarged and made fireproof, and other masonry work was attended to.

It took almost a year for the older men to train new hands to take the places of the younger workers who had been lost to the war effort. Gradually the skill of the shops improved, an additional furnace was put into operation, and the men who had been working only part time during the winter of 1861–1862 had all they could do to keep up with the large orders coming in. One order alone from Buenos Aires totaled $19,000. On June 30, 1862, it was voted by the Board of Directors to authorize the agent to start up the third furnace whenever he thought he had enough skilled men to operate it.

The town was also beginning to feel the effect of the war as it realized that some of its sons would not return. A letter dated June 28, 1862, from Charles Gibbs of Sandwich, on board the steam frigate *Richmond*, was printed in the *Barnstable Patriot*.

I have also to report the death of Thomas Flaherty, formerly an operative in Boston and Sandwich Glass Works. He had both legs and part of one hand shot off and died in about an hour. He was knocked down by a shell while bravely fighting at his gun and died like a hero, without a murmur.

By October, the factory had regained the momentum it had on the day the war began, and, on October 27, the Board restored the salaries that had been reduced in June 1861. Sales were favorable as the year ended with three furnaces running.

By the second anniversary of the war's beginning, the company had returned to full production. Orders coming in to the Boston and Sandwich Glass Company and the Cape Cod Glass Works, mostly for lamps, were far in excess of their ability to produce. Skilled hands were even more scarce, because in July of 1863 the draft took away many more talented glassmakers. Among them were William E. Kern, Michael Buckley, John Swansey, and glass cutter George F. Lapham. The factory agent constantly reminded the Board that salaries of key personnel would have to be increased, or the good help that was left would be lost to the competition. After Agent Sewall Fessenden notified the Board in October 1863, that salaries should also be increased for Boston personnel, the Board granted a raise to Henry F. Spurr, whose pay would now be $1800 yearly. Charles W. Lapham, who had gathered the first piece of glass in 1825, received a $100 increase. The *Barnstable Patriot* jubilantly reported that the community as a whole had not experienced more prosperous times for many years. The two glass factories together employed about eight hundred hands, and needed more.

By January 25, 1864, business had been so good that bonuses were awarded to the Fessenden brothers and to bookkeeper Elisha James, salesman Henry F. Spurr, and head-of-the-factory Theodore Kern. As the high level of trade continued, the company expanded its housing facilities by purchasing several houses and erecting a block of six tenement houses. The brick engine roundhouse, no longer used by the railroad since the line was extended beyond Sandwich, was purchased to be used as a storage facility. Originally offered to the Boston and Sandwich Glass Company in 1859 for $4000, after much negotiation this local landmark was sold for $1800.

During this period, dividends to stockholders were also generous. A 15 percent dividend was paid in 1863, and dividends totalling 13 percent were paid in 1864. By November 28, 1864, Christmas orders were completed, and the agent reported that he was in the process of putting out one of the furnaces. This was the first sign of a slackening workload.

With much of the skilled labor still off to war, it became necessary to simplify the handwork required to finish each piece. Most of the glass at this time was pressed, allowing the company to put out large quantities of glassware with minimum worker skill. Existing tools and machinery were improved and refined, and new machinery was invented that took the place of experienced hand labor.

In 1864, an important milestone occurred at the glass works of Hobbs, Brockunier and Company, in Wheeling, West Virginia. William Leighton, Sr. of that company was successful in perfecting a formula for lime glass, which could be pressed into the same patterns as the more expensive glass made with lead. It would be *nine years* before the Boston and Sandwich Glass Company was forced to admit that, in order to again compete in the pressed pattern tableware market, which had been ignored in their concentration on lamp production, they would have to use a much less expensive glass for those items where quality did not seem to provide a marketing advantage.

Spirits were high in Sandwich as the Civil War neared its end. Families of glassworkers had been allowed to stay in company homes if the head of the household had gone to war, paying no rent until his return. The excellent relationship enjoyed by the glass factory and the townspeople during the war years was further strengthened when, on a slushy March day, fire destroyed William E. Boyden's express office building in the village. The building next door, separated by only a six-foot-wide alley, was saved because Boston and Sandwich Glass Company fire-fighting equipment was sent to the scene with engineer John Clayton to help.

By March 1865, the business climate throughout the North began to soften. A second furnace was shut down. The question of wages once again became the topic of conversation at Board meetings. Key management people were granted sizeable bonuses for past endeavors, but salary increases would wait until a special committee completed a study of the quality of the glass being made. All during the war years, Sandwich had been turning out a product that was saleable, but, in the eyes of the experts, did not match the quality being produced at the New England Glass Company in East Cambridge, Massachusetts. The Board reluctantly acknowledged this, but argued that the company had been hurt by the loss of skilled help during the war. However, even when the experienced workers returned, the quality was not particularly improved. The competitive nature of the trade could not allow the Boston and Sandwich Glass Company to be second best.

On January 19, 1866, according to records now at the Henry Ford Museum, the special committee reported its findings. During an interview at the factory site, Superintendent Theodore Kern claimed glass could be made in Sandwich that was equally as high in quality as at East Cambridge. Kern claimed the problem resulted from the use of purchased cullet of inferior quality. The problem was thought to be remedied, and the committee again visited the works. It was now the committee's opinion that the glass was "very nearly if not quite equal" to the best glass made by the New England Glass Company. Perhaps more care had been taken to mix the batch in their presence, but if Kern maintained such quality standards, the Boston and Sandwich Glass Company would not fall much behind the competition.

However, no mention was made in the report of the difference between the construction of the chimneys of the two companies. It is quite probable that the marked difference in quality was the result of the strong draft created by a chimney built by the New England Glass Company in 1851. It was 240 feet high, higher than the Bunker Hill Monument, and *not* built over the cone of any one furnace. Rather, it was constructed in a central location and connected to each furnace by flues. Careful control of the flues allowed for a more stable fire, creating a constant temperature that was several degrees higher than the Sandwich works could attain with their 90 foot chimneys individually placed over each of the four furnaces. The glass made in East Cambridge had a brilliance and polish not possible at Sandwich under any but the most ideal conditions.

At this time, a certain percentage of pressed glass made by both companies in Sandwich was produced from formulas that called for litharge, a lead substitute. Litharge is an oxide of lead that forms on its surface. The Boston and Sandwich Glass Company manufactured litharge from pig-lead in special furnaces at the factory. Glass made from litharge was less expensive than glass made from lead, an element which had become scarce because of its use in the Civil War. Many items were produced that did not require the best quality flint, such as pressed tableware and lamps. Writing about glassmaking in the 1920's and 1930's, William Germain Dooley, antiques editor for the *Boston Transcript*, interviewed a glassmaker who had worked at Sandwich. The anonymous glassmaker said that lesser quality glass still contained lead, because broken pieces of lead glass were used in the cullet. Some formulas called for a high percentage of cullet. The cullet had to be better than, or at least equal to, the quality that was expected of the batch being made. Glass manufactured from litharge instead of lead was called *demi-crystal* by the industry, although no distinction between the two was made in their advertising. Lead produced their "best metal", and litharge produced their "second best".

The dispute over quality with Theodore Kern was not resolved immediately, ultimately resulting in his resignation as superintendent. It was accepted by the Board at their March 13 meeting, to take effect May 1, 1866. Kern put his house on School Street up for sale, and after emotional goodbyes to his fellow glassmakers, he left Sandwich, taking other key workers with him. They relocated in New Bedford, Massachusetts, and established the New Bedford Glass Company.[2] Ill health forced Kern to retire from the superintendency of the New Bedford plant in April of 1868. He died on April 10, 1870, at the age of sixty-seven.

GEORGE LAFAYETTE FESSENDEN, SUPERINTENDENT
SEWALL HENRY FESSENDEN, AGENT
1866–1882

Theodore Kern's departure from Sandwich marked the rise of George Lafayette Fessenden to a more prominent niche in the management hierarchy. George was born in Sandwich on August 11, 1824, and on February 15, 1849, he married Mary C. Hoxie, the daughter of Clark Hoxie, Deming Jarves' partner in several business ventures.

In Fessenden's own words, Kern left the works on May 1 without telling Fessenden. In the wake of his de-

George Lafayette Fessenden, superintendent.

Sewall Henry Fessenden, agent.

parture, it was left to George to "pick up the pieces", as Kern left no instructions or information that would be helpful to his successor. William Stutson, in his advanced years, had little responsibility other than treasurer, so Fessenden became overseer of the works, "keeping everything drawing". As paymaster, George Fessenden had been liked by his fellow employees, who affectionately called him "Lafe". He had been known for his easy manner and his gentlemanly deportment and courtesy. Now with added responsibility, he was described as "nervous, driving, restless, and untiring, his whole soul evidently in his business, which knew no ten hour limit or easy privileges of physical reprieve or social enjoyment".

As this newest transition of authority was taking place, the stockholders and the public were assured in the *Barnstable Patriot* that business was continuing at a lively pace, reflected in an extra dividend that had been paid in January and $10 per share paid April 2. On June 25, 1866, the Board of Directors authorized Agent Sewall Fessenden to completely rebuild the largest furnace and cone. Converting it into an eleven-pot furnace was one of the few major changes made to the physical structure of the factory under Fessenden management, although company buildings were kept in excellent repair and working conditions were considered the best in the country.

Despite excellent working conditions, good pay, and bonuses for past achievements, the workers formed a glassmakers' protective association, with an initial goal of getting a 15 percent pay increase. With a 10 percent dividend to be paid to the stockholders on September 25, the

workers were beginning to believe that a greater share of the profits should be theirs. The association had a rocky start, however. On September 14, 1866, the association sent a letter to the Board of Directors listing employees who had joined the association but now refused to pay dues. These errant members believed that the association did not stand and fight for them. They saw no advantage in paying dues when they derived no benefits. However, from this small and somewhat bold beginning came the labor troubles that plagued the company sporadically for the rest of its life.

The single greatest fear in any of the more than one hundred glass companies in the United States was fire. The buildings for the most part were made of wood. The fire seldom came from the controlled conditions within the furnace rooms, but from auxiliary heating units that warmed the buildings in winter, or from accidental tipping over of lamps and lanterns. Lightning was also a major factor because of the high chimneys. In the forty-one years that the Boston and Sandwich Glass Company had been in Sandwich, no major fire had consumed any portion of these massive buildings because of its constant state of readiness to fight fire and the continuous updating of fire-fighting equipment. In earlier days, bucket brigades stood ready on a volunteer basis. Cisterns filled with water were placed strategically around the buildings, and every day the firemen on duty would see to it that they were filled. On September 24, 1866, based on recommendation by the insurance company, the agent was instructed by the Board of Directors to build a 50,000 gallon capacity reservoir that would self-fill with salt water at high tide. A suction pipe

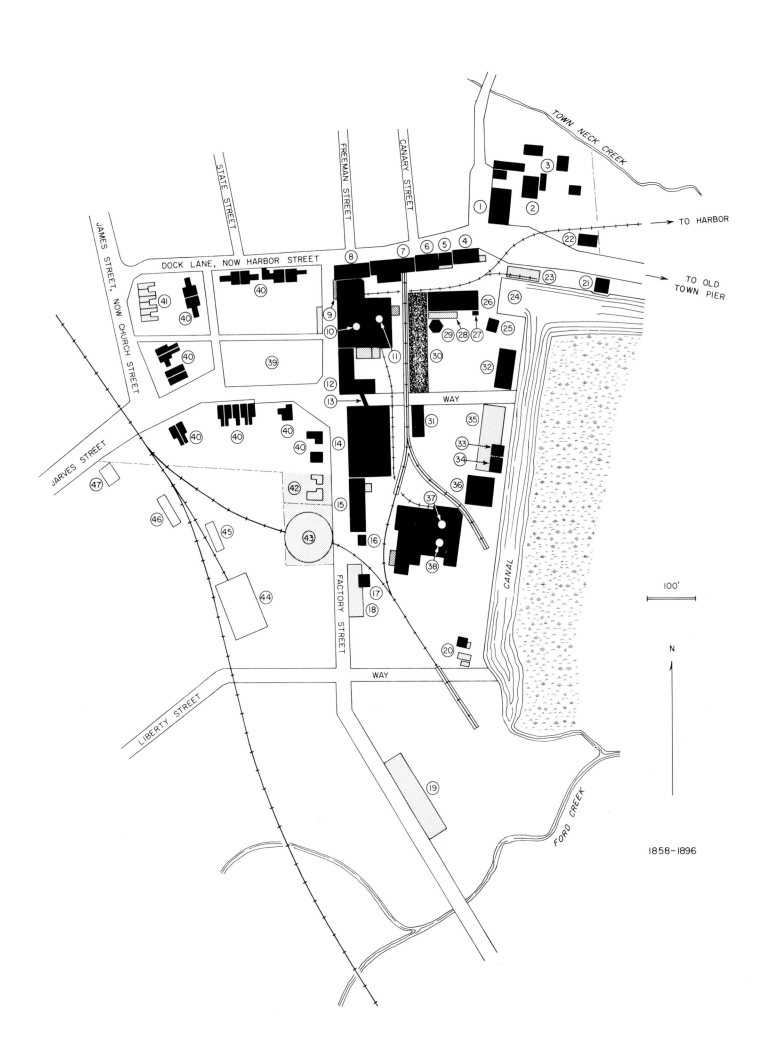

1858–1896

KEY TO MAP ON OPPOSITE PAGE

■ Boston and Sandwich Glass Company as it existed in June 1858.

⊡ Additions and improvements made under the management of the Fessenden brothers from June 1858 to April 1882.

⁄⁄ Minor improvements from 1882 through 1896.

☐ Buildings outside the boundaries of the Boston and Sandwich Glass Company.

╫══╫══╫══╫╌╌╫────Cape Cod Branch Railroad, known as the Cape Cod Railroad in 1854. It became the Old Colony Railroad in 1872, then the New York, New Haven and Hartford Railroad in 1893. Spurs in factory yard belonged to the railroad company.

╫╌╂╌╂╌╂╌╂╌╂╌╂╌╂Factory-owned narrow gauge railroad system, consisting of: Horse railroad to the harbor, removed by 1880.
Suspension railroad used to convey raw materials and coal to the furnaces.

1 Barn for factory horses and oxen.

2 Hay storage for factory animals.

3 Small buildings of cooperage.

4 Storage for packing hay (salt marsh hay).

5 Storage for barrels filled with packing hay. South wall extended in 1861.

6 Storage for trimmings (burners, metal fittings, etc.), cullet shop on west end of first floor.

7 Building erected in 1825 and extended by 1835. Packing rooms on first floor, decorating rooms on second floor.

8 Building erected by April 1826. Packing rooms on first floor, decorating rooms on second floor. West end is shown on Boston and Sandwich Glass Company letterhead, which was printed in 1853.

9 Leers extend into this area, as shown on company letterhead. West wall extended by Electrical Glass Corporation or Boston and Sandwich Glass Company II between 1889 and 1896 (see photo).

10 Larger furnace of Upper Glass House and the largest of all of the furnaces. Built in 1833, altered to burn coal in 1836 and to burn oil in 1895, it remained in operation until the Alton Manufacturing Company ceased production in 1908. Shown on company stationery.

11 Smaller furnace of Upper Glass House, built in 1844 on the site of the original 1825 Sandwich Glass Manufactory furnace. Furnace enlarged and building squared off in 1850. Sometimes called the *canary furnace*. Chimney can be seen on the Boston and Sandwich Glass Company letterhead, behind and to the left of the 1833 chimney.

12 Known as *building number 4*, with the factory bell on the roof. Conference rooms on second floor. First floor consists of: Mold room paralleling Factory Street.
Watch room on the corner of Factory Street and the public right-of-way, which is the sight of the present-day commemorative plaque. Main entrance here, shown in illustration on company stationery.
Blacksmith shop on east end.

13 Second floor bridge over public right-of-way, shown behind horse and wagon on letterhead.

14 Laboratory building erected in 1848, shown as largest building on letterhead. Cutting shop on second floor. First floor consists of: Machine shop.
Lead room.
Ash room.
Sand room.
Engine room.

Boiler room.
Mixing room, from which the batch was transported to the furnaces via the suspended railroad.

15 Former pottery. First floor used for storage, cutting shop extended onto second floor.

16 Shed for railroad tools, shown on letterhead to the left of the railroad engine. Removed after the company bought the railroad engine house.

17 Freight house erected in 1848, shown on letterhead to the right of the railroad engine.

18 New freight house.

19 New cooperage erected in 1874.

20 Lime sheds.

21 Dock shed.

22 Freight shed for horse railroad, removed by 1880.

23 Shed over horse railroad spur.

24 Three-sided box pier built in 1847, with a wooden floor. Workers could repair scows and the pier at low tide without standing in mud.

25 Freight shed.

26 Warehouse built in 1845.

27 Fire engine house.

28 New fire engine house built in 1867.

29 Gas house, began producing gas for lighting in 1853.

30 Coal stockade in close proximity to both railroad systems. Coal was unloaded from the horse railroad that transported it from the harbor, from the box pier, and from the standard gauge railroad spur. Coal was transferred from the large railroad cars to the little factory dump cars at the point where the trestle crosses over the suspended railroad.

31 Boiler house, proposed in 1856 and completed by March 1859.

32 Woodshed.

33 Original blacksmith shop, used for storage. Moved forward against canal bulkhead when lead house numbered 35 was built.

34 Lead house built in 1845.

35 Lead house enlarged and extended in 1863 (see photo).

36 Pot house built in 1852. Second floor used as a cutting shop by later small glass companies.

37 First furnace of the second X house, soon to be called the *Lower Glass House*. Built in 1846.

38 Second furnace of the second X house, constructed in 1851. In later years, the second X house will be referred to in company records as the *Lower Glass House*. It can be seen behind the railroad engine and freight cars on the letterhead. West wall extended in 1882 by Henry F. Spurr.

39 St. John's Park, sometimes called *the fountain lot* in company records. Shown in left foreground of letterhead. Renamed Manilla Park in 1898.

40 Company-owned houses.

41 Company-owned "block of six houses" built in 1864 (see photo).

42 Houses bought from Martin Hall in 1864.

43 Railroad engine house, built in 1847 for use in 1848, when the Cape Cod Branch Railroad terminated in Sandwich. Round roof can be seen in right foreground on letterhead. Bought by the Boston and Sandwich Glass Company in 1864 to use for storage.

44 Railroad depot built in 1847, for use from 1848 to 1878.

45 Railroad freight house built in 1878.

46 New railroad depot built in 1878.

47 St. Peter's Roman Catholic Chapel built in 1830, used until mid-1850's and removed in 1865.

Fig. 1 Map of Boston and Sandwich Glass Company during the Fessenden years. The factory site extended east from Factory Street. Company-owned houses and a park were on the west side. The numbers correspond to the key.

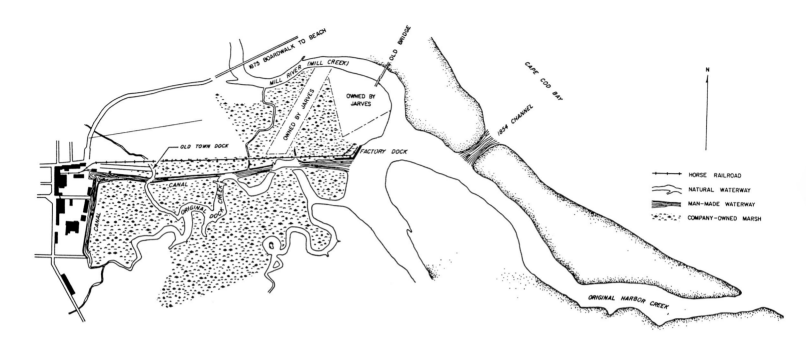

Map of tidal land east of the factory. A narrow gauge horse railroad connected the factory yard to a dock in Sandwich Harbor, crossing over a large creek at the north end of the Sandwich town dock. Salt hay, harvested from company-owned marsh land, was used for packing the glass in barrels that were made at the factory cooperages.

Looking west toward the factory from the marsh. The numbers correspond to the numbers on the map, and to the key.

Looking west from the coal storage area toward the blacksmith shop, located behind the watch room. This photo was taken on August 2, 1930.

Company-owned tenement house on Church Street, still standing today. It is numbered 41 on the locater map.

Looking south down Factory Street from the corner of Factory Street and Dock Lane, now Harbor Street. The two boys are at the corner of the building that is numbered on the map. The boy pulling a wagon is passing the area where the leers are located, numbered 9 on the map. The person leaning against the tree is in front of the Upper Glass House.

Looking east toward numbers 12 and 13 on the locater map. The second story bridge can be seen on the right of the sign.

Boardwalk to the beach, built in 1875 over Mill Creek and rebuilt several times. Refer to the map of tidal land.

Looking south along the west side of the lead house, toward the pot house. The chimneys of the Lower Glass House can be seen in the background. The artists are Mr. and Mrs. Jonathan Leonard. Mr. Leonard was the son of Mary T. Waterman and her second husband, Dr. Jonathan Leonard.

Looking west from number 13 on the map, toward Jarves Street. The park, number 39, is on the right.

would be run from the cistern to the engine room, where a pump would be installed. Run by steam, it would pump water from the suction pipe and feed it to a new fire engine that would be delivered before the end of January, 1867. A fire house was also to be built to protect the engine.

A fire company was organized with its primary interest being the protection of the glass works. It would be allowed to help the town only when fire was no threat to the factory. Though it did not seem like the "olden days" when Deming Jarves had the interest of the town at heart, it must be understood that this restriction on town aid was mandated in the regulations of the insurance company that would cover the company's losses. Henry Vose Spurr was the foreman of the fire company, assisted by John Clayton. Ezra Hamblin was secretary.

No sooner had these plans been made and the fire engine delivered than, on February 12, 1867, a large storage building containing twenty-five tons of packing hay was consumed by fire. The new fire company was on the spot with its engine, but the fire had too much of a head start. Efforts to save the building failed, but the fire company did great service by protecting other buildings at the site. The fire, thought to be the work of an arsonist, reinforced the need for a more adequate water supply.

During this period in early 1867, production dropped to three furnaces. A number of hands were discharged, and some joined Theodore Kern in his soon-to-be-operating New Bedford Glass Company. Overall, however, a reasonable level of productivity was maintained. The stockholders were pleased with George Fessenden's management skills. Records at the Henry Ford Museum show $83,153.74 was in cash on hand, $10,000 paid in dividends during 1866, and $16,176.84 spent on improvements.

Fessenden had to be pleased, knowing he had loyal people in his employ such as Timothy G. Dean (a watchman at the company site), who was the son-in-law of Reverend Joseph Marsh. Grain had been missing from the storehouse, and Dean was placed on guard the night of March 4. He recognized one Peter Devlin entering the granary to fill a bag with grain. When Dean refused a $5 bribe from Devlin, Devlin stabbed Dean with a long, narrow knife. Dean gave chase, but, faint from loss of blood, he made it to the watch house. From there, he was taken home and examined by Dr. M. F. Delano. The wound was severe, and close to his heart. Devlin was arrested at his home, and sentenced to five years of hard labor at the state prison. Dean recovered.

As 1867 came to a close and both glass factories in Sandwich sent out the last of their Christmas orders, the entire industry was sluggish. The Cape Cod Glass Company continued to maintain a full staff by stockpiling glass for the first time. The Boston and Sandwich Glass Company discharged some hands, and remaining employees were obliged to take a 15 percent reduction in wages. By the end of February 1868, five of the seven furnaces in Sandwich were shut down. On April 1, only a 3 percent dividend was paid. As bad as conditions were in Sandwich, they were worse in other parts of the country. New

Jersey houses were running part time, or had suspended operations altogether. Not since the financial crisis of 1857 had the Boston and Sandwich Glass Company experienced such a shortage of orders.

They had simply dried up. Sales personnel in the Boston office were anxiously aware that orders they had become accustomed to filling were going to the competition in Pennsylvania. The greatest volume of sales in the 1860's was for pressed glass, now being produced in Pennsylvania at prices considerably lower than Sandwich, and the quality of the Pennsylvania product was quite satisfactory.

The brothers Fessenden realized that the only shops that were busy were the shops that were blowing special orders for a very narrow segment of the trade. They reasoned that if Sandwich could not recapture their former pressed glass tableware customers, perhaps they could build up a new clientele in a special field of light, well-made blown glass. This was the beginning of a new era known as the Late Blown Period. This type of glass, made until the company's closing and referred to in the industry as *bubble glass*, represented one third of all the glass produced by the Boston and Sandwich Glass Company throughout its entire sixty-three year history. (A detailed study of late blown ware can be found in Volume 4.)

On February 26, 1869, the town was badly damaged by a huge fire. Flames wiped out several business blocks, including a meat market, millinery store, and tenement house. To stop the fire from destroying the entire village, it was necessary to flatten one of the buildings with gunpowder. The town fire department courageously fought the fire, and by daylight it was under control. The new fire apparatus stationed at the glass factory did not come to the aid of the town, but was required to remain on standby at the glass works. In retrospect, historians have condemned the Boston and Sandwich Glass Company for this policy.[3] But the facts prove that this is unfair.

The Board of Directors was granted fire insurance in the amount of $190,000 by a London insurance company. The rate was based on three conditions:

- A 36,000 gallon minimum cistern must be filled with water at all times.
- New fire equipment must be manned on a twenty-four hour basis.
- In case of fire anywhere in the vicinity of the factory, the firemen must station themselves on company ground to protect the wooden buildings from sparks.

The fire company at the glass factory was compelled to follow the directive of the insurance company.

Meanwhile, the dullness of trade, the changing attitudes of labor, and fierce competition from Pittsburgh, Pennsylvania, continued to put great pressure on the productivity of the two glass works in Sandwich.

At the Cape Cod works, although $100,000 in property was in the hands of stockholders, they refused to invest any more money on a labor force that they believed was indifferent to competitive pressure. Therefore, the Cape Cod Glass Company closed on April 15, 1869. A letter written by Treasurer Henry F. Higginson, Deming Jarves' son-in-law, now preserved at the Corning Museum of Glass

Library in Corning, New York, stated that Mr. Jarves would not have closed the Cape Cod works if labor had been fair to the company. Several attempts to reopen that facility for glassmaking in later years failed. (For further details, see Chapter 4 in this book, and Chapter 7 in Volume 4.)

For the first time in ten years, the Boston and Sandwich Glass Company stood alone in Sandwich. The competitive irritation of the Cape Cod Glass Company had ended. And the skilled labor force living in town now had to accept wages and conditions set forth by the Board of Directors, or move away to seek other employment. During a trip to Belgium with Board member S. G. Rogers, George Fessenden sought for better sources of patterns, molds, and foreign rights, plus information on how to manufacture glass more cheaply. In an untypical mood of discouragement, he confided to Mr. Rogers that he was considering quitting the company. Rogers immediately wrote a letter from Brussels, dated May 12, 1869, urging the Board not to accept the resignation because Fessenden's knowledge was invaluable to the company.

The company struggled on, frequently lifted by Fessenden's renewed spirit, and slowly a rebirth of the glass industry in Sandwich took place. Only the highly skilled were considered for employment. Sewall and George Fessenden visualized the company relying more heavily on the blowpipe, creating full sets of tableware that could be engraved and cut. Perhaps it was coincidence that brought Nicholas Lutz, Nehemiah Packwood, and John Jones to Sandwich at this time. Or, just as likely, it was the untiring efforts of the Fessendens to bring skilled artisans, engravers, and cutters into the company to help in the rebuilding.

Even though most of the men were working half time, they stayed on, hoping for better conditions. One advantage enjoyed in Sandwich was that relationships between labor and management were harmonious compared with other parts of the country. In much the same way as the company had taken care of its families during the Civil War, they were now helped by being allowed to draw against their next paycheck whenever necessary. To ensure that such a practice met tests of sound business management, the Board directed Albert Turner to audit the books at the Sandwich counting room. Turner stated in his report dated 1870 that he had never seen such payroll advances allowed in any company he knew. It could encourage fraud and irregularities, he claimed, which the paymaster could easily cover up. Turner assured the Board, however, that he had examined the books and found everything in order and the Board decided to ignore his warnings.

Early in 1871, the Board of Directors realized that the two furnaces that had been running since 1868 would not be able to keep up with the gradually increasing workload, especially with the other two furnaces being in disrepair. Since it would be a costly venture to make them ready for a long run, the Board ordered the construction of a brand new furnace to replace one of the old furnaces in the lower glass house. The foundation was begun on March 28, 1871, and the last brick was laid on May 20. Pots were

set, the fires were put under on August 16, and the pots were filled September 13. The first melt was ready on September 19. All the pots held. Everything was in good order and, according to *The Barnstable Patriot*, the entire undertaking was completed without mishap.

At Sandwich, as well as at other glass factories, many pieces were specially made for individuals or companies that sent their private molds to the factory. Jars in the shape of bears, used to hold bear grease, carried the name of EUGENE BIZE & FRICKE, and were never shown in the Boston showroom. Little bottles manufactured in Sandwich and shipped to Windsor, Vermont, for use by the Windsor Perfume Company, were marked "PAINE'S PERFUME". In April 1872, a heavy medicine tumbler with a glass cover equipped with a spoon rest could be seen at the Homeopathic Hospital Fair. It was called "the Hahnemann tumbler", and the cover was used to keep dust out of the medicine. Many of these items were pressed at the Boston and Sandwich Glass Company using customers' own molds.

At the same time, larger quantities of blown ware were being made — stemware with accompanying decanters, pitchers, fishbowls, colognes, and full sets of tableware that were auxiliary pieces to china dinner sets, such as finger bowls, slop bowls, cheese dishes, and cracker jars.

But, as so frequently happened during the history of the company, the good times were followed by disaster.

At the Boston store orders had slowly built to more than $20,000 each month. An unusually large inventory of glass totalling $60,000 to $70,000 was stored in the warehouse attached to the showroom. And then, on November 9, 1872, disaster struck. A fire on Summer Street, one of the finest residential streets in Boston, raced out of control. It raced south on Summer Street, past Church Green to High Street, and east on High Street to Federal Street. Billowing north on Federal Street, it burned everything in its path on both sides of the street, including the showroom and the warehouse of the Boston and Sandwich Glass Company. Before it was over, sixty-five acres of the City of Boston were destroyed. It caused great damage from Milk Street to the piers north and south, and from Olive Street to Washington Street east and west.

Henry F. Spurr, who was in charge of the Boston operation, was home when the fire began. But an employee named Patrick F. Mahoney, who had come from Sandwich to the Boston store, realized that the store and warehouse would soon be in great danger. He loaded his wagon with boxes and barrels until he was driven from the building by the heat and flames. When he was safely out of the fire area, he stored the wagon and turned the horses over to the fire fighters for their use. His heroic action cut the company's losses by $10,000. Even so, $60,000 worth of inventory was lost, of which only $45,000 was insured. And only $10,000 of this was ever paid by the English insurance company which covered Boston businesses against such losses. It had simply become insolvent due to heavy claims from the Great Chicago Fire which preceded the Boston fire by only thirteen months. The Boston disaster was too much for the insurance company to handle.

The fire had an immediate financial effect on the Boston

nd Sandwich Glass Company. Only a 2 percent stock dividend was paid for the next two years. In time the glass would be replaced, for an extra furnace was quickly put in blast to fill special orders that had been lost. The Boston building, too, would be replaced, but the loss of company records and papers have had a profound effect on historical research today.

The year 1873 was notable for being the first year in which the Boston and Sandwich Glass Company really began to feel the increased pressure from Pittsburgh manufacturers.

It was also the year when the American glass industry changed profoundly, because, on July 1, the American Flint Glass Workers Union, headquartered in Pittsburgh, was formed. Thought of as only a ripple in 1873, the union movement would develop into a tidal wave throughout the industry by 1887.

Also by 1873, lime glass was being produced in Pennsylvania at far less expense than the flint and litharge glass that still made up 100 percent of the production of the Boston houses. Even a somewhat stodgy Board of Boston Directors, with a built-in reluctance to change, had to admit the manufacture of pressed glass needed innovative direction. An obvious but realistic approach to competing with Pittsburgh's huge quantities of lime glass was to also produce lime glass. In anticipation of this, the Fessendens were given the authority to buy any molds, patterns, and equipment that might be used in an effort to expand the pressed pattern departments.

In his articles mentioned previously,[4] William Germain Dooley quoted a Sandwich glassworker as saying, "Later pressed glass used the cheaper ingredient, lime. This was just beginning to be used in 1873 when I came to Sandwich."

When the Portland (Maine) Glass Works closed in 1873,[5] many of its pressed glass molds were bought by the Boston and Sandwich Glass Company as part of its efforts to improve its market position in such glass. This, incidentally, is why many pressed glass patterns, which were previously attributed only to Portland, were made by the Boston and Sandwich Glass Company at a later date.

With the discontinuance of litharge in favor of lime by the Boston and Sandwich Glass Company, it was found that the lime, when heated in the old furnaces of Sandwich, did not make as good a glass as could be made in the modern Pittsburgh furnaces. Even the two furnaces reconstructed by George Fessenden could not reach the temperatures of Pittsburgh. As a result, the glass lacked brilliance and clarity. Early in 1874, barites (barium sulfate) were added to improve the polish, but most of the glass produced at the Boston and Sandwich Glass Company from lime formulas had to have a stippled design, or had to be stained or decorated to hide the lack of clarity. The stippled pattern molds bought from the Portland Glass Company were ideal to hide such lack of quality.

On March 28, 1874, *The Seaside Press* notified the people of Sandwich that the glass works would begin to discharge employees because of insufficient work. This was the beginning of a downturn in business that would ultimately cost George Fessenden his position as Superintendent. Orders that once came to Sandwich were now going to Pennsylvania. Attempts by Sandwich to compete with the pricing structure of companies in Pittsburgh met with utter frustration. For example, lamps that normally sold for 29 cents were underbid as much as 5 cents by Pittsburgh houses.

Fessenden realized that, in order to compete, he had to increase the hourly output per shop without increasing the cost. *The Seaside Press* of August 29, 1874, tells of a pipe ten inches in diameter running from the engine room to the blacksmith shop and the glass blowing rooms. This supplied forced air to speed up cooling of the molds. More rapid cooling, it was hoped, would increase the productivity of each shop. Records do not show whether the expense of the pipe paid off, but it really didn't matter. The dullness of trade in the late months of 1874 affected even the Pennsylvania houses. By September the Great Financial Panic of New York was under way. By the end of the year the whole country had slipped into a severe recession. Demand for the large amounts of glass stored in the warehouses simply disappeared.

The *Crockery Journal* of January 9, 1875, described the Massachusetts Charitable Mechanics Association fair, at which the Boston and Sandwich Glass Company exhibited. To bolster sales, Agent Sewall H. Fessenden personally selected the flint glass to be shown. It included rich cut, engraved and etched tableware and vases, lamps and lamp globes, and flower stands. The space was too small to allow all of the lines to be shown, but what was exhibited showed excellence in quality, design, and workmanship. The New England Glass Company, having applied for space at the last moment, could not exhibit, so the judges decided, in a gesture of industry sportsmanship, to make no awards in the flint glass category.

An interesting observation can be made from the writings in the *Crockery Journal* and from the stereoscopic pictures that were so popular at the time. Very little, if any, pressed tableware was shown at trade fairs, but thinly blown epergnes, cut glass, and lighting devices were considered worthy of display. Pressed glass did not get the attention of the judging committee.

Despite such tactical issues as lime vs. flint glass, the overwhelming fact was that the center of the glass industry was gradually shifting to the Midwest. In Pittsburgh and across the Monongahela River into Ohio, seventy-three glass houses were ready and able to compete for the world market.

Previously, the Atlantic coast glass business had been jealously controlled by the glass houses located in each major geographic market. Boston houses had controlled New England; Brooklyn factories had dominated New York; and Philadelphia and New Jersey glass houses had controlled the Washington, D. C. area and the coastal areas of Pennsylvania.

But, the sluggishness of business was making every geographic area a prime target for the glass houses that could produce quality, at a reduced price, and at a profit.

Distance of the manufacturing location from such markets made little difference. Glass houses simply opened salesrooms in the new markets. By February 6, 1875, the

Pittsburgh firm of Richards and Hartley Flint Glass Company had opened a salesroom at 51 Chardon Street in Boston. On February 20, J. H. Hobbs, Brockunier and Company from Wheeling, West Virginia, advertised a sample room at 49 Washington Street in Boston. The LaBelle Glass Company of Bridgeport, Ohio, had samples at the Richards and Hartley address in Boston. Gillinder and Sons from Philadelphia had samples in Boston, as well as in New York and Baltimore. The Boston area was inundated by companies selling glass at prices that were impossible for the Boston and Sandwich Glass Company to match.

As part of a major strategy to combat the mass production of the Midwest, more and more of the work at Sandwich became specialized. The Boston and Sandwich Glass Company invested heavily in a catalog of lamp goods *printed in color*! As far as the authors know, only two pages of this catalog exist today. Its description, as recorded in the *Crockery Journal* of February 6, 1875, is given in the hope that if even one page comes to light, the authors will be notified.

Upon our table lies an immense catalog, a book whose pages, one hundred of them, are not less than 30" long by 15" wide, are wholly occupied by the most accurately prepared designs of the various lamps and lamp-ware manufactured by the Boston and Sandwich Glass Company. These illustrations, elegantly executed in lithograph, not only give the form and decoration, but the color as well. Lamps for parlor use are shown with wreaths of flowers encircling their globes. Lamps for more humble uses are in green, and blue, and red glass, and these colors are faithfully portrayed. There are hanging lamps, and standing lamps, and if we may use the expression, sitting lamps, for some of them are so low in stature that they hardly seem to stand. In some the pedestal is of bronze, in others, of gilt, in some of marble, and in some of glass, and all of these variations the illustrations faithfully represent. Then, when it comes to lamp ware, such as burners, shade-holders and the like, there is infinite variety, but everything is shown, a counterpart to the original, in bronze color. Some of the efforts are decidedly gorgeous, especially those intended for use in houses of the best class in areas where gas is unattainable. These include chandeliers, with cut glass pendants, and bracket lamps of great elegance of finish. Then there are the highly and somewhat flashy decorated affairs which gambling establishments and saloons in the interior affect and following them every variety of lantern, including the watchman's "bulls-eye" and the reflector lantern for stationary use. What the expense involved in getting up the designs alone, to say nothing of the production of the book itself must have been, those of our readers who have got out costly circulars of their own can best judge, and they will naturally conclude, with us, that an establishment which finds it to its advantage to go into the publishing business upon a scale so costly and gigantic, must have and do a business such as but few "outsiders" have any concept of.

Although the quality of the Boston and Sandwich Glass Company's product was apparent, there was no market. So the Board of Directors, continuing its somewhat desperate efforts, decided to enter into a trade sale of glassware in conjunction with the New England Glass Company, the Suffolk Glass Company, and the Union Glass Company. Together they accumulated five thousand packages of glass and advertised in the *Crockery Journal* to wholesale buyers in the United States and Canada. The ad, dated May 6, 1875, stated that flint glass would be available, both cut and engraved, as well as decorated ware. Again, there was no mention of the pressed glass that had been so large a part of their inventory in the 1840's through 1860's. Also mentioned was the fact that buyers would have an opportunity to visit all of the new buildings in Boston that had been constructed at a cost of $100,000,000 to replace those burned in the 1872 fire.

A western correspondent reported in the *Crockery Journal* of July 29, 1875, that many exciting things were taking place in the Pittsburgh houses, while a Boston man reported, "Two duller weeks cannot be recalled." The contrasting expressions told it all. The coal and natural gas used for fuel in the Pittsburgh-Ohio area was an insurmountable obstacle to eastern companies.

Management in the East did everything possible to keep their factories running and financially sound, with little control over results.

For example, in August, 1875, the Boston and Sandwich Glass Company placed an ad in the *Crockery Journal*, listing agencies in Chicago, Philadelphia, and New York, in addition to the Boston showroom then located at 164 Devonshire Street.

The company took advantage of every opportunity to show its merchandise. At the Franklin Institute in Philadelphia, sales agent J. K. Dunham set up a large and valuable showing, representing a variety of etched and engraved glass, as well as decorated bone glass (white opaque) lamp shades. Dunham received a bronze medal for the display.

In time to boost holiday sales, the *Boston Gazette* placed the following article about the Boston showroom, and the *Crockery Journal* copied it on December 9, under the heading, "A Rare and Beautiful Exhibition".

If Europe has produced the ideas and models, America has the power of learning the lessons rapidly enough, and adapt the best of everything in a facile, practical manner that must astonish toiling inventors the other side of the ocean. A striking example of American progress is now shown in the art of making glass in this country, and to fully appreciate the perfection to which it has arrived within a few years, the reader should pay a visit to the crystal galleries at 164 Devonshire Street, where the Boston and Sandwich Glass Company exhibit their very beautiful productions. The fragile, sparkling devices that crowd their shelves and tables, are as marvelously artistic and lovely as the most fastidious person could desire. The place resembles Baccarat's famous establishment in Paris, and is probably the only one of the kind in this country. At first glance, it seems nothing but a sea of prisms and indiscriminate sparkle; but gradually the systematic arrangement of the brilliant specimens assists the beholder to admire and wonder at his leisure. Perhaps one of the most striking impressions is that such quantities of useful and ornamental articles can be devised simply to utilize this breakable material. Apparently anything, where silver or china were once imperative, can now be made of glass. The designs are thoroughly artistic. Whether the object is a wine glass, thin as a bubble (Editor's note: This was the extremely light-weight blown glass known in the industry as *bubble glass*), or an epergne for fruits and flowers, the workmanship is always perfect. The entire gamut of table furniture is sounded in the present fashion glassware. Dishes for salads, jellies, cheese, trays for ice cream and custards, jars for crackers and pickles, pitchers of all descriptions, champagne coolers, goblets, superb decanters, punch bowls and bottles, are all deliciously suggestive of festive boards, daintily garnished with the good things of life. Among household decorations and ornaments there are magnificent choices for chandeliers and flower vases. The flower troughs that are now so fashionable for the dinner table come in various patterns to be arranged in figures: then there are exquisite jardinieres and baskets, that make charming ornaments for the drawing room. There is also an infinity of toilet sets and cologne stands, so beautifully cut and elaborated that one fain inquires if it is possible to exhaust the subject. One very lovely novelty are the decorated shades or chandeliers and lamps. They are a modern imitation of the Venetian lustre, and are of those artistic devices kindly adopted by people who prefer a mellow light to the glare of unstinted gas. The effect produced on decorated shades is sufficiently becoming to warrant the fashion a great success. But ladies and gentlemen should make a tour of this store, and view the rare articles it contains for themselves. People who are in quest of crystal wedding gifts will find the difficulties of selection agreeably dispersed, and a decided pleasure awaits those who can enjoy a display of native talent and native manufacture, and say, with perfect truth, it is equal to the old world productions.

1875 ended with the entire country suffering from hard times. Warehouses were loaded with unsold goods. Competition from the Midwest was relentless. Reflecting conditions, it was reported on December 30 that "the last day of struggle and endeavor for the year 1875 comes at last."

The Seaside Press on January 15, 1876, reported that dull times were here.

The Boston and Sandwich Glass Company put out one of their furnaces Friday night, leaving only one furnace in operation. Fifty hands were discharged. Those who worked by the piece will have less work, consequently less pay. This reduction is due to the fact that the warehouses are filled with goods and demand is light. Another reason is the fact that glass works in this part cannot compete with manufac-

turing in the west in the manufacture of common kinds of glassware on account of the cost of fuel. But on the production of fine ware they stand a better chance.

The year 1876, the one hundredth birthday of the nation, was to be celebrated with a Centennial Exposition in Philadelphia. The country looked forward to it, as did the glass industry, viewing it as a shot in the arm for a diminishing economy. An enormous amount of space was allocated for glass display in the Main Building at Philadelphia's Fairmount Park, and space was reserved for the major glass companies from the Boston area. Demonstrations of cutting and engraving on glass were planned for Machinery Hall. A working glass factory was erected on the exhibition grounds, to be run by Pennsylvania glass man William T. Gillinder and his sons Frederick and James. While Gillinder and Sons planned to produce on site the pressed glass souvenirs that would be taken home by exhibition goers, the other glass companies worked feverishly to complete the elegant products that would reflect their high quality. Seldom again would the buying public have the opportunity to see glass made, cut and engraved before their eyes, and a finished product displayed in such a setting.

At Sandwich, pieces were specially designed for the great event. Two immense vases were sent to Trenton, New Jersey, with decorator Edward J. Swann, to be decorated and fired in a large kiln. Two large, richly cut punch bowls were perfected by Nehemiah Packwood and his men. Joseph Bonique was given a special order— blowing a glass dish that weighed sixty-eight pounds and was two feet nine inches in diameter. It was the heaviest article of glass thought to have been blown anywhere, taking two men to execute the cutting. It was to be used in conjunction with a glass fountain at the exhibition. Boston's chief salesman Henry F. Spurr was put in charge of the company's display.

The Centennial Exhibition opened May 10, with everything possible done by each glass company to make the public aware that American glass was indeed equal to any glass in the world. But it did not take the full six months of the celebration for the industry to realize that the sorely needed impetus was not forthcoming. Another "Great Trade Sale of Glassware" to get rid of excess inventory was planned for September 6 and 7. Five thousand packages of glass from the Boston and Sandwich Glass Company, the New England Glass Company, and the Union Glass Company were offered on the block. At 9:30 in the morning, auctioneer Samuel Hatch opened the bidding, and prices were later reported to be fair to moderate.

In the fall of 1876, Christmas orders began to come in, and on October 14, *The Seaside Press* carried a jubilant notice that another furnace had been started at Sandwich, giving employment to a number of men who had been out of work for six months or more.

In October, without any known reason, the glass company discontinued supplying the town with gas. Churches, public buildings, and private homes turned to kerosene. The Unitarian Society purchased kerosene lamps for their church from the Boston and Sandwich Glass Company, and considered them an improvement to the church's decor.

At the factory, George Fessenden continued to search for ways to improve the productivity of every man. On November 21, 1876, he patented an improved method of cutting away the excess glass from the rims of bowls and tumblers after they were annealed rather than before. Each refinement in procedure gave the company an edge in the face of the continuing pressure of competition. Improvements implemented into the production line reduced the cost of each line item. This savings in labor was then expended on fuel, balancing the cost of each piece with the cost of a like article from the Pittsburgh houses.

But the Board of Directors could not find the ultimate answers to their competitive dilemma. The location of coal fields in Pennsylvania was an overwhelming obstacle. The Civil War had brought about improvements in railroading that now sped competitive glass to all markets that Sandwich had once monopolized, including Boston. The written word that once took days to cross the country was now transmitted in seconds in dots and dashes. The laborer, once awed and thankful to the mighty factory owner for his very existence, now saw strength in numbers and began to realize that he alone was the catalyst for creating the owner's wealth. That once-mighty owner, who had walked amidst his employees to pass out a fifty-cents bonus, was now being told by the same labor force, "Keep your fifty cents. Share your wealth fairly with those who make your riches possible."

At the end of the year, Jacob J. Nichols resigned from the New York showroom. The agency was continued by Charles E. L. Brinkerhoff, who had worked for Nichols. The New York store remained an important outlet under Brinkerhoff, with glowing reports of his fine displays recorded frequently in the *Crockery Journal*.

Immediately upon taking over as agent, Brinkerhoff suggested to Sewall Fessenden that part of the New York salesrooms could be sublet. Certainly, with business in its present stalemated condition, all of the New York floor space being devoted to Sandwich was not warranted. Brinkerhoff's concern over economic factors signalled the Board that additional belt tightening was needed. Company officials, now close to panic, reduced salaries of key employees in an effort to keep the Boston and Sandwich Glass Company afloat amid news that the New England Glass Company in East Cambridge had decided to fight the trend no longer and was "winding up its business".[6] Brinkerhoff, as well as Henry Spurr and other valued men, had difficulty living within what they considered their meager allotment during the following year. Brinkerhoff could not make his rent payment on his house and asked Sewall Fessenden if the company could advance $250, since his agreement with his landlord had been made before the salary reduction.

It has often been stated that the quality of the glass being produced in the late 1870's was not up to the standards set by Deming Jarves. For example, in her book *Sandwich Glass*, written in 1922, Lenore Wheeler Williams emphatically states that only glass produced before 1853 should be considered Sandwich glass. "These men put their best ef-forts into designs of intricate beauty. There is no comparison between their work and the later commercial pressed glass which took unto itself all the worst features of Victorian decoration and which was never found upon the tables of people of good taste, who turned from pressed glass to English cut during this latter period, or preserved with reverence and used on state occasions the pieces of a generation before."

Our years of research have proven that this statement is not a fair evaluation of the product manufactured by the skilled hands of the men at Sandwich. An article dated May 3, 1877, in the *Crockery Journal* extolls the beauty that deserves recognition today despite the fact that it was not even considered a Sandwich product by some writers who preceded us. Here is the article in its entirety, providing excellent descriptions of the company's production.

The lover of the beautiful and artistic can find no place in this city where he can better gratify his tastes than at Nos. 21 and 23 Barclay Street (New York), where the Boston and Sandwich Glass Company have their agency. Here the eye can feast itself on the most exquisite creations in crystal, and the constant discovery of new beauties would repay one for even making a daily visit. We have written of these goods before in this connection with the exhibit made by the company at the International Exhibition, and can only reiterate what we then said: that we honestly believe they are not excelled by any others of the kind, whether of foreign or domestic manufacture. The stock on hand here is, of course, larger and more varied than that shown in Philadelphia, but this only gives more room for admiration. It is difficult to say which of the specimens we admire the most, for each one possesses peculiar beauties and excellencies of its own. There is a large line of superbly cut decanters, toilet, and other bottles which are exceedingly tempting. These are elegantly cut and engraved, and with their prismatic stoppers, glisten and shine with almost the fire of a diamond. Among the toilet set bottles we notice some superb specimens in blue, ruby, and other colors which would be fitting ornaments for the dressing stands of our fairest belles. In tableware there is endless variety of most graceful styles and designs. Our favorite is the strawberry diamond pattern. This is exceedingly rich, and the interiors of the pieces are to be particularly marked for their exquisite finish. Nothing could be smoother or more brilliant. Tall epergnes, bouquet holders, and fruit bowls, stand as sentinels over hosts of smaller tableware, all charming and original in style, and beautifully ornamented. The lily or fern epergnes are among the finest. They are very elaborate in their finish, and can challenge comparison with the finest imported. The ice cream dishes are among the richest of goods. These are in a great number of patterns and shapes, and all exquisite. In opal glassware they show a full line of finely decorated vases, varying in size from the most diminutive single flower holder to 15 inch high specimens. This company also makes the very finest frosted glassware (Overshot) of which they show a full

Trade shows played a large part in Nineteenth Century industry. Here is the Boston and Sandwich Glass Company display in 1878 at Boston's Mechanics Hall. Note the "flower weights" on the edge of the table near the sign, and the type of globe and shade combined with Onion lamps. *Courtesy, Sandwich Glass Museum, Sandwich Historical Society*

Crystal gas fixtures exhibited by the Boston firm of S. A. Stetson and Company at the same 1878 trade show in Mechanics Hall. The lighting devices were *assembled* by Mitchell Vance and Company of New York, from glass *manufactured* by the Boston and Sandwich Glass Company. *Courtesy, Sandwich Glass Museum, Sandwich Historical Society*

This photo was taken inside the Boston and Sandwich Glass Company showroom at Franklin and Hawley Streets in Boston. The company moved to this address in 1884 (see page 6 of Volume 4). Many of the items are not recognized as Sandwich by present-day collectors. *Courtesy, Sandwich Glass Museum, Sandwich Historical Society*

assortment, including flower baskets, punch bowls, finger bowls, champagne coolers, champagne jugs, etc. They are fully equal to those imported from abroad in every respect. The champagne jug commends itself to those who prefer wine without water (we do). The ice is kept entirely separate from the wine, while it cools it more efficiently than the old plan of drowning it by filling the glass half full of broken lumps, which by melting give as a result a wishy-washy mixture and destroys the flavor. There is another ornamental article which should be noticed, and this is the fish globe. These are in different styles of ornament, and so handsome it makes one to "wish he was a fish" to lodge in such a crystal palace. Besides these they display a complete stock of pressed tableware of the latest designs. In lamp goods they have any amount of different styles. Their decorated opal cone shades and globes are gems of their kind. We might go on and fill columns with descriptions of these goods, but, after all, seeing them is better than reading of them, so we can only advise others to do as we have done, go and examine for themselves. Ladies who are housekeeping must not neglect the glass rolling pin.
The agency in New York is in charge of Mr. C. E. L. Brinkerhoff, who is not only well known to the trade, but has the reputation of not asking more for goods than they are really worth. "A penny saved is a penny earned;" and if goods equally beautiful can be bought for a less price, who cares whether they were made in America or Bohemia.
N.B.—Those who advocate the blue glass cure will find here lamp shades, tumblers, glasses, etc., of the most cerulean hue, and equal in every respect to the rest of the goods.

The "blue glass cure"—sometimes called a "craze"—was reported in the *Crockery Journal* of February 8, 1877. Experiments conducted by General Augustus J. Pleasonton of Philadelphia had "proved" that plants and animals (human and otherwise) matured more quickly when nurtured in close proximity to blue glass. Pleasonton released his findings in a book entitled *Blue and Sun Light; Their Influence Upon Life, Disease, etc.* He began his work in 1860, when he placed blue glass over a grape arbor. The vines reportedly grew forty-five feet long and by the second year, bore unusually large fruit. Pigs raised under blue glass weighed much more than their siblings raised the usual way. A heifer became a mother at the age of fourteen months. A weak, puny child weighing 3½ pounds was placed in a room with blue curtains, and he gained twenty-two pounds in four months. A woman suffering from nervous irritation, exhaustion, and rheumatism found relief by alternating blue and common glass in one window. An interesting side effect was the growth of hair on her balding head! Similar experiments by a French professor resulted in twin girls fully developed and mature by the age of eight. Their senses were so acute that they could *see* the shape and color of *odors*!
In an era of patent cure-alls, medicine shows, and Doomsday predictions, the theory was believable. Many

glass companies both here and abroad began to produce blue items for the gullible public, flooding the market with blue window panes, lamp chimneys, and tumblers. By the latter part of 1878, seeing no ascertainable difference in their livestock or relatives, the public lost interest. Scientists with higher standards of knowledge than Pleasonton were aware that almost any plant grown under glass in sunlight would be superior. The craze for blue glass stopped as quickly as it had started, resulting in great amounts of blue articles no longer needed. Not even worth storage space in the Boston and Sandwich Glass Company warehouses, the glass was returned to Sandwich and dumped onto the factory site for fill. Although digging has been stopped by the town, quantities of blue lamp chimney fragments could be dug from the site until recently.
Throughout 1877, the business climate in the glass industry did not improve. No dramatic layoffs took place, but anyone who left the company was not replaced. The work force dwindled from the 1865 high of 520 employees to less than two hundred. Orders preceding Christmas kept the two hundred workers busy at full capacity, but they were using only two furnaces. There seemed to be no prospect of returning the factory to its former greatness. The value of a share of stock at the close of 1877 had dropped to $17.80.
On January 17, 1878, the *Crockery Journal* discussed marketing problems brought on by the too rapid expansion of the Pittsburgh-Ohio district. Completely disregarding the market's ability to consume, the district had already inundated every corner of the United States. To stay solvent, manufacturers now had to seek foreign outlets. The gutted market was cause for concern.
Once again, the Board of Directors did not know how to confront the problem. Many letters and documents in the company files tell a story of despair in the questions that were asked of various company officials. Why was it impossible for the Boston and Sandwich Glass Company to become as great as it had been in the past? What are the conditions that make it impossible? The questions persisted over the next several years. No one had answers, least of all George Lafayette Fessenden.
In March, the defunct New England Glass Company released to an already saturated market their $200,000 inventory, accepting whatever price it brought. The proceeds were to be divided among the stockholders. Wholesale jobbers bought up the New England Glass Company inventory at as much as 40 percent less than the usual wholesale price. All sales of Sandwich glass came to an abrupt halt, as many large orders already on the books were cancelled in favor of the better New England Glass Company price. This meant that the Boston and Sandwich Glass Company inventory, just sitting in warehouses filled to capacity, was automatically reduced to 40 percent of its value. Immediately, the Board filed a certificate for the reduction in capital from $400,000 to $200,000, forcing each stockholder to take a $25 loss per share—the only alternative other than closing out the business as the New England Glass Company had done.
Meanwhile, the Directors continued to investigate the reasons behind the total devastation of their company.

Committees were created to talk to department heads. They found that employee morale was at an all-time low, caused by a sense of futility in their jobs and depression over a stagnating world economy. Everyone realized that somehow glass would have to be moved even at rock-bottom prices, because conditions were continuing to spiral downward. As late as 1878 every Boston-based enterprise was still feeling the effects of the 1872 Boston fire. The City of Boston had been rebuilt at a cost that was based upon earlier economic prosperity. The overhead for the upkeep of elegant offices in the face of the slow economy was staggering. The *Crockery Journal* noted the lack of ships in Boston Harbor. Businessmen in Boston were at the end of their rope, not knowing how to bring themselves out of the depression. And, at Sandwich, in quiet moments between duties, employer and employee stared at the deteriorating walls, knowing that there were no funds with which to repair them.

On August 12, 1878, a discouraged Arthur Pickering sent his resignation as President to the Board of Directors. He spelled out the single largest problem faced by the company, saying that the Midwest glass companies had now made a cheap glass that had gradually taken over all the markets, leaving only seaports for the Sandwich trade, if the company could find a way to retain its share. A way had to be found to make glass competitively. But Arthur Pickering did not have the way and felt that the best interests of the Boston and Sandwich Glass Company would be served by replacing him. President Pickering's resignation was not accepted, and the Board turned to George Fessenden to lead the company back.

By the end of 1878, all of the glass houses in the Pittsburgh area were in labor turmoil. Unions were dictating who should be employed and at what salary, and who should be discharged. Workers were annoyed over the invention of labor-saving devices, most notably the chimney crimping machine that had been patented by a Pittsburgh man on November 11, 1875. The chimney blowers went out on strike in 1877 to threaten factory owners who shortened their hours—owners who were managing as best they could under the circumstances.

In Sandwich, workers kept a close eye on the relationships that were developing between labor and management within the industry. The nucleus formed in 1866 as a glassmakers' protective association strengthened into a group that was ready to become Local No. 16 of the American Flint Glass Workers Union. At a time when money is short, patience and tempers are also short. The head of a family who cannot keep food on his table does not have the hindsight to realize that worker demands were the final straw that broke the back of the Cape Cod Glass Company in 1869, or the foresight to analyze their long-term effect on the industry. He thinks only of the short-term dilemma, which is that his wife will run out of flour and sugar by next Tuesday. The Sandwich glassworkers really and truly believed that joining the union would give them control of local work schedules and had no idea that National Headquarters would eventually override their decisions and inflict rules that would destroy them. "Obedience to the majority" was their motto, and the "majority" was based in Pittsburgh.

The minutes of Local No. 16 meetings were recorded in a book dated 1879 to 1883, now in the care of the Sandwich Historical Society. At a preliminary meeting held on October 30, 1878, the labor group formed a committee to choose officers. They became formally organized on January 22, 1879, and immediately became involved in the Pittsburgh labor turmoil.

By February, the Pittsburgh flint glass factory owners decided to defy the strike and go back to work, using mostly new hands. The chimney glass blowers, now out for twenty-one months, saw how easily the owners had bypassed the union and decided also to return to work. The three months that the Pittsburgh workers had been out on strike gave the Boston and Sandwich Glass Company a welcome small shot in the arm. Orders that would have gone to less expensive Midwest houses had been sent to factories along the Eastern Seaboard. Sandwich had sufficient orders to allow two furnaces to run most of the time. But some of the employees were contributing part of their earnings to help the cause of labor, and, on April 2, 1879, the union made two decisions—send for their union seal, and send $25 to help Pittsburgh strikers.

In the fall of 1879, the Board of Directors sent Sewall H. Fessenden to the Astor House in New York City to represent the Boston and Sandwich Glass Company in becoming a permanent member of a new organization being formed under the name of The Protective Association of Flint Glass Manufacturers of the Eastern States.

The year closed with the Board satisfied with the number of Christmas orders, resulting in a slight drop in warehouse inventory. A revival seemed to be imminent when several shares of stock sold in Boston for $23 per share, and it appeared that enough orders were on the books to carry the company through the first quarter of 1880.

On February 16, 1880, the New York office and sample rooms were moved to 17 Murray Street, where a new line of threaded ware would be shown. The new quarters were said to be larger for the continued increase in stock. It should be noted, however, that several Boston and Sandwich agencies in other cities had been closed. Funds were

Seal from American Flint Glass Workers Union Local No. 16 in Sandwich.

made available for George Fessenden to enlarge Edward J. Swann's decorating room—a necessary expenditure resulting from the demand for this type of ware. Records show that glass blower John Louvet was making a large number of opal plaques and library shades to be decorated. Swann was actively searching for talented artists, and had recently hired several Sandwich girls, including Mary and Emma Gregory (see Volume 4, Chapter 14). Two new leers were built at the factory, and a 3 percent dividend was paid on March 10. At the annual stockholders meeting on March 31, the president reported that conditions were satisfactory and business was much improved over a year ago. It was reported in the *Crockery Journal* that there were no agents on the road, because the demand for Sandwich glass was such that it took full working capacity of the two furnaces that were operating to fill present orders on time.

As business improved, so did the strength of the union local. For individuals there were decided advantages. If a member was out of work because of illness, his fellow workers were each assessed 15 cents a week—a form of sick pay. As a group, they would ask George Fessenden for permission to attend a funeral, and Fessenden would "close work" until their return.

But the union was also beginning to involve itself in the workings of the factory, affecting decisions that previously would have been made by top management. On April 1, 1880, it was voted that union gaffers "use their best influence to help union men in preference to non-union men". Lists were being made itemizing every article produced in the plant, and the amount of money that members should receive for making them. To union members this all looked good on paper. But they did not realize that the union could demand a reduction in productivity of individuals.

According to writings in the *Crockery Journal* and the union records, business was fair in mid-1880. Cut goods were turned out, rich and elegant flower centerpieces (epergnes), hanging baskets, salad dishes, ice cream trays, pressed black bears and covered match boxes, and a great variety of tumblers and stemware. In the New York showroom, the cut glass and fine crystal was described as "charmingly cool" in the heat of the day. The company had approximately 150 hands employed full time. One furnace ran throughout the summer, and a second furnace intermittently.

The Boston and Sandwich Glass Company held its own throughout the fall, but statistics compiled at the time show why this continued to be difficult. They revealed that, in 1810, there were twenty-two glass factories in the United States. Fifty years later, there were 112. In 1870, there were 114, so it seems that the glass market could support that number of houses. But by 1880, this number had almost doubled—there were 206, of which eleven were in Massachusetts. Glass manufacturing had clearly gone beyond the market saturation point.

By the end of December 1880, some departments were running evenings to fill orders for the holiday trade, but the Board voted not to issue dividends for the stockholders.

The year 1881 marked the beginning of the end for the Fessenden brothers. For many years Sewall and George had completely dominated the Boston office and the works at Sandwich. It appears from the records that the Fessenden brothers lacked the ability or, more likely, were not given Board encouragement to make dynamic *decisions*, even though their *ideas* were generally progressive. They stood up to neither the Board of Directors nor the American Flint Glass Workers Union Local No. 16. One example: A committee from the union had approached George Fessenden about raising the price of fourteen inch library shades, and raising wages in general. It took him three months to make the decision about wages—there would be no increase. It was six months before he told them they could do what they wanted about reducing the number of library shades per move, thereby raising the price.

This tendency to delay decisions was compounded by the indecisiveness of the Board of Directors. Every progressive suggestion made by the Fessendens was eventually turned down by the Board. Only when a situation became desperate was a final decision made by the Board.

George Fessenden, caught between union demands and a Board that would not budge, began to show understandable signs of a nervous breakdown. Frustration and exasperation were his constant companions as he and his brother tried desperately to bring the company back from the brink of disaster. The company had in storage $120,000 in glass for four years or more, some of which had been discounted 40 percent below wholesale and still did not sell. Nothing had been done to modernize the plant and better the working conditions of the disgruntled men still employed.

On January 11, 1881, *The Sandwich Review* reported that all production had stopped so that repairs could be made to the boilers. It was found that two new ones would have to be ordered if production was to be resumed. It would be no easy matter to set new boilers, and labor costs would be considerable. The Board grudgingly decided to make the necessary expenditure. Repairs to the boilers were completed, and glassmaking was started again the first week in February.

On April 4, 1881, the Directors were to cast votes for President for the ensuing year. On the first ballot, Mr. Beal was elected, and he declined to accept the office. It took three more ballots for Arthur Pickering to have a clear cut majority. He was elected by default—no one wanted the job.

Meanwhile, internal strife was the order of the day for the American Flint Glass Workers Union Local No. 16.

Boston and Sandwich Glass Company advertisement, beginning with the May 13, 1880 issue of *Crockery Journal*. This publication was a wholesale trade paper. The ads do little to inform the reader of the skills available in each glass house.

Members who had joined for their own betterment found themselves assessed by National Headquarters for 10 cents a week per man to help strikers in South Boston. Through no fault of their own, experienced glassmakers had been given menial jobs that had previously been assigned to boys. The final irony came when they were told that they could no longer be active union members until they were doing men's work.

It was reported to the union that John Louvet had made more numbers of plaques and chandelier arms than the union allowed. He was ordered to confine himself to the numbers adopted by the society. Some disgusted members stopped going to meetings and were fined. Obvious "turncoats" who sided with the company were refunded their initiation fees. Small skirmishes continued to occur within the locals, and in their relationships with each other and the management of the Eastern and Midwest glass houses.

But each glass company hung on to their piece of the pie—a piece that was getting smaller and smaller with each passing year. Perhaps the saddest evidence of how low the Boston and Sandwich Glass Company had sunk was revealed in the *Crockery Journal* of November 17, 1881. They reported that the factory was pushed to its utmost because of two large orders that were to be given as wedding presents. In earlier days, such orders would not have been worthy of mention. Is it any wonder that George Fessenden was on the verge of a nervous breakdown when only a $2 dividend had been paid on October 1? And it was paid only after a heated argument among Board members, several of whom wanted no dividend paid at all.

The end of 1881 saw fierce competition at all levels of manufacture in the industry. The country was producing more glass than it could absorb, and additional foreign outlets were a must. In truth, however, world production surpassed the need. Only those glass houses with special talents and novel ideas such as the Mount Washington Glass Company, the Union Glass Company, and the New England Glass Works could survive. George Fessenden had no unique ideas, and no way to cash in on the special talents of a demoralized work force.

The Barnstable Patriot of January 17, 1882, stated that the Board of Directors had visited the works on January 10. They seemed pleased that the factory was so busy that the normal winter shutdown was impossible. But the newspaper didn't state that Fessenden's crew was down to seventy-five full-time workers—only half of what it had been the previous June. Nor did it mention that G. C. Boughton had been hired as a travelling salesman who would sell at 5 percent commission. In times of prosperity there *were* no salesmen on the road.

The Directors were once again in a position where they had to make a decision either to close the doors or find a man to lead the company back to greatness. In 1882, after a meeting of the Directors on February 20, the following note appeared in the record book:

The record of a meeting held on February 20, 1882, on pages 28 and 29 and 30, which meeting was desired by the Directors to be considered an informed one, was experged from this book and may be found on file.

We can only wonder what the "experged" information dealt with, but after long hours of debate, the Board named Head Salesman Henry Francis Spurr to superintend the works at Sandwich. At the April 3 meeting of the Board, after Arthur Pickering was again elected president, Spurr was given $300 for expenses in moving to Sandwich.

One week later, on April 10, George Lafayette Fessenden was given a leave of absence with a continuance of his salary. It was noted that "a respite from his duties might be advantageous to himself as well as to the company", his health being poor. Fessenden fought within himself, then submitted his resignation. He quietly made plans to move to California.

When we analyze the documents that exist today, we can only believe that the Board of Directors were more to blame for the shortcomings of this company than has ever been acknowledged. The Board constantly looked for some individual to step forward with magical answers. But there can be no magic nor even credible answers in the presence of *bad management*. At no time did the Board press anyone to create any kind of a long-range business plan. When will the boilers need replacing? What is the expected lifespan of a furnace? What is the future competition and where will it come from? Failure to consider the future meant that the Board reacted to events, rather than aggressively seeking to change events to its own advantage. Records prove they failed to anticipate, and even rejected, the impact the labor movement would have on the industry. Inability to analyze business conditions played a major part in the internal deterioration of the company. These stubborn Bostonians refused to recognize the competition that was coming inexorably from Pittsburgh. Not until Pittsburgh companies opened sales offices in Boston did they become alarmed. The Board was so busy hovering over management during the Fessenden era that management could not manage.

If any one member of the Board of Directors had taken the time to accumulate information from United States statistics, government reports and their own industry trade paper, *Crockery Journal*, they would have become aware that the center of the glass industry had moved away from the Eastern Seaboard and was now firmly established in the Pittsburgh area. Conditions in Pittsburgh were favorable for the manufacture of high quality glass at minimum cost —a combination that no intelligent Board of Directors could ignore, unless they were deliberately looking the other way in their effort to resist change.

William Libbey's New England Glass Works stood in enlightened contrast during this unsettling period. In the early 1880's, William and his son Edward Drummond Libbey took a hard look at business conditions and admitted that their regular line of glassware showed the same weakness in sales that plagued the Boston and Sandwich Glass Company. In response, the Libbeys began to manufacture art glass, which generated a great demand. With complete patent control, William and his son after him were able to charge prices that covered production costs and made a healthy profit.

We must put special emphasis on the effort that George Lafayette Fessenden had given to the Boston and Sandwich Glass Company. Although now broken in body and spirit, he could look back in pride and know that no man could have given more in the face of deteriorating conditions at the factory, including poor attitude of the workers and the decisions made, or not made, by the Board of Directors.

The tenure of Henry Francis Spurr as superintendent and then general manager of the Boston and Sandwich Glass Company is documented in Volume Four of this series.

NOTES TO CHAPTER 1

1. Experts in the past have stated that proof exists that the Boston and Sandwich Glass Company imported glass from other countries to be sold from the Boston showroom and even from the factory site in Sandwich. They maintain that the importing of glass is the reason why we cannot trust documents and dug fragments as proof that the glass was manufactured in Sandwich and not just imported and resold. There are several letters on file that were written to Deming Jarves regarding orders of imported glass. But these letters were written to Jarves as owner of the G. D. Jarves and Cormerais retail store, not to Jarves as agent of the Boston and Sandwich Glass Company. Jarves had been in the retail trade over and above his relationship with the glass industry since 1813. He had several different partners before his association with Henry Cormerais. Even a letter sent to Jarves in care of the Boston and Sandwich Glass Company is not proof that the glass was being imported by the Boston and Sandwich Glass Company. Jarves' habit of using the same address for more than one business is the reason for the confusion.

2. The New Bedford Glass Company was a short-lived operation. It was organized in 1866, backed by New Bedford merchants. The first glass was made in April 1867. Many of the fifty-four workers listed on the payroll can be recognized as Sandwich workers who followed Theodore Kern. Work was suspended at New Bedford in 1868, about the time Kern resigned. The glass trade in general was dull at that time. William L. Libbey purchased the site on January 4, 1870, and moved his Mount Washington Glass Works from South Boston to New Bedford. In 1871, it reorganized as the Mount Washington Glass Company, with Libbey as agent. Libbey resigned in 1872. He became the agent of the New England Glass Company in East Cambridge, Massachusetts, where later his son, Edward D. Libbey, became instrumental in the manufacture of Amberina, Wild Rose, Agata, and Pomona. The Mount Washington Glass Company also became known for various types of art glass, which included Burmese and Peach Blow, under the direction of Frederick S. Shirley. We find no evidence that the Boston and Sandwich Glass Company produced any of these art glass forms.

3. Harriot Buxton Barbour, on page 238 of her book, *Sandwich The Town That Glass Built* wrote, "Gone were the days of the reign of Mr. Jarves when at the first sniff of smoke, the company hand pump would come clanging out of the factory yard. The directors of the Boston and Sandwich Glass Company had issued orders of a different sort. At any sign of fire in the town, the apparatus was to be drawn up beside the factory and kept there in readiness for the threat of flying sparks. And there fire apparatus and company firemen stayed, while half a mile away the heart of the town burned down. The spirit of Mr. Jarves had truly departed from Jarvesville." Miss Barbour accurately recorded the facts, but implied that the glass company did not care for the well-being of the town. Unfortunately, the spirit of Mr. Jarves had very little influence on the insurance company.

4. William Germain Dooley in the *Boston Transcript*.

5. The appointment in August 1873, of William B. Bent as Superintendent of the Portland Glass Works signalled that a decision had been made to close the plant. According to Frank H. Swan, who wrote the definitive book, *Portland Glass Company*, Bent had been listed in the city directory as a "glass packer." His appointment to the superintendency certainly suggests that Portland glass was no longer to be manufactured. His job seems to have been one of cleanup, making finished glass, molds, patterns and machinery available to any interested parties.

6. Most historians have wondered why the Eastern glass companies, including Boston and Sandwich, did not have the good sense to move to the West as did the New England Glass Company. Technically, the New England Glass *Company did not* move to the West. Actually, it had closed its doors in April of 1877, putting 200 men and boys out of work, ten years before the strike that closed the Boston and Sandwich Glass Company. The buildings were placed on the market with real estate offices in Boston and were advertised for sale in the *Crockery Journal* beginning with the issue of April 12, 1877. Bankruptcy proceedings required that the New England Glass Company release all finished stock and goods onto the market at reduced prices. It glutted the market with glass. It was fortunate for the New England Glass Company Board of Directors that William L. Libbey, their agent since 1872, offered to lease the New England Glass Company buildings. Arrangements were quickly made and the buildings were taken off the market.

This was the official demise of the New England Glass *Company*. Their charter remained inactive through the 1880's, and on September 18, 1890, the Board of Directors surrendered the charter.

William L. Libbey started a brand new glass company called the New England Glass *Works*, and in 1877, temporarily housed it in the buildings he leased from the New England Glass Company. He was the sole owner and did not have to report to anyone. He had a son, Edward Drummond Libbey who, it was reported, had the cleverness of his father and the sensitivity of his mother, making him ideally suited to lead this new company to greatness. As soon as he completed his education, he joined his father William in the factory in 1883. William died shortly thereafter and, during the five years that followed, Edward was credited with producing and controlling three of the most popular art glass types of that era: Amberina, patented July 24, 1883, followed by Pomona and Agata. These art glass types were controlled by United States patent rights and were defended in the courts. There can be no question that the Boston and Sandwich Glass Company did not make such art glass, any more than it made another type called Peach Blow. Fragments found in small quantities at the Sandwich factory site should be attributed to a later attempt to reopen the factory.

The only company granted the franchise to produce any of these types of art glass was Hobbs, Brockunier and Company of Wheeling, West Virginia. This company was granted the right to *press* Amberina under Edward Libbey's patent. Hobbs, Brockunier and Company has also been credited with popularizing Peach Blow by producing a facsimile of the Chinese porcelain vase owned by Mary J. Morgan that created a sensation when it was sold at auction on March 8, 1886. This vase, although described in the *Crockery Journal* as "A sickly little bottle with a battered neck, made by a poor devil of a Chinese mudslinger," sold for many thousands of dollars. Variations of the Wheeling Peach Blow were also manufactured in the United States by the New England Glass Works under Libbey, although not particularly promoted by them, and by the Mount Washington factory in New Bedford. The products of all three glass companies are distinguishable from each other, but no Peach Blow can be attributed to the Boston and Sandwich Glass Company. By the mid 1890's these patent rights were copied and infringed on to such a degree that court action was impossible, but by this time the Boston and Sandwich Glass Company had been closed for years. When the strike of 1887 came to the glass industry, Edward D. Libbey seized the opportunity to move his New England Glass *Works* with one hundred of his best personnel to Toledo, Ohio, where he was given free land and free gas, vacating the buildings that had housed the New England Glass Company. As part of Owens-Illinois, Inc., it is still a vital part of the glass industry.

CHAPTER 2

VASES AND FLOWER CONTAINERS

1825–1908

Glass containers for holding flowers date back to Biblical times. With their use, flowers could be displayed in various arrangements, their beauty adding life and color to the surroundings. It is not surprising that when Deming Jarves began to produce glass in Sandwich, containers for flowers were included in his inventory. The earliest records from the Sandwich Glass Manufactory refer to *flower stands*. On December 31, 1825, flower stands with rings were listed by the man who tallied up each week's output in the company sloar book. This began a production run that continued for the sixty-two years that the Boston and Sandwich Glass Company produced glass through the halting of production by the Alton Manufacturing Company in 1908.

The records from that time make very clear that many of the glassmaking terms we use today are not those used at the time of production. For example, the word *lanthorn* preceded *lantern*. Creamers were called *creams*. The reason glass students have had difficulty in differentiating between *pill holders* and *spoon holders* is because they were originally manufactured as spoon holders regardless of their subsequent use. Similarly, a piece that would be identified as a *punch cup* by 1900 saw use as a *custard* in 1870. A new glass collector becomes understandably confused when he cannot distinguish among such various definitions and descriptive terms. The problem has been magnified by impatient researchers and writers who have arbitrarily assigned their own meanings to archaic terms and, in the process, failed to leave a trail that the serious student can trace.

There is no way of determining when the term *vase* came into use at Sandwich. The *Webster's Dictionary* from 1847 defines *vase* as "a vessel for domestic use, or for use in temples; as, a *vase* for sacrifice, an urn. An ancient vessel dug out of the ground or from rubbish, and kept as a curiosity." The 1864 edition adds " . . . especially a vessel of antique or elegant pattern used for ornamental purposes". Neither dictionary describes a vase as a holder for flowers, although present-day dictionaries do. By the time the 1874 Boston and Sandwich Glass Company catalog was released, *vase* was used in reference both to holders

for flowers as well as to ornamental pieces that were *not* designed to hold flowers, and *flower stands* were not mentioned. It is important to understand this change in nomenclature because we frequently look at the form of a vase and wonder how it ever held flowers without toppling over. Or we study a vase that has a design etched or transferred onto it and wonder how the busy design would fight with an arrangement of flowers. The answer is that every vase was not designed to hold flowers, but was meant solely to be used as a decorative ornament by itself.

We must agree that the term *vase* should not be used in connection with the word *celery*. An upright container designed to hold celery, pressed in a pattern or blown into a form that matches other table pieces, was called a *celery stand* or simply a *celery*, but never a "celery vase".

There was yet another use of the term *vase* in the glass industry, as an adjective describing a certain style of kerosene lamp. A *vase* lamp has a large glass bowl, or vase, into the top of which a metal can was inserted. A metal kerosene font was placed in the can, as shown in Volume 4, photo 4112.

The earliest "flower stands" that we have been able to document as Sandwich are free-blown trumpet vases and pressed pattern vases dating back to 1840. Regardless of their size, they are made up of several, separately-made units assembled and ingeniously held together by small wafer-shaped pieces of glass about the diameter and thickness of a quarter. In the early days of glassmaking in the United States, all glass factories heated their furnaces with wood. Heating the molten glass by wood limited the size of a piece of glass that could be pressed, because the glass did not maintain its temperature long enough to flow into all the crevices of the mold. When larger pressed articles were needed, the bases were pressed in one mold, and the upper units—candle sockets, bowls, lamp fonts, or vase trumpets—were blown or pressed into another. The units were joined by standing the base in an upright position, placing a hot wafer-shaped glob of glass on top of it, then placing the upper unit on the wafer and holding it until it adhered without support. Sometimes three units—a

The Enigma of Pairs

A pair of vases is worth more on the antiques market than two similar single vases, so the question inevitably arises—what constitutes a pair?

The answer depends upon the period in which the vases were made. Between 1825 and 1887, construction methods progressed from individually made, free-blown "flower stands" to pressed and Late Blown-molded perfect pairs. The earliest free-blown pieces varied considerably. No one, least of all the gaffers, expected them to be identical in height and diameter. If a vase overheated in the annealing oven and tipped slightly, or if a workman flared out a rim in a slightly different way, two similar flower stands were still thought of as pairs.

With the advent of pressing, the Boston and Sandwich Glass Company strove to make vases exactly alike, but their technique was not yet perfect. Separate upper and lower units had to be put together with a wafer. When one wafer was thicker than another, there was a difference in height. In most instances, no effort was made to line up the panels of pattern on the upper unit with the panels of pattern on the lower unit. Frequently, if two hexagonal vases are placed on a mantle with the straight edge of the lower units parallel to the edge of the mantle, the upper units appear to be askew. When a glassworker reworked a rim, there was often variation in height, diameter, and form as a result of the hand finishing. If the retail salesman found that the finish work drastically altered the forms of two vases pressed from the same molds, he might feel obligated to point this out to the retail customer. But in the final analysis, the judgment of the customer determined whether two vases were close enough in form and color to be considered a pair.

The Sandwich glass collector must use that same judgment today when considering the purchase of a pair of vases that date from the 1840–1860 period. *Consider as a pair only those items that match in color. Then determine whether the hand finishing has drastically changed the original shape, one to the other.* Auctioneers and dealers are inclined to hedge by saying, "A pair of similar vases", so it is still left to the buyer, as it was in the glass company showrooms, to use his own judgment. It is very difficult to assemble an identical pair, and this is the reason for the price difference between an exact matching pair and two similar single vases.

During the Late Blown Period, production methods had so improved that it was possible to blow vases in molds that left no mold marks. It was not necessary to rework them, so each piece was an exact duplicate of the previous one. It was expected that pairs of vases could be mated, so the Sandwich glass collector today should expect a pair of vases to be identical if they were manufactured during the last twenty years of the Boston and Sandwich Glass Company's existence. A study of the 1874 catalog will dramatize this fact.

base, a standard, and an upper unit—were joined to each other with wafers. The completed article was then carried to the leer to be annealed and the separate units were permanently held together. In the late 1830's when coal was used to heat the furnaces and higher temperatures could be maintained, the Boston and Sandwich Glass Company continued to use the wafer method of construction. It gave them great advantage over their competition at a time when costs of production were being watched very carefully. The years following the 1837 financial panic were lean ones, and molds were not replaced if they were still usable. The technology to mold a complete object in one piece existed and was being used by some other glass companies, but at the Boston and Sandwich Glass Company the wafer method was well entrenched. When a better grade of glass sand was discovered in 1845 and formulas were perfected to create new colors, a vast array of standards and upper units could be "mixed and matched" to make a variety of styles and color combinations.

There are many people who are not convinced that the Boston and Sandwich Glass Company continued to use wafers throughout their production years. The controversy compels us to document our research findings carefully. To date, our extensive collection of fragments dug from the factory site includes eighty-nine fragments of standards joined to an upper unit by a wafer. Our collection includes fragments dug by other historians, and there is not a single fragment of a vase with its standard and upper unit molded in one piece. This means that pressed pattern vases attached to marble bases also cannot be attributed to the Boston and Sandwich Glass Company, because we have never seen this type of vase with a wafer between the standard and the upper unit.

During our years of study, we have been fortunate to have access to many collections of Sandwich glass that were assembled at the time of production. General Manager Henry Francis Spurr brought pieces home directly from the works at Sandwich and the showroom in Boston. Lapham, Nye, and Lloyd are only a few prominent Sandwich employees whose descendants still have the pieces that were presented to their families, many with written documentation accompanying them. No pressed vases molded in one piece are included in any of these collections, with the exception of the few styles of very small vases that are nothing more than overgrown salts. *All of the pressed vases that we can attribute to Sandwich workers have wafers.*

A small collection of fragments dug from the site of the New England Glass Company in East Cambridge, Massachusetts, shows several lamps and candlesticks made in a one-piece mold. Patents taken out by or assigned to the New England Glass Company illustrate construction methods without the use of a wafer. A catalog of the New England Glass Company from the late 1860's shows pressed items molded in one piece, but we find no evidence that the Boston and Sandwich Glass Company or the Cape Cod Glass Company used that method. This does not mean that every piece with a wafer was made in Sandwich. The Mount Washington Glass Works joined units together with a wafer as did Pittsburgh houses. But it does mean that *a like item molded in one piece is not Sandwich.*

By the early 1860's, the manufacture of vases declined. For one, the Civil War curtailed production at both the Boston and Sandwich Glass Company and the new Cape Cod Glass Works. For another, kerosene had been discovered, creating a market for new styles of lamps to take the place of lamps that had burned whale oil or other types of burning fluid. The demand for kerosene lamps took precedence over the manufacture of vases and candlesticks, which faded away for almost a decade.

By the early 1870's, the Cape Cod Glass Company was closed, and competition from the Midwest glass houses forced the Boston and Sandwich Glass Company to concentrate upon the manufacture of thin-blown "bubble glass". The glass vases made during this period are well documented in the reprint of the 1874 Boston and Sandwich Glass Company catalog and in the Late Blown Ware chapter in Volume 4.

It cannot be emphasized too strongly that the Boston and Sandwich Glass Company did not excel in the manufacture of art glass vases. When this type of glass was being introduced by other factories, the Boston and Sandwich Glass Company was still concentrating on the very narrow segment of the market that would purchase threaded, acid-etched, and copper wheel engraved pieces for elegant dining. The Vasa Murrhina Art Glass Company, located on the site of the former Cape Cod Glass Company, tried to make and market art glass, and failed. The glass industry in Sandwich simply was not in a position financially to compete with other glass companies in new techniques such as Agata, Amberina, Burmese, Peach Blow, Pomona, or any other art glass form. Traditionally, these new methods were patented and assigned to a manufacturer by the inventor. Frequently these procedures were defended in the courts, but court records show that the Boston and Sandwich Glass Company did not become involved in any litigation resulting from art glass patent infringements.

Furthermore, the Sandwich Historical Society has a book containing minutes recorded at meetings of the American Flint Glass Workers Union, Local No. 16 in Sandwich. The book is dated 1879–1883. In the back of the book is a list of the items that were being manufactured at that time. The names of the items correspond with the names in the original price list that accompanied the 1874 Boston and Sandwich Glass Company catalog, proving that the company under General Manager Henry F. Spurr did not change its glass types and styles toward the end of its production years. The small amounts of Amberina and Peach Blow fragments that have been found in recent years on the surface at the Boston and Sandwich Glass Company site were from an attempt by Frederick S. Shirley to make art glass under the auspices of the Boston and Sandwich Glass Company II in 1896 (see Volume 4, page 82).

Finally, the old outdated furnaces were simply not capable of handling art glass. Vases appear to have been the only art glass articles made by the Alton Manufacturing Company in 1907. Called *Trevaise*, its identifying features are described in Chapter 17 of Volume 4.

THESE SIMPLE HINTS WILL HELP YOU IDENTIFY SANDWICH VASES.

The Boston and Sandwich Glass Company always used a wafer on pressed pattern vases. A like item molded in one piece is not Sandwich.

Each unit of a Sandwich pressed pattern vase is the same color, unlike candlesticks and lamps in which each unit may be a different color.

Pressed vases with marble bases were not made in Sandwich.

Art glass involving the blending and shading of two colors, such as Amberina, Burmese, and Peach Blow, was not produced by the Boston and Sandwich Glass Company.

Study the reprint of the Boston and Sandwich Glass Company catalog from the 1870's.

For vases in specific categories, study Chapters 6, 8, 11, 13, and 17 in Volume 4 of this series.

For many years, both the Town of Sandwich and the Boston and Sandwich Glass Company depended on bucket brigades to protect the Town and the factory against fire. Buckets and ladders were taken to the fire on this wagon, pulled by volunteers. In later years, the wagon was drawn by horses, as shown here. *Collections of Greenfield Village and the Henry Ford Museum, Dearborn, Michigan*

3001 FREE-BLOWN TRUMPET VASE

(a) Vase 10" H. x 3" Dia.
(b) Packing balls 2¾" Dia. 1840–1860

Certainly Sandwich made many free-blown vases, but unless there are family connections it is impossible to attribute a particular one. This vase belonged to the Tobey family in Sandwich. All of the family vases that have been made available to us have this type of base. The rims were reworked and turned outward, but the way the rim is folded cannot determine origin. It was at the discretion of the glassworker. The vase is made up of three pieces—the trumpet, the base, and the knopped standard. The trumpet is joined to the standard by a wafer, and another wafer connects the standard to the base. The packing balls were blown the same color as their vases, but appear to be lighter because they are so thin. For information on the use of packing balls, see Chapter 8.

3002 FREE-BLOWN TRUMPET VASES

(a) Taller 12¾" H. x 4⅝" Dia.
(b) Shorter 12½" H. x 4½" Dia. 1840–1855

Here are two of the best examples of free-blown vases from Sandwich we have ever seen. Each vase was made in three parts—the long trumpet, the standard, and the base. The base and standard were formed, then the trumpet was joined to the standard with the use of a wafer. The rim of the trumpet was folded to the inside and closed into a tight reinforcing ring. Even though there are slight differences in measurements, the vases are a pair. They were made from the same batch, albeit a batch that did not turn out to be the beautiful amethyst that was expected. Color expert James D. Lloyd wrote in his formula book dated August 7, 1868, that a really good amethyst is always clear. If soda is used it will give a brownish tint. The vases shown here are a marbling of amethyst and brown.

3003 FREE-BLOWN TRUMPET VASE
10" H. x 3½" Dia. 1840–1870

Free-blown "flower stands" of this type were made in almost every glass house during this period. Only the vase with glassworker family connections, documented as this one is, can be attributed to a specific factory. Any good glassblower would have the talent to duplicate this piece. It was made over a long period and was a staple in the industry. The trumpet and base were blown separately. The top of the standard is concave to accept a hot wafer of glass. The bottom of the trumpet is adhered to the wafer. In the base is an air bubble 1½" long. It is completely encased with glass. This is not a defect and does not affect the value.

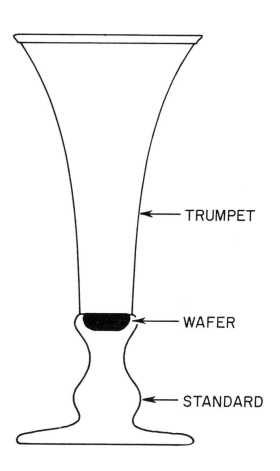

Fig. 3   The wafer is positioned inside the concave top of the standard and is covered by the bottom of the trumpet. It cannot be seen on the exterior of the vase.

3004 FREE-BLOWN TRUMPET VASE
9" H. x 4" Dia. 1840–1870

This vase came in many colors. The trumpet was also made to be inserted into a wooden base for cemetery use. Most of these blown pieces have their rims folded to the outside, away from the piece. This was known as *welted* in the industry. The trumpet was blown first and applied to the base when the base was still soft. If you find one at a sale with no documentation, it cannot be attributed to a specific glass house.

3005 FREE-BLOWN TAPPAN VASE
5¼" H. x 2¾" Dia. 1840–1860
This small vase is often sold by antiques dealers as a straw stem wine. There is no knop in the stem that would identify the piece as a vase in this small size. The base was made first, and the trumpet added to it. There is a rough pontil mark under the base where it was held when the trumpet was attached. If you find this vase without a pontil mark, it was not a vase made in Sandwich but a sherry made elsewhere in the 1920's.

3006 LATE-BLOWN TAPPAN VASE BLANK
18" H. x 6" Dia. 1870–1887
The Boston and Sandwich Glass Company catalog that was printed during the Late Blown Period carried photographs of clear glass before it had been engraved. These plain pieces were called *blanks*. The customer would pick out the piece that was wanted, and could chose from a variety of designs that would be copper-wheel engraved on it. The bottom of the trumpet was drawn out to become a plain stem with no knop. This style was known as Tappan by other glass companies, too. The plain trumpet inserted into a wooden base was used as a cemetery vase. When inserted into a metal fitting, it became the upper-most unit of an epergne.

3007 LATE-BLOWN DROP VASE
4⅞" H. x 2⅛" Dia. 1870–1887
This vase is a Tappan variant. It has the same blown trumpet, but it is connected by a button stem to a paper-weight-shaped base made of solid glass. The Boston and Sandwich Glass Company called it a *drop flower vase*. It came in three sizes, all with the same proportions. A taller one would have a longer trumpet and a larger diameter base. Unlike similar vases produced by Pairpoint in New Bedford, the Sandwich one has a short peg between the button knop and the base, which is solid glass with no controlled bubbles. *Courtesy, Sandwich Glass Museum, Sandwich Historical Society*

3008 LATE-BLOWN VASES WITH PAPERWEIGHT BASE
(a) 7¾" H. X 4" Dia.
(b) 7⅞" H. x 4⅛" Dia. 1870–1887

According to his family, Nicholas Lutz made these for his wife Lizzie. The base is made up of pink, blue and yellow glass shaped into apples, pears and vegetables, and green leaves. These were encased in clear glass to form a paperweight base. The addition of a spool stem and free-blown upper unit completed each piece. This is a variation of the drop vase shown in the Boston and Sandwich Glass Company catalog, but the Lutz family pieces are much heavier than the thinly-blown production pieces. Records at The Bennington Museum indicate that these vases were intended for engraving. *The Bennington Museum, Bennington, Vermont*

3009 FREE-BLOWN VASE FINGER BOWL
5¾" H. x 2¾" Dia. 1825–1835

Vase finger bowls are listed as such in the price list that accompanied a Boston and Sandwich Glass Company catalog that was printed in the 1870's. The piece shown here was made very early in the factory's history. Each unit was made separately. The bowl was blown, then reheated and shaped. A second man in the shop made the trumpet. While both pieces were still extremely hot, the trumpet was positioned inside the bowl, and the two units were fastened together by a glass wafer. The underside of the bowl has a pontil mark. If the piece was to have a design, it was engraved after the units were joined and the completed article was annealed.

3010 FREE-BLOWN VASE FINGER BOWL WITH LOW FOOT
5¼" H. x 2¾" Dia. 1835–1845

With no knowledge of their use, collectors call these pieces "small epergnes". But they were used as finger bowls, and a small bouquet in each vase added color to the table. The trumpet was fastened to the bowl with a wafer. Before the rims were fluted, they were folded for added strength. If it is Sandwich, it will have an unpolished pontil mark in the center of the foot. The engraved design on the trumpet does not extend below the rim of the bowl because the bowl was in the way of the engraving wheel.

3011 FREE-BLOWN GREEK BORDER SAUCER VASE WITH HIGH FOOT
7¼" H. x 4½" Dia. 1840-1850
This vase has wafers above and below the shallow plate. The top wafer holds the trumpet, and the bottom wafer connects the foot. The trumpet is only 4" high and holds a small bouquet of flowers. The saucer may have held after-dinner mints. Don't look for quality in these vases. They were made by the thousands to be used at each place setting on the dining table. Below the border design, clear and frosted panels alternate, with vertical lines bisecting the clear panels.

3012 FREE-BLOWN FERN TRUMPET VASE WITH BOWL
12" H. x 5½" Dia. 1860-1870
Sometimes a trumpet vase was combined with a high or low footed bowl to make an unusual vase. This vase is similar in shape to the Boyd vase shown on page 26 of the Boston and Sandwich Glass Company catalog from the 1870's. It is large enough to be useful and heavy enough to be durable. The trumpet was permanently attached when the piece was made. The fern and leaf design on the trumpet and the matching leaf design on the bowl were engraved after the piece was completed and annealed. Note how the design stops abruptly below the center of the trumpet. This is a common characteristic of Sandwich trumpets, whether used for vases or epergne units.

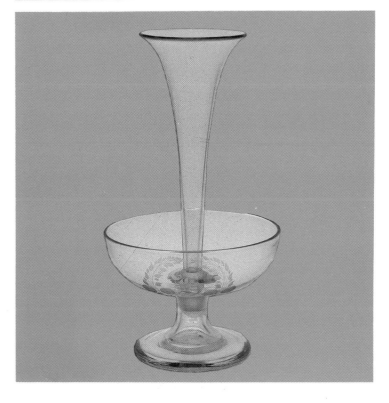

3013 LATE-BLOWN BOYD FLOWER VASE
8½" H. x 4¾" Dia. 1870-1887
Boyd is the name used by the Boston and Sandwich Glass Company for trumpet vases that could be detached from a compote-shaped bottom unit. The bottom unit was blown with a hollow base and standard that opens out to the center of the bowl, creating a socket into which the trumpet was inserted. The detachable trumpet made packing much easier for overseas and cross-country shipping. This piece was copper-wheel engraved with the letter "H" surrounded by a Number 2 wreath. It has been found in the family home of Sandwich glassworkers. The 1874 catalog shows two variations of the Boyd flower vase. This one appears on page 51. Another, shown on page 24, has a large knop toward the bottom of the trumpet, and the bowl is shallow. The number of fragments dug at the site indicate prolific production in clear and opal.

3014 FREE-BLOWN HYACINTH GLASSES
(a) Dark blue 8⅝" H. x 3⅝" Dia.
(b) Light blue 8" H. x 3⅝" Dia. 1830–1850
Hyacinth glasses are simply made. Their form is dictated by the growing habit of the plant. A hyacinth bulb is placed on the bowl-shaped rim so that only the roots come in contact with the water. The base was attached to the body when both units were of equal temperature, so a wafer was not needed. As a result of this crude method of assembly, the top is sometimes off-center. The edge of the base was folded to the inside. We have never seen hyacinth glasses with rigaree, scallops, fluting, or any other form of decoration. The dark blue color of glass A was used from the earliest days of production. It is often claimed that the Boston and Sandwich Glass Company made many things in blue because it was Deming Jarves' favorite color, but blue was the easiest and most inexpensive color to manufacture, and Jarves was a businessman. *Courtesy, Sandwich Glass Museum, Sandwich Historical Society*

3015 FREE-BLOWN HYACINTH GLASSES
(a) Shorter 9" H. x 3¼" Dia.
(b) Taller 9¼" H. x 3" Dia. 1830–1850
Because they were free-blown and finished by hand, the bowl that held the bulb varied in thickness, depth, and diameter. The height could vary as much as 1½". When you find hyacinth glasses in pairs, expect these variations. They may have been made by two different artisans working out of the same pot. Glass B was drawn out in height, accounting for the slightly thinner and therefore lighter colored body. There is a pontil mark underneath where the piece was held by a pontil rod while the top was shaped and the edge of the base was folded under. Fragments in quantity have been found at the factory site showing this wafer construction. Early records call these hyacinth *glasses*, not vases.

3016 FREE-BLOWN HYACINTH GLASS
6⅞" H. x 2¾" Dia. 1860–1887
This glass is from the collection of the descendants of Annie Mathilda Nye, a Boston and Sandwich Glass Company decorator. Many fragments of this base have been dug at the factory site, but many other glass companies also made this type of hyacinth glass. The Sandwich one has a rough pontil mark. It is rarely recognized as a Sandwich piece, which is understandable. Without documentation it cannot be attributed to a particular company.

3017 PRESSED LEAF VASES
11" H. x 6¼" Dia. 1840–1860
The mold for this pattern was most often used for a footed bowl. The flower-holding section of each vase was pressed into a bowl mold. It was then reheated and hand-formed into three upright sections, making three individual receptacles for the flower stems. The top vase section is held to the base with a wafer. The edge of the base has eight scallops. The leaf pattern is pressed on the inside of the base, and the outer side of the base is smooth. Leaf vases can be found in color, and the base was also used on footed Lacy dishes.

3018 PILLAR-MOLDED VASES WITH GAUFFERED RIM AND PRESSED MONUMENT BASE
(a) Deep flutes 11½" H.
(b) Shallow flutes 12" H. 1845–1860
Monument bases were made at both the Boston and Sandwich Glass Company and the New England Glass Company, and both companies are thought to have done a minimal amount of pillar-molding. These vases would be impossible to attribute without documentation, but the ones shown here have ties to Sandwich workers. To *gauffer* means to crimp or flute. A gauffered rim is made by reworking a rim that was perfectly round when it came out of the mold. Although both vases have seven flutes, they are not a pair. Vase A is shorter because the base overheated when the wafer was applied. As the upper unit was set in place the top of the base settled. Also the rim of Vase A was more deeply fluted than Vase B.

3019 PILLAR-MOLDED VASES WITH GAUFFERED RIM, PRESSED MONUMENT BASE AND CUT PUNTIES
(a) Taller, double wafer 12⅜" H. x 5¼" Dia.
(b) Shorter, single wafer 12¼" H. x 5⅝" Dia.
    1845–1860
We agree with Richard Carter Barret, former director-curator of The Bennington Museum, that this pair is perhaps the finest known both in design and workmanship. The difference in height is due to a production error. On Vase A, a wafer was applied to the pillar-molded upper unit, and another was applied to the top of the pressed lower unit. The two wafers were then joined together. After the vases were annealed, three punties were dished out of each vertical rib. Although the museum acquired each vase singly, they are well mated. We do no hesitate to call them a pair. *The Bennington Museum, Bennington, Vermont*

3020 PILLAR-MOLDED VASES WITH GAUFFERED RIM AND PRESSED HEXAGONAL BASE
(a) Round rim 10⅜" H. x 5⅝" Dia.
(b) Wavy rim 10¼" H. x 5¾" Dia. 1850–1860
Expect some variation in form and color when determining that two vases are a matching pair. The hand work necessary to complete these early items often caused them to be slightly different. Vase A is lighter because it was reheated and drawn out more than vase B, thinning the glass. Vase B is closer in form to the shape of the pillar mold. It was not drawn out as much. The rim is thicker where the pillars meet the rim and thinner between the pillars, producing a wavy effect. We sometimes forget that they were meant to be used. When the vase was filled with flowers, the rims would not be visible. *Courtesy, Sandwich Glass Museum, Sandwich Historical Society*

3021 PRESSED TULIP VASES WITH OCTAGONAL BASE

a) Dark amethyst, panels stop above peg extension
   10½" H. x 5" Dia.
b) Light amethyst, panels continue to peg extension
   10" H. x 5¼" Dia. 1845-1865

Tulip vases were made by pressing the top and the base separately and putting them together with a wafer. This pair has eight panels in the top and base, but care was not always taken to assemble them in line. The peg above the wafer varies from ¼" to ½" high. Two types of molds were used at Sandwich to form the Tulip top. On vase A, the panels stop before they reach the peg. On vase B, the panels continue to the peg. To be considered a pair, they must have come from the same type mold. We have seen more than six shades of amethyst and large variations in height and diameter, making it almost impossible to assemble an identical pair.

3022 PRESSED TULIP VASE WITH OCTAGONAL BASE

a) Blue-green vase 10" H. x 5" Dia.
b) Green fragment 1845-1865

Tulip vases may be found in many unusual colors, such as the beautiful blue-green one on the left. The vase on the right is one of the most complete fragments found at the factory site. Only rarely can this vase be found with the scalloped rim flared out only slightly, which was the original shape of the mold. The mold marks will be seen all along the rim. Most vases were reheated and their rims were pulled out into the flower form. To be considered a true pair, two vases must be identical in color, must have come from the same mold, and their scalloped rims should have been reworked so that both vases are reasonably alike in height and diameter. This is why a pair has greater value than two singles.

3023 PRESSED TULIP VASES WITH HEXAGONAL BASE

a) Amethyst 10¾" H. x 5⅛" Dia.
b) Blue-green 10⅞" H. x 5½" Dia. 1845-1865

Tulip vases are seldom found with flaring hexagonal bases. Most of them have an eight-sided base to match the eight panels in the upper unit. But the Boston and Sandwich Glass Company's wafer method of production means that a collector can find any number of combinations, some of which may not be shown in this book. If *both* separate units can be identified as known Sandwich products, and they are joined by a wafer, the vase can be accepted as Sandwich without question. If *only one* of the units has positive Sandwich attribution, more thought must be given to the piece. It could be Mount Washington, because they also used wafers. *Vase B: The Bennington Museum, Bennington, Vermont*

3024 PRESSED TULIP VASE WITH GROOVED CIRCULAR BASE

10" H. 1845–1865

The Sandwich method of using a wafer to join separate units created unusual combinations. This pressed base blank is used on compotes. It is ½" shorter than the common octagonal Tulip base. The vertical grooves are molded into the upper surface of the base. Concentric circles are molded into the underside of the base on the example shown here, but some vases have been found without concentric circles. The wafer can clearly be seen between the two pressed units. Learn to identify the separate units and remember that any combination is possible and acceptable as Sandwich.

3025 PRESSED SIX PANEL VASE WITH GAUFFERED RIM, OCTAGONAL STANDARD AND SQUARE BASE

11½" H. x 4" Dia. 1840–1860

This is a good example of distinctiveness that was frequently created in glass. Note the wafer that holds the vase to the standard. The wafer was too large, and as the vase was pressed onto it the excess glass oozed out. The glassworker quickly twisted the excess glass into petals, giving this piece individuality. In this side view, the edge of the wafer looks like rigaree. The mate to this vase does not have this petaled wafer, but they match in every other way, so are considered a pair. Their value should not be affected. If you want perfection, do not buy glass that dates before 1870.

3026 PRESSED LOOP VASES WITH GAUFFERED RIM, HEXAGONAL STANDARD AND CIRCULAR BASE

(a) Vases 10¼" H. x 4" Dia.

(b) Fragment 1840–1860

The Loop pattern is a popular one that can be found in full sets of tableware as well as in candlesticks. Six elongated loops make up the upper unit, but there are seven plier-marked flutes on the rim. The left vase has shallow flutes, but the difference is not noticeable enough to detract from them as a pair. As in all of the pressed pattern vases, the top was joined to the standard by a wafer. The fragment in the center is the largest in this pattern dug at Sandwich. It is from the former Casey fragment collection, now incorporated into the Barlow collection. Loop vases were also made in one piece, without a wafer, by the New England Glass Company, as were Loop vases with a marble base.

3027 PRESSED TWISTED LOOP VASE WITH GAUFFERED RIM, HEXAGONAL STANDARD AND CIRCULAR BASE

9¼" H. x 4¾" Dia. 1840–1860

When the glass was still hot, elongated loops were twisted about one-third of the way around. The vase has been reworked to the point that the mold mark is not visible. Six loops make up the body, but the rim was expanded to take eight flutes. The base, held to the top by a wafer, was made in a two-piece mold. It is a common base, but the twisted top is very rare. The standard is 1" shorter than the vase shown previously. It is proportioned to the lesser height of the top caused by the twist. Learn to recognize the basic form of a piece as it was molded, and you will be comfortable in attributing the hand-manipulated variations to Sandwich.

3028 PRESSED TWISTED LOOP VASE WITH GAUFFERED RIM, OCTAGONAL STANDARD AND SQUARE BASE

9⅝" H. x 5" Dia. 1840–1860

Here is the Twisted Loop upper unit joined to a 3⅛" square base. Before the rim was gauffered, its edge was folded to the inside. Unusual in these vibrant colors are the streaks of white running through the amethyst, creating a marble effect. This vase is in a private collection. We are grateful to the many collectors who have generously donated their glass and their time to this endeavor.

3029 PRESSED LOOP VASES WITH GAUFFERED RIM, OCTAGONAL STANDARD AND SQUARE BASE

a) Green

b) Blue 9¼" H. x 3⅜" Dia. 1840–1860

These two slender vases are smaller than most of this type. The base is 2½" square. Large quantities of elongated loop pattern fragments have been found in the diggings and we have found that the Boston and Sandwich Glass Company used wafers even on the small pieces shown here. A greater variety of styles of lamps, candlesticks, and vases could be produced when their separate units were interchangeable. Sometimes wafers were used on stemware. Both top and bottom units of each vase came out of the same mold, but no care was taken to line up the mold marks of the top and bottom units of vase A.

3030 PRESSED BIGLER VASES WITH GAUFFERED RIM, OCTAGONAL STANDARD AND SQUARE BASE

11" H. x 4½" Dia. 1840–1860

The name *Bigler* can be found in a McKee and Brothers catalog from the 1860's. The vases are perfectly matched, and each vase is beautiful within itself. The slender upper unit combines nicely with the slender lines of the concave paneled standard. Each upper unit is joined to its base with the type of wafer most often seen on lamps with blown fonts and pressed bases. The two rows of pattern are separated horizontally by a bar and vertically by a groove. We place special emphasis on the horizontal bar because its high relief distinguishes Bigler from similar patterns. *The Bennington Museum, Bennington, Vermont*

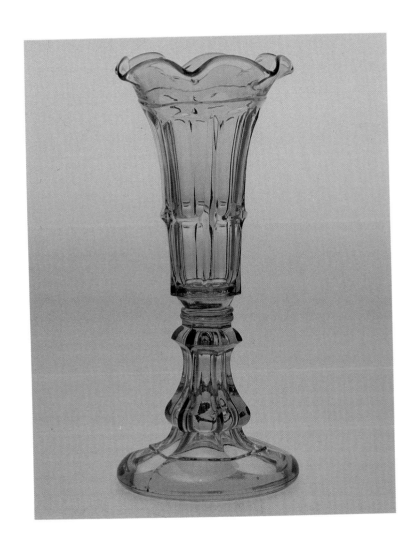

3031 PRESSED BIGLER VASE WITH GAUFFERED RIM, HEXAGONAL STANDARD AND CIRCULAR BASE

9½" H. x 4⅜" Dia. 1840–1860

For pieces that were made from two units, the pattern name refers to the upper unit. The gauffered rim was common at Sandwich. Don't let the number of flutes be a determining method of origin. They were hand formed at the discretion of the glassmaker. There may be six or eight panels of pattern pressed into the vase, and between six and nine flutes formed after the piece was removed from the mold. These early pieces were referred to at the time of production as *flower stands. Courtesy, Sandwich Glass Museum, Sandwich Historical Society*

3032 PRESSED THUMBPRINT AND ARCH VASE WITH GAUFFERED RIM AND MONUMENT BASE

12¼" H. x 4⅜" Dia. 1840-1860

If any vase can be called *masculine*, it would be this one. Its pattern lends itself very well to a straight-sided piece. There are six panels of pattern, and eight flutes in the rim. After the rims were reworked, they often dipped to one side. This is a characteristic of glass made in the 1800's, but it is uncommon today. The base is extremely heavy—the walls may be as much as ¾" thick. The monument base is often attributed to the New England Glass Company, but there is no question that it was also made by the Boston and Sandwich Glass Company. This pattern is often called a variant of Bigler. However, there is an area of smooth glass between the upper "thumbprint" and the lower "arch" in each of the six panels instead of the horizontal bar. We would prefer to call it *Two-Printie*, for reasons that will become clear in the following *Three-Printie* and *Four-Printie* photos. *Courtesy, Sandwich Glass Museum, Sandwich Historical Society*

3033 PRESSED THREE-PRINTIE VASES WITH GAUFFERED RIM AND HEXAGONAL BASE

10¾" H. x 5½" Dia. 1840-1860

The term *printie* refers to the concave indentations. There are three such indentations running vertically in each of six panels. These panels were not lined up with the panels on the base, but the vases are as close a pair as you will ever find. Both rims were fluted to the same depth. The hexagonal base was used on lamps and occasionally on candlesticks. It can be seen on a candlestick on page 48 of Volume 4. These pieces had to have come out of the factory as a pair, and should be kept together. If separated, the two vases would be worth only two-thirds of the value of the pair. *Courtesy, Sandwich Glass Museum, Sandwich Historical Society*

3034 PRESSED THREE-PRINTIE VASES WITH HEXAGONAL BASE

10½" H. x 5¼" Dia. 1840–1860

Even though these are pressed, it is unusual to see a perfectly matched pair. The less they have been reworked, the better are the chances of finding an exact pair. Generally the top unit was placed on the wafer with complete disregard for lining up the panels or mold marks. This is a pair in perfect alignment. The rims were flared out slightly, thinning the glass and lightening the color. Three Printie pattern and Bigler pattern both have vertical grooves (splits) between each panel, but no horizontal grooves. *Courtesy, Sandwich Glass Museum, Sandwich Historical Society*

3035 PRESSED THREE-PRINTIE BLOCK VASE WITH EXPANDED RIM, OCTAGONAL STANDARD AND SQUARE BASE

10" H. x 5" Dia. 1845–1860

Compare this pattern with the Three-Printie vases shown previously. In this vase, the addition of horizontal grooves between the three concave circles forms a block pattern. The upper unit that holds the flowers was made in a mold designed for the Three-Printie Block lamp font. That part which was flared out to make the rim of the vase would have been closed in to form the domed top of the lamp font. The knop beneath the pattern is part of the upper unit, and the wafer is below the knop. The 3" square base that works well when applied to a lamp is too small when used with this greatly expanded vase. When flowers are put in this piece, it is difficult to keep it from toppling over. It may have been an ornamental vase, not intended to be used as a flower stand.

036 PRESSED THREE-PRINTIE BLOCK VASE WITH GAUFFERED RIM, OCTAGONAL TANDARD AND SQUARE BASE
" H. x 3⅜" Dia. 1840–1860

The 2½" square base is the same one used on the longated Loop vases in photo 3029, but the upper unit s a variant of Three-Printie Block. The mold was designed with ovals instead of round printies. The ovals were n the mold and were not the result of distorting round printies by reworking the vase. Six panels of pattern make up the upper unit, with seven gauffered flutes around the im. The number of flutes can vary. *Courtesy, Sandwich Glass Museum, Sandwich Historical Society*

3037 PRESSED FOUR-PRINTIE BLOCK
a) Vase with gauffered rim and hexagonal base
   11½" H. x 4½" Dia.
b) Lamp 11" H. x 3½" Dia. 1840–1860

At first glance, this pattern looks like the one shown previously, but an additional fourth row barely a half block vide can be seen above the knop. This vase was one of the argest made in Sandwich for commercial purposes. The ame molds were used to make both the vase and the amp. The vase is taller because the glass was drawn up and out, elongating the top row of blocks. Expect minor variations in the hand-tooled rims. There are six panels of pattern molded into the vase, and six flutes gauffered nto the rim. The rim could just as easily have had eight or nine flutes, depending on the whim of the gaffer. Both he vase and the lamp must be connected to their bases vith a wafer to be considered Sandwich.

3038 PRESSED FOUR-PRINTIE BLOCK VASE WITH SCALLOPED RIM, HEXAGONAL STANDARD AND CIRCULAR BASE

10" H. x 5¼" Dia. 1840–1860

There are eight panels and eight scallops lined up over each block. Scallops are part of the mold. Mold marks sometimes can be seen on the edge of the rim, depending on how much the glass was reheated and flared out. The number of scallops cannot vary if the same mold is used to make another vase. Gauffered rims are hand fluted plain rims. There is no way to line up an eight-paneled vase with a six-paneled standard. This is not a defect and does not affect value. The usually graceful lines of Sandwich bases have been interrupted by the sharply-edged band surrounding the standard. *Courtesy, Sandwich Glass Museum, Sandwich Historical Society*

3039 BLOWN MOLDED HEART VASES WITH GAUFFERED RIM AND PRESSED HEXAGONAL BASE

9¾" H. x 4" Dia. 1840–1860

This pattern is common on Sandwich lamps, but occasionally the factory used a mold designed for lamp fonts and adapted it to other pieces. After the glass was removed from the mold, it had to be considerably reworked in order to shape it into a vase. The pattern was lengthened, distorting it somewhat. The glass that would have formed the dome of a lamp font was flared out and hand tooled into seven flutes, even though there are six hearts around the body. Do not mistake this pattern for the later Heart with Thumbprint (Bulls Eye in Heart) pattern that was made in Pennsylvania. In the Sandwich version, three hearts have thumbprints in them, alternating with hearts that have diamonds enclosed. The wafers can clearly be seen in the photo. *Courtesy, Sandwich Glass Museum, Sandwich Historical Society*

3040 BLOWN MOLDED HEART VASE WITH GAUFFERED RIM AND PRESSED HEXAGONAL BASE

9¼" H. x 4¼" Dia. 1840-1860

This vase appears to be the same as the last pair, but note how it was joined to the wafer. There should be a peg molded into the bottom of the upper unit. In the process of reshaping the glass from a lamp font form into a vase form, the peg, while in a molten condition, was absorbed into the body. This changed the height and appearance of the finished piece. If this vase was one of two and the only difference was the overheating of the peg, they would still be considered a pair. *Courtesy, Sandwich Glass Museum, Sandwich Historical Society*

3041 PRESSED ELONGATED LOOP WITH BISECTING LINES VASES

(a) Transparent green 4¾" H. x 3⅛" Dia. 1840-1850
(b) Fiery opalescent 4⅞" H. x 3¼" Dia. 1835-1840

The Boston and Sandwich Glass Company made very few small "flower stands" during the early years of pressing. There did not appear to be a market for them, and their scarcity today makes them very desirable. The hexagonal base is not hollow underneath—the vase was molded in one piece with no wafer, in the same manner as an egg cup or salt. The green vase is not as old as the opalescent one. There is more detail in the green vase. A reinforcing ridge can be felt along the inside of the scallops and, where the scallops come together, the ridge was machined smooth in the cutting shop. The dug fragments match the green vase in color and date. A similar item was also made in France by Cristalleries de Baccarat.

3042 PRESSED BALL AND GROOVE VASES

(a) Clear 5" H. x 3½" Dia.
(b) Amethyst 6" H. x 3¾" Dia. 1845-1865

If this vase had a name, it is lost to history. We are naming it *Ball and Groove* for obvious reason. By remembering the name, you will be able to differentiate easily between this Sandwich vase and a similar one made in Pennsylvania. The knob that protrudes out from the panels between the grooves is almost round. On the Pennsylvania piece, the knobs are egg-shaped, the smaller end at the top. Their other variations are minor. The vases from both areas were made in a mold with a scalloped rim. They were reheated and reworked, pulling the scallops up and out, much like the large Tulip vases. Unscrupulous antiques dealers sometimes buy these pieces with broken tops and have the tops cut off by a glass repair shop. The remaining portion is sold as a pressed salt.

3043 BLOWN MOLDED OVAL HOBNAIL WITH LEAF VASES
(a) Small pair 8" H.
(b) Medium single 10" H. 1850–1870
This style was made in three sizes. The hobnails are about the same size, but the small one has eleven rows of hobnails, the medium one has thirteen rows, and the large one (not shown) has sixteen rows. There are three long leaves that alternate with and overlap three short leaves. All of the vases in the Sandwich Oval Hobnail series have a pontil mark in the bottom where they were held as the rims were expanded. They were blown into the mold from the top down. This vase was also made in France. It can be seen in the book *L'Opaline Francaise au XIXe Siecle* with the hobnail bowl in a dark color and the trumpet and leaves in a lighter color. The ring separating the hobnails and leaves is less pronounced on the French piece. According to author Yolande Amic, the French vase can be found in a three-color combination. The Sandwich vase, however, was made only in a single color.

3044 BLOWN MOLDED OVAL HOBNAIL WITH LEAF
(a) Vases 8" H.
(b) Blown molded finial for newel posts and curtain rods 5¾" H. x 2¾" Dia. 1850–1870
Certain patterns lend themselves to multiple applications. When you are at an antiques show, keep your mind open to the surprise of finding unusual items in patterns you know to be Sandwich. There can be no doubt that, since the vase forms are documented as Sandwich, the finial is also. Finials can also be found in white and in green. We have a cologne in very light green, so don't limit your thinking to a particular color. The exciting part of collecting is never knowing what is in the next booth. The finial shown here was dug at the Boston and Sandwich Glass Company site.

3045 BLOWN MOLDED OVAL HOBNAIL VASE
5½" H. x 2¾" Dia. 1850–1870
This vase is very similar in design to the cologne in photo 3118. It is from the family of Charles W. Spurr, whose brother Henry was head salesman and then general manager of the Boston and Sandwich Glass Company. The top was reheated and expanded. The green rim was applied in the same manner that blue or red rims were applied to smoke bells. We have yet to see a piece in this pattern that is not extremely attractive.

3046 FREE-BLOWN VASES WITH BLOWN MOLDED CENTER

(a) Green with white Sawtooth (Mitre Diamond) center
    9" H. x 3½" Dia.
(b) White with green Oval Hobnail center
    9" H. x 3¼" Dia. 1850–1870

It is our opinion that these vases were not intended to have water in them. They are ornamental vases, not flower holders. Each vase is a composite of three distinct pieces. The center was blown into a patterned mold. The base was blown and fastened to the center with a wafer. The trumpet was blown with a wafer-like projection at its lower end, which was then attached to the top of the patterned center. On some of these vases, there is a hole through the center of the projection that allows water to enter the patterned center, but the hole is so small that it is impossible to clean the center. On some of the vases we studied, the hole was plugged up by excess glass from the trumpet, so only the trumpet would fill with water. Vase A is difficult to find, and Vase B is the only example of its kind we have encountered.

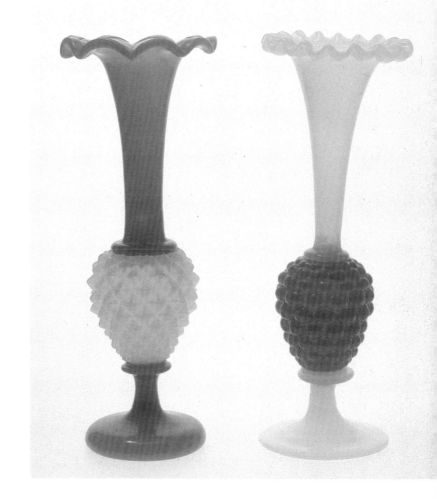

3047 FREE-BLOWN VASES WITH BLOWN MOLDED SAWTOOTH (MITRE DIAMOND) CENTER

(a) Blue 9" H. x 3½" Dia.
(b) Green 8¼" H. x 3½" Dia. 1850–1870

Although accurate measurements are given, they cannot be used as a method of attribution for pieces that have been free-blown or have had extensive hand finishing. These vases are alike to the top of the Mitre Diamond center, which was blown into a mold. The height changes by varying the length of the trumpet, which was free-blown. Before the rim of the trumpet was fluted, it was folded to the inside, making it a dirt catcher. Do not attempt to attribute origin by the direction in which a rim is folded. It was done at the discretion of the gaffer. *Courtesy, Sandwich Glass Museum, Sandwich Historical Society*

3048 ROSETTE
(a) Blown molded vase 5½" H. x 2¼" Dia.
(b) Blown molded cologne 4⅜" H. x 2⅛" Dia.
    1850–1870
Sandwich produced both a five-petaled and six-petaled Rosette pattern. These pieces have five-petaled Rosettes. The body of the vase was made from the same shape mold as the cologne, but the vase has a raised base. After the vase was removed from the mold, the top was reworked into its trumpet shape. *Courtesy, Sandwich Glass Museum, Sandwich Historical Society*

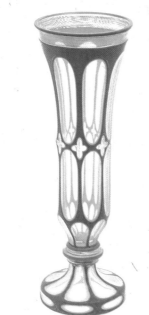

3049 CUT DOUBLE OVERLAY VASE PRESENTED TO ISAAC HOXIE
13¼" H. x 4½" Dia. 1856
Not many ornate Overlay vases were made for commercial purposes. Most were one-of-a-kind, to commemorate a specific occasion. This vase was one of a pair given to Isaac Hoxie on the day of his retirement. The base and trumpet were blown separately, and joined by a wafer. The design cut into the trumpet was well executed, but the base was not. The white layer of glass was too cool when it was blown into the pink, so it remained thick. When the design was cut into the base, too much of the white showed. Do not look for perfection in Sandwich Overlay —much of it is crude. A good way to study double Overlay is to look into the trumpet. The white middle layer can be seen from the inside, and from the outside the white layer appears as a white line separating the pink outer layer from the clear inner layer. The vase was gilded after it was cut.

3050 LATE-BLOWN VASE BLANK
9¼" H. x 5⅞" Dia. 1870–1887
The 1874 Boston and Sandwich Glass Company catalog lists this piece as "6065 plain vase". It can be seen on page 44 of the catalog in six sizes, ranging in height from 4 to 10 inches. Here, the claw feet curl outward, but they may sometimes be found curling inward. The top was reworked to provide a flat area to support the stems of the flowers. A berry prunt covers the pontil mark, but may not be present on every piece. The plain vases were called *blanks*, because they could be etched or copper-wheel engraved with standard factory designs as seen in the catalog or with wreaths and monograms as specified by the customer. This style was also made in opal, which was decorated with butterflies, flowers, or leaves. It can be seen with etched ferns in Volume 4, photo 4206. *Courtesy, Sandwich Glass Museum, Sandwich Historical Society*

3051 LATE-BLOWN VASE WITH ACID-ETCHED CASTLE TRANSFER PRINT

6" H. x 3¼" Dia. 1870–1887

This vase, made during the Late Blown Period, was listed by the Boston and Sandwich Glass Company as "6051 vase". It can be seen on page 44 of the catalog in four sizes ranging from 5" to 8". The claw feet curl outward, but occasionally pieces can be found with the feet curling inward. The feet and the lower ends of the reeded handles were applied to the body by pulling each ridge out until their appearance resembled scallop shells. The handles were drawn thin and attached at their upper ends. This vase has a castle acid-etched on one side and a small fern on the other. Don't dismiss a good piece of Sandwich glass because the design is unusual. The designs were purchased and could change from year to year. Many show European influence. This piece is in the family collection of descendants of James Lloyd and Hiram Dillaway.

3052 BLOWN MOLDED OPAL RING VASE DECORATED WITH STORYBOOK CHARACTERS

7" H. x 2½" Dia. 1885

According to descendants of Boston and Sandwich Glass Company General Manager Henry Francis Spurr, it was his novel idea to copy illustrations from children's books onto glass. This Palmer Cox illustration of a frog riding a mouse is entitled, "A Morning Ride". It was taken from the book *Art in the Nursery*, published by D. Lothrop & Company in Boston, Massachusetts, in 1879. Spurr's family believed it was reproduced on glass about 1885.

3053 BLOWN MOLDED OPAL RING VASE DECORATED WITH STORYBOOK CHARACTERS

7" H. x 2½" Dia. 1885

This vase has a Palmer Cox illustration entitled, "Merrily, Oh!". It was copied from the same book as the vase above. It shows a rabbit being led merrily away by a fox, and the outcome was left to the reader's imagination. It is believed that many of these were made from early story illustrations. They are *not* transfer designs—each one was individually painted, so do not pass one by at an antiques show because the design is not familiar. Animals and landscapes painted with a rather heavy hand can be attributed with a fair amount of confidence to Edmund Kimball Chipman, whose work can be seen in Volume 4, photo 4259.

3054 BLOWN MOLDED DECORATED OPAL RING VASES

(a) Storybook characters 7" H. x 2½" Dia. 1885
(b) Raspberries from brier patch 8" H. x 3" Dia.
   1870–1887

Several illustrations in the storybook *Art in the Nursery* depict the brier patch. Although the center vase is larger, and the design is painted above and below the rings, and there is no gilding on the rim, it has been identified by a Spurr family descendant as part of the same series. Note the dug fragment. It was made in the same mold as the larger vase and its color matches all of the vases perfectly. Many of these fragments are available in other colors, indicating prolific production in Sandwich.

3055 BLOWN MOLDED OPAL RING VASES DECORATED WITH RASPBERRIES

(a) Raspberries from brier patch
(b) Raspberries without thorns 8" H. x 3" Dia.
   1870–1887

When we are able to authenticate Sandwich glass pieces as we were able to document the Spurr storybook vases shown previously, we can then attribute related pieces with accuracy. The vase on the right was found at an antiques show, but there is no doubt of its origin. Note the leaves below the rim, and the shadowy leaves in the background. There are minor variations on vase B, such as a lack of thorns and excessive ground cover. Slight differences reflect individual workmanship and do not affect the value.

3056 BLOWN MOLDED OPAL RING VASE DECORATED WITH APPLE BLOSSOMS

6⅞" H. x 2⅝" Dia. 1870–1887

Ring vases with floral designs depicting flowers, shrubs, and trees indigenous to the New England area were commonly produced by the Boston and Sandwich Glass Company. It was not unusual to see Sandwich artists in the meadows and fields of Cape Cod painting animals and plants in their natural surroundings. In the decorating room, the designs were simplified and adapted to glass. Vases with hand-painted designs that do not depict local nature cannot be attributed to Sandwich. In addition to the gilding on the rings, this piece has narrow gold lines delineating the floated blue ground. *Courtesy, Sandwich Glass Museum, Sandwich Historical Society*

3057 BLOWN MOLDED OPAL RING VASE DECORATED WITH QUEEN ANNE'S LACE

4⅝" H. x 1¾" Dia. 1870–1887

Ring vases were made in several sizes. This is the smallest. The delicate tracery of wild flowers combined with a pastel yellow ground provide a pleasing design for this diminutive vase. Many times only the center of the vase is painted, but on this piece the blade of grass begins beneath the bottom rings. The artist carried the design to within ¼" of the rim. Designs painted with a very light touch show the influence of Edward J. Swann, who came to Sandwich late in 1872. Swann expanded the decorating department of the Boston and Sandwich Glass Company and added variety by searching out local talent having different painting techniques. *Courtesy, Sandwich Glass Museum, Sandwich Historical Society*

3058 BLOWN MOLDED OPAL RING VASE DECORATED WITH BUTTERFLY

6¾" H. x 2⅝" Dia. 1870–1887

This type of ring vase with four gilded rings and a completely decorated center was made in quantity at Sandwich. This vase would have been described in their catalogs as having a *floated center*. The green ground color was floated on only between the rings. The butterfly and its landing area were hand-painted. A transfer (decal) was not used on this piece, although transfers were used on a great many. There is greater value in a vase painted completely by hand than in one on which color was added by a transfer. Ring vases were also hand-painted at Mount Washington. *Courtesy, Sandwich Glass Museum, Sandwich Historical Society*

3059 BLOWN MOLDED OPAL RING VASE DECORATED WITH BLUEBIRD AND DRAGONFLY

8" H. x 3" Dia. 1870–1887

White opal glass was often tinted to make other soft colors, so the color of the vase blank should not be a determining factor in identifying a Sandwich piece. This bluebird is a good example of the detail originating from the Boston and Sandwich Glass Company decorating department. The bird is taking off to chase the dragonfly. Friedman Miller, a skilled decorator and naturalist, went to the fields and forests of Cape Cod to paint scenes in their natural colors. His work was copied by the other artists in the decorating room, who adapted his designs to vases, flower pots, and even smoke bells. The ferns and foliage completely surround the vase.

3060 BLOWN MOLDED OPAL RING VASES DECORATED WITH GREAT BLUE HERON

5⅞" H. x 2⅜" Dia. 1870–1887

The great blue heron is the most common design painted on ring vases. This type of decorating was initiated by the Smith Brothers when they worked at Sandwich. It was continued by them at the Mount Washington Glass Works in New Bedford and at their own decorating shop in New Bedford, where they utilized Mount Washington blanks. Ring vases were also made by Samuel Bowie in New Bedford and by Gillinder and Sons in Philadelphia. Based on fragments dug at Sandwich, we are able to document three variations of the heron design. In this first variation, the green reed shows between the heron's legs, passing behind and over his body. There are no brown cattails. Other variations appear in photos 3061 and 3072. If the vases are a true pair, the birds will face each other.

The Smith brothers. Harry A. Smith is on the left and Alfred E. Smith is on the right. *Courtesy, Sandwich Glass Museum, Sandwich Historical Society*

3061 BLOWN MOLDED OPAL RING VASE DECORATED WITH GREAT BLUE HERON

7¾" H. x 2½" Dia. 1880–1887

This vase was painted by Annie Mathilda Nye, who worked at the Boston and Sandwich Glass Company from 1880 until the last of the decorating work was completed in 1888. This variation has heavy stalks on each side of the heron, and brown cattails. The salmon background color was *floated* on. Some decorated vases had floated centers and were plain at the top and bottom. Some had floated tops and bottoms and were white between the rings.

3062 BLOWN MOLDED OPAL RING VASE DECORATED WITH ELK TRANSFER PRINT

7" H. x 2½" Dia. 1870–1887

The elk, the rocks in the foreground, and the water are part of the transfer print. The clouds and sky were touched up by hand to "dress" the piece. The color above and below the rings and the gilded lines on both sides of the rings were painted on by a decorator called a *liner*. The fragment matches the vase in shape, but its base has six indentations. Both types were made in Sandwich.

3063 BLOWN MOLDED RING VASE WITH ACID-ETCHED BIRD TRANSFER PRINT

6" H. x 2⅜" Dia. 1870–1887

Sandwich made very few pieces commemorating a particular holiday. The words "A MERRY CHRISTMAS" are on the branch behind the bird's feet. The tree is bare of leaves. There is a vine of five-lobed leaves along the right side of the branch and across the bottom. The rings are etched, as is the border design at the top and bottom. These vases were not expensive. They were packed on their sides in layers protected by a layer of straw. Packing balls were not used. If, in transit, the rings of one vase touched the rings of another, they were not likely to break.
Courtesy, Sandwich Glass Museum, Sandwich Historical Society

3064 BLOWN MOLDED OPAL RING VASE DECORATED WITH CHARIOT TRANSFER PRINT

7" H. x 2½" Dia. 1870–1887

The Boston and Sandwich Glass Company catalog price list describes this piece as "colored top and bottom, black figure vase". The picture of a chariot drawn by two horses was acid-etched into the white glass blank, and the lines were filled with black enamel. The black line on each ring was put on by a decorator called a *liner*. After all the color work was completed, the vase was sent to the decorating kiln. Study page 59 of the catalog reprint for other black figure designs. The chariot design was also used on a cone shade shown on page 66 of the catalog.

3065 BLOWN MOLDED RING VASE WITH ACID-ETCHED CHARIOT TRANSFER PRINT
7" H. x 2½" Dia. 1870–1887

Many clear glass ring vases were made and acid-etched in Sandwich. They are not often recognized by inexperienced collectors. Study the "black figure" designs that are on the opal ring vases shown in the factory catalog on page 59. Don't be afraid of slight variations in designs, because the prints were purchased and changed from year to year. The Greek Border variation etched around the top and bottom is an unusual touch. It can be found on an opal decorated flower pot in the catalog. Original catalogs are invaluable in the documentation of a company's product. We carry a copy with us when we shop for Sandwich glass.

3066 ETCHING PLATE, FIRST DESIGN
1870–1887

A glass etching plate at the Sandwich Glass Museum has several designs that were used on clear and opal articles during the later years of production. This chariot design is the one most often found and can be seen on the ring vases shown previously. Note the Greek Border on the horse's girth and the stars on the cape. The etching plate originally belonged to the Russell family, two generations of whom had a member working at the factory. *Courtesy, Sandwich Glass Museum, Sandwich Historical Society*

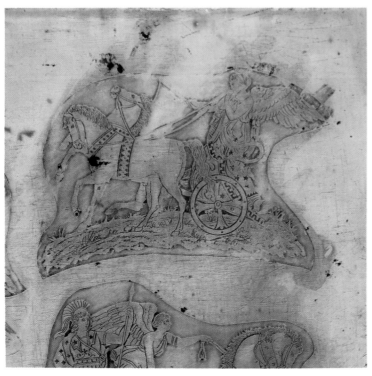

3067 A SECOND DESIGN ON ABOVE ETCHING PLATE

All of the designs on the etching plate are related in some way. A similar winged goddess is holding the reins. Note the stars on the clothing. The chariot is bordered with a Roman Key design, used frequently on Late Blown Ware (see Volume 4, Chapter 11).

3068 THIRD DESIGN ON ABOVE ETCHING PLATE

Here is a single horse whose rider is wearing a cape embellished with stars. A study of the 1874 catalog shows that the decorated items were not described according to design. The opal vases were listed as *black figure*.

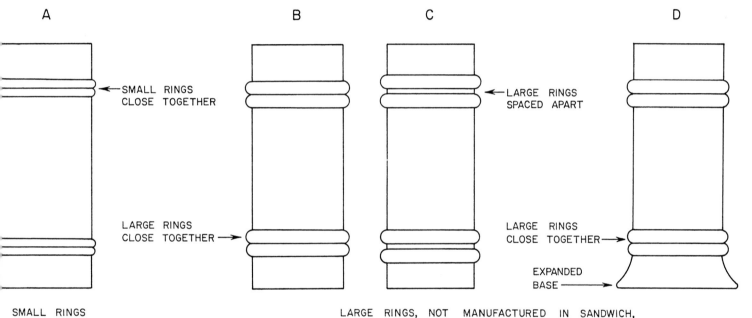

A   B   C   D

←SMALL RINGS CLOSE TOGETHER

←LARGE RINGS SPACED APART

LARGE RINGS CLOSE TOGETHER →

LARGE RINGS CLOSE TOGETHER→

EXPANDED BASE ——→

SMALL RINGS CAN BE SANDWICH

LARGE RINGS, NOT MANUFACTURED IN SANDWICH, BUT SOME WERE DECORATED THERE

Fig. 4 All of the vases we have been able to document as having been *manufactured* by the Boston and Sandwich Glass Company have small rings, as shown in illustration A, although other glass companies also made them. Note the size of the rings in proportion to the vases. The large-ringed vases were not manufactured in Sandwich and most of them were not decorated in Sandwich. The small percentage of large-ringed vases that found their way to Sandwich were blanks that were purchased from other sources by Edward J. Swann and Charles W. Spurr, both of whom operated decorating shops after the Boston and Sandwich Glass Company closed. Do not attribute a large-ringed vase to a Sandwich decorating shop unless it is accompanied by irrefutable documentation. A vase with the expanded base shown in illustration D was found at the site of Spurr's decorating shop. It can be seen in Volume 4 on page 128.

Fig. 5 Only two types of bases have been found on ring vases *manufactured* by the Boston and Sandwich Glass Company. Family pieces and dug fragments show that some vases have a bottom that is perfectly flat, as shown in the illustration on the left. Others have a recessed base with indentations made from cleats in the bottom of the mold in which they were blown. The number of the indentations may vary, but each indentation is trapezoidal in shape—wide toward the outside of the base and narrow toward the center. Other glass houses also made these two types, so there is no way of identifying Sandwich ring vases by examining the bottom.

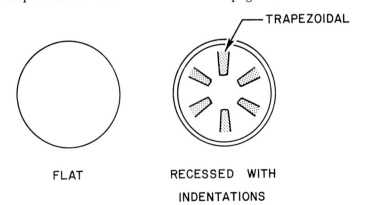

——TRAPEZOIDAL

FLAT   RECESSED WITH INDENTATIONS

3069 PRESSED OPAL VASE DECORATED WITH AUTUMN LEAVES
4¾" H. x 2¼" Dia. 1875-1887
To reliably attribute Sandwich glass, we must have more than one method of proof. Even this strikingly simple vase can be traced two ways. First, it was passed on from the family of Annie Mathilda Nye, who worked in the decorating department under Edward J. Swann. Second, a of the fragments dug at the site of the factory have the stems of autumn leaves twisted together, even if there are only two leaves. The light pink background was applied first. After the leaves were painted, the color was made permanent by firing the piece in the decorating kiln. The leaves vary in color from piece to piece.

3070 PRESSED OPAL VASE DECORATED WITH WHITE VIOLETS
4" H. x 2" Dia. 1875-1887
These pieces are often mistaken as being made by the English firms of Stevens and Williams, or Richards. Many of the flowers native to Sandwich are also grown in England. This is one reason why identification is difficult. The leaves of this white violet plant provide us with a clue. Note the shading in the leaves to give them depth. Their similarity to work done by Edward J. Swann tells us that an artist under his tutelage painted this vase. The color of the glass can be determined by looking into the vase. The blue background is a floated color. The rim is gilded.

3071 PRESSED OPAL CYLINDER VASE DECORATED WITH GREAT BLUE HERON
6" H. x 2¾" Dia. 1875-1887
Straight-sided vases without rings are not shown in the 1874 Boston and Sandwich Glass Company catalog, but the heavy cattail reed between the legs of the bird is an identifying feature that can also be found on ring vases made by the company. A sprig of wheat is painted on the other side, echoing the painting on the front. The rim is gilded. Learn the styles of blanks that were used at Sandwich. Any of the designs that can be authenticated at Sandwich can be found on any authenticated style of blank. This includes blanks for cone shades, gas globes, finger bowls, and flower pots. *Courtesy, Sandwich Glass Museum, Sandwich Historical Society*

4072 PRESSED OPAL VASE DECORATED WITH GREAT BLUE HERON

¼" H. x 2⅝" L. x 1¾" W. 1907-1908

All of the long-legged birds painted in Sandwich or New Bedford are great blue herons, although some resemble storks and are often sold as such. Designs were painted from nature, and there are no storks along the Massachusetts coast. This is a third type of heron design found on the fragments dug at the factory site. The reeds are heavy and look like cornstalks. Note the poor quality of the floated blue background and the lack of detail. It is easy to tell that Edward J. Swann was not in charge of *this* decorating department! We believe this piece was a product of the Alton Manufacturing Company in a last attempt to manufacture glass in Sandwich.

4073 BLOWN MOLDED OPAL VASE DECORATED WITH GREAT BLUE HERON

⅛" H. x 4¾" Dia. 1880-1887

This vase is usually attributed to the New England Glass Works in East Cambridge, and to the Smith Brothers in New Bedford. However, family records from Sandwich decorators and fragments dug at the site prove that the Boston and Sandwich Glass Company produced this shape *after* the Smiths left Sandwich. Annie Mathilda Nye painted this vase. She was born in 1860 and began working at the factory in July 1880, according to Emma Gregory's diary. This vase was made in one piece out of opal glass. The color was painted on, but the white of the heron and the water lilies is the color of the glass. Only one heron is on each vase in all of the heron series. A pair of vases has one heron on each vase facing each other. If the herons are facing the same direction, the vases are two singles and should be priced individually.

Annie Mathilda Nye, decorator.

**3074 BLOWN MOLDED OPAL VASE
DECORATED WITH RASPBERRY SPRIG
AND INSECT**
7⅛" H. x 3¾" Dia. 1875-1887
The shape of this vase cannot be found in the 1874 Boston and Sandwich Glass Company catalog, so it is not often recognized by collectors. *All* the shapes shown here and in subsequent photos have family documents that tie them to Sandwich. Also, look for fine detail in Sandwich vases, such as the insect coming in for a landing from the left and the barbs on the stem. The background is a soft pastel, and the base is painted black. Gilding separates the two colors. Another gilded line is on the rim. *Courtesy, Sandwich Glass Museum, Sandwich Historical Society*

**3075 BLOWN MOLDED OPAL VASE
DECORATED WITH DAISIES, BUTTERFLY
AND LADYBUG**
10" H. x 3¼" Dia. 1875-1887
Note the ladybug on the blade of grass to the right. The butterfly with full wing expansion is on a daisy to the left. Sandwich artists were able to capture a moment suspended, very much as a high-speed camera can freeze living action today. A band of gilding separates the background color from the black base, and the rim of the vase is gilded. After being blown into a mold, the opal vase blank was annealed, then sent to Edward J. Swann's decorating room. After the artist completed his work, the vase was fired in a decorating kiln to permanently fix the color. *Courtesy, Sandwich Glass Museum, Sandwich Historical Society*

3076 BLOWN MOLDED OPAL RAISED FLOWER VASE

10" H. x 5" Dia. 1870–1887

By today's definition, this vase would be called "milk glass". It was made by blowing the hot glass into a mold. The glass conformed to the shape of the mold, so that the leaves and flowers can be felt on the inside in reverse. The sculptured effect leads many to believe this was a product of Pennsylvania's Phoenix Glass Company, but three variations of this piece can be seen in the Boston and Sandwich Glass Company catalog reprint on page 60. A cigar holder of similar style belonged to the family of James D. Lloyd, Deming Jarves' color expert. Other than cigar holders and vases, the company generally did not employ this type of "puffy" construction.

3077 BLOWN MOLDED OPAL RAISED COLORED FLOWER VASE

10" H. x 5" Dia. 1870–1887

The background color is brushed on between the raised flowers and leaves. We have found it in blue as shown here, and in lavender and brown. The white border and floral pattern stand out in relief, giving a cameo effect. A gilded line surrounds the rim, and the ring above the band of leaves is gilded. The catalog also shows this piece in reverse—the flowers are decorated and the background was left white. This third variation was called "opal raised painted flower vase". Sandwich was *not* noted for using white enamel. When white was needed as part of the design, the blank would be made from white glass.

3078 PRESSED CHRYSANTHEMUM LEAF VASES
(a) Large 10⅛" H. x 4" Dia.
(b) Medium 8⅜" H. x 3¼" Dia.
(c) Small 6⅛" H. x 2⅝" Dia. 1875–1887
There is always an exception to the rule, such as these pressed vases molded without the use of a wafer. They are similar in construction to a goblet. This pattern was the last commercially made at the Boston and Sandwich Glass Company. Very few early patterns of tableware have matching vases. There are six leaf panels. Each leaf is slightly different in shape. The row of dots in each stem is in no way related to a chrysanthemum leaf in its natural form. Sometimes the stem is gilded or ruby stained. The color adds greatly to the value of the vase. *Courtesy, Sandwich Glass Museum, Sandwich Historical Society*

3079 PRESSED CHRYSANTHEMUM LEAF VASE
7" H. x 7½" Dia. 1875–1887
The bulbous shape of this piece resembles vase styles of the early 1900's. The wide base made flower arranging easier. It would not tip over even if the design of the arrangement leaned heavily toward one side. We know of no other glass company that made this pattern in clear glass with or without gilding or staining. However, both styles of vases can be found in Chocolate glass, which was manufactured in the Midwest after the Boston and Sandwich Glass Company closed and sold its molds to Jones, McDuffee, and Stratton in the Spring of 1889 (see Volume 4, page 19). This piece is sometimes called a carafe, but its short, wide neck makes it almost impossible to hold for the purpose of pouring. *Courtesy, Sandwich Glass Museum, Sandwich Historical Society*

080 SPANGLE VASE

½" H. x 3¾" Dia. 1880–1887

Fragments of spangle glass are found in quantity at the Boston and Sandwich Glass Company site and at the Vasa Murrhina Art Glass Company site (see Volume 4, Chapter 8). Much of it was produced, but very little reached the market because of its inherent tendency to crack. Most spangle glass came from Hobbs, Brockunier and Company, where it was manufactured under a patent issued to William Leighton, Jr. on January 29, 1884. John C. DeVoy's patent for Vasa Murrhina was issued only five months later. During this time period, patents were granted regardless of their similarity and were later fought out in the courts if either patentee was unhappy. Note the simplicity of this piece—no attempt was made to flute the rim or apply a base or handle. Pieces that were reworked can be attributed to the Wheeling, West Virginia firm.

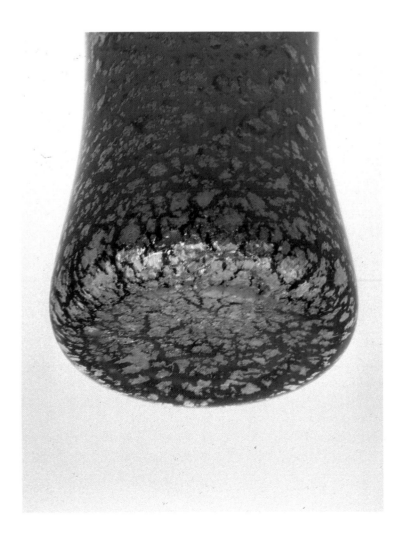

3081 BASE OF ABOVE VASE

The metallic flakes are mica that was coated with silver. A gather of glass that was to become the inner layer of the vase was rolled on the marver to pick up the flakes. This gather was then reheated and blown into an already formed outer layer of clear glass. Note the heavy concentration of flakes on the bottom. This was caused by an uneven pickup of flakes when the gaffer rolled the gather on the marver. The uneven distribution caused stress between the layers, making these pieces impossible to rework without cracking at the old, inefficient Sandwich furnaces.

3082 VASA MURRHINA VASE
5⅞" H. x 4⅝" Dia. 1883–1884
This is an excellent example of the Vasa Murrhina glass that was made by the Vasa Murrhina Art Glass Company at the site of the Cape Cod Glass Company. It has an outside surface of gold and magenta, and is cased on the inside with transparent blue. Vasa Murrhina made in Sandwich was seldom reworked. When the glass was reheated to flute the rims or apply handles, it almost always cracked. This problem caused the downfall of the company only eighteen months after its inception. See Chapter 8 in Volume 4. *Courtesy, Sandwich Glass Museum, Sandwich Historical Society*

3083 TREVAISE VASE
4½" H. x 4⅜" Dia. 1907–1908
Trevaise closely resembles the Art Nouveau style of glass made by Louis C. Tiffany. It was produced at the Alton Manufacturing Company in Sandwich, under the direction of a Tiffany employee. Its most notable identifying characteristic is a wafer-shaped piece of glass applied to the center of the base. In most instances, the center of the wafer was dished out and polished, resulting in a *donut.* Some pieces of Tiffany also have a donut, but Tiffany pieces are signed. Volume 4 includes the complete history of the Alton Manufacturing Company in Chapter 4, and the study of Trevaise vases in Chapter 17.

3084 BLOWN MOLDED OPAL FLOWER POT DECORATED WITH BIRD TRANSFER PRINTS

7" H. x 7¾" Dia. 1874–1887

This style of flower pot was described as "new shape" in the Boston and Sandwich 1874 catalog. Pots with straight sides could be several years older. A ½" hole in the center of the base was not for drainage, but for attaching to an ornate jardinier stand. The robin shown can be seen on a hanging flower basket pictured on page 57 of the catalog. Today we might not combine orange lines with a lilac floated band, but the overall effect is very attractive.

Courtesy, Sandwich Glass Museum, Sandwich Historical Society

3085 ANOTHER VIEW OF ABOVE FLOWER POT

If you find this hummingbird on another opal piece such as a lamp shade, gas globe, vase, or water bottle and tumbler, it is very likely that the piece is Sandwich.

3086 THIRD VIEW OF ABOVE FLOWER POT

There are three different birds on this same pot. Although all three basic designs were transferred, an artist embellished the designs with shading and detail on the background leaves. The parrot can be seen in the catalog on several styles of vases and a cone shade. Parrots were not native to Cape Cod, but were more common as a household pet than they are today.

3087 BLOWN MOLDED OPAL FLOWER POT DECORATED WITH DOGWOOD AND BEE
7½" H. x 7⅞" Dia. 1880–1887
Decorator Annie Nye began working for the Boston and Sandwich Glass Company in 1880. She was one of the last employees to leave, staying on to complete orders remaining after the factory officially closed. This piece is attributed to her by family descendants. Because there are other family pieces painted in this finely detailed style with a muted background, we concur. Note the veins in the bee's wings and dogwood petals. Again, look for this type of artistry on lamp pedestals and other articles.

3088 JARDINIER STAND ACCOMPANIED BY BLOWN MOLDED OPAL FLOWER POTS
(a) Jardinier stand 1870–1887
(b) Great Blue Heron "new shape" flower pot 1874–1887
(c) Four decorated straight-sided flower pots 1870–1887
This photo was copied from the original Boston and Sandwich Glass Company 1874 catalog. The company sold this stand, but did not manufacture it. The flower pot was mounted by placing a rubber washer on the threaded fitting of the stand, then positioning the hole in the pot over the fitting. Another washer and a threaded nut, and the pot was firmly in place with a watertight seal. Stones were placed in the decorated glass pot. A plant already planted in a clay pot with a drainage hole was inserted. If the diameter of the clay pot was only slightly less than the inside diameter of the glass pot, excess moisture that drained onto the stones would not evaporate but would find its way back into the soil. This was the advantage of the "new shape" pot. The straight-sided pots that preceded the "new shape" pots by several years could not hold as much water. The catalog identifies the designs only by number. The birds were hand painted, but the figure at the upper right was probably a transfer. *Courtesy, Sandwich Glass Museum, Sandwich Historical Society*

3089 PRESSED STRAIGHT FLOWER TROUGHS

(a) 2" H. x 18" L. x 2" W.
(b) 2" H. x 11½" L. x 2" W.
(c) 2" H. x 8½" L. x 2" W. 1870–1887

Flower troughs were placed end to end on banquet tables, keeping floral arrangements low enough so as not to interfere with conversation. They came in a variety of shapes but were all the same width and pattern of coarse ribs so they could be strung together in any number of configurations. The ones shown in the 1874 catalog are raised on small feet. Some sat flat on the table. They were made in a later mold. Straight troughs varied in length to accommodate the various lengths of tables.

3090 PRESSED BRIDGE FLOWER TROUGH

5½" H. x 11½" L. x 2" W. 1870–1887

Bridges had several uses. They were placed every several feet in the "run" with flowers in the end compartments. Mints or bonbons in the center compartment and stick candy or candy canes fanned out from the vertical compartments, delighting both adults and children. They were also used to bridge the gap between two tables that were not the same height.

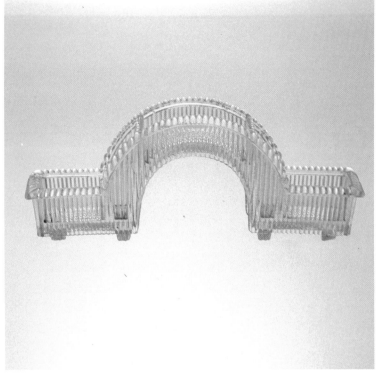

3091 PRESSED GONDOLA

5" H. x 11¾" L. x 2" W. 1870–1887

The gondola is designed like the bridge. Four partitions divide it into five chambers. It was not used for flowers, but was positioned in the "run" at right angles. "Red hots" were placed in the end sections where they could be easily scooped out. The candy sticks and treats in the other compartments could only be eaten with permission from Mother, who could reach over the ends without rocking the gondola.

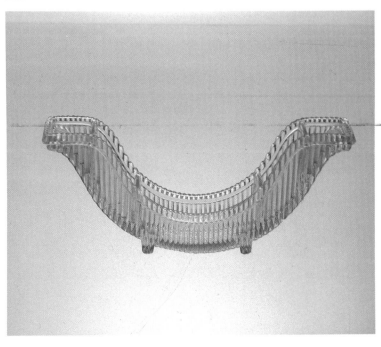

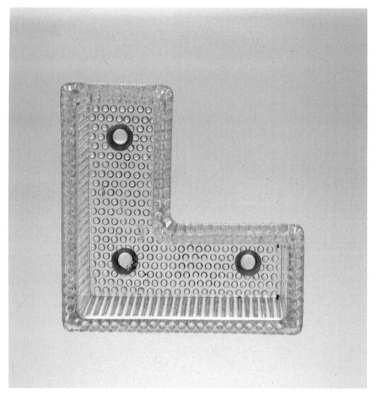

3092 PRESSED ANGLE FLOWER TROUGH
2" H. x 4¾" L. x 4¾" W. 1870–1887

Train and boat excursions to political rallies and camp meetings were a large part of Nineteenth Century social life. As many as one thousand people would attend a celebration or jubilee. An elderly lady recalling a strawberry festival in an enormous barn told about red clover and purple vetch being arranged in troughs. For a harvest supper in the Fall, bittersweet and bursting milkweed pods were used. The angle trough units were most commonly used when a row of tables made a 90 degree turn. Four units could make a square in the center of a square table or a rectangle when combined with straight units.

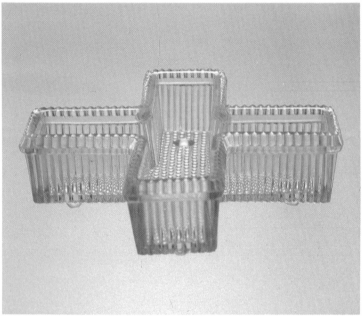

3093 PRESSED CROSS FLOWER TROUGH
2" H. x 7" L. x 7" W. 1870–1887

We have known of this piece being combined with a straight unit to make a cross at a church function. Flower troughs meant to be combined were made in clear glass. Fresh flowers were used in Spring and Summer. For a large gathering, it was difficult to use fresh flowers because the shallow containers did not hold enough water and the flowers wilted if they were arranged the day before.

3094 PRESSED TRIANGLE FLOWER TROUGH
2" H.; 5" L. on short sides; 6½" L. on long side
1870–1887

Triangles were used to fill in when the centerpieces required it. This one has three feet. It can also be found with a flat base, like the other units. Note the dug fragment. It is the 90 degree corner and shows the same defect as the complete piece. Unlike the beaded rims of the other pieces, the corners of the triangle are smooth. The hot glass did not flow readily into the corners, especially the 45 degree ones. A later change in mold design corrected the problem.

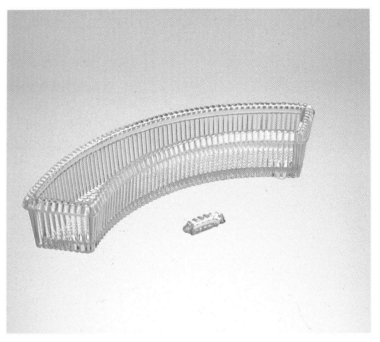

3095 PRESSED QUARTER CIRCLE FLOWER TROUGHS

To make a 14" Dia. circle 1870–1887

Quarter circles and half circles were arranged around a centerpiece, which might be a salver or an elaborate epergne if the social function was in a home or hotel. Epergnes held fruit and nuts and even more flowers. Salvers are called *cake plates* today, but in Victorian times several arranged vertically held dessert jellies and sweets. It has been suggested to us that the Victorian table must have resembled a junk yard.

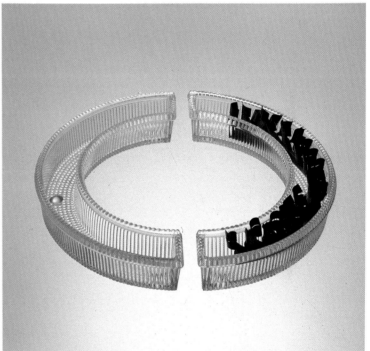

3096 PRESSED HALF CIRCLE FLOWER TROUGHS

To make a 12" Dia. circle 1870–1887

Several sizes of half circles were marketed to make different diameter full circles. A smaller size in our collection makes a 9½" circle. Metal flower holders that could be cut to any length were inserted as shown here.

3097 METAL FLOWER HOLDER FOR TROUGHS

Two types of flower holders were made to be used in flower troughs. The two shown here were made by coating a sheet of copper with hot lead. The lead adhered to the copper, giving it weight. The copper sheet was cut into strips ½" wide. The strips were twisted into stem holders. Later inserts were made of wire springs.

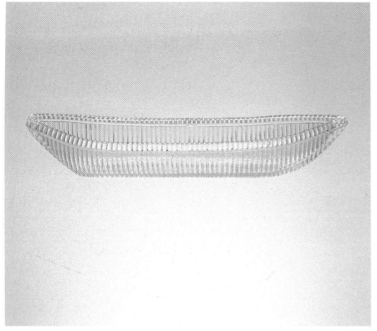

3098 PRESSED BOAT DISH
2" H. x 12" L. x 2" W. 1870–1887

The boat was sold as an accessory to the troughs but was not used in the "run". It was used as a dish for sweets elsewhere on the table. For a small gathering, there is no reason why it could not have doubled as a relish dish. Each unit was marketed and priced individually. The customer made his selection to fit his needs.

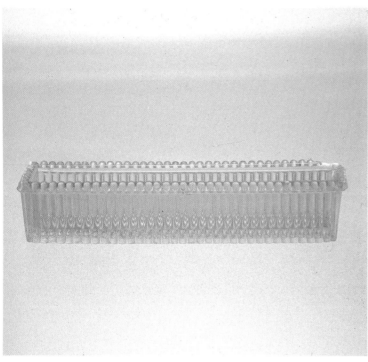

3099 PRESSED FIERY OPALESCENT STRAIGHT FLOWER TROUGH
2" H. x 9" L. x 2" W. 1870–1887

The troughs meant to be purchased in bulk were made from clear glass. Occasionally a unit was selected to be made in color to be used singly. This piece has an underfilled corner. Underfill can be found anywhere around the rims of troughs because, even in color, this was an inexpensive item and quality control was not a consideration. If it was used in an office and broken, who cared? The underfill would be hidden by the floral arrangement. Underfill is caused by not pressing enough glass into the mold.

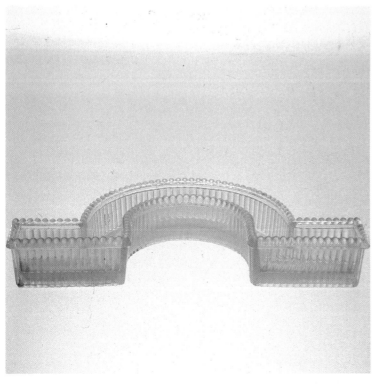

3100 PRESSED FIERY OPALESCENT HALF CIRCLE WITH EXTENSIONS FLOWER TROUGH
2" H. x 12" L. x 5¼" W. 1870–1887

There are no partitions between the half circle and the two extensions. One long metal insert could be easily bent to follow the shape of the unit. We have one documented use of this shape trough. Two units were placed back to back across the top of a roll top desk in a business establishment. An inkwell was in each half-circle for the use of anyone who walked up to the desk to sign papers for the clerk who was sitting behind the desk. The troughs, filled with flowers, held the inkwell in place.

CHAPTER 3

CAPE COD GLASS WORKS

John W. Jarves and Company
1858–1864

One of Deming Jarves' greatest strengths was his ability to turn adversity into triumph.

As the result of his long feud with the Board of Directors of the Boston and Sandwich Glass Company, he terminated his employment as agent of the company he had founded. His letter of resignation was read and accepted by the Board on June 9, 1858. He took with him his son John William, who, since December 1853, had been a chemist in the company's laboratory. John's letter of resignation was accepted by the Board at their June 21 meeting and was to take affect July 1.

Jarves had come to Sandwich in the early 1820's, intending to build a family dynasty that would run a glass factory fashioned after the Pittsburgh factory established by his idol, Benjamin Bakewell. His departure from the Boston and Sandwich Glass Company some thirty years later would, for most people, be a traumatic experience that could do irreparable harm to one's pride and confidence in the future.

Instead, Deming Jarves and his family thought of it as an opportunity to achieve an earlier dream—a return to the original concept embodied in the Sandwich Glass Manufactory which Deming had abandoned in 1826.

Now financially secure, and uninhibited by a sometimes unfriendly Board of Directors and a frequently cantankerous work force, Deming now returned to his original dream of establishing a family industrial empire. Still vigorous at age sixty-seven, he saw in his sons John and Deming, Jr. and in his son-in-law, Henry Francis Higginson, the partners he wanted to help him develop a fresh, new business devoted to the manufacture of fine glass, and one with unlimited, unrestricted opportunities for growth.

If he built a new glass factory, he believed, it would not be run in the same manner as the Boston and Sandwich Glass Company. It would have no Board of Directors—the family would reign supreme. It would not fight for a slice of the retail trade, but would be devoted to the wholesale jobber market, eliminating the expense of showrooms in major cities. Sales personnel would not be necessary, and

John William Jarves (left) in his laboratory. The man on the right is not identified. *Courtesy, Sandwich Glass Museum, Sandwich Historical Society*

certainly Jarves, with his vast experience in the glass market, would be able to recognize the styles and kinds of glass that were in constant demand.

In John, Deming saw himself as a young man—enthusiastic, persevering, well-trained in his field. For seven years before starting his Sandwich Glass Manufactory, Deming had been associated with the New England Glass Company in Cambridge, Massachusetts. John's years of acquiring skill in the experimental and practical aspects of glassmaking paralleled his father's. Certainly he was now ready to take charge of a family-owned glass works. Married to Mary Thayer Waterman on September 5, 1855, and already living in Sandwich, he could continue in his chosen profession without disturbing plans he and his wife had made together.

In Henry F. Higginson, who had married Mary Jarves, Jarves saw a man with the business intelligence necessary to maintain an already available Boston office at 51 Federal Street.

This office was one of two Deming Jarves had built and retained title to, with the understanding that the Boston and Sandwich Glass Company would rent one, and a part of the other, for its showrooms.

As explained in Chapter 1, these buildings were also used as an independent venture by Deming Jarves and his partner, Henry Cormerais (see Appendix), dealing in domestic and imported glass, plated ware, imported table cutlery and similar goods.

Moreover, the partnership had secured a manufacturing plant in South Boston, which was known as the Mount Washington Glass Works, where it manufactured a line of domestic glass. With his canny skill in juggling involved business matters, Deming Jarves had originally established this plant in South Boston in the late 1830's. So the partnership of G. D. Jarves and Cormerais was actually leasing the manufacturing facility from Deming Jarves.

Other pieces in the growing family enterprise began to fall into place, because Deming Jarves had envisioned the need several years before. Barrel staves could be made at Jarves' North Sandwich stave mill, his mill at Spring Hill, or supplied by Howland, Hatch and Company, who ran a lumber yard and planing mill on Jarves' property. His North Sandwich foundry had been heavily damaged by a fire in 1857, but, if rebuilt, could supply molds and castings. The sand companies in Cheshire, Massachusetts, would continue their accounts with Jarves. Deming could see no obstacles standing in the way of the future he planned for his family.

His partnership with Cormerais was to continue for another three years, but his real attention was directed toward developing the family business.

As of July 1, 1858, Jarveses were no longer employed by the Boston and Sandwich Glass Company.

The major decision that had to be made was where to locate the factory. Jarves was blessed with two sites suitable for a thriving glass house, both of which had been put up for sale during the winter of 1856–1857, but had not sold because of the depressed condition of the economy. The Jarveses owned the large tract of land in North Sandwich, three miles from Sandwich Village, on which was located a stave mill, a planing mill, and the foundry. It straddled the Herring River and was bounded on the south by the Cape Cod Railroad. But an unexpected opportunity arose to sell this land to a New York firm planning to build a woolen mill with the potential for employing five hundred. It made much more sense to sell the foundry site and use the funds made available from the sale to finance the building of the factory at a second site.

Jarves also owned a four acre tract in Sandwich Village that was bounded by Mill Creek. The railroad right-of-way passed through the property, giving him access to transportation. On this land was a lumber yard and planing mill that had been run by H. H. Thayer. The second floor of Thayer's building had been occupied by W. C. and I. K. Chipman, who manufactured sashes, shutters and doors.

If Jarves had the planing mill moved to another location on the property, ample room would be available to place the new glass works close to the railroad and to an existing work force. The decision to locate here was quickly made.

The coming of a second glass factory to Sandwich could not have happened at a better time. The entire country had been dealt a severe financial blow known as the panic of 1857. In Sandwich, many workers had been laid off as the result of slow times in the trade. Another factory that promised to employ one hundred hands created great excitement and hope in the town.

Tryphosa French, aunt of the Boston and Sandwich Glass Company's famous glass decorator, Mary Gregory, wrote a letter to her sister, Hannah Gregory in Providence, Rhode Island:

> Mr. Jarvis has commenced this week to put up a new Factory it is going to be where the lumber yard is the Planing Machine is going to be moved to make room for it. it will make business good here now they say he is going to put on all the help he can get, he means to get it ready to work in by winter—you se what folks can do that has a plenty of money. I have heard he was a going to give to John after him. . . .

Second page of Tryphosa French's letter to Hannah Gregory. The letter is dated August 4, 1858.

Deming Jarves began construction promptly in the fall of 1858. By September 1, ground was broken for a building that would be 140 feet long and fifty-five feet wide and would eventually house two large furnaces, the cones of which would be sixty-five feet above the working surface. The *Yarmouth Register* of November 12, 1858, carried the following article.

CAPE COD GLASS WORKS

We have recently had an opportunity to go over the premises in Sandwich, on which Deming Jarves, Esq., is erecting the new Glass Factory which will bear this name. The busy hum of industry, and the clatter of the mechanic's hammer resounds all around the vicinity, and it is evident that the work is being pushed with all the vigor and energy so characteristic of the enterprising founder of these works.

The factory premises occupy some three acres of land, a little to the southward of the Catholic Church, directly on the line of the Cape Cod Railroad. The main building is to be a beautiful structure, both architecturally and mechanically considered, is built in the most substantial manner, due regard being had to convenience and symmetry of plan. The whole of the main building, comprising the Glass House proper, Ware Room, Counting Room, Mixing Room, &c., is 140 feet in length. The Glass House is fifty-five feet wide; the remainder of the building, fifty feet wide. We were pleased to notice among other new and excellent features of the structure, that due regard is to be paid to the health of the workmen, excellent arrangements being made for a thorough and scientific ventilation of the operatives' department, so that the noxious gasses that are so liable to be generated in an establishment of the kind, can be readily carried off. Besides the main building, there are connected with the establishment, a machine-shop, a pottery, for the manufacture of the vessels in which the glass is manufactured, &c, &c. From fifty to sixty laborers are employed in the work, and about $500 are disbursed every fortnight for labor alone. This is a most seasonable and timely relief for those of the population of Sandwich who are dependent on their daily labor for a subsistence. When the new works are in operation, as they probably will be some time in January, they will employ from seventy to one hundred men. This will be in all respects a model establishment; and enjoying the advantage of the remarkable business talents of Mr. Jarves, will doubtless take the foremost rank among the Glass manufactories in New England. Mr. John W. Jarves, son of the proprietor, who superintends the work of erection, and Mr. C. C. P. Waterman, former paymaster of the old company, who has had long and valuable experience in the business, will be connected with the establishment. Success to the Cape Cod Glass Works!

The early stages of construction went well. The main structure was closed in before the deepest part of the Cape winter arrived. Charles C. P. Waterman, who had been dismissed from the Boston and Sandwich Glass Company the day that John Jarves' resignation became effective, supervised the building of the cone, twenty-one feet in diameter, which was erected in twelve days under the shelter of a sail during the most severe weather of the season, and completed on December 3, 1858. A large coal furnace was placed on a platform inside and was raised each morning as the cone grew higher. The heat was trapped by the sail, allowing the men to complete the cone.

John was asked when he thought the first glass would be produced. He was quoted as saying he hoped for the first day of February.

According to the *Yarmouth Register* dated February 4, 1859, a small amount of glass was melted in the factory for the first time on January 27. John W. Jarves, Esq. was satisfied with the melt and told a reporter from the *Barnstable Patriot* that the Cape Cod Glass Works would be prepared to execute orders for all kinds of glassware by April 1.

On February 8, the *Cape Cod Advocate and Nautical Intelligencer*, another local newspaper, suggested that the February 1 statement in the *Barnstable Patriot* was a hoax to the public and that, in their opinion, glass had not been made at the Cape Cod Glass Works and probably never would. Obviously the new company was not without enemies. Many people feared that competition between the two companies would lead to a rivalry that would hurt Sandwich's glass industry.

Charles Cotesworth Pinckney Waterman, Deming Jarves' right-hand man and father of John Jarves' wife Mary. *Courtesy, Sandwich Glass Museum, Sandwich Historical Society*

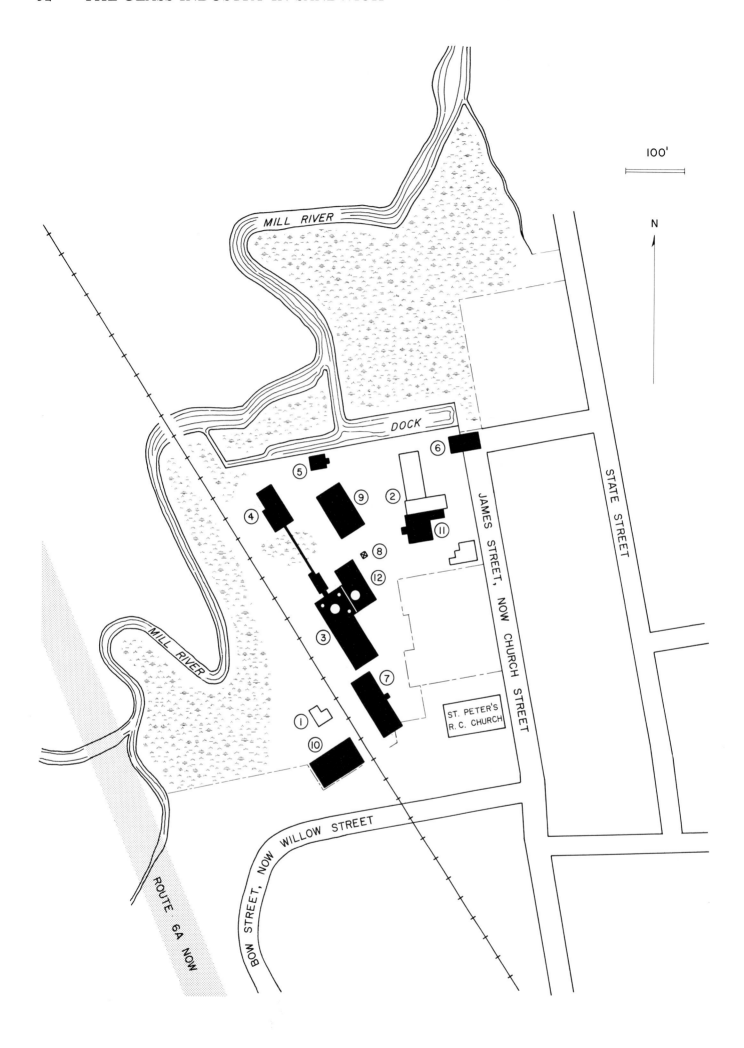

EY TO MAP AND PHOTO

] Buildings on the site prior to the Cape Cod Glass Works.

◖ Cape Cod Glass Works.

◖ "Factory Village" house owned by Deming Jarves.

2 Howland, Hatch and Company planing mill at its new location.

3 Main building, consisting of:
Glass house with one ten-pot furnace and three "new-style" glory holes.
First floor (basement floor) with rooms for cullet, potash, sand, and storage.
Second floor includes the counting room (office), mixing room, mold room, and ware room.

4 Pot house, connected to main building by a one hundred foot long bridge. Former location of planing mill.

5 Original machine shop.

6 Cooperage, extending over the property line onto the road.

7 Building erected in 1859, consisting of:
Watch house.
Cutting shop.
Second machine shop.
Rooms for grinding, sifting, and pounding the clay used for making pots and brick.

8 Water tower.

9 Storage house.

10 Storage house.

11 Shed, under which was the small experimental furnace with Delano furnace feeder.

12 Second large furnace.

Although taken at a later date, this photo shows the Cape Cod Glass Works essentially as it appeared in the 1860's, as seen from the north-west. The additions on the rear of the glass house have been joined. The numbers correspond to the numbers on the map and key.

Fig. 6   Map of Cape Cod Glass Works. The numbers correspond to the key.

No. 4.

The Cape Cod Glass Works followed closely the lines of the factory shown here. This picture appeared in the *Barnstable Patriot* dated August 31, 1852. It was captioned, "Interior View of an American Model Glass Factory." It accompanied one of a series of articles about glassmaking written by Deming Jarves that was eventually published under the title *Reminiscences of Glass-making*. According to Jarves, necessity paved the way for improved furnace design in the effort to secure a less expensive method of melting glass which would enable the American manufacturer to sustain his business against foreign competition. The wages of glassmakers in the United States were 2½ times the wages paid on the continent. It was found that with more efficient furnaces, larger melts of glass could be made at little additional expense, offsetting the differences in labor costs.

But John W. Jarves, Esq. ignored the sniping and moved ahead, preparing his new factory to go into full operation. He signed a contract with the railroad for loading, shipping, and unloading freight. He built a dock in the tidal waters, and patiently waited for the special steel furnace crown and accompanying brick work that had been ordered from Scotland.

The *Yarmouth Register* reported the company's first setback on April 8, 1859. The ship carrying the furnace crown and bricks ran into a severe North Atlantic winter storm. Badly damaged, it had to return to a European port for repairs. Other transportation could not be found, and it was thought that months might pass before its arrival. Once this news had been received, Deming Jarves and his people decided to close the crown with American-made ten-inch fire brick.

On April 12, 1859, a legal notice appeared in the *Barnstable Patriot*, advising that on April 1 a co-partnership had been formed between John W. Jarves and H. F. Higginson. It would be known as John W. Jarves and Company. The address of the business was 51 Federal Street, Deming

Jarves' Boston office location. This document brought the company that would manage the business into legal status, and on May 24, 1859, a long dissertation was placed in the *Barnstable Patriot*, announcing, among other things, the making of glass on May 16.

The opening of these works at Sandwich for the manufacture of glassware, is an event of considerable importance to our County and to the town of Sandwich in particular.

On Monday last, the 16th inst., the first glassware was made, though some glass had been melted before. The event was celebrated by a social meeting, and by speeches and sentiments of congratulation and encouragement. It was certainly an occasion on which the people interested, employer and employed, might well pause and be grateful. But it was not our purpose to speak of those interesting performances, so much as it is to give a general notice of this new addition to the wealth and prospects of our County. The land on which the Cape Cod Glass Works stand extends along the line of the Cape Cod Railroad about twelve hundred feet, and is from one hundred to six hundred feet in width. It lies immediately west of the new Catholic Church edifice. The main building is 140 feet long by fifty-five feet in width, containing the Glass House proper, mixing room, mould room, and ware room on the second floor; and the rooms for cullet, sand and potash, and large storage room on the first or basement floor. Another building for the making of pots and fire brick, seventy-four feet by forty feet, is erected and connected with the Glass House by a bridge one hundred feet long. There is also another building for making casks and all the co-operage work. Another building is in process of erection 120 feet long by thirty-four feet wide to be used as a cutting shop and for machine shop, and also for grinding, pounding and sifting the clay used in making pots and brick. The motive power in this building 'is to be supplied by an Ericsson Caloric Engine, the first introduced in this region. It is also in contemplation to erect another large store house building the present summer. The situation of these works by the side of the railroad track affords the best facilities for traffic and transportation. The proprietors have already set about fifty shade trees about the establishment, and its general arrangement is such as will finally make it an ornament to the town. Many new features, suggested by the experience and sagacity of Mr. Jarves have been introduced. In fact, we venture to say that this is a model Glass House in its main arrangement. It is expected that about one hundred persons will find constant employment in and around the establishment.

Mr. Joseph Marsh is to have superintendence of the glass house. His long experience and well known character for energy, integrity and high moral principle certainly will fit him for the position. His influence with the workmen cannot fail to be salutary and potent. We are sure that he will inculcate by precept and example all those moral attributes without which the best mechanic is but a poor man. We shall hope to hear that intemperance, profanity and all unmanly conduct will find no foothold in the Cape Cod Glass Works. If at the outset the right ground is taken, and persisted in, how much influence for good may emanate from the employees of this manufactory.

It speaks well for the arrangements and appointments of the new works, that they have more applications from competent workmen than they have places to fill. The payroll and other similar duties will be in charge of C. P. Waterman, Esq., who performed the like services for the Boston and Sandwich Glass Company for about a third of a century.

In May 1859, news was received that the repaired vessel carrying the crown to be used in the Cape Cod Glass Works had arrived. The temporary crown that the men had installed in the winter of 1858–1859 had worked well, and John Jarves could see no reason to tear it out until it gave him trouble. The new glass works, with all its modern conveniences and extremely large pots, each of which held at least 1,800 pounds of metal, was producing

REV. JOSEPH MARSH.
BORN APRIL 3, 1796.

Reverend Joseph Marsh, superintendent of the glass house. *Courtesy of Town of Sandwich, Massachusetts, Archives and Historical Center*

Contract dated May 16, 1859, between J. W. Jarves and Company and cooper Joseph French. French agreed to make casks for eight cents each and repair them at the rate of $1.25 per day.

large quantities of excellent quality glass, so the Scottish crown was set aside for the time.

On May 16, 1859, John W. Jarves and Company entered into a one year contract with Mary Gregory's uncle, Joseph French, who agreed to assemble casks for 8 cents each. This was only one example of the intertwining of families in the workings of both glass companies and the use by both companies of key personnel critical to the industry. The contract was witnessed by C. H. Waterman, a Cape Cod Works employee who was the son of C. C. P. Waterman and the brother of John Jarves' wife Mary.

Summer saw the completion of the building housing the machine shop and cutting shop. It had been erected in front of the factory, close to Willow Street. With every modern convenience to support the production of glass efficiently and at minimal cost, the newspaper reported it "was worthy of a visit from the curious".

By the Fourth of July the Sandwich townspeople were beginning to feel comfortable with the security given to them by the old Boston and Sandwich Glass Company, and delighted in the excitement brought to them by the attitude of the new Cape Cod Glass Works. The conventional holiday parade that year was indeed a celebration. A new competitive spirit appeared in that part of the parade devoted to the trades. On board the Boston and Sandwich Glass Company wagon was an example of many things made by that company and, in the eyes of the onlookers, it "made a good appearance". However, the most prominent feature of the parade was the wagon entered by the Cape Cod Glass Works. It displayed a furnace belching smoke, and the men and boys "went through all the evolutions of glass making". They passed out trinkets to the people standing by to celebrate the occasion.

The summer passed with all hands in both companies actively engaged in their trade. By September the life of the temporary crown was coming to an end. It became necessary for John to direct its removal and install the Scottish crown that would be the permanent heating device used in the factory. The work proceeded throughout September, taking about six weeks. The factory was back in full operation in October.

Town of Sandwich tax records for 1860 show that the new Cape Cod Glass Works had completed the main glass house, the cutting shop building, a pot house building, a blacksmith shop, a cooper shop for the making of casks, and several store houses. The necessity of completing all of these subordinant buildings that housed various departments drained the coffers of Deming Jarves. The sale of the foundry property in North Sandwich to the New York woolen mill firm did not materialize, and the anticipated funds from this sale were sorely needed. But, true to form, Deming Jarves was able to secure financing and was soon able to complete the most modern and workable glass house in the United States in its time.

The *Barnstable Patriot* dated February 21, 1860, carried the following information taken from the *New Bedford Mercury*:

These were established in May 1859, by J. W. Jarves and Company. 120 men are employed, and one ten-pot furnace used. For motive power besides the steam engine, are four caloric engines of 5 hp. each which use one barrel of wood each day. Many late improvements have been introduced into these Works, a new style of "glory holes" made with cast iron and lined with firebrick, a new kind of pressing frame, where, on our visit, were being moulded lamps, handles and all. Nest eggs were being made too, faster than hens ever laid the common ones. Thirty pots of glass material, each containing from 2500 to three thousand pounds of metal, are used each week.[1] One great branch of business here is the manufacture of deck lights, also aquaria. Lamp cappings (Editor's note: The collars into which the burners are inserted.) are fitted in a room devoted to the purpose, there are besides a room for the making of glass bottle-stoppers, cutting room, packing room, etc. In the spring it is intended to erect a gas works to supply these works with burning material.

These works are situated by the railroad track, rendering transportation easy and convenient. On the other side of the track is a storage building 90' by 50'. Most of the materials used are brought to Cohasset, eleven miles distant, and then sent to Sandwich by railroad.

C. C. P. Waterman is the assistant superintendent and bookkeeper of the works, and C. H. Waterman manager of the glass works. To his kindness and attention in explaining the various processes is due much of the interest, if any, of this article.

This article give us great insight into the factory itself The Cape Cod Glass Works was a much larger operation than most historians have described. The Boston and Sandwich Glass Company, with its four furnaces, was capable of producing 100,000 pounds of finished product each week during this period. To do this, over five hundred men and boys were employed. The new glass factory, with updated improvements, was capable of producing 75,000 pounds of finished product each week employing a maximum of two hundred hands. The savings in labor alone was substantial.

Jarves' new enterprise had come into the industrial mainstream at a time when the glass industry was in an upswing. The need for millions of kerosene lamps to replace whale oil and fluid lamps rapidly going out of favor gave the new company a new market. The Jarveses could plan on making fonts and bases with no fear of overstocking the trade.

A study of the factory records show that the bulk of production was in items that were most likely to be purchased in large quantity by business and industry. It appears that the Cape Cod Glass Works, soon to become the Cape Cod Glass Company, geared its production to the needs of large eating establishments (hotels, convention centers, and railroad dining cars) and to the needs of the transportation industry. Their customers were reminded that the company was ready and willing to fill orders for private molds "Parties owning Moulds for Lantern Globes, Sidewalk Lights, Lenses, Bottles, etc., can rely on our working them as reasonable as any one in the market." Occasionally one-of-a-kind pieces surfaced as the result of James Dan

rth Lloyd's formula improvements. Lloyd, a favored
otégé of Deming Jarves, became a highly-respected color
nsultant under Jarves' tutelage, working wherever his ex-
rtise was required in both Sandwich and at the Mount
ashington works in South Boston.

Glass hen's eggs, formerly made for use as samples of
g sizes in grocery stores, were now in demand by the
ultry industry. The eggs were placed in nests to teach
ung pullets where to lay their eggs. Also, in areas where
s was available, shades were needed in large quantity.
rves could not have selected a better time to build this
ctory for the Jarves family. As the United States came
t of a prolonged depression, inventories of glass were at
low, but the financial stability of the working nation had
proved to the point where Jarves was confident of
ccess.

But he was not a miracle worker. He sometimes made
rors. History has tended to record only his skills and suc-
sses and to ignore the documents which revealed that his
dgment was less than perfect. For example, he reportedly
st more than $30,000 as a result of his somewhat sim-
istic belief that maximum production resulted in mini-
um cost, and that it was possible to wholesale barrels of
ass at auction when production exceeded demand. When
her glass companies found themselves with excess inven-
ry, they would participate in an auction called a "trade
le". Although this method of selling was generally un-
ofitable, Jarves continued to participate, which ac-
unted for his heavy financial losses.[2]

Only eighteen months after John W. Jarves and Com-
any began production, the buildings were found to be
adequate to house the rapidly increasing business. A
ed had to be built in the yard to protect a smaller experi-
ental furnace utilizing a Delano furnace feeder. Delano's
tent feeder burned both hard and soft coal at extremely
gh temperatures. So intense was its fire that it consumed
l of the noxious gas and smoke that normally plagued
assworkers. This small furnace was not adjacent to a
er, so it was used mostly to manufacture chimneys that
d not require annealing. But, in order to use the glass
ft in the bottom of the pots and to press small items that
quired annealing, Waterman stretched a wire from a
indow in the Delano furnace shed to a window one
ndred feet away in the main furnace room. From this
ire he hung wheels which were used to carry a sheet iron
x. The box could be drawn along the wire from one
ilding to the other, carrying the glass that needed to be
nealed.

Soon, even this proved to be inadequate. The *Barnstable
atriot* of October 9, 1860, told about the increased de-
and for lamp bases, a new and beautiful article manu-
ctured by both companies in Sandwich. To meet this
emand, it became necessary for both companies to
pand.

A twenty foot extension was added to the north side of
e Cape Cod's main glass house. Another large furnace
as constructed, with certain innovative touches by Water-
an, that allowed the company to prolong the life of the
ots. Despite its inadequate working space, the Cape Cod
lass Works became known as an efficient, smoothly run

establishment. Deming Jarves believed that the younger
generation of Jarveses was well on its way toward leaving
its mark in the glass industry. The youngest of the Jarves
children, Deming Jarves, Jr., entered the glass business
in 1860, at the age of twenty-one. He became a clerk at
51 Federal Street. This completed the Jarves dynasty as
Deming saw it.

With the addition to the furnace room completed, the
Cape Cod Glass Works closed out the year with maximum
production. Its future in the glass industry was well established.

The competitive spirit of both companies had by this
time settled into a friendly rivalry, with only an occasional
flareup from one side or the other. John Jarves had served
his father well. He had taken a rather primitive planing
mill and moved it out of the way, and, in its place, had
built an edifice that Deming, Sr., had long dreamed of.
John had set the Jarves dynasty on its feet and brought it
financial independence, but, at the same time, he was to
suffer great personal loss.

Deming Jarves, Jr., in uniform as second lieutenant of the
24th Massachusetts Infantry. The photo was taken in September 1863. *Photo from Trayser Memorial Museum Collection
in Barnstable; Courtesy of Marion Vuilleumier, Cape Cod a
Pictorial History*

John had watched his brother, George, succumb to the nightmare of lung disease in 1850, and he well knew the symptoms. A tendency to this disease was prevalent on his mother's side of the family. The fear that it could strike again hung heavy over the Jarveses. Although John had learned to live with this knowledge, he eventually developed a chronic hacking cough, which was diagnosed as tuberculosis. Papers dated April 27, 1865, written by C. C. P. Waterman, now in the care of the Town of Sandwich Archives and the Sandwich Historical Society, indicate that John became ill in the fall of 1860, about the time the addition was put on for the second large furnace. He was later to die of this dread disease, which was probably exacerbated by the prolonged hard work and stress of developing the new business.

The spring of 1861 saw the country in turmoil over the issue of slavery. On April 12, 1861, the southern states, formed into a Confederacy, fired on Fort Sumter. The country was plummeted into all-out war. Deming, Jr., who had previously been made a corporal in the New England Guards, was commissioned as a second lieutenant of Company "B" 24th Massachusetts Infantry. He was later transferred to the Signal Corps, where, after serving in North Carolina and Virginia, he was assigned to Washington, D. C. in September 1862.

Both glass companies felt the loss of the young men as they left to fulfill their military obligations. Additional girls were hired to work in the cutting and decorating (enameling) departments, and to grind chimneys. New methods had to be devised which would cut the cost of production. Among them, on August 27, 1861, C. C. P. Waterman patented a machine that would allow many glass shades at a time to be ground smooth, a great saving in time and labor.

The older men left behind did what they could to help the war effort. Waterman was active in setting up a citizens committee that devised ways to support the families of men who were away. Deming, Sr., devastated by the political instability of the country, offered free rent to families living in the houses that he owned, if their men had volunteered or were planning to. He himself had served his country in the War of 1812 in the New England Guards. He was made recruiting officer for Sandwich and actively advertised in the local paper for men to join his old regiment, which had again been activated. One of his large ads appeared in the *Barnstable Patriot* of October 29, 1861.

One would think that with the country at war, each industry in its own way would commit itself to the war effort and be deluged by the workload. This was not true in the glass industry. The loss of the young men broke up work teams, some of which had taken years to train. The simplest tasks around the hot furnaces were poorly done, or not done at all. To add to the difficulties, orders began to slacken as companies that normally handled Sandwich products turned away from civilian needs and toward military obligations. Railroad cars usually carrying civilian freight were pressed into the military. Ingredients used in glassmaking, such as saltpeter, iron oxides, magnesium, copper, lead, and cobalt, became difficult to obtain. Large

orders of glassware that were to have been shipped southern warehouses for local sale now lay unwanted i Sandwich warehouses. Both companies could see nothir but lean times ahead as the result of the outbreak of tł Civil War.

The slowdown in production at the Cape Cod glass fa tory was cited by the *Barnstable Patriot* of December 3 1861, as one of the principle reasons for the decline in rai road freight earnings during that period. Freight busine from the Boston and Sandwich Glass Company was al greatly reduced. This downturn in the business cycle at tł start of the war forced company officials to regroup, c back production, and maintain a production level con siderably below maximum capacity. By the time the Civ War entered its second year, the business climate sta bilized, and gradually the glass business returned to profitable level with a minimum labor force. On May 2(1862, the *Patriot* carried the following entry:

> The Cape Cod works are doing a safe business, but employing a limited number of hands. They are constantly receiving orders, and as the season advances their business will probably be extended.

This slow beginning was soon replaced by demands fc glass unheard of in the industry because the tin, coppe and pewter that made up the bulk of lighting devices wei scrapped for the war effort and replaced by glass lamp At the close of 1862, both companies were working fu time.

With John Jarves ill with tuberculosis, he and his wif Mary, spent much of their time in Lebanon, New Hamp shire, hoping that rest and dry, clean air away from tł chimneys of Sandwich would stabilize his deterioratin condition. The responsibility of day-to-day routine at tł factory fell to his father. The elderly man once more ro: to the occasion, placing key personnel in positions c authority and surrounding himself with talented ind viduals, as he had done many times in the past. Under h leadership, the Cape Cod Glass Works expanded. Sprin of 1863 saw it in full production around the clock, attemp ing to fill orders that were back-logged for weeks.

John William Jarves succumbed to tuberculosis i Boston on May 21, 1863, leaving his wife, Mary, and tw children, Arthur and Bertha. The town of Sandwich wa saddened. He was only twenty-eight years old.

Records at Barnstable County Registry of Deeds sho that John, as early as January 1862, began to transfer h holdings in Sandwich to his father-in-law, C. C. P. Wate man. Some of the transactions took place in Lebanor New Hampshire, with deeds made out in Grafton County They were placed on file in Barnstable County showin land located in Sandwich being sold to Waterman. Wit John's impending death inevitable, this practice continue into the early months of 1863.[3] A legal notice date December 2, 1862, appeared in the *Barnstable Patriot* de claring John an insolvent debtor. Interestingly, only on month before, Deming had transferred to John the Nort Sandwich water privilege known as the Upper Factory and his three-quarter interest in the water privilege Spring Hill.[4] John's creditors were informed that a mee

...g would be held at a Court of Insolvency on December 1, at which they could present their claims to the estate. ...ssignees of his seized estate were George A. King and ...harles B. Hall.

John's death legally brought an end to John W. Jarves ...nd Company. The partnership of John Jarves and Henry ...igginson was dissolved on May 22, 1863. This in no way ...ffected the output of the Cape Cod Glass Works, which ...ntinued to run at maximum capacity. On July 7, 1863, ...nly six weeks later, the *Barnstable Patriot* reported:

We are pleased to learn that such is the demand for the wares of the Boston and Sandwich Glass Company that a fire has been put in another furnace the past week. The *Advocate* says that the universal industry noticeable throughout the town, is a remarkable feature of these "war times". All who wish can find

employment suited to their various capacity and taste, and our community, as a whole, has not experienced more prosperous times for many years. The two glass factories are both in full operation both day and night. They employ, together, about eight hundred operatives, and are in want of more.

The period of highest production of glass in Sandwich was, undoubtedly, 1863 to 1865. The Boston and Sandwich Glass Company was running smoothly, showing great profit for its stockholders. The Cape Cod Glass Works had lost its leader, but continued to function because, once again, Deming Jarves stepped into the void left by the death of a son. The business, inevitably perhaps, turned from a family-run enterprise to a corporation run by a Board of Directors. Deming Jarves had, once again, come full circle.

NOTES TO CHAPTER 3

. Research indicates that this figure differs substantially from company records.

. Notes written by C. C. P. Waterman and placed in the Sandwich Centennial Box, dated November 1876 (Town of Sandwich Archives and Sandwich Historical Society).

. Barnstable County (Massachusetts) Registry of Deeds

Book 75, page 187
Book 79, pages 32–33
Book 79, page 496
Book 79, page 527
Book 99, pages 498–501.

4. Barnstable Registry, book 80, page 290.

Deming Jarves as he appeared in the later years of his life, after the family-owned John W. Jarves and Company was restructured and incorporated as the Cape Cod Glass Company. *Reproduced by permission of the Stetson Kindred of America, Inc. from Booklet No. 6, compiled by Nelson M. Stetson, Campello, Massachusetts, 1923*

CHAPTER 4

CAPE COD GLASS COMPANY

1864-1869

In the months following John Jarves' death, Deming Jarves methodically organized a group of businessmen to buy out the Jarves interest in the Cape Cod Glass Works. This group was organized as the Cape Cod Glass Company, with capital stock of $150,000. At a meeting held in Boston on February 18, 1864, the following gentlemen were chosen to be on the new Board of Directors: Deming Jarves, who was elected president, Isaac Livermore, George B. Upton, John S. Tyler and James Read. Henry F. Higginson became the treasurer, and continued to man the Boston office. Louis A. Felix was the new clerk. Jarves, because of his experience as an agent, functioned in this capacity once again, much as he had for the Boston and Sandwich Glass Company.

The forming of a new corporation required the legal transfer of property, even though the corporation would continue to manufacture glass at the same facility.

A deed dated March 9, 1864, recorded at Barnstable County Registry of Deeds, shows that the Cape Cod Glass Works property and buildings belonging to Deming Jarves were transferred to the new Cape Cod Glass Company for $30,000.[1] A plan of the Cape Cod factory site was included with the legal document. A separate deed, also dated March 9, recorded the transfer of the Spring Hill and North Sandwich water privileges.[2]

The company's capacity to grow was limited by its physical size. So the first order of business was to double its manufacturing capacity by adding a building to the east side of the original structure. This allowed the corporation to hire and fully utilize many more employees. With the completion of the new addition, the company immediately achieved a sizeable and profitable growth. On June 14, 1864, the *Barnstable Patriot* announced the payment of a 5 percent dividend on its capital stock for the previous six-month period.

As business picked up, both glass companies in Sandwich realized that they would have to find a way to compensate for the scarcity and expense of the lead used in the production of flint glass. They relied more heavily on formulas that had been developed in Europe, which used litharge as a substitute for lead. Litharge is an oxide of lead, made from pig-lead in a furnace designed for that purpose. It was significantly less expensive and was used to make flint glass of lesser quality. This second grade of flint glass was called *demi-crystal* in the industry, and was used in the pressing of lamps and tableware.

On January 5, 1865, Hiram Dillaway, who was employed at the Boston and Sandwich Glass Company, signed a contract[3] agreeing "to serve the Cape Cod Glass Company as a Machinist to keep all of the running machinery, moulds, tools and other property in the factory in good working order as far as his ability will admit." Dillaway was to be paid $1560 per year in quarterly payments for a period of three years. This was substantially more than he was receiving as superintendent of the machine shop at the Boston and Sandwich Glass Company, and there was no stipulation as to the number of hours he had to be on the premises. However, he also continued to work at Boston and Sandwich. Minutes of that company's meeting held on June 26, 1865, contain remarks by George L. Fessenden "on the subject of Hiram Dillaway's compensation".

The unusual employment arrangement of Dillaway's is small but clear evidence that the Boston and Sandwich Glass Company and the Cape Cod Glass Company by this time had learned to live together. Although they remained competitive and sought ways to outdo each other, they were also willing to work toward a harmonious relationship.

The Cape Cod Glass Works had never owned the land all the way to Willow Street, formerly called Bow Street. They had used it freely for access to the factory, and a building they had erected extended onto it. The property was part of the land Jarves had sold to Father William Moran in 1853,[4] on which St. Peter's Catholic Church had been built. Deming Jarves approached Bishop John B. Fitzpatrick of Boston about its purchase. The land was sold to Deming Jarves with strict regulations regarding its use. The deed limited severely the height and number of structures that could be built on the site. This transaction took place on September 12, 1865, and on October 10, Jarves transferred this parcel to the Cape Cod Glass Company for $500.[5]

In October 1865, Jarves wrote a letter to the Board of

101

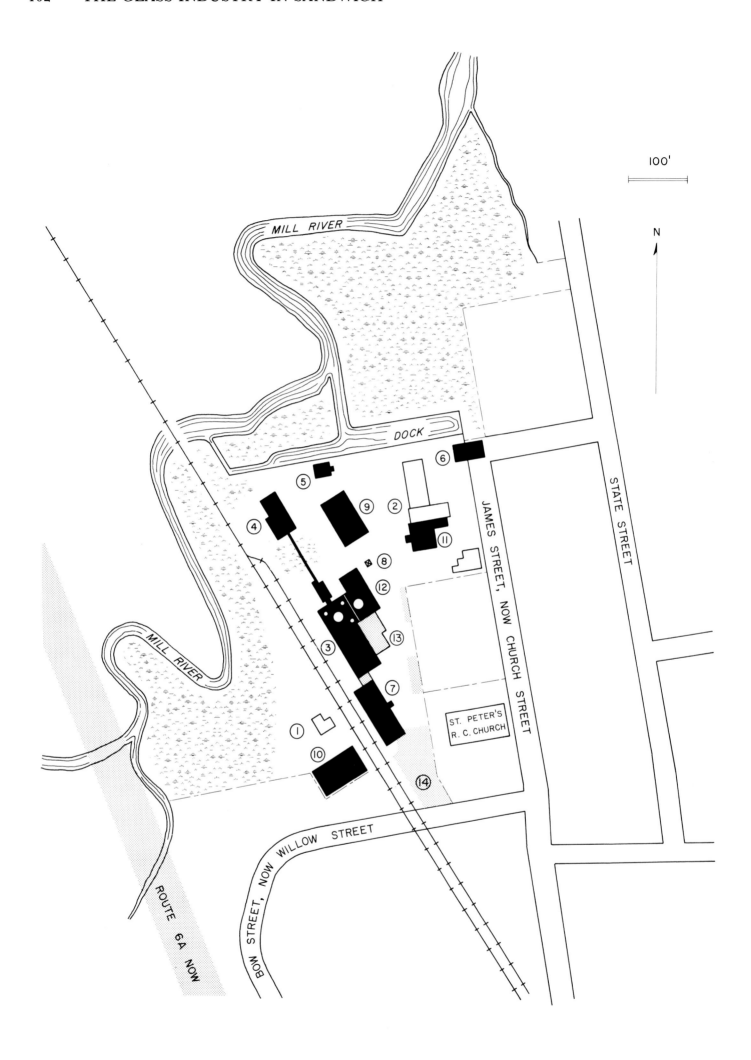

KEY TO MAP AND PHOTO

☐ Buildings on the site prior to the Cape Cod Glass Works.

▨ Cape Cod Glass Works.

▧ Improvements made under the direction of the Cape Cod Glass Company.

1 "Factory Village" house owned by Deming Jarves.

2 Howland, Hatch and Company planing mill at its new location.

3 Main building, consisting of:
Glass house with one ten-pot furnace and three "new-style" glory holes.
First floor (basement floor) with rooms for cullet, potash, sand, and storage.
Second floor includes the counting room (office), mixing room, mold room, and ware room.

4 Pot house, connected to main building by a one hundred foot long bridge. Former location of planing mill.

5 Original machine shop.

6 Cooperage, extending over the property line onto the road.

7 Building erected in 1859, consisting of:
Watch house.
Cutting shop.
Second machine shop.
Rooms for grinding, sifting, and pounding the clay used for making pots and brick.

8 Water tower.

9 Storage house.

10 Storage house.

11 Shed, under which was the small experimental furnace with the Delano furnace feeder.

12 Second large furnace.

13 Addition to main building in 1864.

14 Parcel of land acquired from the Roman Catholic Church in 1865, because the corner of building 7 overran the property line by fifteen feet.

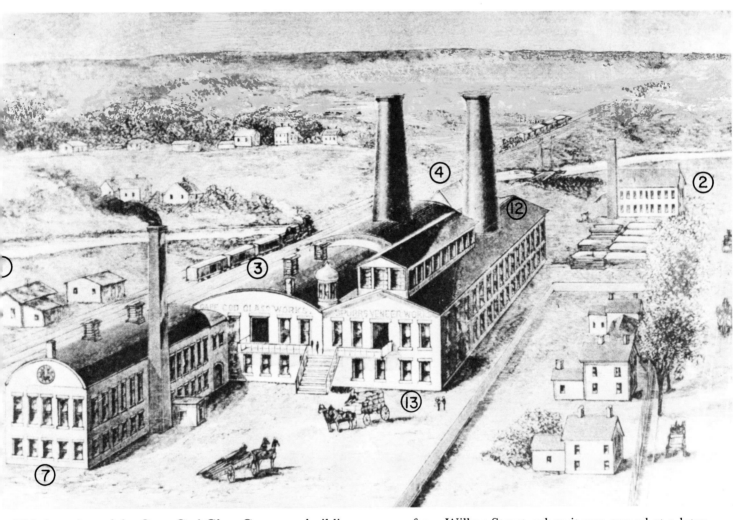

This is a view of the Cape Cod Glass Company buildings as seen from Willow Street, when it was owned at a later time by Charles W. Spurr. Some changes can be seen on the right building, used by Spurr for his veneer business. The shed housing the Delano experimental furnace has been taken down. The numbers correspond to the numbers on the map and the key.

Fig. 7   Map of Cape Cod Glass Company. The numbers correspond to the key.

Directors of the Boston and Sandwich Glass Company, asking if the Cape Cod Glass Company could buy gas now being pumped into the pipelines that were supplying some of the residences and businesses in the village. Boston and Sandwich Glass Company voted to notify Jarves that, if the pipes from its company to the Cape Cod Glass Company were laid satisfactorily, the Cape Cod company could become a gas customer. The Boston and Sandwich Glass Company further stated that it would attempt at all times to serve Jarves in good faith, but Jarves would have to waive all claims of insufficient supply or stoppage of gas service. When the installation of the gas lines was completed, it allowed the Cape Cod Glass Company to light its buildings so that accuracy could be maintained on night shifts, and its output was increased to the highest level in its history.

On March 30, 1866, the remaining one-quarter interest in the Spring Hill mill and water privilege (see Volume 4, Chapter 10, for details of this operation) was transferred from William Stutson to the Cape Cod Glass Company. The company had already decided not to repair the mill,[6] which had been used for many years to make barrel staves.

In the spring of 1866, a gentleman who resided in Plymouth, Massachusetts, visited the glass works, and wrote a letter to the *Barnstable Patriot* of May 22. It included the following:

CAPE COD WORKS

The details of glass manufacture have always been a mystery to us, unsolved by personal vision. Through the kindliest attentions of Mr. Waterman, of the Cape Cod Works, we enjoyed two hours of the night in personal inspection among the blast-furnaces, molten fires, moulds, dies, blowers, and finishers of this miniature infernails. The crimson glare reflected from the faces of the workmen, the lively call, the running boys and clanking machinery, were alike novel and exciting. Molten lumps dropped from long rods into moulds of any shape, down comes the lever and punch, and out flies beer mugs, goblets, tumblers and glassware of all patterns and stamps in half the time we can spare to tell of it. So with the skill and slight of hand of the blowers who work as if by magic the tempered mass into forms of beauty and graceful curves, flare, groove, and finish, with a dexterity that astonishes the beholder.

This establishment is of recent organization, located near the Cape Cod railroad track, and employs two hundred hands.

Although Deming Jarves maintained a position of leadership in the Cape Cod Glass Company, and was responsible for its success for several years, the day-to-day functioning of the plant was under the watchful eye of capable, trustworthy employees. James D. Lloyd and C. C. P. Waterman continued to serve Jarves, as they had for so many years. But Jarves' last opportunity to build a family dynasty, his dream when he started the Cape Cod factory, had once again eluded him. Death had taken George and John, and then the Civil War took Deming,

Jr., away from the Boston office. Of the family members, only son-in-law H. F. Higginson remained.

Although Jarves was now an elderly man of seventy-five, his abiding interest in glassmaking never left him. He was spending more of his time in Boston at his home on Boylston Street, but he continued to monitor the workings of both the Cape Cod Glass Company and the Mount Washington Glass Works from their respective offices in Boston. The Cape Cod Glass Company office was now located at 102 Milk Street, and the Mount Washington Glass Works, under the management of William L. Libbey and Timothy Howe, had an office at 61 Milk Street.

In September 1866, Jarves sent James Lloyd to the Mount Washington plant in South Boston to assess operating costs. A letter written by Jarves on Cape Cod Glass Company stationery to Lloyd on September 28, 1866, provides an interesting insight into the interrelationship of these companies. In his letter Jarves wrote, "Our mould cleaner must be careful not to rub off the fine work *on our Cape Cod moulds.*" From this, it is reasonable to assume that, for at least a short period of time from September 1866, until October 10, 1867 (when Libbey leased the Mount Washington Glass Works), both glass factories made the same patterns.[7]

Deming and Anna Jarves spent the summers of 1866 and 1867 in a cottage they had built in Marion, Massachusetts,[8] next to the inn known as the Marion House. He continued to draw money by selling land and holdings that he had accumulated over the years.

Meanwhile, as the depression of 1868 spread across the land, business conditions at the Boston and Sandwich Glass Company were beginning to fail. It began to lose orders and was forced to discharge many employees. The Cape Cod Glass Company, financially sound, informed their employees that, as the daily workload slackened and each shop ran out of orders to complete, items should be made in anticipation of future sales. In this manner, William E. Kern, now superintendent at the works, could keep his work force intact.

Large quantities of finished product were stockpiled for the first time. As this practice continued, stockholders began to feel the financial pressure. Labor unrest, which usually accompanies difficult times, erupted in Sandwich as delegations of glassmakers convened at Sandwich's Harper House, giving local workers the opportunity to compare their own working conditions to those of other shops throughout the industry. In February 1868, the *Barnstable Patriot* reported that workers had struck "on account of set tasks".

C. C. P. Waterman, sensing the decline of the trade in New England, had long since left for a job in New Jersey, only to find that New Jersey glass houses had also suspended work or were running part time.

Newspapers continued to report declining trade throughout the country. The February 25 issue of the *Barnstable Patriot* stated that, out of the seven furnaces maintained by the two manufactories in Sandwich, only two were in operation. It was expected that soon those two would be reduced to one furnace running at half capacity.

us began a period of hard times, labor disputes, and
ancial ruin in Sandwich history.

Workers continued to hold meetings at which reduction
wages and loss of jobs were discussed. Although they
ew these conditions were not unique to Sandwich, they
ok it upon themselves to slow down the number of pieces
at each shop made in a given hour. This offset their pay
ductions, guaranteeing them longer working hours to fill
e same order. At the Cape Cod factory work stopped en-
ely but began again late in March. The year 1868
nained a slow one, and the gap between labor and man-
ement grew wider.

James D. Lloyd took advantage of the lull to assemble
of his perfected formulas into a book dated in Sandwich
gust 7, 1868. This book, now carefully tied with a red
bon, reposes in the Tannahill Research Library. Lloyd
corded tidbits of information that would be useful to
ure batch mixers attempting to make delicate pastel
ades, such as opal iris, pearl-gray, and lilac. His ex-
rtise as a consultant would be depended upon even into
: 1900's, when several fledgling glass companies would
:k to reestablish the glass industry in Sandwich.

On the night of November 27, 1868, someone entered
: counting room and took cash and checks totaling
)00 that were to have been used for the payroll. The loss
t an added burden on the already foundering company.
By this time Deming Jarves had developed a heart ail-
:nt and had lost all interest in the daily running of the
siness. The added responsibility had to be assumed by
:nry Higginson. On February 23, 1869, the *Barnstable
triot* reported that Jarves had sent a letter to the Board
Directors, resigning his position as agent. The Board
pointed the returning C. C. P. Waterman to the posi-
n made vacant by Jarves. The newspaper noted that
aterman was one of the most skillful and efficient glass
unufacturers in the country.

A week after Waterman's return, at midnight on Febru-
' 27, a fire broke out in a large storage building on the
tory grounds. It was thought to have been set delib-
itely. The Sewall Engine Company, exhausted from
hting an extensive fire in the business section of Sand-
:h only one day earlier, managed to keep the blaze from
'eading too far, but several houses were damaged and
: storage building was completely destroyed. It contained
t to fifteen tons of salt marsh hay, used for the packing
glass.

The poor business climate, the payroll theft, the slowing
vn of the workers, the resignation of Jarves, and the loss
the storage building and hay were too much for the
ckholders to handle. Although there was more than
50,000 in buildings and equipment, the stockholders reed to invest further. According to Waterman, "They ex-
:ssed sorrow for their almost heartbroken old friend,
aning Mr. Jarves."

Henry F. Higginson sent a letter to Superintendent
lliam E. Kern, dated April 5, 1869. It is now in the
e of the Corning Museum of Glass Library in Corning,
w York.

Dear Sir,

I regret very much the necessity which obliges me to

James Danforth Lloyd, Jarves' color expert who perfected
many of the formulas for pastel opal glass. *Courtesy, Sandwich Glass Museum, Sandwich Historical Society*

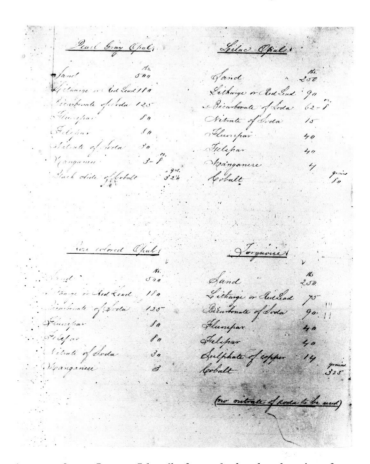

A page from James Lloyd's formula book, showing formulas for pearl gray opal, lilac opal, rose-colored opal and
turquoise. Lloyd's book is dated August 7, 1868.

write you that after the fire in the furnace is out entirely, and the Glass House no longer at work, the Company will be obliged to dispense with your valuable services as Superintendent of the Glass House, and as Gaffer of the Castor Place. (Editor's note: The *castor place* is where glass was pressed.)

There being no probability that work will be resumed by the present Company it only remains for them to wind up its affairs in the most economical and advantageous manner.

Mr. Jarves desires me to express to you his entire satisfaction with the manner in which you have fulfilled your duties while in the employ of the Company and his hope that you may readily find employment for your skill elsewhere, after your connection with this Co. is terminated, and he trusts that you will for the short time that remains devote yourself as heretofore to the interests of the Factory. With the best wishes for your future success from myself.

I am Yours Very Truly H. F. Higginson Treas'r

Mr. Jarves desires me to add that he should not have given his consent to the stoppage of the Factory if the workmen, especially the pressed and blow over chairs, had been ready or willing to make as many pieces per move as were made at other factories—but as they were almost continually short in numbers it involved the Company in heavy and continuous losses.

Yrs. H. F. H. T'r

Higginson's letter leaves no doubt that Deming Jarves,

by his own words, instructed Higginson to close the Cape Cod Glass Company, bringing to an end his dream of a business run by the Jarves dynasty. Kern understood clearly that the factory would never again produce glass under the name of Jarves.

William Kern complied with the instructions Higginson had written. He let the fires go out, thanked the remaining men for their service, and busied himself with the tasks necessary to close a $150,000 business permanently.

On April 15, as Kern finished the last of his work, Deming Jarves succumbed to heart failure in his home at 64 Boylston Street. According to records, he was seventy-eight years and five months old.

There remained one final letter to Mr. Kern from the Milk Street office:

Dear Sir,
As the fires are now out and everything appears to be . . . in good order, I suppose you will consider your engagement with the company terminates on the 1st May—I know of nothing else that will require your services after that time at the factory. . . .

On May 11, 1869, the *Barnstable Patriot* announced that the Cape Cod Glass Company was being wound up, and its buildings were to be sold. However, it remained for Anna Jarves, and a gentleman named Benjamin W. Robinson, to unravel the mysteries of Deming Jarves' holdings at the Barnstable County Registry of Deeds. It would be a decade before the buildings would come to life once again.

NOTES TO CHAPTER 4

1. Barnstable County (Massachusetts) Registry of Deeds, book 83, pages 129-131.
2. Barnstable Registry, book 84, page 193.
3. Contract signed by Deming Jarves as president of the Cape Cod Glass Company, and by Hiram Dillaway, dated January 5, 1865. The three year period was to commence when Dillaway began work. (Dillaway family documents).
4. Barnstable Registry, book 55, pages 140-141.
5. Barnstable Registry, book 87, pages 270-271.
6. Letter dated April 27, 1865, written by Deming Jarves to Mr. Howland. Howland operated the planing mill in the Cape Cod Glass Company factory yard. (Sandwich Historical Society, Sandwich Glass Museum).
7. A letter dated September 28, 1866, addressed to J. D. Lloyd and signed by D. Jarves, states: "When you can give the estimate of fuel at the working places & Mt W & get the exact weight melted per

week & the number of pots the quantity fills I can then get at the weekly cost of running the works. I hope to visit the factory next week. For mode of paying you I can end of each month send you a check which will be more convenient and no risk." (Lloyd family documents).
Jarves was discussing the fine detail of Cape Cod pattern molds. The Cape Cod pattern is now known as Hamilton and is finely detailed. A sugar bowl in this pattern is illustrated on the Cape Cod Glass Company list of glassware.
A letter dated September 16, 1889, was written by James D. Lloyd to "friend William". Lloyd's formula for ruby glass was enclosed, and in the letter Lloyd said, "If you were making ruby right along as I did at So Boston---." (Corning Museum of Glass Library).
8. Plymouth County (Massachusetts) Registry of Deeds, book 337, page 268.

Memo of articles to be made for future sales November 21, 1867

Butters 10 casks N(umber) 21 Feather and Diamond
     10 ”   43 Star and Bee
     10 ”   31 Vine
     10 ”   32 Sunk Diamond
     10 ”   200 Gaines
     20 ”   Mount Washington
     10 ”   ”   7 inch
     15 ”   64 Cape Cod
     10 ”   ”   5 inch
     15 ”   Mount Vernon
     10 ”   94 Leaf

Plates 6 ”   6 inch Grape

Bowls 20 ”   8 inch 200
     20 ”   9 inch ”
     10 ”   10 inch ”
     10 ”   8 inch Comet
     20 ”   8 inch Washington
     20 ”   9 inch   ”
     10 ”   10 inch   ”   all tall feet
     20 ”   7 inch Cape Cod
     20 ”   8 inch   ”
     20 ”   7 inch 94 Leaf
     10 ”   8 inch   ”
     10 ”   8 inch   ”   and cover
     10 ”   8 inch 98 Medley

Bitter Bottles 10 barrels Belt screw cap

Bird Boxes 10 barrels or kegs or boxes S(tar and) B(ee) pattern
               10 ”   Baths

Beer Mugs 30 casks Short Flute #18
         30 ”   Utica   96 plain top
         10 ”   New York   84
20   ”   ”   poney 84
         20 ”   ”   ” 200

Castor Bottles 30 boxes or barrels of hexagonal Glenny or octagonal
               20 ”   Washington

Saloon Peppers 20 boxes   screw cap

Champagnes   10 barrels Huber
           10 ”   N 200

Creams and Sugars 10 casks Washington equal number
               10 ”   200   ”
               10 ”   Vernon   ”
               10 ”   Rose Leaf

Dishes 20 small casks 7 inch 200
     20 ”   8 inch ”
     25 ”   7 inch 64
     10 ”   8 inch ”
     20 ”   7 inch Leaf 94
     10 ”   8 inch ” 94

Decanters 10   ”   quart 200 and stop
       5   ”   pint   ”   ”

Egg Glasses 10 barrels Huber
          10 ”   Washington
10   ”   200

Eggs   100 barrels or boxes like contents

Goblets 10 casks each Comet, Huber, 200 large, 200 small,
             Mount Vernon, Cape Cod
       30 ”   N 101 Raised Diamond

Jugs 6 casks three pint N 54 not to weigh over three pounds each
     6 ”   quart   ”   ”   2½   ”
    10 ”   three pint N 200
    10 ”   quart   ”

Jars 20 hogshead Fluted gallon
   30 ”   ”   half gallon
   50 ”   ”   quart   lime metal
   30 ”   N 16 gallon
   40 ”   ”   half gallon
   40 ”   ”   quarts

Lemonades 10 kegs or barrels 6 Flute
         10 ”   Flute and Split
         10 ”   Cape Cod

Nappies   20 kegs   3 inch any pattern
       40 barrels   4 inch   ”
       20 ”   5 inch   ”
       50 ”   6 inch   ”
       20 small casks 7 inch   ”

Salts   20 barrels each N 60, 64, 65
      40 ”   87
      20 ”   200, 64, 94, Washington
      30 kegs each   45 individual, 45 on feet, 700, 108,85

Tumblers 100 casks N 10 5 ounce
      20 ”   Wygand ale 9 ounce
     100 ”   N 18   8 ounce
      20 ”   Albion   9 ounce
      20 ”   N 70   9 to 10 ounce
      30 ”   73 bar   8 ounce
      10 ”   206 knob   10 ounce
      20 ”   204 bar   9 ounce
      50 ”   216 half pint Ashburton 7 to 8 ounce
      20 ”   218 Fifth Avenue 10 to 11 ounce

If we cannot get the above made not to exceed the weight named let me know. To make of greater weight we loose.

Noggins 20 small casks twenty-five gill

Wines   10 barrels each Ashburton, Huber, Gaines, Washington,
           Old Colony, Cape Cod, Leaf

Enamelled Glass deep color

Eggs   100 boxes or barrels

I must call your particular attention to the weight. In no case should they exceed the flint. Make deep color enamelled.

     10 casks 200 sugars
     10 ”   ”   creams
      5 ”   ”   8 inch nappie on feet
      5 barrels ” 4 inch   ”
      3 casks ” spoon holders
     40 ”   N 2 chimneys
     20 ”   1   ”
     10 ”   Reed lamp shades crimped top
     20 ”   N 2 Mount Washington molasses jug
     10 ”   57   ”
     10 barrels   bird boxes
      5 ”   200 salts
     20 small casks Dolphin candlesticks
     10 ”   Dolphin French candlesticks
     10 ”   #78 raised work spoon holder

Deming Jarves itemized the articles that should be made at the Cape Cod Glass Company when the men had no orders to fill. The original memo is dated November 21, 1867. *Boston and Sandwich Glass Company Records, Archives and Research Library, Henry Ford Museum, The Edison Institute*

LIST OF GLASS WARE

MANUFACTURED BY

CAPE COD GLASS COMPANY.

OFFICE No. 102 MILK STREET,

BOSTON, MASS.

Utica Pattern.

Cape Cod Pattern.

No. 64 Cape Cod Pattern.

Sugars,
Creams,
Butters,
Spoonholders,
Egg Cups,
3 pt. Water Pitcher,
Lemonades,
Goblets,
Champagnes,
Wines,
Gill Tumblers, punted,
½ pt. " "
7 in. Oval Dishes,
8 in. "
Salt Cellars,
4 in. Nappies,
5 in. "
6 in. "
7 in. " cast foot,
8 in. " " "
7 in. Bowls, tall, "
8 in. " " "
9 in. " " flanged,
Quart Bar Decanters, slide stops,
" Table, " glass "

No. 94 Rose Leaf Pattern.

Sugars,
Creams,
Butters,
Spoonholders,
Egg Cups,
Salts,
Lemonades,
Goblets,
Champagnes,
Wines,
Gill Tumblers, punted,
½ pt. " "
7 in. Oval Dishes,
8 in. "
4 in. Nappies,
6 in. "
7 in. " cast foot,
8 in. " " "
7 in. Bowls. tall "
8 in. " " "
8 in. Covered Bowls, tall foot.

No. 96, Utica Pattern.

Sugars,
Creams,
Butters,
Spoonholders,
Egg Cups,
3 pt. Water Pitcher,
Lemonades,
Goblets,
Champagnes,
Wines,
Gill Tumblers, punted,
½ pt. " "
7 in. Oval Dishes,
8 in. "
Salt Cellars,
4 in. Nappies,
5 in. "
6 in. "
7 in. " cast foot,
8 in. " " "
7 in. Bowls, tall "
8 in. " " "
9 in. " " "
8 in. Covered Bowls. tall foot,
Quart Bar Decanters, slide stops,
" Table " glass "

No. 45, Star and Punty.

Sugars,
Creams,
Spoonholders,
8 in. Bowls, tall foot,
9 in. " " " flanged,

No. 19, Mirror Pattern.

Sugars,
Creams,
Spoonholders,
Butters,
Egg Cups,
Goblets,
Champagnes,
Wines,
½ pt. Tumblers, flatted,
3'd qt. " "
4 in. Nappies,
6 in. "
7 in. " cast foot,
8 in. " " "

No. 19, Mirror Pattern.

CONTINUED.

8 in. Nappies, tall foot .
Quart Bar Decanters, slide stops, .
" Table " glass "

No. 22, Huber Pattern.

Sugars,
Creams,
Egg Cups,
Goblets, (large)
Champagnes,
Wines,
½ pt. Tumblers, punted,
6 in. Nappies,

No. 200, Gaines Pattern.

Cpal.   Flint.

Sugars,
Creams,
Butters,
Spoonholders,
Egg Cups,
3 pt. Water Pitchers,
Lemonades,
Salts, (on foot)
Salts, (on foot with covers)
Goblets, (hotel sizes) .
Goblets, (large sizes) .
Champagnes,
Wines,
Celeries,
Gill Tumblers, flatted,
½ pt. " "
Pint " "
Bitter Bottles, (cork or screw tubes)
7 in. Oval Dishes,
8 in. "
9 in. "
10 in. "
3 in. Nappies,
4 in. "
5 in. "
6 in. "
7 in. " cast foot.
8 in. "
8 in. Bowls, tall foot,
9 in. "
10 in. "
Pt. Bar Decanters, slide stops.

Page 1 of a four-page list of glassware manufactured by the Cape Cod Glass Company. *Courtesy, Sandwich Glass Museum, Sandwich Historical Society*

LIST OF GLASS WARE.
CAPE COD GLASS COMPANY.

No. 200, Gaines Pattern.
CONTINUED.

	Opal.	Flint.
Qt. Bar Decanters, slide stops		
Pt. Table " glass stops		
Qt. " " "		

(All Decanters with *cut necks* if desired.)

Mt. Washington Pattern.

Sugars, ...
Creams, ...
Butters, (6 in.) . .
Butters, (7 in.) . .
Spoonholders, .
Egg Cups, . . .
Quart Pitcher, (plain neck) .
Quart Pitcher, (reeded neck)
Lemonades, . .
Salts, (on foot) .
Goblets, (str't.) .
Goblets, (bbl. shape) .
Champagnes, . .
Wines, . . .
No. 1 Molasses Jugs B. C.
No. 2   "   "   "
Celeries, . . .
Gill Tumblers punted, .
½ pt.   "   "
3 in. Nappies, .
4 in.   "
5 in.   "
6 in.   "
7 in.   "   cast foot,
8 in.   "   "
8 in. Bowls tall foot, .
9 in.   "   "
10 in. "   "
Pint Bar Decanters, slide stops, .
Pint Table   "   glass   "
Qt. Bar   "   slide   "
Qt. Table   "   glass   "
(All Decanters with *cut necks* if desired.)

No. 400, Zouave Pattern.

Sugars, . . .
Creams, . . .
Butters, .
Spoonholders, .
Goblets, .
4 in. Nappies, .
6 in.   "
7 in.   "   cast foot,
8 in.   "   "

No. 150, Mt. Vernon Pattern.
Grape Vine.

Sugars, . . .
Creams, . . .
Butters, . .
Spoonholders, . .
Goblets, . .
Salts, . . .
4 in. Nappies, .
6 in.   "
8 in.   "   cast foot,
Cheese Plate, (6 in.) .

Miscellaneous Wares.
Beer Mugs.

No. 16 Hoop and stave, (poney) .
" 16 Hoop and stave, (large) .
" 18 Flute, (short) . .
" 18 Flute, (tall) . .
" 71 Edwards, . .
" 84 New York, .
" 96 Utica, (plain) . .
" 96 Utica, (old mould) .
" 108 Patch diamond, .
" 200 Gaines, (poney) .

Ale Glasses.

No. 14 Wygand, . .
" 200 Alsop, (small) .
" 200 Alsop, (medium) .
" 200 Alsop, (large) .
" 206 Knob, . .
" 206 Knob, (handled)

Butters.

No. 32 Sunk diamond, . .
" 42 Feather and diamond, .
" 43 Star and punty, .
" 58 Plain Ring, . .
" 67 Grecian border, (5-inch) .
" 67 Oval, Grecian border, .
" 92 Quincy, (3-in. individual) .
" 35 Plain, (3-in. individual) .
" 46 Panel, (3-in. individual) .
(All 6-inch Butters on *cast* or *tall* foot if desired.)

Decanters.

No. 14 Qt. Bulls-eye, . .
" 54 Qt. Ring and Ball, (bar or table) . . . .
(For balance see under No. 200 and Mt. Washington Patterns.)

Tumblers.

No. 10 3d pt. Worcester, post .
" 11 3d pt. Revere, post .
" 11 ½ pt. Revere, post .
" 12 3d pt. Pillar flute, punted .
" 12 ½ pt. Pillar flute, punted .
" 12 1 pt. Pillar flute, punted .
" 13 3d pt. Finger flute, (taper) post . . . .
" 13 ½ pt. Finger flute, (ship) post .
" 15 ½ Flute and split, post .
" 16 ½ pt. Hoop and stave, punted .
" 17 ½ pt. Finger and dia., flatted .
" 18 ½ pt. Short 9 flute, flatted .
" 18 3d pt. Short 9 flute, flatted
" 20 gill Flute, flatted .
" 21 ½ pt. 8 Flute, flatted .
" 25 gill Plain Bar, flatted .
" 25 3d pt. Plain Bar, flatted .
" 25 ½ pt. Plain Bar, flatted .
" 28 ½ pt. Gem, flatted .
" 28 3d qt. Gem, flatted .
" 29 gill Column, flatted .
" 29 ½ pt. Column, flatted .
" 30 3d pt. Albion soda, flatted .
" 31 ½ pt. Vine, punted .
" 34 ½ pt. Balloon, post .
" 51 ½ pt. 6 flute, flatted .
" 56 ½ pt. French flute, punted .
" 59 pint Belt, punted .
" 63 ½ pt. Albany, flatted .
" 68 3d qt. Reversed Flute, punted .
" 68 pint Reversed Flute, punted .
" 69 ½ pt. 12-square Flute, punted .
" 70 ½ pt Charleston, punted .
" 72 1-2 pt. Short fingered flute, punted . . . .
" 73 3d pt. New York Bar, punted .
" 73 1-2 pt. New York Bar, punted .
" 74 1-2 pt. Tall flute, punted .
" 75 1-2 Pillar flute, punted .
" 105 1-2 pt. Albany, flatted .
" 201 1-2 pt. Arch, punted .
" 204 1-2 pt. Empire bar, flatted .
" 205 gill Flute and split, punted .
" 205 1-2 pt. Flute and split, punted .
" 209 3d pt. Bar, punted .
" 213 3d pt. A. B. bar, punted .
" 215 1-2 pt. Fine split, punted .
" 216 1-2 pt. A. B. Table, punted .

Goblets.

No. 15 Flute and Split, .
" 17 Finger and diamond, .
" 40 Comet, . . .
" 50 A. B. .
" 62 Old Colony, .

Page 2 of a four-page list of glassware manufactured by the Cape Cod Glass Company. *Courtesy, Sandwich Glass Museum, Sandwich Historical Society*

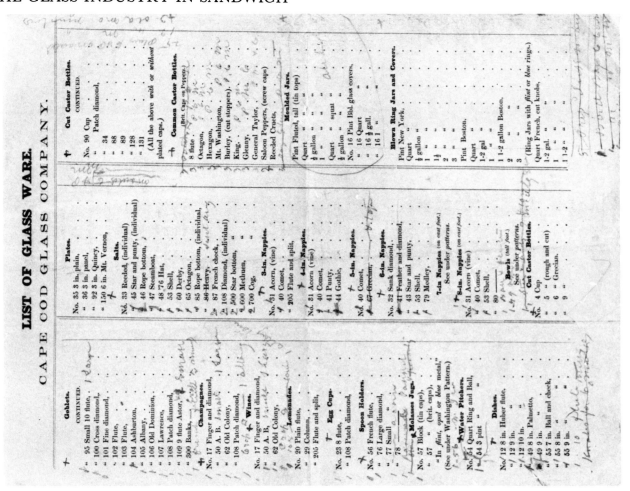

Page 3 of a four-page list of glassware manufactured by the Cape Cod Glass Company. *Courtesy, Sandwich Glass Museum, Sandwich Historical Society*

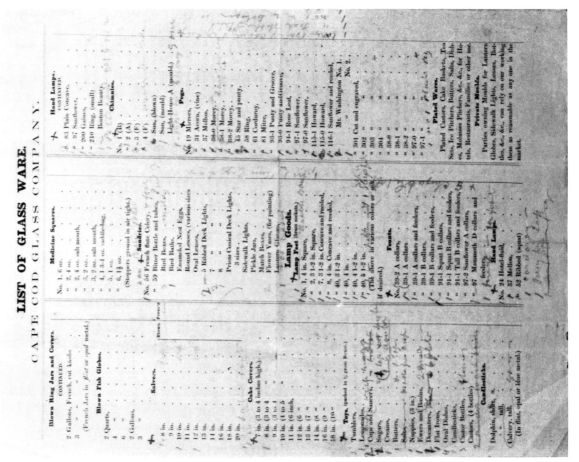

Page 4 of a four-page list of glassware manufactured by the Cape Cod Glass Company. *Courtesy, Sandwich Glass Museum, Sandwich Historical Society*

CHAPTER 5

COLOGNES

1840–1887

Bottles can be divided generally into three categories. First are the traditional commercial types such as flasks, wines, medicine, and extract bottles. Although records do show that the Board of Directors of the Boston and Sandwich Glass Company authorized the making of green bottle glass, this was only during a period of severe depression. The usual commercial bottles did not represent a large part of the company's production, nor did they at the Cape Cod Glass Works. These orders were best filled by glass houses specializing in bottles, utilizing a less expensive glass made from an inferior grade of sand. The second category covers highly specialized commercial bottles that were designed for a specific purpose, either by the glass companies or by wholesale houses that sent their private bottle molds to the glass factory. After receiving the empty bottles from the manufacturer, the wholesale houses filled them with their own product, such as smelling salts or perfume. These specialized commercial bottles were made in relatively large quantities at Sandwich, and will be treated in another chapter. In the third category are the decorative bottles that contained cologne, which was perfume diluted with alcohol. Cologne bottles were made from high quality glass that required the special talents of individual workmen. Although an order for colognes would be occasionally sent out to a retailer to be labeled and filled with his product, most were sold through glass company showrooms or outlying agencies directly to the retail customer, to be used on bureaus and dressing tables.

The colognes shown here represent only a small fraction of Sandwich's output. The quantity of stoppers of elegant form and color that were dug at the Boston and Sandwich Glass Company site strengthens the belief that production of cologne bottles was extensive. Living in today's society, it is difficult for us to realize that, in the Nineteenth Century, cologne was a most practical necessity. People did not have the convenience of hot and cold running water for bathing. Nor did they have washers and dryers to automatically launder their clothing. Personal hygiene was a constant problem, intensified by the heat of a summer day and made unbearable by the heavy woolen cloth-ing of winter. The use of cologne was as common as today's use of deodorants. In addition to its use at home, cologne was regularly carried by women in their purses for that "pause that refreshes". The small purse-size bottles were filled with a tiny funnel.

Information on the earliest cologne bottles is scanty. They are listed late in 1825 in Sandwich Glass Manufactory records, but with no description other than that some had mushroom stoppers. All of the colognes designed for milady's dressing table which will be discussed in this chapter were manufactured from approximately 1840. They all have glass stoppers that match the bottle in form and color. The plug of the stopper and/or the throat (the inside of the neck) of the cologne were machined to create a perfect fit, to prevent evaporation of the contents. After a stopper was fitted to a bottle, it very often was numbered. The same number was inscribed on the bottle, either in the neck, lip, or base. All of the colognes that can positively be attributed to Sandwich are inscribed with Arabic numerals. There are a number of Overlay colognes with Roman numerals, but these are closely identified with Nineteenth Century French Overlay pieces shown in Yolande Amic's *L'Opaline Francaise au XIXe Siecle*, published in Paris in 1952.

Occasionally a cologne is found with a stopper that appears to be its mate, but does not seat snugly. It may wobble slightly, or goes either too deeply or not deeply enough into the throat. If it is numbered and the numbers match, we must be satisfied that the piece is correct and that not enough care had gone into its fitting. If the number of the stopper does not match the number on the cologne, it is very possible that the cologne was one of a pair or a set, and the stoppers were switched. If you are buying one of a pair, and the seller has both, check the stoppers of each to make sure that each stopper is in the correct bottle. *Half the value of a cologne is in its stopper.* Even an inexpensive clear glass cologne is substantially decreased in value if its stopper is not original. (Because stoppers are an important means of identifying Sandwich glass, we have devoted an entire chapter to the more than eight thousand stoppers dug from the site of the Boston and Sandwich Glass Company.) If a cologne stopper can be positively identified as Sandwich, and appears to fit properly into a bottle that matches in color and form, it is possible that the entire unit can be attributed to Sandwich.

Many Sandwich colognes can readily be identified by associating their patterns and designs with other known Sandwich articles. For example, several colognes are identical in pattern to lamp fonts, such as Heart and Waisted Loop. Oval Hobnail pattern was made in colognes, puff boxes, newel post finials and vases. Designs that were copper wheel engraved on tableware during the Late Blown Period can also be found on Sandwich colognes.

There are almost one hundred Overshot, copper wheel engraved, and cut glass colognes pictured in the 1874 Boston and Sandwich Glass Company catalog. They are identified as colognes in the price list to the catalog, preserved at the Sandwich Glass Museum. Most of them are on pages 3, 9, and 10 of the catalog. There are also several plain colognes in the catalog which were used as *blanks* for Threaded Glass colognes after 1880.

As we studied Sandwich colognes, we were able to verify a fact that had been established by Ruth Webb Lee in 1939: no octagonal colognes can be attributed to Sandwich. Sandwich bottles are hexagonal, round, square, or square with chamferred corners. An occasional *cut* octagonal cologne may be found, but a *round* bottle was used for a blank.

It is essential that Sandwich glass attribution be based upon *at least* two methods of identification (described below) for an important reason: the Boston and Sandwich Glass Company, like other glass manufacturers in this country, routinely copied patterns when they saw something they liked. It was a common industry practice.

That is why many of the patterns we know for certain were made in Sandwich also appear in French catalogs of the 1840's, such as those of Cristalleries de Baccarat and Cristalleries de Saint Louis.

As early as 1927, Rhea Mansfield Knittle pointed out in her book *Early American Glass* that some patterns made in Sandwich could not be distinguished from those turned out by Launay & Cie of France.

The records show, furthermore, that the Boston and Sandwich Glass Company sent representatives several times to Europe to study methods of glassmaking. George Franklin Lapham went to study etching, and, in 1869, Superintendent George Lafayette Fessenden went to actually *acquire* patent rights for foreign molds and patterns.

So, when a piece of glass is found illustrated in an original factory catalog, it is a mistake, *on that basis alone*, to attribute that piece exclusively to that factory.

Throughout our research and writing, therefore, we have constantly attributed Sandwich glass only with the security that comes from the use of two or more of the following methods of identification:

- Fragments of bottles dug at factory sites.
- Whole stoppers dug at factory sites.
- Catalogs printed at the time of production.
- Company invoices, records, and other documents.
- Family heirlooms belonging to descendants of glass workers, with accompanying documentation.
- Newspaper advertisements and articles written at the time of production.

In 1925, Bangs Burgess wrote an article telling about going into the Boston and Sandwich Glass Company factory. Miss Burgess was the niece of glassworker Thomas Heffernan, who had taken her on a tour of the factory when she was a child. Her father and grandfather had also worked in the factory, so she was well versed in the art of glassmaking.

> There was one lovely old man whom I remember as a child called Mr. Bonique, who was the gaffer of the castor place shop, so-called. What he really did was made odds and ends from patterns. *I once saw him copying a perfumery bottle*, that had a broken stopper, of a then celebrated actress. Her order was that they were to drill a hole in the old bottle and get the perfumery out without waste.

The important statement here was the fact that he took the time to copy the bottle. We would assume that if he was copying the design of the bottle, it was not a Sandwich bottle, but soon would be. So copying each other's product whenever the opportunity presented itself was an everyday occurrence at a glass factory.

THESE SIMPLE HINTS WILL HELP YOU IDENTIFY SANDWICH COLOGNES.

Colognes have glass stoppers.

Study the chapter on stoppers. Stopper identification is a useful tool.

Check to determine if the attributed stopper is original to the cologne.

If a number is inscribed on the cologne, the same number should be inscribed on the stopper.

Colognes with Roman numerals cut into them are not Sandwich.

Study the Boston and Sandwich Glass Company 1874 catalog.

Identify by association. Study other articles of identical design and pattern, such as lamp fonts, finials, salts, and vases.

101 BLOWN MOLDED RING AND STAR (STAR AND PUNTY) COLOGNES

a) Small neck 5⅛" H. without stopper
b) Large neck 5¼" H. without stopper 1841–1870

We have deliberately removed the stoppers so that you can study the neck of each cologne. The neck on the right bottle is thicker and higher. All of these pieces were worked to some extent by hand, which accounts for the variation in dimensions. Even though the necks vary, the colognes are considered a pair. We give you exact measurements of the piece we are working with, but the student of glass who attributes a piece to a certain company based on dimensions alone is usually wrong. Be careful when handling stoppers not to mix them up. They are individually machined to fit each bottle and are so numbered. Mixed stoppers downgrade a cologne's value. The stopper shown here does not have an air pocket because it was pressed in a stopper wheel mold.

102 BLOWN MOLDED RING AND STAR (STAR AND PUNTY) COLOGNE

¾" H. x 2¾" Dia. 1840–1870

This pattern was very popular, and is often seen in this color. The same pattern was also used to make lamp fonts, pitchers, and spoon holders. This cologne is very heavy because the walls are exceptionally thick. A pontil rod was used on all pieces made in this pattern while they were being reworked into various configurations, so a polished pontil mark is on the base of the cologne. The cologne and its stopper both have the same number inscribed. Note the stopper. It has a large air pocket that is clearly visible and was unquestionably blown into a stopper mold.

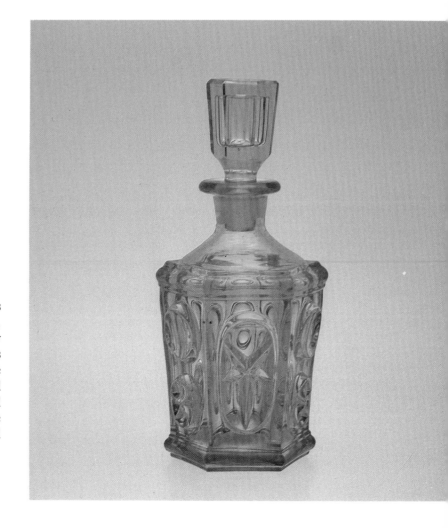

3103 BLOWN MOLDED LYRE (HARP) COLOGNE

6⅛" H. x 3⅛" Dia. 1840-1870

This pattern is sometimes called Harp, as it was in th 1859-1860 catalog of McKee and Brothers from Pitts burgh, Pennsylvania. This piece, however, was made i Sandwich. The overall shape of this cologne is the sam as Star and Punty in photo 3101. Only the design in th panels changes. There are six lyres (harps), one in eac panel. The mold used to make this cologne was badl worn. The base of the instruments and the strings are nc well defined. This does not detract from the value of th piece. The flat, square stopper has chamferred corners. I is a pressed stopper, and is numbered to match the cc logne. *Courtesy, Sandwich Glass Museum, Sandwich Historic Society*

3104 BLOWN MOLDED HEART COLOGNE

7⅛" H. x 3¾" Dia. 1840-1860

In order to truly appreciate the design of this pressed cc logne, turn the picture upside down. Only then will yo realize that it was made from the mold for the font of th Heart lamp. Used as a cologne, the hearts are upsid down. The base of the cologne is where the dome on th top of the font would be. What would have been the exter sion underneath the font has been formed into the nec of the cologne. A pressed, cut stopper was inserted. Th shape of the stopper is not critical to this piece. It can b found with other stoppers, but the stopper and bottl should be inscribed with the same number.

3105 BLOWN MOLDED BABY THUMBPRINT COLOGNE

7" H. x 3" Dia. 1840-1860

This cologne is covered with round thumbprints on th *outside* of the bottle. If the outside surface is smooth, an the pattern shows through from the inside, the piece woul not be Sandwich. No fragments have ever been found a the factory site with a surface pattern that came in conta with its contents, such as the inside of a pitcher or vas or the upper surface of a plate. The stopper and the bottl are inscribed with the same number. The bottle and th stopper tip slightly off center, the result of overheating i the annealing oven (leer). This does not detract from i value. Small imperfections are characteristic of antiqu glass, and are useful identification marks when describin your glass on the inventory pages of this book.

106 BLOWN MOLDED LOOP (LEAF) COLOGNE
½" H. x 3" Dia. 1840-1860

The pattern known as Loop today was called Leaf by the glass companies that made it. This includes the Boston and Sandwich Glass Company, Cape Cod Glass Company, and McKee and Brothers from Pittsburgh, Pennsylvania. This cologne was made in Sandwich, using the mold for a lamp font. The glass that would have formed the knop under the lamp font was reshaped to become the foot of the bottle. The glass that would have been the dome of the font was drawn to make the neck. Note how light the color is in the part of the glass that was drawn. It is so thin that little pigment is left, making the glass look almost clear. The stopper and bottle have matching numbers.

107 BLOWN MOLDED WASTED LOOP COLOGNE WITH FLOWER STOPPER
" H. x 2½" Dia. 1840-1870

This cologne holds two ounces of liquid. A puff box was made to match. The flower stopper appears just as it came out of the mold. Sometimes the petals were reworked to flare out or to close into a bud. We point this out to impress on you why it is important to study how glass articles were constructed. Note also that Sandwich colognes have six, not eight, sides. This flower stopper and bottle was also produced by Cristalleries de Baccarat in France, and can be seen in the Launay Hautin & Compagnie catalogs. We have not seen a reworked stopper on the French pieces that we have examined.

108 BLOWN MOLDED ELONGATED LOOP COLOGNES
" H. x 3" Dia. 1840-1870

The Boston and Sandwich Glass Company very often used a flower motif. The Petal candle socket, the Easter Lily towel holder, and the Tulip vase are several examples. To fully enjoy the floral effect of this cologne, turn the photo upside down. The graceful flow of the design becomes apparent. Each of the six panels has an elongated loop. The panel is carried to the lip. The petal protrusions at the base stand out ¾" from the body. The stopper, normally the same width as the lip, was made larger to repeat the petal design. This piece is often gilded, as on the stopper fragment.

3109 BLOWN MOLDED ELONGATED LOOP COLOGNE

6½" H. x 3" Dia. 1840–1870

The spike on the stopper varies in height up to ½", de
pending on the mold. On some pieces, the elongated loop
have bars across their centers. Keep in mind that color i
no way determines where a piece was manufactured. Th
cologne is "depression green", and was passed over b
many experienced collectors because of its color. This bot
tle and stopper was also made by Cristalleries de Baccara
in France. The bottle with a different stopper is illustrate
in an 1868 catalog from the New England Glass Con
pany. A similar bottle was reproduced by perfume house
in 1983. The Sandwich and Baccarat colognes have po
ished pontil marks. The New England Glass Company co
logne and the reproduction do not.

3110 BLOWN MOLDED OVAL PANELLED FRAMES COLOGNES WITH LILY STOPPER

(a) Amber with gilding and cut neck 6¾" H. x 3¼"
Dia. 1845–1870

(b) Green canary 7" H. x 3¼" Dia. 1840–1870

This cologne is often attributed to France because a simila
one was made by Cristalleries de Baccarat in the 1840's
Note the reinforcing ring half way down the neck. Thi
ring is not on the Baccarat piece, as shown in the illustra
tion. Many fragments of the bottle and stopper were du
at the Boston and Sandwich Glass Company site, an
descendants of Sandwich glassworkers have this cologn
in their family collections. No gilding was done at Sand
wich prior to the arrival of gilder William Smith by 184!
This accounts for the difference in the dating of the tw
Sandwich colognes in the photo. The term *vaseline* was no
used in the 1800's. Yellow with a green tinge was calle
green canary.

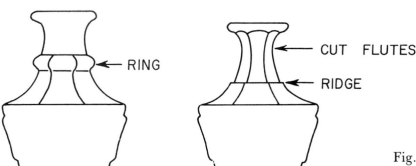

SANDWICH   BACCARAT

Fig. 8 The Sandwich cologne has a reinforcing rir
around a plain neck. The neck of the Baccarat cologne
cut into six flutes beginning at the lip and terminatir
abruptly in a horizontal line that makes a slight rid;
above the shoulder. Both colognes have a Lily stopper

William Smith, first gilder at the Boston and Sandwich Glass Company, arrived in Boston from England on January 7, 1844. He was the father of the Smith Brothers, who were known for decorating on opal glass. *Courtesy, Sandwich Glass Museum, Sandwich Historical Society*

3111 BLOWN MOLDED COLOGNE

5½" H. x 2½" Dia. 1840-1870

Clear fragments of this cologne and this stopper have been found at the Boston and Sandwich Glass Company site in large quantities, but the cologne shown here is the only one we have seen in color. The stopper is machined to fit unusually tight. When stoppers fit this tightly, care should be taken to move them periodically to prevent them from sealing. Expect this cologne to be heavy for its size, because the thickness of the walls limits its contents to less than one ounce. Although blown, the stopper matches the drawing in Hiram Dillaway's patent number 2226 for a pressed stopper wheel, dated August 21, 1841, which can be seen in the stoppers chapter in this book.

3112 BLOWN MOLDED COLOGNE

5½" H. 1840-1870

A clear glass cologne identical to the one shown here was dug in almost perfect condition at the site of the Boston and Sandwich Glass Company. It is so heavy that it holds very little. There are six large convex circles around the body, with six almond-shaped ovals above. The stopper has an air trap in its center, indicating that it was blown into a mold.

3113 BLOWN MOLDED PANELLED DIAMOND POINT COLOGNE

5⅝" H. x 3¾" Dia. 1840–1860

Decorative bottles with alternating panels were very popular during this period, and were produced by most glass manufacturers. The Sandwich cologne can accurately be identified only by matching it with fragments from the factory site. Alternating rows of six and seven full diamonds in each panel are common in the Sandwich diggings. The stopper and the three rings on the shoulder of this cologne have also been found at the site. The soft green color is found in the fragments, although not in the form of a cologne. The slight protrusion of the raised base indicates there may have been an underplate similar to 3121.

3114 BLOWN MOLDED COLOGNE WITH FLOWER STOPPER

7¼" H. x 2¾" Dia. 1850–1870

This is an example of a cologne with a different color stopper which is original to the bottle. Using different colored stoppers was an accepted procedure at the time of manufacture. The number on the stopper matches the number on the bottle. Once again, do not determine origin by color. This cologne in brassy green would be thought by many to be French, but it was produced at the Boston and Sandwich Glass Company. *Courtesy, Sandwich Glass Museum, Sandwich Historical Society*

3115 BLOWN MOLDED ROSETTE COLOGNE

7½" H. x 3⅛" Dia. 1845–1870

This cologne is made up of five-petaled rosettes placed in nine rows around the body. Some areas have large flat spaces between the rosettes. The top row near the shoulder shows some flattening of the petals, caused by reheating the bottle to form the neck. A very deeply polished pontil mark is on the base, and there is gilding on the shoulder, neck, and base. The flower stopper was married to the bottle at a later date. There is a number inscribed on the base of the cologne, but no number on the stopper, which looks top-heavy. *Courtesy, Sandwich Glass Museum, Sandwich Historical Society*

3116 BLOWN MOLDED ROSETTE COLOGNE WITH UMBRELLA STOPPER

7¾" H. x 3¼" Dia. 1840–1870

This cologne is the same as the previous one, but was not gilded. The raised foot on both bottles was blown as part of the original piece. By looking down into the bottle, a penetration into the foot can be seen. The pressed umbrella stopper has eight segments, and a three-ringed knop in the center of the shank. The stopper was also produced by Cristalleries de Saint Louis in France. *Courtesy, Sandwich Glass Museum, Sandwich Historical Society*

3117 BLOWN MOLDED ROSETTE COLOGNE
4⅜" H. x 2⅛" Dia. 1840–1870
The shape of this cologne lends itself to nine rows o
evenly-spaced five-petaled rosettes. The rosettes are smal
on the shoulder and near the base, and larger in the cen
ter. The six-lobed stopper is original and can be found or
many other colognes made in Sandwich. *Courtesy, Sandwicl
Glass Museum, Sandwich Historical Society*

**3118 BLOWN MOLDED OVAL HOBNAIL
COLOGNES**
(a) Rings on shoulder, six-lobed stopper
    5½" H. x 2½" Dia.
(b) No rings on shoulder, Hobnail stopper
    4½" H. x 1⅞" Dia. 1840–1870
This hobnail pattern is unique because it does not imitate
the round flattened hobnail made by other manufacturers.
Therefore, we have added the word *Oval* in its description.
Colognes with this pattern were made in several sizes. A
puff box (powder jar) was made to match, and can be seen
in the chapter on covered containers. A pair of colognes
and a puff box were sometimes sold as a three piece toilet
set. The stopper on cologne A is identical to the one on
the previous Rosette cologne. The stopper on cologne B
has a hobnail pattern. This cologne is a family heirloom
from the descendants of head gaffer Theodore Kern.

3119 BLOWN MOLDED OVAL HOBNAIL COLOGNE

5" H. x 2½" Dia. 1845–1870

The French influence can be seen in Sandwich glass in both color and pattern. Quantities of fragments dug at the Boston and Sandwich Glass Company site show the upper rows of hobnails and the ring above them. The gilding around the base indicates that the cologne did not have an underplate. The stopper has been dug in a variety of colors and was used on other colognes as well. *Courtesy, Sandwich Glass Museum, Sandwich Historical Society*

3120 BLOWN MOLDED OVAL HOBNAIL COLOGNE WITH FLOWER STOPPER

5½" H. x 3" Dia. 1845–1870

The flower stopper is a standard type used on many pieces produced by the Boston and Sandwich Glass Company. The mixed color combination is correct because the stopper fits perfectly and is numbered to match the number on the cologne. The tips of the hobnails are gilded, and a band of gilding can be seen surrounding the base. The Oval Hobnail pattern was used on other pieces as well, including lamp fonts. This cologne is closely related in design to several of the vases shown in this book, and to the finial shown later.

3121 OVAL HOBNAIL

a) Blown molded cologne with pressed flower stopper
   8" H. x 4" Dia.
b) Pressed underplate 1" H. x 5" Dia.
c) Blown molded finial for newel posts and curtain rods 5¾" H. x 2¾" Dia. 1840–1870

The Boston and Sandwich Glass Company frequently used the same pattern to make several different items. It is important, therefore, to become familiar with the other items. The cologne and the underplate have polished pontil marks, indicating that they were blown into the mold. The cologne was reworked in the neck, throat, and expanded lip. The clambroth underplate and stoppers are fragments dug at the site of the factory and match the blue pieces perfectly.

3122 BLOWN MOLDED SNAKE ENTWINED COLOGNE

6" H. x 2¾" Dia. 1841–1860

Once again we see the simple lines of Sandwich molds. This smoky clambroth cologne was blown into a mold, like the one in the next photo. The snake was applied with its head at the bottom. The Dillaway stopper, matching in color and fitting perfectly, completes the piece. The shape of the stopper is illustrated in Hiram Dillaway's patent for making many pressed stoppers simultaneously. His patent can be seen in Chapter 6 about stoppers in this book. Keep in mind that foreign glass companies shipped great quantities of colognes with serpents wrapped around them into this country. It is difficult to identify Sandwich bottles of this style without family connections.

3123 BLOWN MOLDED RING-NECKED COLOGNE

3½" H. x 2" Dia. 1850–1860

This cologne combines a blown bottle with a pressed stopper, both opaque white. At one time, each was gilded, but most of the gilding has worn away. A translucent blue ring encircles the piece near the shoulder. Generally, the simple lines of bottles such as this make attribution to a specific glass house difficult. We can attribute this cologne to Sandwich, however, because the stopper has been found in the diggings, and several necks with both blue and green rings have been found in the area of the dump believed to have been used in 1850. The stopper is numbered to match the number on the bottle.

3124 BLOWN MOLDED COVERED BASKET COLOGNE

4⅞" H. x 2½" Dia. 1850–1870

Although this cologne was molded in one piece, it was designed to look like two pieces. Note the double line around the bottle, representing the rims of the basket and its cover. A plain neck was added to the basket cover. The stopper takes its ribbed pattern from the basket cover. Gilded lines surround the neck of the cologne and the shoulder of the stopper, which is inscribed with a number that matches the number on the cologne. This is one of the few examples of figural glass made in Sandwich. Several types of baskets were made, all from glass of excellent quality and all with patterns of wicker basket weave. The difference between the Sandwich weave and the weave made at Compagnie des Cristalleries de Baccarat, located in Baccarat, France, is shown in the illustration below. Both patterns were made during the same period out of exceptionally beautiful glass. Midwest and French companies later used Sandwich's pattern on figural match or toothpick holders of lesser quality. *Courtesy, Sandwich Glass Museum, Sandwich Historical Society*

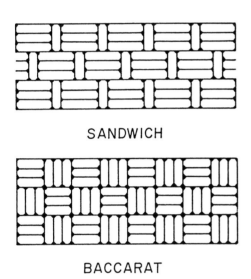

SANDWICH

BACCARAT

Fig. 9   The Sandwich basket pattern is a wicker weave composed of three pliable horizontal rods woven over and under widely spaced, single, rigid vertical rods. The Baccarat weave of three horizontal rods woven under and over three closely spaced vertical rods gives the effect of a splint basket.

3125 BLOWN MOLDED RIBBED COLOGNE

5" H. x 2½" Dia. 1850–1870

The similarities between this cologne and the previous one can easily be seen. The ribs, also used on the Boston and Sandwich Glass Company's Onion lamp, run up the side, over the shoulder, and stop at the neck. The plain neck sits atop the bottle like an afterthought, in the same manner as 3124. The stopper repeats the design of the cologne. It is the same stopper as the previous one, and in size is interchangeable. But it was machined to fit this cologne and is numbered to match it.

3126 BLOWN MOLDED ARTICHOKE COLOGNE
7" H. 1845–1860
This is one of Sandwich's most striking cologne patterns. Note the rib on each artichoke scale, both on the cologne and stopper. Although this shade of green is extremely rare, it is the only color in which this cologne has been found. The gilding is well preserved on both units. Do not let a lack of gilding discourage your purchase of this bottle. Fragments dug at the factory site show no gilding. The stopper is numbered, and the matching number is inscribed on the polished pontil mark. A similar cologne was made by Cristalleries de Baccarat. The French bottle has a plain rim and the neck is fluted. Note the differences in the illustration.

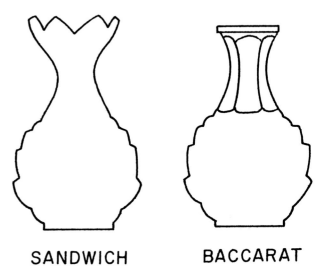

SANDWICH   BACCARAT

Fig. 10 The Sandwich Artichoke cologne has a plain neck and a petaled rim. The Baccarat cologne has a fluted neck and a plain rim.

3127 CUT PRISM AND SHARP DIAMOND COLOGNE WITH SIGNED STOPPER
9½" H. x 3½" Dia. 1841
George Franklin Lapham joined the Boston and Sandwich Glass Company in 1836, when he was fourteen years old. Five years later, with his apprenticeship completed, he had become a skilled glass cutter at the age of nineteen. This cut glass cologne is one of many exquisite Sandwich pieces from the Lapham family collection. The bottle was cut with panels, and the lower part was cut into a diamond motif. The stopper was cut to match the panels in the neck. Note the ring around the neck, a characteristic of Sandwich colognes.

3128 SIGNED STOPPER FROM ABOVE COLOGNE
The bottom of the stopper plug is inscribed "Oct 1841 F Lapham", the signature of George Franklin Lapham, called Frank. The fact that he signed as many pieces as he did for his private collection is evidence of the pride he had in his work.

George Franklin Lapham, glass cutter.

3129 CUT SHARP DIAMOND COLOGNE

3½" H. x 3¾" Dia. 1840–1860

This is an example of a cologne that was originally identified by its stopper. Several such stoppers were dug at the site of the Boston and Sandwich Glass Company, but we did not know at the time what type of bottle the stopper was designed to go with. The stopper blank was shaped like a mushroom. Large diamonds were cut into it, which were then crudely crosshatched. The diamond design shown on the cologne is not repeated on the stopper. This was a common practice at Sandwich. The stopper is numbered to match the cologne. The cut Sharp Diamond design is sharp to the touch and is very well preserved. Cut prisms radiate from a polished pontil mark on the base to the Sharp Diamond design.

3130 CUT SHARP DIAMOND GLOBE COLOGNE

7½" H. x 4¾" Dia. without stopper 1870–1887

Globe colognes were made in many sizes and in several cut designs. There is a Fine Diamond design, which has a small diamond, and the Octagon Diamond design seen in photo 3154. The neck is paneled and there are concentric circles on the shoulder. There should be a faceted stopper with a rather long shank. Other glass companies *pressed* reproductions in the same pattern. They are often sold as Sandwich, but only the *cut* colognes have been authenticated as Sandwich. The pressed reproductions have pressed stoppers with a matching diamond pattern. The Boston and Sandwich Glass Company made matching puff boxes. The finial on the puff box cover is cut into facets to match the cologne stopper. *Courtesy, Sandwich Glass Museum, Sandwich Historical Society*

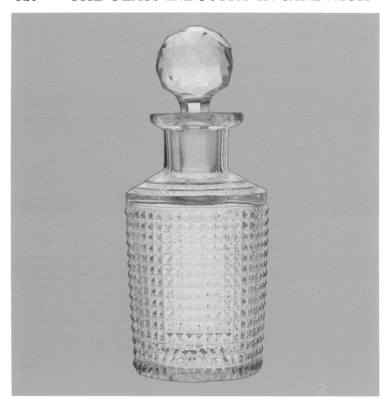

3131 CUT SHARP DIAMOND COLOGNE
5¾" H. x 2½" Dia. 1870-1887

A study of the 1874 catalog reveals that, by 1870, cut designs with several elements had given way to geometric designs repeated over the whole body. The blanks were made in as many as eight sizes, both round and square. Mass produced lapidary stoppers were fitted to each bottle rather than custom made stoppers. This saved on production costs, because if a stopper was chipped during fitting, a new one did not have to be cut with a matching design. The Sharp Diamond design was cut in horizontal rows as shown here and, more often, in diagonal rows as shown in the catalog. The steps on the shoulder were made by cutting concentric rings around the bottle. Be aware that the designs shown on colognes in the Boston and Sandwich Glass Company catalog are *cut* designs.

3132 CUT BLOCK DIAMOND COLOGNE
7⅜" H.; 2½" square at base 1870-1887

At one point, this piece was a square bottle blank. The lines to be cut were drawn on the surface, and the design was then cut and polished. This blank can be seen in the Boston and Sandwich Glass Company 1874 catalog. The Block Diamond design can be seen on a pickle jar in the same catalog. In the 1870's, straight-forward geometric designs were cut over the entire body of a piece. Square puff boxes were made to match the colognes. The puff boxes are very seldom found today. *Courtesy, Sandwich Glass Museum, Sandwich Historical Society*

3133 CUT BLOCK DIAMOND WITH STAR COLOGNE
8¼" H.; 2¾" square at base 1870-1887

This cologne has the simple squares of the Block Diamond design with an eight-pointed star cut and polished in each block. Note the steps made by cutting into the shoulder of the bottle. If this bottle blank had been round, the cutting on the shoulder would appear to be concentric rings. This piece has nine horizontal rows of blocks and six vertical rows on each side. When this design is cut into a smaller blank, each block would be about the same size as on this piece, but there would be fewer rows. The whole bottle has a sameness of design which was characteristic of cut glass designs in the 1870's and 1880's. *Courtesy, Sandwich Glass Museum, Sandwich Historical Society*

3134 CUT QUATREFOIL AND HONEYCOMB COLOGNE

5½" H. x 2¼" Dia. 1860-1880

This cologne is identifiable as Sandwich because of the five quatrefoils cut into the sidewalls, a design which is frequently found on Sandwich Overlay lamp fonts. Three rows of honeycomb are cut into the lower third of the bottle, extending to the base. The lapidary stopper is inscribed with a number that matches the number inscribed on the cologne. The blank for this cologne can be found on page 10 of the Boston and Sandwich Glass Company catalog.

3135 CUT OVERLAY COLOGNE

6¼" H. x 3⅛" Dia. 1845-1860

Overlay is glass cased on the outside with a different color, which is then cut back to reveal the glass beneath. A piece that was cased with one layer of glass was called *plated*, and a piece with two layers of outside casing was called *double plated*. Do not look for perfection in Sandwich Overlay. For example, this cologne was cased with blue glass, then sent to the cutting shop, where the design was marked. Careless cutting created great irregularities in the design. The spacing between the circles (punties) varies, and the blue lines vary in thickness. The stopper was blown and cased with a blue overlay. Its hollow core can be seen in the photo. *On loan to Sandwich Glass Museum, Sandwich Historical Society from the Hollander Family Collection*

3136 CUT OVERLAY COLOGNE

6¼" H. x 3⅜" Dia. 1845-1860

One of the most gratifying experiences of digging at Sandwich for fragments was finding fragments to a piece we already had and knowing they will match. Quantities of fragments matching this cologne were found in red, blue, and green. The red fragment shown here matches the neck of the bottle. The stopper matches the bottle in form, design, and color. It is inscribed with the same number that is on the bottle. In 1844, the Boston and Sandwich Glass Company erected a small furnace for the manufacture of colored glass to be used in plated ware. The earliest Overlay pieces are crude. It took some time to perfect the technique. Pieces of the outer layer would flake during annealing.

3137 CUT OVERLAY PUNTY COLOGNE

8" H. x 2½" Dia. 1845–1865

During thirty years of digging at the site of the Boston and Sandwich Glass Company, we unearthed only a very few perfect pieces. This cologne is by far the greatest find. It was five feet under the ground, near the factory end of the horse railroad. It took five weeks to free the stopper from the bottle, both of which are inscribed with the same number. Other than a slight sickness inside the bottle, it remains today in mint condition. The design is a simple one of circular cutouts called *punties*. The blue overlay is very thick. A polished pontil mark is on the base. The reinforcing ring around the neck is found on many Sandwich colognes.

3138 CUT OVERLAY COLOGNE

5½" H. x 3¼" Dia. 1848–1860

In the late 1840's and early 1850's the quality of the glass company's products improved. Here is an outstanding example of that excellence. In addition to the cut panels on the side, this cologne has a rayed star on the base. This bottle can also be found with a clear cut faceted stopper. Watch for a wide protruding lip that shows the predominant color, in this instance, blue. Often the lip becomes nicked and is then cut down, taking away the colored outer layer. If the lip is gone, you may be sure that you are looking at a badly damaged piece. Repairing glass does *not* add to its value. In the eyes of the advanced collector, it is a damaged piece.

3139 CUT OVERLAY COLOGNE

5½" H. to flattened finial; 2¾" Dia. 1850–1870

This cologne demonstrates the greater skills of Sandwich workers in later years. This bottle is an outstanding example of aesthetic sensibility in combining color and form. The lip of this cologne has been turned up and scalloped, giving the piece a flower effect. The neck has been cut into panels to show the plug of the stopper. A teardrop blown into the plug is centered in the neck panels. Unfortunately, the stopper was at some point cut down and is flat on top. It should have a point similar to the stopper in photo 3127. The amount of overlay left on the edge of each panel can vary significantly. Keep in mind that primitive cutting machinery was used in making these early pieces.

3140 CUT OVERLAY FLORAL DESIGN COLOGNE

9" H. x 4½" Dia. 1850–1870

A band of daisy-like flowers surrounds this elegant cologne near the base. Leaves are cut into the ring on the neck, repeating the small leaves on the vine between the flowers. All of the Sandwich colognes with long, slender necks have this ring. It was used as a thumb and finger rest when pouring out the contents, and, when the bottle was carried, it took the weight off the lip. A polished pontil mark is on the base. The blown stopper matches the bottle in color and form, and seats properly in the throat of the bottle. The familiar Sandwich quatrefoil, seen frequently on lamps, is cut into the stopper. Because the green outer casing is thin, the cutting appears to be well executed.

3141 CUT OVERLAY COLOGNE

9⅞" H. x 3⅝" Dia. 1848–1870

On occasion, a cologne like this will be found that is cut into a random, almost haphazard design. Several different size cutting wheels were used to carve away the blue outer layer of glass. Some of the ovals are vertical, some are horizontal, and they vary in size. If you should find a bottle like this, study the shape of the bottle and the stopper for identification. The cut designs vary from bottle to bottle and cannot be used for positive ID. The stopper, blown into a mold, has a hollow core. Sometimes the top of the stopper was cut away, and the remaining glass was reshaped into a tulip by cutting the scallops into it. This stopper is numbered to match the cologne. *On loan to Sandwich Glass Museum, Sandwich Historical Society from the Hollander Family Collection*

3142 CUT OVERLAY COLOGNE WITH TULIP STOPPER
8⅛" H. x 3" Dia. 1850–1870

This cologne is without question a magnificent bottle in shape and design, but detailed study reveals poor workmanship. Note how erratically the blue lines run up the cologne, wide in some areas and almost nonexistent on the neck. The blue outer layer of glass varies in thickness, and the cutter did not compensate. Keep in mind that the goal of the cutter was to make the cologne highly desirable — as quickly as possible. In this way, he maintained high productivity. Originally, the stopper was similar to 3141, with an airtrap in the center. The top was cut away and the remainder was shaped into scallops. Ovals were cut to repeat the design of the bottle. Do not confuse the construction of this cut stopper with the lily stopper, which was pressed. *Courtesy, Sandwich Glass Museum, Sandwich Historical Society*

3143 CUT OVERLAY COLOGNE WITH SIGNED TULIP STOPPER
10" H. x 3¾" Dia. 1850

George Franklin Lapham joined the Boston and Sandwich Glass Company at age fourteen to learn the art of glass cutting. He was twenty-eight when he cut this bottle. It is in the private collection of the Lapham family and is one of the most striking examples of cutting done in Sandwich. Note the depth of the punty that makes up the inside of the four rings near the base. The rings alternate with four panels of Strawberry Diamond. This cologne was made five years after the company began to obtain sand from the Berkshire Mountains in Massachusetts. To understand how the quality of this sand changed the quality of the cutting, read about the Cheshire, Massachusetts, sand in Volume 2. We have also seen this piece in blue. Note the copper wheel engraving in the long panels below the ring on the neck.

3144 SIGNED STOPPER FROM ABOVE COLOGNE

This exquisite tulip stopper matches the cologne in every way, and if broken would greatly diminish its value. Note the teardrop running into the body of the stopper. The plug is signed "F. Lapham 1850". Mr. Lapham was known as Frank.

3145 CUT OVERLAY COLOGNE
10¼" H. x 3½" Dia. 1850–1870
The cut design of punties and diamonds is often seen on Sandwich pieces. When it is found on pressed tableware, the pattern is known as Diamond Thumbprint. Note the four large pointed arches that make up the design at the base of the bottle. This motif was repeated on the rim by cutting it into a pointed quatrefoil, which could be seen by looking straight down from the top. The reinforcing ring has four V-grooves to match the design of the lip. The matching stopper number, as well as its cut design, prove that the stopper is original. It is lighter in color than the bottle because the ruby layer of glass is very thin. This change in tone does not affect the value of this magnificent piece. *Courtesy, Sandwich Glass Museum, Sandwich Historical Society*

3146 CUT OVERLAY COLOGNE
11⅜" H. x 4" Dia. 1850–1870
Note the slender lines of this blown molded blank. Characteristic of Sandwich colognes are the ring around the neck for reinforcement and the slender neck that opens down and out to become the body of the bottle. The cut design generally changes at the widest point of the body and extends onto the bottom. A star is cut into the bottom so that every surface of the blank is cut and polished. The design of the bottle is repeated on an original stopper, and also changes at the widest point. The lip is cut into six points. The slightest nick on even one of the points will decrease the value of the piece by more than 50 percent. *Courtesy, Sandwich Glass Museum, Sandwich Historical Society*

3147 CUT OVERLAY COLOGNE
11½" H. x 3½" Dia. 1850–1870
This piece deserves detailed study. The neck of the bottl
has five horizontal rows of punties above the reinforcin
ring, with six punties in each row. This motif is repeate
in the five rows below the ring. At this point the desig
completely changes. There are six vesicas cut into each o
the next ten rows. Each vesica is longer from point t
point to maintain the design as the neck widens. The de
sign changes again, as the vesicas give way to diamond
and punties. The cuts are deeper, taking away a greate
proportion of the red layer of glass. Around the base is
leaf design. The leaf design and the rows of vesicas are re
peated on the stopper, which is inscribed with the sam
number that is inscribed on the rim of the bottle. We stres
the importance of maintaining a matching stopper, an
here is an excellent example. If this stopper were lost o
broken, the cologne would have very little value.

3148 CUT OVERLAY VESICA COLOGNE
6⅛" H. x 4⅛" Dia. 1859–1869
This cologne belonged to Ida Nye Lloyd, daughter-in-la
of James Lloyd, Deming Jarves' color expert. It was mad
when Lloyd was at the Cape Cod Glass Works in Sand
wich. The design consists of eight vesicas: four with
Strawberry Diamond motif, two with sunbursts and tw
with ovals. The intricate cutting and long hours of labo
indicate that this was not a production piece. The vesic
with oval is repeated four times on the stopper, which i
inscribed with a number that matches the number in
scribed on the bottle. Sandwich colognes of this qualit
had as much attention paid to the base as was paid to th
rest of the piece. A mark of good design is beauty whe
viewed from any angle. *On loan to Sandwich Glass Museun
Sandwich Historical Society from the Hollander Family Collectio*

3149 CUT OVERLAY STAR IN FROSTED OVAL COLOGNE

4½" H. without stopper; 2½" Dia. 1850–1870

Overlay glass is made by taking a gather of colored glass and blowing it into a shell mold. Immediately a second gather of transparent glass is inserted into the mold and blown. The two layers, now fused together, are reheated. This gather is then blown into the mold that will shape the piece. Single overlay was called *plated*. If a total of three layers of glass were blown into the shell mold, the result was double overlay, *or double plated*. The design of this cutting is most interesting, and without question is unique to Sandwich. It is made up of four crosses alternating with four large punties. A small punty is above and below each cross, as well as a frosted oval with a cut eight-pointed star. Additional cutting was done on the neck and shoulder, and under the base there is a large polished pontil mark. The stopper is a replacement, and is not Sandwich. *Courtesy, Sandwich Glass Museum, Sandwich Historical Society*

3150 CUT OVERLAY STAR IN FROSTED PANEL COLOGNE

5⅝" H. x 2½" Dia. 1850–1870

Note the similarity in the cutting of the red panel to the overall cutting of the cologne in 3149. There are four panels with the punty and cross design, alternating with four frosted panels. Four eight-pointed stars are cut and polished into the frosted panels, but they are not precisely spaced. The cut panels on the neck and shoulder are irregular. The blown stopper matches in design, and is probably the best example of why an original stopper should be retained. If you lose the stopper, 50 percent of the value of the cologne would be lost. The blue stopper is similar, but is cut into six rather than eight panels. There are punties in the blue panels, but no crosses. *Courtesy, Sandwich Glass Museum, Sandwich Historical Society*

3151 CUT OVERLAY STAR IN FROSTED PANEL COLOGNE STOPPERS

(a) Eight panels, from above cologne
(b) Six panels 1850–1870

In most cases, highly sophisticated stoppers which match their colognes in color, design, and quality are impossible to replace. Therefore, they should be handled with great care. Note the similarity of the two stoppers. The red one is cut into eight panels. The four red panels have a punty and cross design. The blue stopper has six panels with no crosses. Yet it is obvious that the stopper blanks were alike, and the variation was created in the cutting shop. *Courtesy, Sandwich Glass Museum, Sandwich Historical Society*

3152 CUT OVERLAY PANEL AND STAR COLOGNES
7¼" H. x 2¾" Dia. 1850–1870

Stoppered pieces that have been paired from the time they were originally purchased from the glass company are often numbered consecutively. On this pair, the number 10 is on the base of one bottle and a corresponding 10 is on the plug of its stopper. The other cologne has the number 11 on both units. If the original intent had been to have an exact matching pair, the blanks would have been blown from the same batches of clear and colored glass into the same mold, and one cutter would execute the design on all four units. Seldom will you find Sandwich cut colognes of this quality that do not have a design cut into the base, even though it cannot be seen when the bottle is in an upright position. Other factories made this cologne in pressed glass with a matching pressed stopper. Sometimes they *stained* the panels, shoulder, and neck in blue or red, making the cologne look like Sandwich cut Overlay.

3153 CUT PANEL AND STAR COLOGNE
7¼" H. x 2¾" Dia. 1870–1887

As competition increased from the Midwest, the Boston and Sandwich Glass Company decreased the cost of the cologne by leaving off the outer layer of colored glass and using a clear glass faceted stopper. The design, however, was cut with the same high level of skill. The price list accompanying the 1874 catalog, now in the care of the Sandwich Historical Society, identifies the design. It was cut into eight different size bottles. Each "star" is a rayed design that fills each square. There are three horizontal rows of rayed squares on each bottle. The height of the rows of panels varies with the height of each size bottle.

3154 CUT OVERLAY OCTAGON DIAMOND COLOGNE

7 ¾" H. x 3" Dia. 1860-1887

Octagon Diamond is the original factory name given to this cut glass design, as recorded in the Boston and Sandwich Glass Company price list of the 1870's. Eight panels cut into the neck leave red overlay to define their sides. Four concentric rings are cut around the shoulder, accentuating a circular, red design which greatly enhances the cologne. The Octagon Diamond design that covers the body can be seen in the factory catalog on several differently shaped colognes. It was also made in blue and, rarest of all, in green. This design was also made at the Mount Washington Glass Company in New Bedford, where it was called *Two Cut Octagon Diamond*. The Mount Washington pieces do not have the stepped concentric rings surrounding the shoulder. Other glass companies made this design in a pressed pattern.

3155 CUT OVERLAY STRAWBERRY DIAMOND AND FAN COLOGNE

6" H. x 2½" Dia. 1859-1869

This is an exceptionally fine piece of glass cut at the Cape Cod Glass Company. It was extensively reproduced in France in five sizes, from two to sixteen ounces. On this original Cape Cod piece, note the uneven cutting in the Strawberry Diamond design near the base, and the uneven cutting in the fans. The colored glass left between the panels cut into the neck and shoulder varies in width. If you find this cologne with excellent, even cuttings, be wary of a reproduction. A star was cut into the base of this Cape Cod bottle after the pontil mark was polished. The original stopper was cut with fifty-four facets, and is numbered to match the bottle.

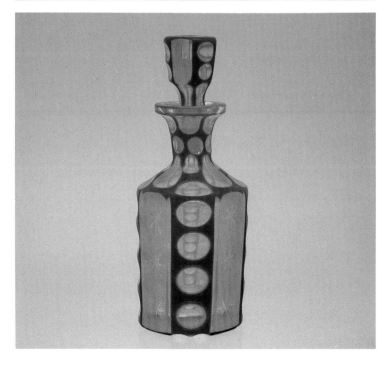

3156 CUT OVERLAY STAR IN FROSTED PANEL COLOGNE

6½" H. x 3½" Dia. 1850-1870

At one time, this bottle was a pink blank, because only the outer pink layer of glass could be seen. After it was shaped and annealed, it was sent to the cutting shop to have the outer layer cut away in the predetermined design shown here. Note the panel with four round punties. There are four red panels on the bottle, but only three matching panels with punties on the stopper. Three eight-pointed stars are cut and polished in the four frosted panels, matching three frosted panels in the stopper. The hexagonal stopper that was used as a blank can be seen on the Ring and Star cologne in photo 3102.

3157 CUT OVERLAY STAR IN FROSTED OVAL COLOGNE

10¼" H. x 3¾" Dia. 1850–1870

This cologne was given to the Sandwich Glass Museum by a descendant of the Holway family. It had been given to the Holways by Charlotte Hall Chipman, the granddaughter of gaffer Charles W. Lapham, who had gathered the first piece of glass for the Sandwich Glass Manufactory on July 4, 1825. Many Sandwich colognes have this shape. Note the ring around the slender neck. It was used as a thumb and finger rest to facilitate carrying and pouring. Eight-pointed stars are cut into the large frosted ovals near the base. This design is repeated four times, giving the cologne a square appearance. The two rows of punties cut into the stopper match the rows of punties on the neck above the ring. The stopper and bottle have matching numbers. *Courtesy, Sandwich Glass Museum, Sandwich Historical Society*

3158 CUT DOUBLE OVERLAY COLOGNE

2" H. x 1¼" Dia. 1850–1870

In 1947, when digging near the Lower House, we discovered this little cologne with its broken stopper 3½' underground. Although whole pieces are rarely found at the site, this bottle is a rare and perfect exception. The stopper is unfinished—it broke in the process of fitting it to the bottle. If the stopper had been the only one left made from the same batch of glass, and it broke, it may have rendered the bottle useless, accounting for its being discarded. Note the cross and four punties that were cut into the stopper. This design is closely related to several Overlay colognes shown in this chapter. Careful study of cut designs will soon enable you to identify those from Sandwich. There is a layer of white glass under the layer of deep pink. At the time this bottle was made, double Overlay was called *doubled plated*. A Boston and Sandwich Glass Company statement dated December 14, 1849, lists "3 dozen double plated double cut colognes" for $2.50 a dozen.

3159 CUT DOUBLE OVERLAY VINTAGE GRAPE COLOGNE

4⅞" H. x 2" Dia. 1850–1870

The arches cut into the side of this bottle are the simplest form of cut designs, easy to execute and pleasing to the eye. The design is delineated by the layer of white glass between the pink and the clear. The leaves of the copper wheel engraved, Vintage Grape design are frosted, while the grapes were polished for added clarity. There are three bunches of grapes, maintaining the three-panel motif that is characteristic of engraved and decorated ware at Sandwich. These grapes are nestled among the leaves, but some cutters would "hang" the grapes away from the leaves, attaching them to the vine by a twig. A horizontal line separates the design on the body from the design on the neck and shoulder. There is a sixteen point star cut into the base. The stopper has a six petal rosette on top, and is matching numbered. Sometimes Overlay colognes were marketed with clear lapidary stoppers. Make sure the numbers match. *On loan to Sandwich Glass Museum, Sandwich Historical Society from the Hollander Family Collection*

160 RUBY STAINED VINTAGE GRAPE COLOGNES

a) Light Stain 6¾" H. x 2½" Dia.
b) Dark Stain 6½" H. x 2½" Dia. 1880–1887

These colognes were stained with a solution that was painted on the glass after it was annealed. They were then put into a decorating kiln and fired to make the stain permanent. There is a significant difference in the color of the two colognes. It was sometimes claimed that the amount of use would drastically change the color, so that the one on the left would be considered well used, while the cologne on the right remained little used and unwashed. A study of the light piece shows that none of the stain has wear. It was stained with a weaker solution than the cologne on the right, and has always been lighter. Note also the raised bases. Ruby stained glass is frequently thought as being Bohemian in manufacture. However, as we will see, the same technique was used in the manufacture of ruby stained glass at the Boston and Sandwich Glass Company.

161 RUBY STAINED VINTAGE GRAPE COLOGNE

6½" H. x 3" Dia. 1880–1887

This cologne has a flat base instead of the raised base seen in most. Colognes in the ruby stained series have acid-etched leaves and polished grapes. This is a good clue that they were made at the Boston and Sandwich Glass Company, and not in Bohemia. (This applies, however, only to *ruby* stained items.) The grapes were polished back through the stain to provide some sparkle to an otherwise dull piece. The fragments were dug at the factory site. The stoppers and colognes that we have studied *in the inexpensive ruby stained series* were *not* inscribed with numbers.

162 RUBY STAINED VINTAGE GRAPE COLOGNES

a) Ring-necked, flat base 6½" H. x 2½" Dia.
b) No ring, raised base 7" H. x 2½" Dia.
c) No ring, raised base 6¾" H. x 2½" Dia.
   1880–1887

Each cologne was made from a different mold, yet each holds the same amount of liquid. Expect great variations in shape, and radical differences in staining patterns. Note the varied shapes of the leaves acid-etched onto the colognes. The cologne in the center has a long, narrow neck, while the bottle on the right obviously has a shorter, wide neck, again reflecting the great variety of shapes you may encounter.

3163 RUBY STAINED VINTAGE GRAPE COLOGNE

8" H. x 4" Dia. 1880–1887

This is the largest cologne in the ruby stained series. Th two rings surrounding the shoulder were part of the mol and were not applied. An intricate design of acid-etche leaves and polished grapes surrounds the body of the co logne, and, below, a chain of cut punties encircles th piece at its widest point. An acid-etched vine below th punties repeats the design in miniature. A slightly raise base completes the bottle.

3164 RUBY STAINED COPPER WHEEL ENGRAVED COLOGNE

5¾" H. x 2½" Dia. 1880–1887

Ruby stained glass was made in many shapes and sizes The design, copper wheel engraved into this cologne, i unique but matches many fragments that were dug at th Boston and Sandwich Glass Company. The tiny ovals en graved into the corners of the plaid design make eac square resemble the German cross of the pressed tablewar pattern known as Sandwich Star. But note the botto square to the left of center. In the hasty manner of work manship in the dying years of the company, the engrave left out one tiny oval. The stopper is not original. It doe not match the cologne in form and color and descends to far into the throat.

3165 RUBY STAINED CUT COLOGNES

7½" H. x 3½" Dia. 1880–1887

One of the most sought after colors in the late era at San wich was red. The most inexpensive method for makin clear glass red was to stain it. Great quantities of rub stained glass were produced at the Boston and Sandwic Glass Company, and, on rare occasions, pieces can b found in amber and blue. This pair of bottles was mad and annealed, after which punties and vesicas were cut t give them a design. The red stain was then brushed on be tween the cut designs, overlapping into the cut areas. Th gave the illusion of depth. The stain overlap can be mi taken for the outer layer of glass on Overlay pieces. The they were placed in a kiln and fired to fix the color.

166 RUBY STAINED MORNING GLORY LEAF COLOGNE

½" H. x 3½" Dia. 1880–1887

The Bohemian influence on the Sandwich glass industry can be seen in many pieces of ruby stained glass. But Sandwich had the knack of combining the Bohemian method with designs that were used on American glass, such as in the leaf made famous on Morning Glory pressed pattern tableware. Leaves on the same vine point in opposite directions and there are no flowers. The ovoids below the vine are common to both American and Bohemian work. *Courtesy, Sandwich Glass Museum, Sandwich Historical Society*

3167 OVERSHOT COLOGNE

8" H.; 2½" square at base 1870–1887

The glass we call Overshot today was marketed as Frosted Ware by the Boston and Sandwich Glass Company. The square colognes shown here can be seen in an original factory catalog from the 1870's. They were made in five sizes and could be purchased singly or as two units of a three-piece toilet set. We seldom find one with its original Overshot stopper, because it has usually been replaced by a clear faceted one. Overshot was made by applying clear ground glass particles to a hot gather of glass either before or after it had been shaped. The finished product appeared to be cool and frosty, accounting for its name.

168 OVERSHOT COLOGNE

⅝" H.; 2" square at base 1870–1887

This excellent cologne shows how color was achieved in the making of Overshot. A thin layer of colored glass (in this instance, deep pink) was used to case the inside of both the bottle and the stopper. Proof of this can be seen in the neck. When the throat of the bottle was polished to fit the stopper, the inside layer of pink was taken away, returning the neck to clear glass. On the stopper, the pink inner casing can easily be seen just above the lip of the bottle. For more information on Overshot, see Chapter 6 of Volume 4. *Courtesy, Sandwich Glass Museum, Sandwich Historical Society*

3169 ACID-ETCHED FANNED IN FERN GLOBE COLOGNE

3⅝" H. x 2½" Dia. 1870–1887

The 1874 Boston and Sandwich Glass Company catalo shows blown globe colognes in eight sizes. This on appears to be the smallest. The stopper was pressed in mold and then cut into diamond-shaped facets. A star cu into the top of the stopper matches the star cut into th base of the bottle. After careful study, you will be able t recognize Sandwich pieces even if you have not previous! seen that particular piece. This cologne relates in shape t photo 4207 and is identical in design to photo 4203.

3170 COPPER WHEEL ENGRAVED BAND AND LINE WITH GRAPES COLOGNE

5" H. x 1½" Dia. 1875–1887

The grape design was a popular one during the Lat Blown Period at Sandwich. A matching design can be see on the slop bowl in photo 4209 in Volume 4. Eight pane were cut into the neck of the bottle. A polished pontil mar is on the underside. Gilded bands surround the cologne and the gilding was carried onto the panels of the stoppe which is numbered to match. This stopper is closely ident fied with the New England Glass Company, but can b found on several documented Sandwich colognes. Remem ber, we cannot always attribute a particular shape to onl one company, because several companies used the sam shaped molds.

3171 THREADED COLOGNE

3⅜" H. x 2⅛" Dia. 1880-1887

Many times in the study of glass we find a design that is the essence of beauty and simplicity. By threading just the stopper and the bottom half of this cologne, and calling it complete, a worker made this piece one of the finest examples of Sandwich workmanship. The plain bottles that were used as blanks for Threaded Glass can be seen in the 1874 Boston and Sandwich Glass Company factory catalog. The bottle, stopper, and threading were made from the same batch of green glass. The stopper is inscribed with a number matching that on the cologne. See Chapter 13 in Volume 4 for information about the threading of glass. *Courtesy, Sandwich Glass Museum, Sandwich Historical Society*

3172 THREADED COLOGNE WITH ENGRAVED IVY AND BERRIES

6¼" H. x 2½" Dia. 1880-1887

The threading on Sandwich pieces starts at the pontil mark and in most cases continues one-third up the side. The upper part remains clear. In this cologne, an ivy vine with groups of three berries was copper wheel engraved on the unthreaded section. Do not limit your thinking to a particular engraved or etched design. Study the shape of the bottle, as well as the method of threading, and accept *any* design in the unthreaded part. An attempt to cut ovals into the threads of the stopper was not successful, and the threads shattered. The stopper does not appear to match the bottle, which has no ovals cut into it. However, both pieces are inscribed with identical numbers. *Courtesy, Sandwich Glass Museum, Sandwich Historical Society*

3173 THREADED GLOBE COLOGNE

4½" H. without stopper; 3¼" Dia. 1880-1887

It is not often that we find Sandwich pieces completely threaded. It took more time, more glass, and added little to the value of the piece. Normally, the threading stops about one-third up the side of the bottle, where the threading in the photo looks the darkest. The neck was cut into panels that continue down to the shoulder. There are two clues that the stopper is a replacement. First, it does not match the cologne in size. The original was probably threaded and was larger. Second, a number is inscribed on the bottle, but there is no number on the stopper. *Courtesy, Sandwich Glass Museum, Sandwich Historical Society*

INVENTORY OF SANDWICH GLASS

No.	Description	Condition	Date Purchased	Amount	Date Sold	Amount

CHAPTER 6

A STUDY OF STOPPERS

Stoppers excavated at the site of the Boston and Sandwich Glass Company 1825–1887

As mundane as they may seem, stoppers have just as much importance as the bottles they protect.

To the serious collector, a bottle is not truly complete unless it is surmounted either with its original stopper, or, if the original has been lost, with a stopper of the period which displays the style, the color (if any), and the proportions which the glassmaker intended.

An original stopper can increase the market value of a bottle by as much as four times. Conversely, without a correct stopper, a bottle can command only half the price or less.

So the serious glass student will expend as much effort getting the right stopper as in finding the perfect bottle.

Because stoppers are somewhat homely items compared the richness of design and manufacture of decanters or colognes, little attention has been given to their identification and to the niceties of their manufacture. The problem has been compounded by the fact that stoppers, like bottles various types, were widely copied by New England manufacturers among each other and from European sources.

Because they were relatively cheap to make and were manufactured in vast quantities, the collector becomes further confused. Stoppers which fell to the floor during manufacture were not considered worth retrieving, so they were swept into the dump literally by the thousands. Collectors and the curious acquired cartons of them by picking the site of the Boston and Sandwich Glass Company. The fragment collection of Francis (Bill) Wynn, who was well known to the glass research field, contained 752 stoppers. Four hundred were included in the Casey fragment collection. Gradually, these collections and several others were added to our Barlow collection, representing more than eight thousand perfect stoppers and five hundred pounds of stopper fragments (If this amount of stoppers had been discarded by the factory because of no apparent salvage value, think of the enormous amount which must have been made and shipped).

Because so many American and foreign glass companies copied each other's stopper designs, we are reluctantly convinced that a bottle cannot be attributed to a specific glass house on the basis of its stopper design *alone*.

However, all of the stoppers shown in this chapter came from the Boston and Sandwich Glass Company dump site. We can therefore say, without too much fear of contradiction, that any stoppers you have which match these are at least of the period (assuming they are not obvious reproductions), that they could have been made at Sandwich, and that your ability to identify what you have, based on the text and illustrations herein, brings you closer to the attribution of the total piece than you might otherwise have achieved.

At the very least, we hope that the information on stoppers will provide you with some interesting insights which have not heretofore been available.

Stopper production began on the first full day of glassmaking at the Sandwich Glass Manufactory on July 9, 1825. Toy decanters were made, which took small loosely fitting hand-formed ball stoppers and Sunburst stoppers, which were called *star stoppers* in the factory sloar book. During the first month, Sunburst stoppers for quart decanters were made, as were flathead stoppers and stoppers for cruets. Sixty-eight large flathead stoppers *for initialling* are listed in November 1825. This original company document finally dispels the myth that Sandwich glassmaking had a shaky beginning because they had to use local sand from a pile in the factory yard!

As glass production increased, so did the stopper count. By the time the Sandwich Glass Manufactory became incorporated as the Boston and Sandwich Glass Company, over one thousand stoppers were being made each week in one shop at the eight-pot furnace. These early stoppers were free-blown, blown molded or formed by hand from a solid glob of glass.

Every glass factory that manufactured containers in the early 1800's may not have made accompanying stoppers, because the Sandwich factory sloar book reveals that Sandwich produced stoppers to be shipped out to other factories. Records indicate great numbers of stoppers were made compared to the numbers of containers that they would fit. For example, during the week of March 15, 1828, Michael Doyle's shop made 150 quart three-ring decanters and 387 no-ring decanters—a total of less than six hundred decanters. The rest of the time Doyle's shop made lamps and dishes. The other shops around the furnace made witch balls, champagnes, lemonades, tumblers, wines, lamp globes, some cruets which took stoppers, some caster bottles which may or may not have taken stoppers, and peppers which did not. Compare this to the more than one thousand stoppers that were produced during the same week. In the shop of Samuel Barnes, one man was asked to stay, after he had completed his regular work, to make 301 cruet stoppers, 305 ball stoppers, 228 more cruet stoppers, and 312 half-pint cruet stoppers. Samuel Kern made 178 mushroom stoppers and George Hartshorn made ninety-one ball stoppers. Over 1500 stoppers were produced, yet during the same time period only 750 items that would take a stopper were made. If this was an occasional occurrence it would have no significance, but between 1825 and 1828 this practice continued week after week, doubling, tripling, and sometimes quadrupling the number of stoppers produced compared with the number of items in which a stopper could be used. It is very clear that the factory was either stockpiling great quantities for future use, or they were selling them to other glass factories. If the latter is true, it means that Sandwich stoppers may be fitted to containers that were made at other glass houses. The unanswered questions that arise from research of this magnitude can be frustrating, but our feeling is that the earliest decanters and cruets *cannot* be attributed to a particular glass factory on the basis of the shape, pattern, or cutting of the stopper alone.

As pressing techniques were perfected in the 1830's, stoppers were made by forcing the hot glass with a plunger into a mold that consisted of a rectangular reservoir connected to three or four stopper-shaped cavities. This mold produced a block of glass with the stoppers attached to it at their plug ends. After the glass was removed from the mold, the stoppers were broken away from the block of glass. The block of glass was returned to the cullet shop, where it was stored until it was remelted in another batch of metal. The use of this block mold increased production, but did not curtail the blowing of stoppers. Unlike production methods for other styles and patterns of Sandwich-made articles that can be related to various time periods, each new method in stopper technology was carried on *in addition* to older methods. The simplest ball stopper was blown molded from the first days of production to the last, with improvements on the plug end to help distinguish among them.

By the 1840's, another improvement in the pressing of stoppers came into use. On August 6, 1841, Hiram Dillaway, a mold maker who would later become head of the Boston and Sandwich Glass Company machine shop and engine room, sent to the United States Patent Office specifications for a mold designed to revolutionize stopper pressing. His "new and useful improvement in the art of pressing solid articles of glassware in molds" allowed up to twenty-four stoppers to be made at the same time.

Dillaway's patent replaced the rectangular block with cylinder that he called a *fountain* (see Dillaway's patent Each stopper form radiated from and was connected by plug end to the center fountain, the way spokes radia from the hub of a wheel. A plunger forced the molten gla into the fountain, and then into each stopper form. Aft the wheel of stoppers was removed from the mold, t stoppers were broken away from the center hub by tappi them with a mallet. If a stopper bounced to the floor i stead of into the stopper bin, it was not worth retrievin This is why so many stoppers are dug at the site that st have mold marks on the side of the plug. The mold mar on the plug of stoppers found at the site are proof that t stoppers were manufactured by the Boston and Sandwi Glass Company, and were not discarded after use by t townspeople or brought into the factory as part of a lo of purchased cullet. After the stoppers were broken awa the glass that made up the hub was stored for later use cullet.

As noted previously, minutes of the June 6, 1846, Boa of Directors' meeting record an accusation by the Ne England Glass Company that the Boston and Sandwi Glass Company was infringing on a stopper pate Several times throughout the history of both companie this claim was made in regard to other aspects of glas making—the pressing of knobs and the making of silver glass (mercury glass). Recurring claims of patent infring ment seemed to be a normal part of the glass business th sometimes caused no more than a minor irritation. B more detail in this instance is needed to show why t attribution of glass can be difficult.

Hiram Dillaway, around whom much of the patent co troversy swirled, was born in Uxbridge, Massachusetts, 1813. At the age of fifteen, he served for one year as apprentice to E. M. Bartholomew, a South Boston mo maker. His apprenticeship began on August 26, 1828. I early career during the following ten year period is n clear. He did renew his apprenticeship with Bartholome

Wooden patterns of block molds from the Boston a Sandwich Glass Company. These patterns were sent to t foundry as the first step in casting the molds in whi stoppers would be made.

Hiram Dillaway, who trained under a Boston mold maker, became head of the machine shop and engine room. *Courtesy, Sandwich Glass Museum, Sandwich Historical Society*

Boston and Sandwich Glass Company machine shop. *On loan to Sandwich Glass Museum, Sandwich Historical Society by Carol Morrow*

He is not listed as being in business for himself in the Boston Business Directory, but one Enoch S. Dillaway is listed as a brass founder as early as 1827, and as a machinist by 1838. Dillaway family papers state that Hiram Dillaway came to Sandwich from the "Mount Washington Glass Manufactory". Deming Jarves established his Mount Washington works in 1837. It appears likely that after Hiram Dillaway left Bartholomew he worked with Enoch Dillaway, then spent a year in Mount Washington. The earliest records placing Dillaway in Sandwich are both dated December 1838. The marriage of Hiram Dillaway of Sandwich to Mary Le(h)man of Boston was announced in the *Barnstable Patriot, and Commercial Advertiser* dated December 19, 1838, and, according to payroll records preserved by the Sandwich Historical Society, he is first listed on the factory payroll for the period of December 17–29, 1838. Although Hiram and Mary Dillaway made their home in Sandwich, and over the next several years their three children were born in Sandwich, it appears that Dillaway himself may have returned to Boston. He had come to Sandwich at a time when the glass industry was in deep trouble, following the financial panic of 1837. In 1839, the Board of Directors of the Boston and Sandwich Glass Company discussed severing connections with the factory in Sandwich and ordering Superintendent William Stutson not to fill the pots. On March 26, 1840, the *Yarmouth Register* announced with regret the suspension of glassmaking due to "difficulties of the times". The name of Hiram Dillaway was removed from the company payroll.

On August 6, 1841, when Dillaway patented his stopper mold, his address was given as Boston. He could have

been with Enoch S. Dillaway, who in later years would list his address as 51 Federal Street, the building that housed the offices of all of Deming Jarves' enterprises. Or, he could have returned to the Jarves-owned factory in South Boston that was called the Mount Washington Glass Manufactory, later to become the Mount Washington Glass Works.

As a private individual who was granted a patent, Hiram Dillaway was free to allow one or several companies, including the New England Glass Company, to press stoppers by his improved method. Possibly by 1843, and definitely by 1845, Dillaway once again settled in Sandwich—this time permanently. The Boston and Sandwich Glass Company had access to Dillaway's brilliance, and the New England Glass Company may have resented it.

Some time after the New England Glass Company made the 1846 accusation of patent infringement, both companies tried to come to terms with each other and with Dillaway, but records from May and June 1848, say that a legal problem arose regarding the purchase of Dillaway's patent for stoppers by the Boston and Sandwich Glass Company "and others". The outcome was hazy in the minutes of the Board of Directors' meetings, but on May 1, 1855, the patent was reissued to private citizen Hiram Dillaway of Sandwich, Massachusetts.

In 1865, Dillaway worked under contract for the Cape Cod Glass Company while he was still on salary at the Boston and Sandwich Glass Company. It appears that he did not assign his patents to any one company, but continued to collect royalties for his inventions. Eventually many glass companies in New England and in the Pittsburgh area adopted the Dillaway method of pressing stoppers without paying royalties. It took little change in mold construction for a glass company to circumvent a patent right.

Some of the stoppers dug from the factory site were inscribed with a number. This was common practice for better quality pieces. After a stopper was fitted to a bottle, both units were inscribed with the same number, allowing the finished stopper to travel through the factory and be packaged and shipped with its intended bottle at the end. It would be an oversimplification to say that, if a bottle and its stopper have matching numbers, it is Sandwich. Unfortunately for Sandwich collectors, many glass houses in this country and abroad used this system. But regardless of which company made a certain piece, finding the same number on a bottle and its stopper helps to determine that the stopper is original. This is particularly important if the decanter, oil bottle, or cologne you are buying is or was one of a pair. If you are buying a single piece, such as a decanter, and the seller has two, make sure that the stoppers have not been accidentally switched. An ill-fitting stopper with a different number greatly decreases the value of the bottle. Your money is invested much more wisely when you purchase the pair rather than convince the

owner to sell you only one. Items that were originally sold in pairs, such as matching decanters, candlesticks, and vases, are more valuable today when they are kept a pairs. For example, if a cologne is valued at $100, and second identical $100 cologne can be matched to i another $100 is added for a total value of $300.

Generally, the numbers inscribed at the factory a quite legible. Occasionally a piece is found with both num bers identical but very poorly executed. The last tw sentences of the following magazine article explain wh The article was taken from an issue of *Peterson's*, probab issued in October 1872.

To Take Stoppers Out of Bottles and Decanters.— Take the bottle or decanter by the neck with the left hand, and place the first finger at the back of the stopper. Take a piece of wood in the right hand, and tap the stopper first one side, then the other, turning the decanter round in the hand. A quick succession of little, short taps is the most effective. If this plan fails, wind a bit of rough string once around the neck, one end of the string being held by one person, the other by another; pull backward and forward till the neck becomes hot with friction. Then tap as before. Stoppers often become wedged into decanters from the wrong stopper being used. To avoid this the bottom of the stopper should be scratched with a number, and a corresponding number scratched under the bottom of the decanter.

There is one type of stopper that is today called a *cove* so we have not dealt with it at length in this study. Th is the upper unit that was fitted to wide-mouthed jars fc pickles, spices, and medicinal salts. Catalogs illustra medicine jars, square in shape, that were called *medici squares*. They had a large opening for contents that we not liquid, such as smelling salts, lavender salts, and othe pharmaceuticals. This large opening was called a *sa mouth*. It took a cover with a deep inner rim that fit insid the wide neck of the jar. The outside of the inner rim wa roughly ground to make a tight fit in the same manner a our spice jars of today. These jars were listed as "stoj pered", not covered. Regardless of their diameter, a cove that was machined to fit like the plug of a stopper wa called a *stop*.

THESE SIMPLE HINTS WILL HELP YOU IDENTIFY SANDWICH STOPPERS.

The reprint of the Boston and Sandwich Glass Con pany 1874 catalog is your best friend. Study the stoppere pieces to learn the type of stopper that was original to eac piece.

Study the shapes of the blanks used for cutting and er graving. Although variations occur among different cu ters, the shape of the original blank is the determining clu to its having been made at Sandwich.

UNITED STATES PATENT OFFICE.

HIRAM DILLAWAY, OF SANDWICH, MASSACHUSETTS.

IMPROVEMENT IN THE CONSTRUCTION OF MOLDS FOR PRESSING GLASS.

Specification forming part of Letters Patent No. 2,226, dated August 21, 1841; Reissue No. **308**, dated May 1, 1855.

All whom it may concern:

Be it known that I, HIRAM DILLAWAY, late of Boston, in the county of Suffolk, but now of Sandwich, in the county of Barnstable, and commonwealth of Massachusetts, have invented a new and useful Improvement in Molds for the Manufacture of Articles of Glassware; and I do hereby declare that the following is a full and exact description of the same.

My said invention is to be found in such a formation of the mold as shall cause the forms—by which I mean the cavities—into which the articles are to be pressed or molded to be filled with the melted glass to great advantage by means of a pressure applied to a mass of the material in a larger fountain connected with the forms, and it may be applied either in pressing a single article or a number of articles at one operation.

I will describe that mold which I have found convenient for pressing a number of small articles at once, but the relative position of the forms may be varied according to circumstances in molding different articles so far as they are arranged so as to lead out the lower part of the fountain. A block, of circular or other convenient form, proportioned to the size of the article and number of them to be formed at once, is made with a central elevation or neck on the top, in diameter equal to about one-half, and in height equal to about the whole, of that of the body of the block. The block is divided horizontally through the middle so as to make an upper and lower section, which constitute the two parts of an open and shut mold. Through the center of this elevation or neck the upper section is bored vertically so as to have a cylindrical hollow, of a diameter about half of that of the neck, passing entirely through it. The lower section is also bored vertically through the center, but so as to have a bore of a diameter a little larger than that of the bore of the upper section. The lower edge of the bore of the upper section is then hollowed or grooved so as to make it meet and match that of the lower section when the two parts are put together. All that part of the cylindrical hollow thus made through the entire block, which is not occupied by the bottom piece hereinafter described, I call the "fountain." The forms or the articles to be pressed are made by cavi-

ties on the inner surfaces of the upper and lower sections of the block cut to the shape designed, those in the upper matching with those in the lower section, and so disposed as to communicate with the central cylindrical hollow, and, when it is desirable to cast more than one article by one operation, the forms or cavities may be made to radiate or diverge from the central bore toward the outer circle of the block, as in the mold I am now describing. It may be found convenient to have in that part of the forms next to the central bore a small elevation, *n n*, (see the drawings hereinafter referred to,) with a sharpened edge sufficient to form a slight indentation around the end of the article pressed. These forms may be as numerous as the size of the article to be made and of the block containing them will admit, those in the mold exhibited in the drawings being for making glass stoppers for bottles. To the bore of the lower section is fitted a bottom piece, *f*, reaching as high as the lower edge of the forms and entirely filling the bore to that point, this bottom piece to be made movable. A plunger is fitted to the hollow in the neck of the upper section so as to pass down the bore to the bottom piece. When the plunger is brought down entirely home to the bottom piece, the diameter of the bore of the lower section being larger than that of the bore of the upper, and consequently than that of the plunger which is fitted to it, and the lower edge of this upper bore being hollowed out to meet the upper edge of the lower one, as above described, there is left around the bottom of the plunger a vacant chamber, *h h*, into which all the forms open, so that the plunger, however far pressed down, cannot close or obstruct the mouths of the forms. It may be found convenient to have, as in the mold I am now describing, on the inner surface of the upper section, at convenient points near its circumference, elongated square elevations, and on that of the lower one corresponding depressions, matching the one into the other, for the purpose of keeping each part of the mold secure in its proper place. The block may be made of cast-iron, or other metal sufficiently firm for the purpose and capable of bearing heat, and the central hollow and plunger may be made square, instead of cylindrical, when a number of articles are to

308

made at once, of such a shape as to make that form most convenient.

For the better specification of my said improvement I refer to the accompanying drawings as follows:

Figure 1 is the block, showing the horizontal division C D, and the top of the plunger dropped entirely down to reach the bottom piece. Fig. 2 is a vertical section of the block A B, showing the plunger *e* and movable bottom piece, *f*, and a sectional division of the forms or matrices *g*, and of the hollowing out of the lower edge of the bore in the upper section to meet the larger diameter of the bore in the lower section, the whole being to form the outer or auxiliary chamber, *h*. Figs. 3 and 4 horizontal sections of the mold on C D, showing plan of the forms or matrices *g* in inner surfaces of the upper and lower sections of the mold; also, the elevations *i* and depressions *k*. Fig. 5 is a movable bottom piece. Fig. 6 is a plunger. Fig. 7 is a top view of the mold without the plunger, showing the aperture *l*, into which the plunger passes. Fig. 8 is an under-side view of the mold without the movable bottom piece, and showing the aperture into which it is placed. The mode of using my said mold is described as follows: The mold being properly closed, a quantity of metal sufficient to fill all the forms or matrices, and a portion of the central hollow or fountain besides, is gathered and dropped in at the neck of the upper section. The plunger is then brought down upon it with a pressure sufficient to force the metal laterally from the central hollow into all the forms or matrices communicating with it, and the quantity gathered and dropped at any time be so little more than enough to fill the forms as to allow the plunger to be forced down below their upper edges, the metal not required to fill the forms remaining in and filling the chamber above described will be sufficient to prevent any imperfection in the pressing. After the metal is partially cooled the upper section is removed, and the pressed glass taken from the lower one, and the articles broken from the central mass at the indentations made by the edged elevation

before referred to. The object of making the bottom piece movable is that if the glass hangs or adheres to the lower section the bottom piece may be moved by force or pressure applied from below, and sufficient to start from the mold the glass with the articles attached, such being sometimes found necessary.

Any number of articles, according to their size and that of the block containing the forms, may be pressed at one time from one central fountain and by one plunger. The size, weight, and thickness of the articles made at each successive use of the same mold will be the same, the difference between the quantity of metal supplied at one time and another being left in the central mass instead of being forced into the article formed.

I claim—

1. So combining with a mold fountain or reservoir provided with a plunger, one or more matrices or molds that a liquid mass of glass, when pressed in said fountain or reservoir by the plunger, may be made to flow or pass therefrom and into such matrix or matrices.

2. Combining with a series of matrices and a press chamber or reservoir surrounded by them an auxiliary annular and concentric chamber, as seen at *h h*, in Fig. 2, formed in the two mold plates and made to perform the function of preventing the plunger from clogging the mouths of the matrices under circumstances as above stated, and also to prevent the chilled glass from obstructing the downward movement of the plunger.

3. So combining with the lower mold-plate a movable bottom block, *f*, that the same may not only serve to form a bottom to the main and auxiliary mold-chambers, or to the former, but also enable a person to detach the pressed glass or metal from the lower mold-plate under circumstances and in manner as above set forth.

In testimony whereof I have hereunto set my signature this 16th day of March, A. D. 1855.

HIRAM DILLAWAY.

Witnesses:
R. H. EDDY,
F. P. HALE, Jr.

H. DILLAWAY.
GLASS MOLD.

Re. 308
No. 2,226.   Patented Aug. 21, 1841.

Fig. 1. *Elevation of Mould, showing top of plunger.*
Fig. 2. *Section of Mould on A B, showing plunger and movable bottom piece.*
Fig. 3. *Horizontal Section on C D, showing underside view of top part of Mould.*
Fig. 4. *Horizontal Section on C D, showing top view of lower part of Mould.*
Fig. 5. *Movable bottom piece.*
Fig. 6. *Plunger.*
Fig. 7. *Top view of Mould without the plunger.*
Fig. 8. *Underside view of Mould without the movable bottom piece.*

Hiram Dillaway's patent for pressing many stoppers at one time, dated August 21, 1841, and reissued with minor improvements on May 1, 1855.

3174 HAND-FORMED BALL STOPPERS
1" H.-2" H. 1825–1828
Here is the simplest form of stopper made at Sandwich. Some have no shank—the plug is tight against the ball finial. Some have a short shank. Hand-formed ball stoppers were sometimes used on plain toy decanters, made from the first day of production at Deming Jarves' Sandwich Glass Manufactory.

3175 FREE-BLOWN BALL STOPPERS
1" H.-2" H. 1825–1828
All six stoppers were dug at the Sandwich site. Note the size of the plugs. Five stoppers have not been machined to fit into bottles. The stopper on the right was. Did it come from a bottle shipped into the factory which was later thrown away? We can't tell for sure, but it *does* match the other stoppers in every detail.

3176 BALL STOPPERS
(a) Free-blown 2" H.
(b) Pressed 2" H.
(c) Pressed 1½" H. 1830–1835
In early days, all the stoppers of this size with a ball finial were free-blown individually, and roughly pre-shaped. They required excessive machining to shape the plug, and there was always the danger of cutting into the airtrap. A normal day's production for one shop was 350 stoppers. In later years, with the advent of pressing, perfect stoppers far superior to those free-blown were turned out at the rate of one thousand per hour.

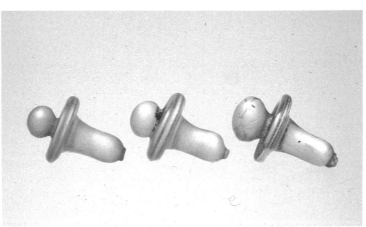

3177 HAND-FORMED TAM-O'-SHANTER STOPPERS
1½" H. 1825–1830
These are the stoppers that were used in vinegar cruets in the late 1820's. They were made in clear, blue, and amethyst. They show the individuality of each man who worked on them. Note the differences in the ball finial. The stopper in the center has no shank between the ball and the disk. All three have a pontil mark at the bottom. There are no mold marks on these early stoppers, and no airtrap in their centers, proving they were hand-formed—neither blown into a mold nor pressed.

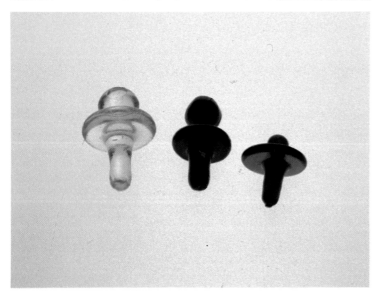

3178 HAND-FORMED TAM-O'-SHANTER STOPPERS
(a) 2" H. x 1¼" Dia.
(b) 1¾" H. x 1" Dia.
(c) 1¼" H. x ¾" Dia. 1825–1830
These stoppers show the clarity and color of the glass made in Sandwich. All three stoppers have a pontil mark on the end of the plug. The disk beneath the ball finial can vary from ¾" diameter to 1½" diameter, as shown here. These early stoppers were not made to fit individual cruets. Their only purpose was to slow down evaporation and keep dirt and insects from entering the bottle. The disk rested loosely on the rim of the bottle.

3179 HAND-FORMED RIBBED TAM-O'-SHANTER STOPPERS

a) Plain, for comparison 2" H. x 1¼" Dia.
b) Ribbed, large ball finial 1½" H. x 1" Dia.
c) Ribbed, small ball finial 1¾" H. x 1⅛" Dia.
    1825–1830

All three stoppers were made at a temperature when the glass could be worked like putty. Study the plug on stopper C. The spirals are the last signs of the crimping that formed the ribs. As the plug was worked into shape, the ribs gradually disappeared.

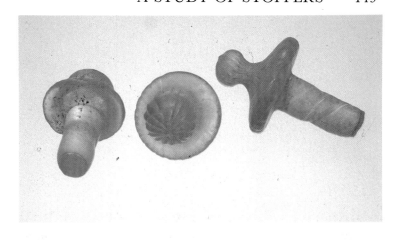

3180 FREE-BLOWN TAM-O'-SHANTER STOPPERS

a) Plug too short 1½" H. x ¾" Dia.
b) Hole in plug 2" H. x 1" Dia. 1825–1830

When searching for a free-blown stopper, look for a plain, very smooth exterior with an airtrap in the center. Stopper A was dug at the site of the Boston and Sandwich Glass Company. It was discarded because the plug was too short for the size of the stopper and could easily fall out. Stopper B was also dug at the site, discarded because, although the plug is the proper length, it has a hole in the end. Sediment could enter the airtrap where it could not be cleaned, so the stopper became useless. It is, however, an excellent example of what was made in the earliest days of production.

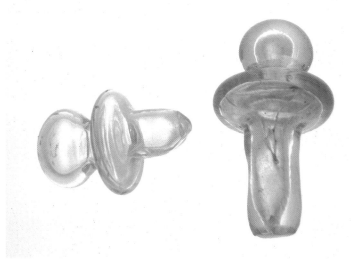

3181 BLOWN MOLDED RIBBED BALL DECANTER STOPPERS

3½" H. 1825–1830

The great number of stoppers found at the Sandwich dig site with this pattern were discarded because of a hole in the bottom of the plug, similar to the one that can be seen on the right stopper. It appears that some finish work was done on the plugs, and as the bottom was machined, they cut through to the airtrap. Because dirt and sediment could enter the plug, they were thrown away. There is no other damage. Today, finding a decanter with a stopper that has a hole in it should not affect the value of the piece.

3182 BLOWN MOLDED DECANTER STOPPERS

a) Ridged 3¼" H.
b) Ribbed 4" H. 1825–1830

Both stoppers were thrown away during production because holes broke through to the inside when they were disconnected from the blowpipe. The dark discoloration in stopper A is caused by sediment on the inside of the plug. Mold marks can clearly be seen on the plug of stopper B, indicating that it was never machined and completed. Today, we are satisfied to see the correct pattern stopper on an early decanter even if their is an opening into the airtrap. However, it is not the original stopper, because the Boston and Sandwich Glass Company did not ship open stoppers out of the factory. The ripples seen on the lower part of the ball of stopper A are the ridges reflected through from the other side.

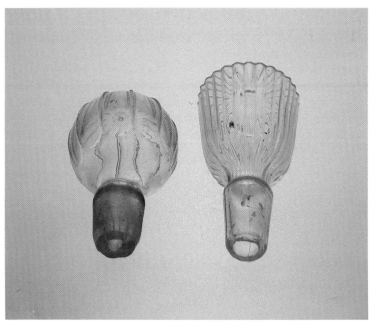

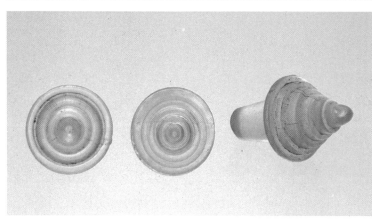

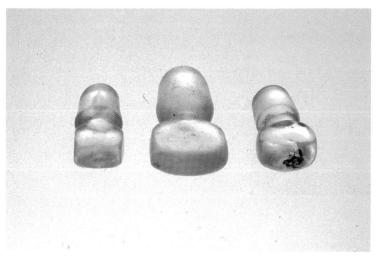

3183 PRESSED DIAMOND POINT STOPPERS

(a, b) Diamond Point 3¼" H.
(c, d) Fine Diamond Point 2" H. 1841–1850

The stoppers shown here were pressed in a Diamond Point pattern, with a smooth cap. They came from three different size wheel molds—stoppers A and B came from the same size, and stoppers C and D each came from different wheel molds. Up to twenty-four stoppers were made at one time using this method of production, but all of the stoppers on a wheel were identical in size, shape, and style.

3184 PRESSED MUSHROOM DECANTER STOPPERS

(a) Ribbed 3¼" H. x 2¼" Dia. 1825–1830
(b) Lacy 2¾" H. x 2⅜" Dia. 1835–1845

Mushroom stoppers were used on early quart decanters. These two patterns are the only pressed mushroom stoppers dug at the factory site in sufficient quantity to guarantee that they were made by the Boston and Sandwich Glass Company. Cover the top half of each stopper, and you will see a simple ball stopper. The mushroom is connected to the ball by a plain shank, and the ball becomes a knop between the shank and the plug.

3185 PRESSED CONCENTRIC RINGED STOPPERS

(a) Three rings 1¼" H.
(b) Five rings 1⅛" H.
(c) Five stepped rings 2" H. 1828–1835

These stoppers are crude and were made very early at Sandwich. They pre-date the stopper wheel and came from a primitive mold that pressed several stoppers at a time on top of a rectangular block. This type fits loosely into its bottle in the same manner as the early Tam-o'-shanter stopper. When properly machined, the plug runs straight down from underneath the largest ring, allowing the bottom of the largest ring to rest on the rim of its bottle.

3186 HAND-FORMED FLAT-SIDED STOPPERS

1⅛" H.-2¼" H. 1825–1840

All nine of these stoppers have pontil marks on the plug end. Some were hand made in their entirety, while others were pre-shaped in a mold. All were made before the invention of the wheel mold, which was patented by Hiram Dillaway in 1841.

3187 HAND-FORMED FLAT-SIDED STOPPERS

(a) Finial and plug are same width 1⅛" H.
(b) Finial is wider than plug 1½" H.
(c) Incomplete finial 1⅛" H. 1825–1830

These clear glass stoppers were dug at the 1830 dump area in Sandwich. They are poor in quality and are incomplete. Stopper A has a small hole in the bottom of the plug, making it useless. Stopper B is a good example of a hand-formed flat-sided stopper. Stopper C has an incomplete finial because the glass cooled before the shaping was completed. When the glassworker attempted to reheat it, he picked up carbon by striking the stopper on the edge of the glory hole. The carbon is still embedded in the finial. We did not dig at the factory site to find perfect pieces but to gain knowledge through the imperfect pieces discarded at the time.

3188 PRESSED FLAT-SIDED STOPPERS

a) Square finial, long plug
b) Rounded finial, long plug
c) Rounded finial, short plug 1¼" H. 1830–1835

Stopper A shows the bottom of the plug not yet machined, but the side of the plug has been machined to fit a bottle. Stopper B is completely machined and is ready for use. Stopper C has a large part of the stopper block still attached. It has not been machined at all. Incomplete pieces were most important to find at the factory site, because even the most exacting critic cannot deny that they were manufactured by the Boston and Sandwich Glass Company.

3189 WHEEL OF PRESSED FLAT-SIDED STOPPERS

2¾" H. each stopper 1841–1850

Although this method of pressing stoppers was used by many companies, the two wheels shown in this chapter are believed to be Sandwich because many matching stoppers of this type have been dug there. Keep in mind that stoppers that have been machined to fit bottles are not *proof* of production. They could have come from containers that brought material into the factory and were thrown into the dump when empty. The loose stoppers here do not show machining. Their plugs still have mold marks. They were dropped at the time the stoppers were broken away from the center fountain. When found at a glass factory site in large quantities, they can be considered part of the production run. As many as twenty-four stoppers could be pressed at one time. The discoloration on dug stoppers is caused by iron oxides in the soil.

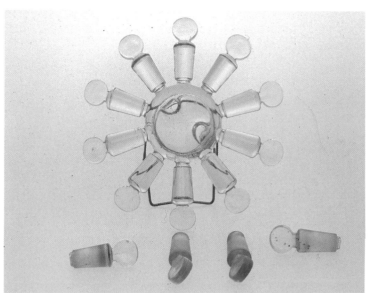

3190 FLAT-SIDED STOPPERS

a) Hand-formed 2⅛" H.
b) Hand-formed 2½" H. 1825–1845
c) Pressed by wheel method 2⅞" H. 1841–1850

Note the differences between the hand-formed stoppers and the pressed stopper. The finials on stoppers A and B are rounded, as if shaped from a lump of putty. The finial on stopper C has sharp edges around the circumference and a distinct mold mark. In order to identify a possibly defective mold cavity, some stoppers from a wheel have a number *molded* into them in the center just above the plug, as appears on stopper C. Each stopper cavity had a different number. If some stoppers came out defective, the problem mold form could be identified. Do not mistake this number for a number *inscribed* on a fitted stopper that would match a number inscribed on its bottle.

3191 WHEEL OF PRESSED FLAT-SIDED STOPPERS

2⅛" H. each stopper 1841–1850

This wheel of stoppers is one of the best ever found from this time period. The amber color was common to the Keene-Stoddard area, but we do not attribute glass to a particular factory by color alone. This color matches the candlestick shown on photo 4042 of Volume 4. The candlestick has family ties to a Sandwich glassworker, and many stoppers that match in shape and color have been dug at Sandwich. Most of the dug stoppers still have a mold mark down the side of the plug, assuring us that they were manufactured by the Boston and Sandwich Glass Company.

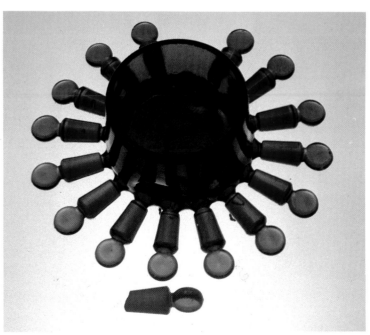

3192 PRESSED FLAT-SIDED STOPPERS
2⅛" H. 1841–1850

Hundreds of these stoppers that match the stoppers sti
attached to the wheel have been salvaged from the site
Most have not been machined. They were dropped at th
time they were broken off the center fountain of the whee
They ended up on the floor and were swept out with th
trash to be salvaged by us 125 years later. Only the cent
hub of the wheel was returned to be used for cullet. Stop
pers were not worth the effort.

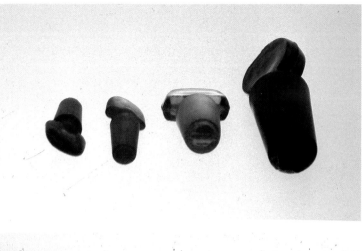

3193 PRESSED FLAT-SIDED STOPPERS
1⅜" H.–2¾" H. 1830–1835

Hundreds of these stoppers in dark "bottle" colors of amb
and green have been dug at the Boston and Sandwic
Glass Company site, yet few of their matching bottles c
necks of bottles were found. Four sizes of stoppers ar
shown here, all in dark amber. They are solid glass
broken away from a stopper block. The lack of matchin
bottles remains an unsolved mystery of the digging sit
Are they still beneath the soil, or were they returned to th
cullet shop to be used in future batches? Or, were stopper
made in large quantities and sent to Deming Jarves' Ne
England Glass Bottle Company in East Cambridge?

3194 PRESSED FLAT-SIDED PERFUME STOPPER
¾" H. 1830–1835

This stopper is compared to the size of a penny. Note th
bottom of the plug where the stopper was broken off th
block. When completed, this area would have been ma
chined off, leaving a smooth area on the end where
number would be inscribed to match the number inscribe
on its bottle. This tiny stopper was for a perfume used in
purse.

3195 HAND-FORMED SUNBURST AND WAFFL
DECANTER STOPPERS
(a) Blank
(b) Sunburst
(c, d, e) Waffle 1½" H.–2¼" H. 1825–1828

Stopper A shows the shape of the finial before the patter
was pressed into it. After reheating, the desired patter
was pressed into it by means of two patterned dies, on
on each side of a pair of pincers. Stopper B has bee
pressed into a Sunburst pattern and stoppers C, D, an
E have three variations of Waffle pattern.

3196 HAND-FORMED SUNBURST DECANTER STOPPERS
2¼" H.–3⅜" H. 1825–1835

All of the stoppers shown here were dug at the site of th
Boston and Sandwich Glass Company, and each one ha
a different variation of the Sunburst pattern on its finia
All of the finials have one thing in common—the center
of the Sunbursts are clear. It has sometimes been claime
that the pattern on decanter stoppers can reveal whic
glass house in New England made them. In our opinion
this is not true. Many variations of the Sunburst wer
made in Sandwich, as well as at other factories.

197 HAND-FORMED SUNBURST DECANTER STOPPERS

a, c) Clear center
b) Clear center, ring around edge 3" H. 1825-1835
Here are three variations of the Sunburst, all with clear centers. The same pattern is always repeated on the other side of the finial. Stopper B is considerably different from the others. There is a ring around the finial near the outer edge that cuts through the rays of the Sunburst pattern. Little or no machining was done to make the stoppers fit snugly in their decanters.

198 HAND-FORMED SUNBURST DECANTER STOPPERS WITH TWO-RING CENTER

a) Small finial with thick shank
b) Large finial with thick shank
c) Small finial with no shank 2⅜" H. 1825-1828
Two concentric rings and a protruding knob can be seen in the center of each Sunburst pattern. These stoppers should have little or no machining on the plug, because very early stoppers were made to fit loosely into their decanters. Their only purpose was to act as a cover to keep out dirt and insects.

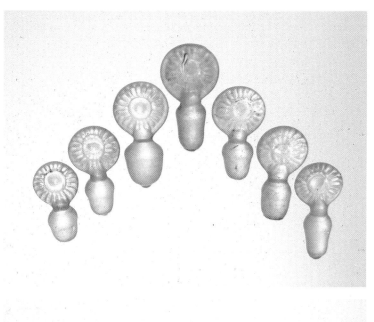

199 HAND-FORMED SUNBURST TOY DECANTER STOPPERS

" H.-1½" H. 1825-1830
Toy decanters are listed in the Sandwich Glass Manufactory sloar book (also called a *turn book*) on July 9, 1825, the first full day glass was made in Sandwich. All seven stoppers shown here are a variation of the Sunburst pattern, pressed into their finials by a variety of dies on the pincers. More than sixty Sunburst toy decanter stoppers in perfect condition have been dug at the Sandwich site, in these seven Sunburst patterns.

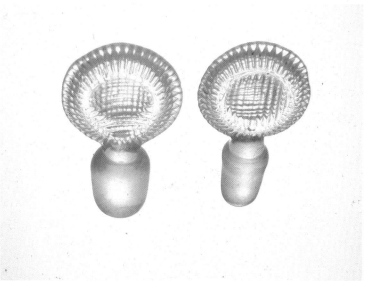

200 HAND-FORMED SUNBURST DECANTER STOPPERS WITH WAFFLE CENTER

a) Large plug 3¼" H.
b) Small plug 2⅞" H. 1825-1835
The pattern on these stoppers is often thought to be solely the work of Thomas Cains, who was affiliated first with the South Boston Flint Glass Company and then with the Phoenix Glass Works, which he built across the street. We are sure Cains used this pattern, but so did Sandwich. We see no way to distinguish between them. Note the flattened edge of both finials. On stopper A, it can be seen left of the center, near the top. Stopper B is flat at the extreme right. The flat edges were made by the ends of the pincers where the dies were attached.

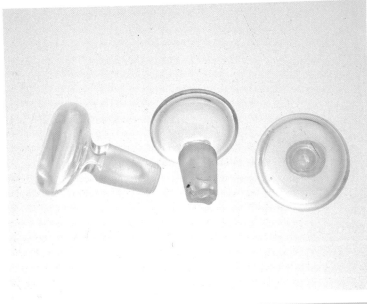

3201 BLOWN FLAT-TOPPED DECANTER STOPPERS
(a) Fitted to a decanter
(b) Dug from site
(c) Top view 2⅛" H. 1840–1860
Many stoppers blown in this shape have been dug at Sandwich, and are used on pint and half-pint decanters. The stopper on the left was taken from a known Sandwich decanter. The center stopper was dug in an area of the factory dump where known 1850–1860 debris was discarded. It matches the left stopper in every detail. The stopper on the right was also dug. This top view shows the airtrap in the finial.

3202 BLOWN MOLDED FLAT STOPPERS
(a) Flat-sided finial 1" H. x 1⅛" Dia.
(b) Flat-topped finial, bottom view, closed across bottom of plug 1¼" H. x 1¼" Dia.
(c) Flat-topped finial 1¼" H. x 1¼" Dia. 1830–1870
Stoppers like these were used on tincture bottles and salt mouths. All those dug at the Boston and Sandwich Glass Company site have been clear, ranging in size from ¾" to 6" in diameter. They are machined to fit snugly into a jar and were often left roughly ground to increase friction. Stopper B has been positioned to show the hollow center. It is closed across the bottom, making an airtrap in the plug. Some were accidentally left open across the bottom and were discarded.

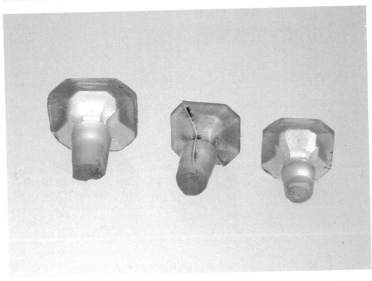

3203 PRESSED SQUARE COLOGNE STOPPERS WITH CHAMFERRED CORNERS
(a) Plug broken when machined 1⅜" H.
(b) Perfect plug ready to be machined 1¼" H.
(c) Finished and fitted to cologne 1⅛" H. 1850–1860
Here is the same type of stopper in three stages of development. Stopper A was broken when the plug was being worked on. Stopper B shows where the plug was broken away from the block or wheel fountain. The mold mark can clearly be seen running across the bottom of the finial and down the side of the plug. Stopper C is a completed perfect stopper taken from a cologne. The finial has been polished. Both the stopper and the cologne are inscribed with the number 6.

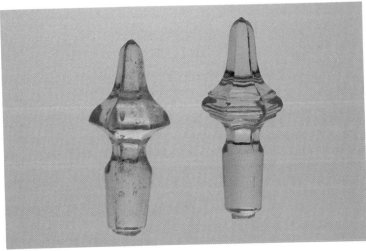

3204 PRESSED FLARING HEXAGONAL STOPPERS
(a) Plain 2¼" H. 1830–1887
(b) Detailed 2¼" H. 1840–1887
Stopper A can be found on very early cruet bottles for caster sets that pre-date revolving caster stands. It was made as small as 1¼" H. for use in toy caster sets that were made up to the time of the closing of the Boston and Sandwich Glass Company. Stopper B has a ridge above and below the widest point of the finial. It is usually found on caster sets that rotate. Both stoppers have been dug in quantity. Over two hundred are in our collection alone — some in green, canary, and dark red. In our opinion, colored caster sets were made on special order.

3205 PRESSED CRUET STOPPERS

3" H.-3 ¾" H. 1840-1870

Here is a group of stoppers that were used in vinegar cruets and caster bottles. They are all solid glass, so were undoubtedly pressed in stopper molds that used either the wheel configuration or a block. Although some appear to have cut facets, close examination reveals that the only finish work done was the machining of the plugs.

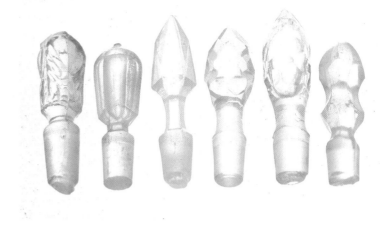

3206 BLOWN MOLDED COLOGNE STOPPERS

(a) Short stocky finial 3" H.
(b) Taller finial, blunted point 3½" H.
(c) Like B but sharp point 3⅝" H. 1840-1870

These stoppers were blown into a mold, annealed, and then six flutes were cut around the top of the finials. Note that each cutter shaped the same stopper blank differently. Stopper C is the most difficult to maintain in perfect condition. The slightest pressure against the sharp point would chip it. Learn to identify Sandwich glass by studying the shape of the blanks. The stoppers in the photo have variations in cutting, but the shape of the blanks is identical.

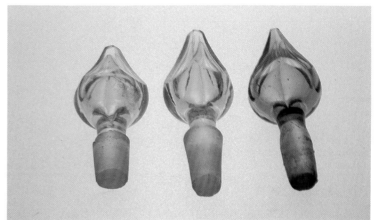

3207 COLOGNE STOPPERS

(a) Light blue, blown molded 3⅜" H. 1840-1870
(b) Dark blue, pressed 3⅝" H. 1841-1870

These stoppers are essentially the same. They were put to the same use and have the same market value. But stopper A was blown. There is an airtrap in the finial and no mold marks below the flutes, which were cut into the stopper after it was annealed. Stopper B was pressed and is the style illustrated in Hiram Dillaway's patent number 2226 that is dated August 21, 1841. There is no airtrap in the finial and a mold mark can be seen in the shank between the cut facets of the finial and the machined sides of the plug. Dillaway illustrates ten stoppers being pressed at one time using his wheel method. Blown stoppers could not be made as quickly.

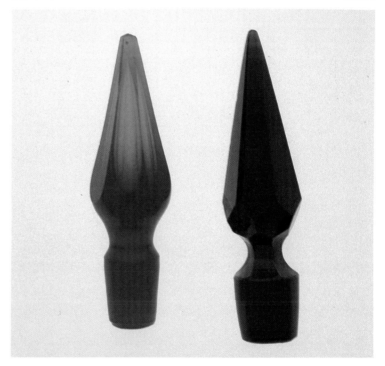

3208 BLOWN MOLDED COLOGNE STOPPERS

a) Six flutes, facets below 2¾" H. 1845-1860
b) Eight flutes, facets below 4⅛" H. 1855-1870

Stopper A is similar in shape to the stoppers illustrated in Hiram Dillaway's patent for *pressing* many stoppers at a time, but this one is *blown* into a mold. Six flutes are cut into the pointed end of the stopper blank, with facets below. The finial was polished after the cutting was completed. Stopper B is a beautifully blown one, with eight flutes cut into it. Both stoppers were used on numerous Sandwich colognes. Although the blanks for both stoppers are similar in shape, the cutting changed the contour.

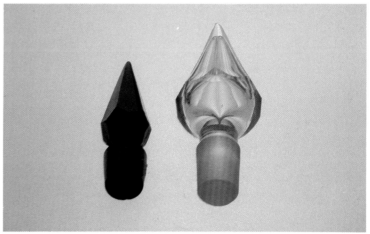

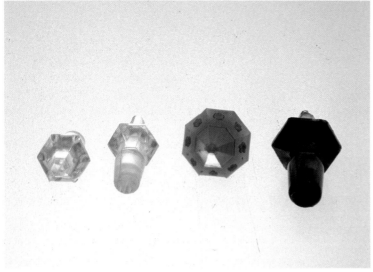

3209 PRESSED GILDED STOPPERS
(a) Light blue 2¼" H.
(b) Clear 2¼" H.
(c) Blue 2½" H.
(d) Dark green 2½" H. 1845–1860

Based on shape and color, these stoppers could have been made as early as 1840. But the man called "William Smith, the gilder" did not come to the Boston and Sandwich Glass Company until the mid-1840's to head the company's new decorating shop. The gilding can best be seen on stopper C, a large dot on each of the panels. A gold dot is also applied on the very top of the finial. None of these stoppers have been machined to fit a bottle. Stopper B shows the mold mark running down the side of the plug just left of center.

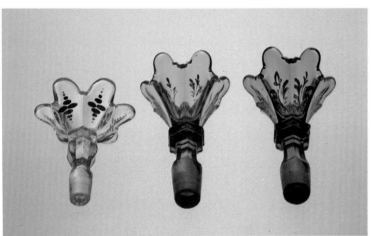

3210 PRESSED GILDED COLOGNE STOPPERS
(a) Flower 2½" H. x 2¼" Dia.
(b, c) Lily 3¾" H. x 2" Dia. 1845–1870

Stopper A has a protuberance below the petals much like a real flower. Sometimes the petals were reworked to flare out, or close up into a bud. The Lily stoppers have two hexagonal rings below and are the trumpet shape of a real lily. Note the gilding on all three stoppers. The light, sandy soil of Sandwich has preserved the decorations so that rubbing with toothpaste on a soft cloth, even after one hundred years in the ground, restored the gilding perfectly.

3211 PRESSED FLOWER COLOGNE STOPPERS
(a) Large 3" H. x 3" Dia.
(b) Medium 2½" H. x 2¾" Dia.
(c) Small 2¼" H. x 2½" Dia. 1840–1870

Flower stoppers are beautifully made and add a special quality to the cologne. Stopper A fits a cologne that holds one quart and has an underplate. Stopper B was used on a one pint cologne and stopper C on a half pint bottle. No other American glass factory made a stopper that is even close to this configuration, but a similar one was made in France. It has not been reproduced.

3212 CUT OVERLAY COLOGNE STOPPERS
(a) Green, plug not machined 3¾" H.
(b) Blue, plug partly machined 3½" H.
(c) Blue, ready for use 2⅜" H. 1845–1870

Overlay is glass cased on the outside with one or two different colors. The outer layer (or layers) are cut back to reveal the glass beneath. When stopper A was blown, the layer of green was carried down over the plug. The stopper was never fitted to a bottle, so the green remains. Stopper B has the blue overlay removed. Two other identical stoppers were dug at the same time along with the bottle shown in photo 3137 in the chapter on colognes. Stopper C was ready to be inserted into a cologne bottle. It is inscribed with a number and is in perfect condition. There was no reason to discard it, unless its matching bottle was damaged and discarded.

3213 PRESSED FACETED STOPPERS

(a) Amber, machined plug 2½" H.
(b) Light canary, machined plug 2½" H.
(c) Light amethyst, machined plug 3" H.
(d) Light blue, plug not machined 3¼" H. 1870–1887

Three types of faceted stoppers were made in Sandwich: pressed faceted, pressed lapidary, and blown molded lapidary. *Pressed* faceted stoppers were formed in a mold that had the pattern of facets in it. The only work that had to be done after it was removed from the faceted mold and annealed was machining the plug. They had the least clarity and were the least expensive. All of the stoppers shown here were pressed by the wheel method. Each is from a different mold, but the same number of facets are pressed into each finial. Stopper D was not machined. The mold mark can be seen running down the side of the plug.

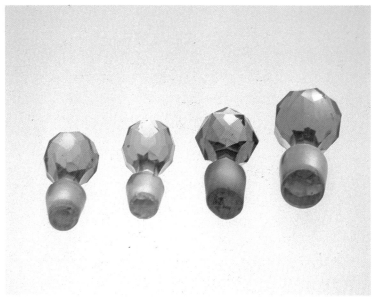

3214 PRESSED FACETED STOPPERS

(a) Light amber, machined plug
(b) Amber, plug not machined 3" H. 1860–1887

Stopper A is a finished stopper. It was machined to fit a bottle, and a number is inscribed on the bottom of the plug. The same number would have been inscribed on the bottle to which the stopper was fitted. We cannot be absolutely sure that this stopper was made by the Boston and Sandwich Glass Company even though it was dug there, unless additional identical stoppers are found that still show the mold mark. The stopper could have been on a bottle that was brought to the factory by a worker who purchased it elsewhere. When the bottle was empty, it could have been thrown in the dump, and therefore historians should not attribute it to Sandwich. Stopper B was made at Sandwich. Note the mold mark on the plug. It was dropped when the cutter was shaping the end of the plug.

3215 PRESSED LAPIDARY STOPPERS

(a) Polished finial, machined plug 3" H.
(b) Unpolished finial, machined plug 3" H.
(c) Polished finial, cut hexagonal shank, partly machined plug 4¾" H. 1870–1887

A second type of faceted stopper is the pressed lapidary stopper made by *polishing* the facets of a pressed faceted stopper. This extra step resulted in added clarity. All three stoppers shown here were intended to have their facets polished. Stopper A is complete except for the missing inscribed number. Stopper B has a machined plug, but the first attempt to polish the facets chipped it. As the plug on stopper C was machined, it went out of round and was rendered useless. Note that stoppers A and B have no shank. Stopper C has a long shank, cut into six sides to enhance its beauty. There could be as many as fifty-two facets on each finial.

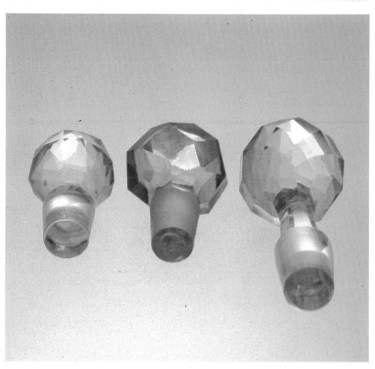

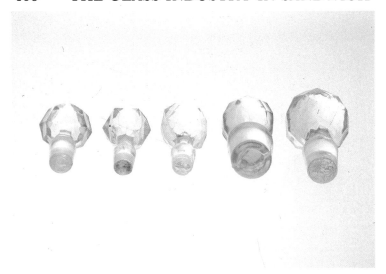

3216 PRESSED LAPIDARY STOPPERS
2¼" H.-3" H. 1870-1887
These stoppers were pressed on a stopper wheel; there are no airtraps in their centers. Note the variations in the size of the plugs, which extend from the finials with no shank between. The facets of all five stoppers were polished after they were removed from the wheel and annealed. They were considered excellent substitutes for blown lapidary stoppers.

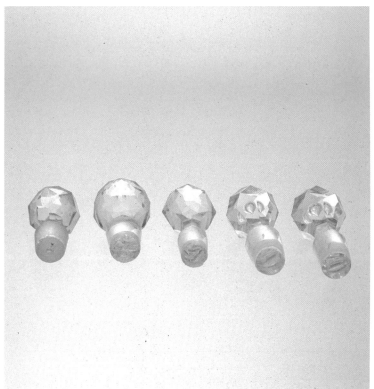

3217 LAPIDARY STOPPERS
(a, b, c) Pressed, no airtrap
(d, e) Blown molded, with airtrap 2¼" H.-2¾" H.
    1870-1887
A third type of faceted stopper was made by blowing glass into a mold that had the pattern of facets in it. Stoppers D and E were made in this manner. Note the airtrap in their centers. If they were pressed, they would be solid, as are stoppers A, B, and C. Blown faceted stoppers have greater brilliance than pressed faceted stoppers. They were made from the highest quality glass and reached their zenith during what is known as the *Brilliant Period* in cut glass manufacture. They represent some of the finest faceting executed in Sandwich.

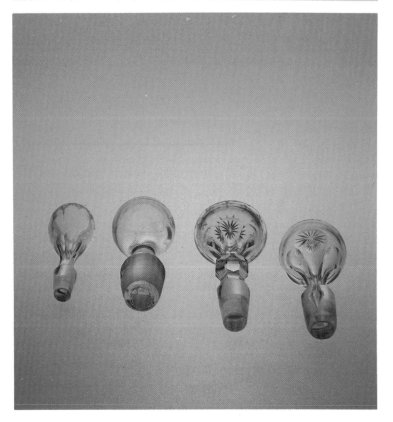

3218 BLOWN MOLDED STOPPERS FOR LATE BLOWN WARE
(a) Curtain design, copper wheel engraved on finial, six flutes cut into shank 4¼" H.
(b) Fern design, copper wheel engraved on finial, plain shank 4¼" H.
(c) Copper wheel engraved design and cut star on finial, long shank with faceted knop center 4½" H.
(d) Cut star on finial with cut flutes below, and airtrap extending into plug 1870-1887
The Late Blown Period in the history of the Boston and Sandwich Glass Company coincided with the Brilliant Period in cut glass manufacture. The finials were blown "thin as a bubble". Note the airtrap that extends into the plug of stopper D. The plug of stopper B was damaged when it was machined.

3219 BLOWN MOLDED STOPPERS

a) Bands of ribbing and diamond diapering 3½" H. 1830

b) Diamond Thumbprint pattern 3¾" H. 1840

c) Threaded glass 2½" H. 1880

d) Late blown ware, Etched 500 design 4" H. 1885

Compare stopper A with stopper D, and note the improvement in workmanship. Note also the evolution of the plug, from a loosely fitting one that only protected the contents of the bottle from dirt and insects, to a sophisticated plug individually fitted to one particular bottle, preventing evaporation of its contents. The patterns on stoppers A and B were completed simply by blowing the glass into patterned molds. The threading on stopper C was applied after the stopper was removed from an unpatterned mold, then the stopper was annealed. Stopper D was blown into an unpatterned mold, annealed, then the design was etched into its surface.

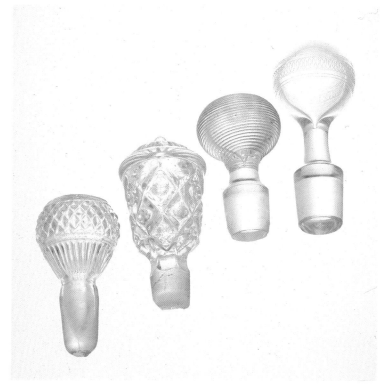

3220 PRESSED FLAT-SIDED WHISKEY JUG STOPPERS

a, c) Lacy Teardrop design copper wheel engraved on finial

b) Blank 2¾" H. 1870–1887

The decanters to which these stoppers were fitted were the short, squat, handled ones listed as *whiskey jugs* in the 1874 catalog of the Boston and Sandwich Glass Company. They can be seen on page 14 of the catalog reprint. Any of the Late Blown Period designs could be copper wheel engraved on the stopper blank, or have just a simple letter that indicated the contents of the jug. The letter "B" stands for brandy, and "W" denotes whiskey—they are *not* someone's monogram!

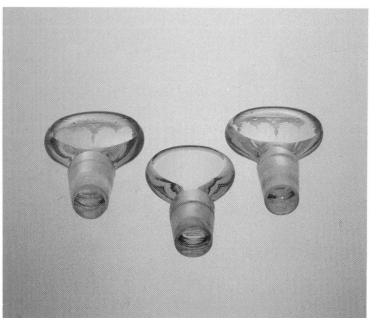

3221 BLOWN MOLDED THREADED STOPPERS

a) Small finial, long hexagonal shank 3¾" H.

b) Large finial, shorter plain shank 3¾" H.

c) Short plain shank 2¾" H.

d) Short plain shank 2¼" H. 1880–1887

The Late Blown Period provided some of the most beautiful glass. Although large quantities of cologne fragments were dug that have blue, green, and canary threading, all of the stoppers we found have pink threading. Out of the dozens with pink threading, only these four have perfect threads. The shank of stopper A was cut into six panels and polished. One hundred years in the soil made the threads *sick*—discolored to a pale pink. All of the threaded stoppers dug at Sandwich have threading completely covering the finials. If you buy a partly threaded stopper, it may be English.

3222 SLIDE STOPPERS
(a) Permanent cage 1¾" H. from finial to bar lip
(b) Threaded removable cage 2" H. from finial to bar lip 1850–1870

Pressed decanters were made in two styles. *Table* decanter were fitted with "glass stops", and *bar* decanters wer shipped with "slide stops". To date, the four slide stopper shown here are the only types that have been dug at th factory site. The opening in the pewter stopper tha allowed the liquid to be poured out of the decanter wa made in three sizes, requiring three different size marble The marble was inserted in a cage-like device that wa permanently attached to the stopper as in A, or threade to the stopper as in B. When the decanter was in an up right position, the marble closed the opening. When th decanter was tilted for pouring, the marble slid toward th top of the cage.

3223 SLIDE STOPPERS
(a) Wire cage 2" H. from top of cage to bar lip
(b) Permanent cage 1⅞" H. from finial to bar lip 1850–1870

Slide stoppers with wire cages are not plentiful, so the command a higher price in the antiques market. The cag of stopper B is permanently attached, but the finial is nc the same as those shown in the previous photo. All fou types use cork to keep them in place. The glass marble were not made in Sandwich. Records show that the Bosto and Sandwich Glass Company purchased them fror German glass houses in four hundred pound casks with guarantee that 70 percent would be usable. Glassmake sometimes made marbles for the boys who worked at th factory or for their own children, but marbles were nc manufactured for commercial purposes.

3224 SLIDE STOPPER FRAGMENTS
1850–1870

Although time has eaten away the pewter slide stoppe dug at the factory site, there is in this photo enough infor mation to tell us what types were used and how they wer assembled. The stopper at the top took the largest marbl and was used on a quart decanter. The stopper below i in the center, took the smallest marble and was used o a half pint decanter. The other three were used on pint ba decanters and utilized a medium size marble. A "slide sto was shipped with every bar decanter, so your decanter not complete without this upper unit.

CHAPTER 7

THE NORTH SANDWICH INDUSTRIAL AREA

Its Importance to the Glass Industry
1847–1895

The era of the specialist had not yet arrived during the heyday of the Boston and Sandwich Glass Company. In order to operate such a business successfully, it was imperative for its manager to be a man of many talents, able to understand and oversee the subsidiary industries upon which his business depended.

And so it was with Deming Jarves. As agent of the Boston and Sandwich Glass Company, he had many specialized jobs to be done, but he did not look for specialists to do them. When he needed lumber, he owned sawmills. When he needed bricks, he bought a brickyard. It was necessary in the glass business to have a constant supply of cast iron molds, so Jarves established and ran an iron foundry. In this manner, Jarves had the security of knowing all of these things were available to him when he needed them, and, if a profit could be made from such other industries, he was not reluctant to enjoy this benefit.

This chapter records the development of the area along the Herring River in North Sandwich. Although it was separated from the glass factory by three miles, it became the site of a nail factory, a barrel stave mill, several ax and edge tool factories, and, most important, the foundry that supplied Sandwich's glass companies with molds, furnace doors and grates, and even ox carts.

The early settlers of Sandwich were well aware of the value of fast-moving streams for water power. As early as 1695, the area around Indian Burial Hill in North Sandwich teemed with activity because of two large ponds located north of the Barnstable County line in Plymouth County. The smaller of the two, Little Herring Pond, was north of Cedarville. Great Herring Pond extended from Cedarville south to the county line, where it emptied into Herring River. The ponds were high enough to cause the water coming from the outlet of Great Herring Pond to move at a speed that could be harnessed for power. The ponds derived their name from the fact that herring, a small bony fish, return each spring to spawn. After the eggs had hatched and the young herring had matured during the summer, the herring then swam through Herring River, Monument River and Buzzards Bay, to complete their life cycle in the sea.

On December 17, 1695, the Selectmen of Sandwich granted to Elisha Bourne the right to build a gristmill on the banks of Herring River, provided he did not jeopardize the migration of the herring. A method was devised of taking water through a sluiceway, allowing the gristmill to run on water power without interfering with the fish. During this period, the town built a herring house straddling Herring River. It was so constructed that the fish, in order to reach the ponds, had to pass through a narrow waterway under the herring house. Large quantities of herring were netted for food and bait, each family in town being supplied with one free barrel. Additional barrels could be purchased for ten cents each.

As the gristmill continued to operate, the Board of Selectmen, in 1717, granted Benjamin Bourne permission to build a sawmill between the gristmill and the mouth of Great Herring Pond. Mr. Bourne was instructed by the Selectmen not to allow the sawmill to prejudice herring going up or coming down Herring River. These mills caused great problems for the Selectmen in relation to the herring run. Their heavy use of water dried up the river bed and the herring could not migrate. Finally, in the spring of 1743, the Board of Selectmen of Sandwich ordered the "Bourne boys" to stop all activities on the river from April 1 to May 20 for every year thereafter, unless Medad Tucker or Samuel Gibbs, appointed fish wardens, were there to see that the fish were not obstructed.

This is the only recorded use of the waterway until 1821, when a trip hammer mill and ax factory was erected, using the flume remaining from an earlier enterprise. A new mill race and a small dam were built, raising the water six feet and back-flooding the lowlands. This created a third pond of ten acres, known as Mill Pond.

By 1830, Thomas Swift took over the old gristmill site and made an addition to the building, converting it into a woolen mill. The woolen factory became the property of Ariel Boyden, Ira Guild, and Mason White, and served the town of Sandwich well for several years, but on December 10, 1834, it was sold at auction. The auction notice in the *Barnstable Patriot* of November 19, 1834, tells of a large water wheel that was capable of running a num-

Herring run at the west end of the dam at Mill Pond. This photo was taken in 1903 by Edward Nickerson, who re corded the history of North Sandwich (Bournedale) in great detail.

ber of machines, and describes the site as one of the best water privileges in the country.

The new owner was Ephraim Ellis. He purchased the woolen mill, and a large tract of land bounded by the western and southern shore of Mill Pond, and extending south on both sides of Herring River all the way to what would later become the Cape Cod Railroad. In February 1836, he, with many others, formed a new company under the name of E. Ellis and Company. A blacksmith shop, built on the edge of the Herring River to utilize the water privilege, was used to manufacture cut nails. Some limited wool carding and cloth dressing was continued in the woolen factory.

Ellis' new company began to expand into other areas of industry. The river, as it meandered southward through the Ellis property, had a thirteen foot fall. Realizing the potential of this water power and having capital to work with, Ellis and his partners spent the next few years improving conditions around the area. Further south, new buildings were added for a rolling mill, which rolled out heated metal into sheets and rails. New machinery, furnaces, and forges were installed. A dam was built across Herring River, guaranteeing ample water power for the rolling mill. This created a fourth pond, which became known as Foundry Pond. The area was now divided by Foundry Pond into the northern site known as the Upper Factory, and the new southern site, called the Lower Works. The river at the Lower Works now had two channels—a flume to drive the machinery for the rolling mill and the original river bed with a fish ladder used for the first time to protect the herring migrations.

One of the many partners in the firm of E. Ellis and Company was Sandwich businessman, Clark Hoxie. On November 6, 1845, Hoxie bought out the company,[1] acquiring 24/25 part of the Upper Factory and three quarters interest of the Lower Works that was east of the Herring River, between the river and the road to Monument,

Massachusetts. He now owned 100 percent interest in these two parcels, for which he had paid $3056. Shortl thereafter, Hoxie transferred one-half interest to Bosto and Sandwich Glass Company Agent Deming Jarves, an one-quarter interest to Jarves' brother-in-law and superin tendent of the glass factory, William Stutson. These thre men began to lay the groundwork that would satisfy a acute need in the Sandwich area. They would expand th Ellis rolling mill into a full-fledged iron foundry.

MANOMET IRON COMPANY
1847–1858

On March 6, 1847, Clark Hoxie, William Stutson, an B. F. Leonard met with Deming Jarves at his Boston stor to finalize plans for the formation of a company to b known as the Manomet Iron Company. Each of the me would turn over to the Manomet Iron Company his in terest in the property that had been purchased from E Ellis and Company. William Stutson and Clark Hoxi were each paid $3450 for their one-quarter interest, an Deming Jarves received $6900 for his one-half interest. The parcel of land that had been retained by the Elli group was transferred to the Manomet Iron Company o May 20, 1847, for $400.[3] Ellis retained a right of wa through the property at the Lower Works that was wes of Herring River, and "also a piece of land called th Island, lying east of the described premises". The Islan was the land between the two channels of the river. Thi final transaction placed the water privilege above and be low Foundry Pond entirely under the control of Manome Iron Company and its Board of Directors. Stock was sol to several people. Among those who bought were Henr Cormerais of the G. D. Jarves and Cormerais partnership and C. C. P. Waterman, who became the first clerk an paymaster. B. F. Leonard became the new superintenden and was given authority to follow the building program se forth by the Board.

The buildings at the Upper Factory were completed first. According to the *Sandwich Observer* of June 26, 1847, there was a planing machine, stave machine, a sawmill and gristmill. A wagon maker and blacksmith were also on the premises.

All through 1848, the building program continued and was completed in 1849. A local newspaper was invited to make an inspection of the new plant. On February 3, 1849, the following editorial was released.

MANOMET IRON WORKS

We had the pleasure, a short time since, of examining this company's works at Herring River; and, as everything indicative of enterprise and improvement is matter of interest to our readers, we shall give some account of this establishment. The real estate was formerly owned by Ephraim Ellis & Co., and was the seat of their nail works. It consists of two water privileges; the upper, upon which a large building was erected by the former owner, in which were nail machines, and a carding machine; and the lower, upon which the same Company had their rolling mill. Under the auspices of the present owners, the whole aspect of the place has been changed. The upper works, near the house of Col. Gibbs, have been enlarged and put in complete repair. A stave mill is in constant operation—a large wood planer, and nail machines. And the dam, the flumes, the races, have all been put in perfect order, and the grounds beautified with trees. But at the lower establishment the most entire change has been effected. The old rolling mill still stands, though even that would hardly be recognized. Here, where everything before was rough, wild and inconvenient, one of the best ordered establishments in the State has sprung up. Without unnecessary expense, everything has been done in the most perfect manner, and with that economy which looks beyond the present. The buildings consist of a blacksmith shop, 30 feet by 40 feet; a machine shop, 40 by 50; a foundry, 40 by 75; a hammer shop, 40 by 70; a large pattern shop; a car shop; a large boarding house; barn; and three very neat cottages. We cannot go into detail, in stating the convenient manner in which everything is arranged.

The Company, we learn, are now fully employed in every department. The foundry turns out about six tons castings each week; and yet this does not meet the demand. In the machine shop, car axles, nail machines, lathes, shafting, screw plates and every variety of machinery are manufactured. The nail machines built by them are said to be the best ever made. Mr. B. F. Leonard, the superintendent of this shop, is a most skillful and ingenious machinist, and is devoted to his business. The hammer shop excited our special interest. In it is a scrapping furnace, and one of Lewis Kirk's patent steam hammers, the right of which for New England is owned by this Company. The scrap iron is laid together in masses of about 75 lbs. each, and placed in the furnace. When fully heated, it is taken out, placed under the hammer, and brought into blooms. These blooms are again heated, and then under the hammer are brought into any shape required for the market. The hammer turns out between four and five tons of blooms daily. It works to a charm—striking with great rapidity or very slowly—a hard or light blow—as is wanted. The value of this invention to the iron manufacturer can hardly be overestimated. It must take the place of the water hammer, as it can perform (we should think) four or five times as much, and in a better manner. It is worth any ones trouble to visit the works and see the operation of this hammer. In one of the shops, we saw a steam hammer just finished by the Company for the Washington Navy Yard. It is most beautifully finished, and does great credit to the men employed, as well as the Company. We never saw better work. And if Uncle Sam is not pleased with his purchase, he does not know when he is well used.

We have not time to notice further in detail. The works are now in successful operation in every part. About fifty hands are employed; though the number is increasing. A most admirable system has been adopted by the Agent, by which the actual condition of the establishment and each department is always known. With each shop a regular account is kept, and from the foreman of each a weekly report is received. Thus creating a sense of responsibility, and enabling the Agent to manage the whole systematically and easily. We wish the Company abundant success in their enterprise. They have added largely to the taxable property of our town—they are employing its labor—they are fostering the spirit of enterprise and improvement in others—and we trust their efforts will be remunerated. And if there be not an entire prostration of the business of the country, and a total failure of close and prudent calculations, the stock of this Company must soon become as good as any manufacturing stock in the State.

The cost of creating the new enterprise and completing it in so short a time was an unexpected financial burden to the stockholders. At several times during construction they were assessed additional funds, and the prospect of a quick return seemed remote. Only Deming Jarves could see the potential, but it was obvious that there was infighting among the partners. Clark Hoxie bowed out in October 1849. His finances were so depleted that he also sold to Jarves his interest in another business they had together, a stave mill on a water privilege at Spring Hill (see Volume 4, page 175). He was declared an insolvent debtor, and in 1850, even his home was offered for sale. He moved to California, and his position as agent was taken over by Superintendent Leonard, amid continual upheaval. A notice in the *Sandwich Observer* signed by Waterman called for people who had demands on the company to present them for payment, and others to settle their debts. By 1850, the company was put up for sale, but there were no takers.

Despite the iron company's problems, the North Sandwich area continued to develop. The availability of water power created yet another business, an ax factory built by Lewis Howes further down the river.

Deming Jarves alone knew the importance of the North Sandwich water privilege to the Boston and Sandwich Glass Company. All of the orders going out of the glass factory for maintenance, castings, and iron molds were sent to the Manomet Iron Company. Even the sale of barrel staves, produced at the Upper Factory mill, was funneled to the glass company through the Manomet Iron Company. Jarves' absolute control over these various businesses provided him with handsome profits. The bill of lading, illustrated, reveals to what extent the Boston and Sandwich Glass Company relied upon the North Sandwich foundry. The statement appears to be for a six month period.

Part of the Manomet works' financial difficulty was created because, in addition to supplying the glass company with molds, it had counted on manufacturing complete freight cars and parlor cars for the Cape Cod Railroad. Jarves, Hoxie, and Stutson had not chosen the foundry site by chance but because of its proximity to the new railroad. Not only could supplies be transported into the foundry and finished product be transported out, but new railroad cars could be placed right on the track where they would be used. But even though Jarves was on the Board of Directors of the railroad company, the president was buying cars from factories in distant towns, at an additional cost of $75 per car. So Jarves became deeply embroiled in controversy with the railroad as part of his attempts to expand the growth of the iron company.

THE MANOMET IRON AND MACHINE COMPANY

"N. Sandwich, Jan. 7, 1851.   Boston & Sandwich Glass Co.

1 mould casting	7 pounds	@ 8c		.56
1 chaldron	763 "	@ 4c		30.52
3 side door castings	577 "	@ 3c		17.31
19 Lear Machine rolls	63 "	@ 3½c		2.21
1 B. Smith fireback	50 "	@ 3c		1.50
1 press plate	267 "	@ 3c		8.01
3 pot bottoms	639 "	@ 3c		19.17
1 day turning spindle for lathe				3.00
12½ pr. mould hinges		@ 20c		2.50
1 side lear run	183 pounds	@ 3c		5.49
2 furnace doors	428 "	@ 3c		12.84
8 wheels	255 "	@ 3c		7.65
18 moulds	307 "	@ 8c		24.56
1½ days turning on clay machine				4.50
16 grates	438 pounds	@ 3c		13.14
4 casks of nails	400 "			14.00
8 casks of spikes	800 "			28.00
1 deck light mould	46 "	@ 8c		3.68
1 Ox cart delivered in the Glass Yards per Mr. Jarves order....				
(Not to be included in this bill rendered July, 1st, 1851)				
47,492 Staves	32 inches @ 12½c			593.65

Bill of lading showing the Boston and Sandwich Glass Company account with Manomet Iron Company for the first half of 1851. Note the leer machine rolls and leer run, which coincide with Boston and Sandwich Glass Company records dated September 28 and October 30, 1850, authorizing the building of a new furnace south of the X house (Lower House), enlarging the glass house for that purpose. The west wall of the X house was to be extended for a leer to the new furnace. This construction was completed by May 14, 1851. Note also the mold castings, all at 8 cents per pound.

Production continued to be highly diversified. It made nail machines to sell to other cut nail factories, railroad cars, castings of all types, furnace grates and doors, iron-strapped wheels, ploughs, and even gates and fences. The *Barnstable Patriot* of August 12, 1851, carried the following article, taken from the *Sandwich Observer*, which makes reference to Anna Jarves, Deming's wife.

ORNAMENTAL IRON FENCE. — The agent of the Manomet Iron Works, Zenas R. Hinckley, Esq., has exhibited to us patterns of the fence which was noticed last week. The fence is composed of diamond lattice work — the interstices being 4½ inches long and 2⅞ inches wide — and is cast in pieces nearly 3 feet in height and 4½ feet in length. — The posts, which are set at the distance of 9 feet from each other, are cast in 8 pieces; their four sides are of smaller diamond lattice work, with the figures arranged perpendicularly instead of horizontally as in the other portion of the fence. The posts have appropriate feet and caps, and are set diagonally to the line of the fence so as to present diamond points. The base is intended to rest on a stone foundation. The various parts are symmetrical, and in combination the effect of the whole is fine. The specimen which has been put up in Mount Auburn is pronounced the most beautiful fence in the place.

The design of this fence originated with the lady of Mr. Jarves, for whom the first order has been supplied. During a ride she was struck with the appearance of some lattice work attached to a building; and at her suggestion the experiment was made to ascertain how the same style would do in a fence. Much labor was expended in embodying the idea, and the result is the production of a perfect article. Among the gentlemen who are entitled to special credit for their efforts in getting it up, may be mentioned Mr. S. T. Silsby, who has had most to do in completing the patterns, and Mr. Charles Burgess, who superintended the castings.

This fence can be furnished at $1.25 per foot, exclusive of the posts which come higher; and that is less than elsewhere charged for an inferior article.

With modifications this fence will answer for other enclosures besides cemeteries. In some parts of the country ornamental iron fences are coming into use for front yards to houses. We noticed some of this kind in North Bridgewater a few days since. The Company at No. Sandwich are prepared to execute all orders. We hope this notice will have some inspiration inducing persons of wealth and taste to give plenty of work to our deserving neighbors at Herring River.

Orders from abroad soon arrived as the company's reputation spread. The growth pattern was such that Jarves was assured of success, but, as was true with other businesses in which he had an interest, his associates still had doubts. Jarves suggested that they sell out to him, making him sole owner. Early in 1852 the stockholders at their meeting agreed to allow Jarves to buy out the

Manomet Iron Company for $33,375. The transaction took place on February 20.[4] But Jarves' great hope that the foundry would grow and show a profit for his family failed to materialize. He had expanded to a point far in excess of the needs of the time. He had built individual buildings to house each operation, and, as the years passed, he realized that the Cape and surrounding areas could not support this massive iron foundry to the degree necessary to cover operating costs. By September 5, 1854, the Manomet Iron Company was again offered for sale, although Jarves continued to run it. By 1856, his business fortunes, as well as those of many other people, declined. Many of his properties were put up for sale, but world conditions did not encourage large investments. So his holdings remained on the market, including the entire Manomet Iron Company, both the Upper Factory and the Lower Works, which he listed for $20,000.

By the summer of 1857, the foundry was working around the clock. But, on September 13, at 3:00 AM, the dreaded word *fire* rang through North Sandwich. The machine shop and foundry at the Manomet Iron Works were totally destroyed. The buildings were partly insured, but the loss was between $25,000 and $30,000. Many of the outbuildings were saved, but the fire gutted the heart of the business and of Jarves. He dissolved the Manomet Iron Company as a corporation in February 1858.

THE MANOMET IRON WORKS SITE 1858-1868

After the fire, the site remained dormant for several years. In the early 1860's, after John became ill from a lung disease, Deming sold the small tract of land that was the Upper Factory, between Mill Pond and the Bournedale Road, to John W. Jarves and Company. The deed, dated November 1, 1862, shows that both the Upper Factory water privilege and the Spring Hill water privilege were transferred for $2800.[5] The water privileges were transferred on March 9, 1864, to the Cape Cod Glass Company,[6] during its reorganization after John's death. The Cape Cod Glass Company had the right to use, but not control, the Upper Factory water privilege. The stave mill continued to turn out staves for the Cape Cod Glass Company until the glass works closed in 1869.

HOWARD FOUNDRY COMPANY 1868-1884

On July 2, 1868, Deming Jarves sold the burnt out Manomet Iron Company property known as the Lower Works to Ezra C. Howard for only $4000.[7] The sale was subject to a lease held by Nelson Barrows and Jarves' former superintendent B. F. Leonard that was due to expire April 1, 1869.

Ezra Coleman Howard was born in Pocasset, Massachusetts, in 1813. He learned his trade as an iron molder in Providence, Rhode Island, and subsequently worked in shops in Fairhaven, Massachusetts, and Pocasset. As a result of the fire, and the subsequent abandonment of some of the outbuildings, he bought the Manomet Iron Company property for a pittance.

Ezra Coleman Howard

He began his new business in 1869, in the small foundry building that had been leased by Barrows and Leonard. The sluiceways and flumes, damaged by winter frost and ice, needed repair. But Howard soon brought the foundry back into full operation. His ties with the fast-growing Keith Car Company of West Sandwich brought in sufficient orders for castings, undercarriages for railroad cars, and sundry iron work to operate the foundry full time, with plenty of work for all hands. The nail business was also reactivated.

By 1874, Howard was receiving substantial orders from the Boston and Sandwich Glass Company. His account book, now in the Bourne Town Archives, shows that more than $2500 was received in January alone. The largest portion of this, $1,275.50, was for molds. *The Seaside Press* on January 9, 1875, shows that the iron foundry was running full time with sufficient work to keep busy over an extended period. It was Ezra Howard's good fortune that the rapid growth of the railroad industry in the United States resulted in the expansion of the Keith Car Company at a rate unheard of in the industrial East. The Howard Foundry became a supplier, and work for the car company dominated the iron foundry for the next several years. A larger foundry was built, and several buildings were extended.

The profit dreamed of by Deming Jarves was realized in small part by Ezra Howard and by his nephew after him. In 1884, the year in which North Sandwich became Bournedale, Howard leased the iron works to his nephew, William A. Nye, and sold it to him on October 30, 1884.[8] However, Howard retained the building that housed various shops as part of his private property. Howard died in April of that year.

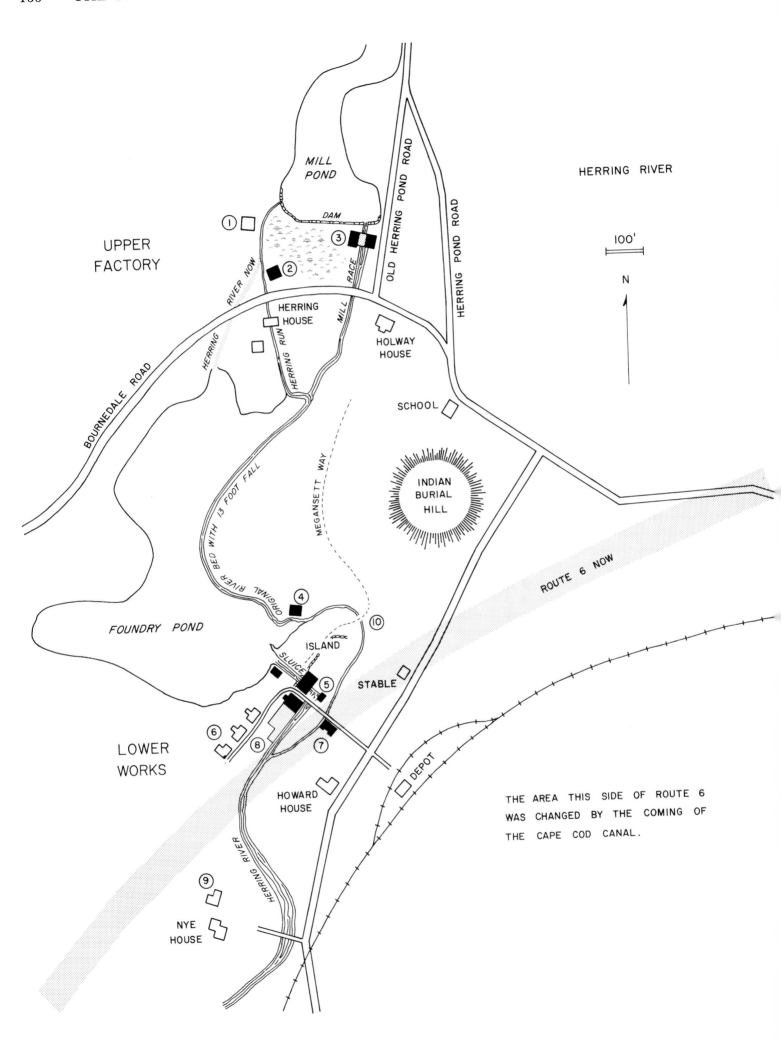

HERRING RIVER

MILL POND

UPPER FACTORY

DAM

① □

③ ◼

② ◼

RIVER NOW

HERRING

MILL RACE

OLD HERRING POND ROAD

HERRING POND ROAD

100'

N

HERRING HOUSE

HERRING RUN

HOLWAY HOUSE

BOURNEDALE ROAD

HERRING

SCHOOL □

ORIGINAL RIVER BED WITH 13 FOOT FALL

MEGANSETT WAY

INDIAN BURIAL HILL

ROUTE 6 NOW

④ ◼

FOUNDRY POND

⑩

ISLAND

SLUICE

◼
◼ ⑤
◼
◼
⑦

STABLE □

⑥ ◻
⑧ ◻

LOWER WORKS

HOWARD HOUSE

DEPOT □

THE AREA THIS SIDE OF ROUTE 6 WAS CHANGED BY THE COMING OF THE CAPE COD CANAL.

⑨ ◻

HERRING RIVER

NYE HOUSE ◻

EY TO MAP

Buildings used for production.
Additions.
Buildings outside company boundaries and company-owned houses.
Woolen mill.
E. Ellis and Company cut nail factory.
Manomet Iron Company sawmill and gristmill on both sides of mill race, powered by a water wheel, retained by Deming Jarves to cut staves for the Cape Cod Glass Works. The mills were rebuilt and connected over the mill race to be used as an ax factory by Seth W. Holway, powered by a turbine wheel.
E. Ellis and Company rolling mill.
Three Manomet Iron Company buildings not damaged by fire, as

purchased by Ezra C. Howard.

6 Three "very neat cottages". They can still be used as a landmark.

7 Howard Foundry Company building that housed various shops, retained by Howard as private property after he sold to William A. Nye.

8 Building erected in the 1880's, on site of Manomet Iron Company building that was destroyed by fire in 1857.

9 William A. Nye's barn, where the glassmaking equipment from the Electrical Glass Corporation were stored until used again by Albert V. Johnston.

10 Footbridge where Megansett Way, the Indian footpath, crossed over Herring River. Photo of the foundry site was taken from here.

Looking southwest toward the Lower Works. The foundry and shops are on the left, and "three neat cottages" are on the right. Repaired in 1908, they were still used as private residences in 1985. Megansett Way, an Indian footpath, crosses over Herring River at the bridge in the foreground. The numbers correspond to the numbers on the locater map.

Fig. 11   Map of the North Sandwich industrial area on the Herring River. The numbers correspond to the key.

Looking southeast toward the main road, through the cluster of buildings marked number 5 on the map. The buildings on the left were structurally sound when Ezra C. Howard purchased the Lower Works in 1868. The building on the right, with the squared-off roof, was reconstructed to become part of the large building that is number 8 on the map. Howard painted it dark red.

WILLIAM A. NYE
1884–1895

William A. Nye, nephew to Ezra Howard, and the new township of Bourne's first town clerk, had been at the foundry since 1871. As Howard grew older, he trained Nye, first to supervise and then to manage the foundry. Nye later purchased the foundry from his uncle, although it continued to be called the Howard Foundry by the newspapers.

Under the ownership of Nye, the foundry prospered. The *Sandwich Observer* of August 25, 1887, reported that eleven molders were working full time. By July 1888, twenty to twenty-five molders were employed, melting tons of pig iron to make castings for the Keith Car Company.

Interestingly, Nye played a controversial role in the history of the closing days of the Boston and Sandwich Glass Company. It was stated by Frank W. Chipman in his book *The Romance of Old Sandwich Glass* and Harriot Buxton Barbour in *Sandwich The Town That Glass Built* that the Sandwich glass molds were destroyed when the glass company went out of business in 1888. Barbour maintained on page 302 of her book, "Jones, Macduffie, and Stratton sold the precious iron molds to be melted up as scrap in the iron foundry of Senator Nye in Bourne". This erroneous statement has caused much difficulty in the identification of Sandwich glass. The fact is that the molds and stock of finished glass were sold to the Boston wholesale

house of Jones, McDuffee and Stratton, who advertised in the *Crockery and Glass Journal* that they could supply customers with any patterns that had formerly been supplied by the Boston and Sandwich Glass Company (see Volume 4, page 19). Some of the molds were subsequently sold to other glass companies, accounting for a Sandwich pattern being made at a later time by another factory. For example, Chrysanthemum Leaf was pressed in clear glass at Sandwich prior to 1888, and pressed in chocolate glass at a Midwest factory after 1888.

Included in William Nye's private papers, now in the authors' files, is a "memorandum of stock of Electric Glass Co. with prices of value". Many iron articles are listed under "Glass Makers Tools &c.", and the prices Nye was willing to pay for them (see Nye's memorandum at end of chapter). The Electrical Glass Corporation was in business at the Boston and Sandwich Glass Company site until 1890 (see Volume 4, page 73). It was iron from this company that was sent to Nye's foundry, not the molds from the Boston and Sandwich Glass Company, which Nye never did melt down. He stored them in a barn on his property, and sold them to Albert V. Johnston in January 1893, to be used again at the Boston and Sandwich Glass Company site (see Volume 4, page 76).[9]

In 1890, Nye expanded to the manufacture of twist drills, and entered into a licensing arrangement in 189_ with the Strange Forge Twist Drill Company of New Bedford, Massachusetts, to manufacture twist drills, bits and hucks. But in 1895, the foundry was consumed by fire. The *Sandwich Observer* of February 26 reported that it was totally destroyed. Machinery and a large number of valuable patterns were lost, and twenty men were thrown out of work.

The fire was the death knell of this little industrial area. On December 15, 1897, Nye mortgaged the Lower Works to N. S. Bartlett and Company. However, Nye continued to be listed as the owner in the *Bourne, Falmouth and Sandwich Directory* in 1900. According to the newspapers, Nye repaired the "very neat cottages" in January 1908. Later that year, the mortgage was discharged and one of the old buildings was taken down. The Keith Car and Manufacturing Company purchased the Lower Works from Nye on February 3, 1910.[10] It remained in their hands until December 1928.[11]

Slowly all traces of the flourishing enterprise disappeared, until today the location of this old foundry is difficult to find. The construction of the Cape Cod Canal dramatically changed the contour of the land in this area, making it nearly impossible to locate the exact foundation of the foundry. Route 6 passes directly over the site of some of the buildings that made up the Manomet Iron Works. However, the dam, sluiceways and three cottages stand in 1985 as a monument to this endeavor.

THE UPPER FACTORY
1869-1908

When the Cape Cod Glass Company closed in 1869 and Deming Jarves died, the Herring River stave mill was no longer needed. The property, together with all of the Cape Cod Glass Company holdings, became part of Jarves' estate. All of the land belonging to the Cape Cod Glass Company was incorporated into a single deed. In 1873, Deming's wife Anna was legally free to dispose of these holdings. They changed ownership three times during that year (see Volume 4, page 124) and remained in the name of John T. Richards until 1879. To accommodate a bankruptcy auction, the Cape Cod Glass Company property was divided into three parcels recorded in three separate deeds. Sandwich businessman George T. McLaughlin was the high bidder for parcel number three, which consisted of the Herring River water privilege at the Upper Factory and the Spring Hill water privilege east of Sandwich Village. McLaughlin sold the Herring River water privilege to Harry L. Buswell on September 27, 1887.[12]

During the time of these transfers, the mills at the Upper Factory lay idle, except for a small ax factory operated by Seth Weeks Holway. Holway had previously run the ax factory started by Lewis Howes in 1850. He took over from Howes in 1860. The records are unclear exactly when Holway came to the Upper Factory. *The Seaside Press* of May 29, 1875, shows him at that location, but the *Sandwich Observer* of September 4, 1888, makes a point of saying that S. W. Holway, the veteran ax maker, rented the shop of the owner, Mr. Buswell.

On March 25, 1890, Buswell sold the Upper Factory site to William Nye.[13] Nye sold the "swampy piece that the blacksmith shop stood upon", the land between the

Remains of building destroyed in 1895 fire. The photo was taken by Edward D. Nickerson in 1899.

channels of the river that was bounded by the westerly wall of the ax factory, to Walter G. Beal.[14] Beal built a home that was a local landmark for some years. Nye retained the land east of the ax factory, between the mill race and Old Herring Pond Road. In conjunction with his foundry business, he erected a new building on the site for the manufacture of twist drills. Three years later, in 1893, the drill business had expanded to the degree that Nye refurbished the shop room of the ax factory building as part of his agreement with the Strange Forge Twist Drill Company to manufacture twist drills, under their license.

We were fortunate to find a picture of Mr. Holway standing in the doorway of what had been the stave mill. The picture was taken in 1903 by Edward D. Nickerson. Here is his first-hand description of conditions in 1903.

Very near the Beal homestead in lower Bournedale, and right on the river, was this little shop operated by Mr. Seth Holway. He is the elderly gentleman in the doorway, beside him is his son Albert Holway. The shop was operated by water power, the "water wheel" being behind the men and to the right of them. It was a weather-beaten little shop, entirely devoid of paint. There were no frills or "fixens" anywhere about it. Yet, from this little place came the "Holway" ax. Considered the finest implement of its kind that could be bought anywhere. I still own one, in perfect condition after years and years of use. Mr. Holway sold all he could make, but he made them himself, never increasing production by hiring anyone, occasionally his son "Bert" seen here, helped his father, as he was doing the day I came along with my camera and they stopped work to pose for me in the doorway.

All that remained of the sluiceway at the Lower Works, as seen by the authors in 1985.

Seth W. Holway, standing in the doorway of what had been the stave mill. He is holding an adz in his hand. On the right is his son Albert, holding a sledge hammer. This photo was taken in 1903, by Edward "Ned" Nickerson of Bournedale.

On May 1, 1905, Nye sold the land and buildings between the mill race and Old Herring Pond Road to Beal.[15] *The Hyannis Patriot* on August 24, 1908, recorded the demise of the ax factory building.

> Walter G. Beal is taking down the old historic ax factory at Bournedale, so long occupied by Seth Holway. Mr. Holway has removed all his machinery and given up his business.

The buildings are all gone now. The Beal house was destroyed by fire. There is a pretty little park where the buildings once stood. Children wiggle their toes in the waters of the river, and visitors watch the herring go upstream to spawn. Only pieces of drills and bits and the skeleton of a turbine wheel remain to remind us that there was ever a flourishing manufacturing center there at all.

Remains of the turbine wheel and mill race at the Upper Factory. This is the site of Seth Holway's axe works as seen by the authors in 1985, numbered 3 on the map.

NOTES TO CHAPTER 7

1. Barnstable County (Massachusetts) Registry of Deeds, book 36, pages 342–345.
2. Barnstable Registry, book 41, pages 537–539.
3. Barnstable Registry, Book 46, page 187.
4. Barnstable Registry, book 79, pages 521–523.
5. Barnstable Registry, book 80, page 290.
6. Barnstable Registry, book 84, page 193.
7. Barnstable Registry, book 96, page 451.
8. Barnstable Registry, book 165, page 40.
9. According to an article in the March 1927 issue of *The Magazine Antiques*, James E. Johnston of Sandwich (heir to Albert V. Johnston's estate) turned the patterns over to Colonel A. H. Heisey, founder of the firm of A. H. Heisey and Company.
10. Barnstable Registry, book 301, page 216.
11. Barnstable Registry, book 462, pages 37–39.
12. Barnstable Registry, book 175, pages 284–286.
13. Barnstable Registry, book 188, page 202.
14. Barnstable Registry, book 262, page 360.
15. Barnstable Registry, book 272, page 150.

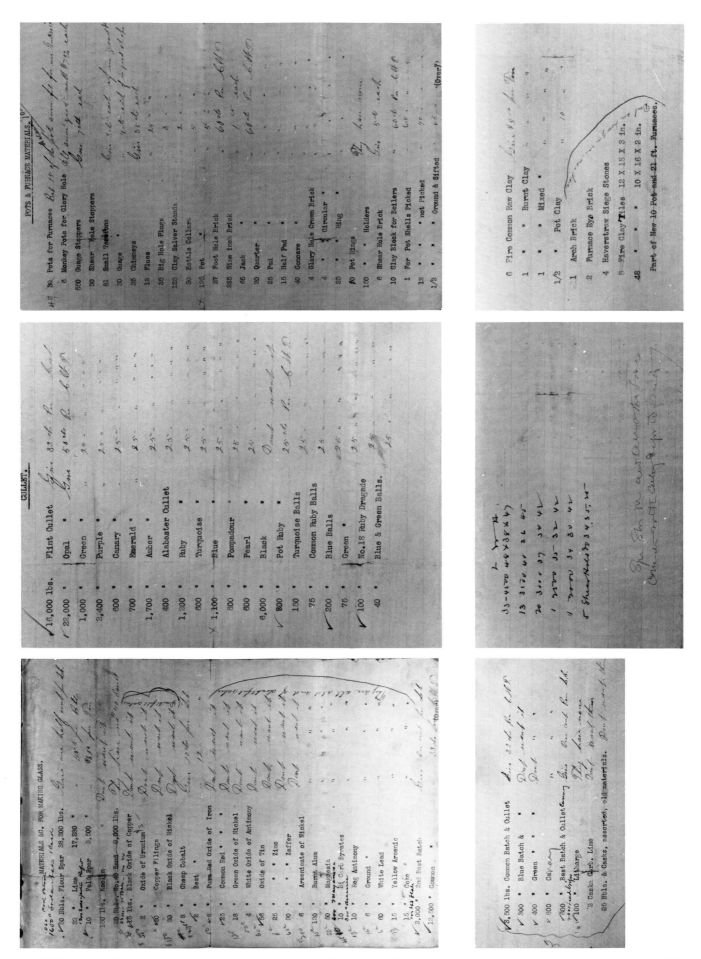

William A. Nye's memorandum of stock of the Electrical Glass Corporation at the time of its sale in 1890.

Glass Makers Tools, &c.

84	3/4 inch	Shade Irons	*Gro $1.00 each*
43	5/8 "	By place or Chimney irons	*Gro 75ct each*
18	1/2 "	Bottle Irons	*Gro 62c each*
14	1/2 "	Gathering Irons, leather handles	*Gro 87ct each*
6	5/8 "	" " " " "	*" $1.00 each*
45	1/2 "	Punts Stuck up in round heads	*" 10ct each*
49	5/8 "	" " " " "	*" 10ct each*
32	3/4 "	" " " " "	*" 10ct*
17	3/8 "	Bit or Peg irons	*" 10"*
17	1/2 "	Ring Punt "	*" 10"*
7		Extra large Irons, leatherhandles	*" $1.25"*
3		Shearers rakes	*" $2.00"*
4		" Bars	*" 2.00"*
3		" Rakes	*" 2.00"*
7		Furnace Hooks	*" 30cts"*
10		Metal "	*" 10"*
40		Glass Makers Chairs	*" $2.50"*
8		Iron Chests	*" 3.00"*
6		Sand Horses	*" 50ct"*
8		Iron Files	*Don't want them*
14		Marver Irons	*Don't know what*
6		Chipping Pans	*Gro 50ct each*
2		Drawing Pans	*" $3.00 each*
2		Large Skimming Kettles	*" $18.00 each*
1		Small "	*" $12.50*
4		Cleaning off "	*" $4.00 each*
2		Large Lazy Bones	*" $18.00"*
2		Small "	*" $6.00*
			(Over)

2	Large Pot Setting Carriages	*Gro $15.00 each*
5	" " " Bars 200 lbs. & Over	*$7.00 each*
2	Pot setting Bars, 100 lbs. and over	*" 6.00 each*
4	Small Pot setting bars	*" $7.00 "*
1	Pot setting Hook	*$2.00*
1	Ladle	*$1.50*
1	Pot setting Rake	*" $2.00*
1	" " Maker	*$2.00*
4	Scrapers	*1.50*
17	Pig Irons	*" 70ct Per 6/14*
20	Tower Irons	*" 70"*
190	Snaps & Plugs, mostly for stem ware	*Don't want them*
15	Glass Presses	*Try and by them for all ...*
20	Batch Carriages	*Gro $4.00 each*
3	Iron Coal "	*6.00 for lot*
2	" Wheelbarrows	*$1.00 each*

Miscellaneous.

1	Side Belt, Leather		*About all gone doubtful*
2	Sides Lace, "		
	Lot Rubber Gaskets	$5.00	
4	Kegs Nails		*Thy have none*
25	lbs. Galvanized Shingle Nails		
2	Gallons Paint Oil		
20	" Roof Coating		
640	Ft. Hard Pine Lumber		
87	" Pine & Cypress matched boards		
120	" Elm Wood		
60	" Oak Plank		
90	" Birch Joist		
110	" Boards		
2	Sawed Cedar Shingles		
4	6 Ft. Cedar Posts		
85	Tons Gas Coal		
15	" Packing Hay, $10.00 per ton		*We pay $7.00 per ton*
16	Oil Bbls.		*Don't want them*
23	Lead "		
225	Flour ", 25 # each		*all gone*
1	Horse (Billy)	$60.00	*all gone*
2	" Carts	50 each	
2	" Trucks	50 each	
	Harnesses	10.00	
	Shovels, picks & Bars	10.00	*doubtful*
120	lbs. Russia Tallow		*don't want it*
55	" Japan Wax		*don't want*

450	lb. Ground Emery	
2000	Paste board Boxes for salts & Peppers, etc.	
1650	lbs. Common Paper	*all gone*
200	" Best Paper	
2	Large platform Scales	
2	Small " "	
	Lot of Decalcomanies, original cost over $1000.	
	Lot of Plates for Etching	
1	"Fairbanks" Hay Scales	
850	Gas & Steam fittings, assorted sizes, 1/4 in. to 2 in. (elbows, ties, nipples, etc.)	
75	Water Buckets filled with water.	

William A. Nye's memorandum of stock of the Electrical Glass Corporation at the time of its sale in 1890.

CHAPTER 8

WHICH BALLS ARE WITCH BALLS?

1825–1887

One of the simplest forms to make out of glass is a ball. A glob of hot glass is gathered on the end of a blowpipe and the blowpipe is rotated slowly as the ball is inflated. Depending on its use, it may be allowed to cool naturally or may be sent to the leer and cooled slowly to eliminate stress in the glass.

Some of the earliest of these round pieces also had necks and were used to hold holy water. A knob on the end of the neck allowed the primitive bottle to be hung. It was common belief that such bottles with their contents provided protection against evil spirits. Such spirits, from mischievous fairies to evil witches, were feared for their ability to cause sickness, deformities, and even death to both man and beast. In America, this fear culminated in the nightmare of witch-hangings in Salem, Massachusetts — a black chapter during the early years of the colonies.

Witches were thought to fear certain herbs and, strangely, "roundness". Logically, herbs placed in a sphere would provide a double whammy. One theory had it that evil beings were attracted to herbs. By placing herbs in a ball, witches might be dissuaded from bothering the occupants of a house or barn, or perhaps the witch would enter the ball instead and become trapped in a tangle of leaves and twigs, rendering it harmless. Either way, whether the balls were needed to trap the witch or ward it off, early glass companies had a ready market for such mystical devices.

By the early 1800's, a glass works at Nailsea in the Bristol area of England, was producing balls that could be filled with herbs to counteract the havoc of the unknown. The first of these were made of clear glass, crudely splashed with specks of blue and white. Soon after, designs of crude loopings and swirls were developed. The practice of making witch balls spread to other glass houses throughout England and across the sea to the New World. Within sixty days of the incorporation of the Boston and Sandwich Glass Company, witch balls were being produced. The document known as the *sloar book* (called a *turn book* by some students) shows that on May 20, 1826, 170 witch balls were made. They were 2½" in diameter, and in sub-sequent entries would be described as "small". On May 27, 1826, fifty-six 3½" witch balls were made, later to be entered as "large" witch balls. Throughout 1827 and into 1828, witch balls made up a surprisingly large part of production. Most were made in the shop headed by Michael Doyle.

So far as is known, all Sandwich witch balls were made to be hung. There is no indication in the sloar book that matching witch ball stands were manufactured, or are there fragments dug at the site that could be identified as such. The balls were hung by inserting a small piece of wood into the same hole used to fill the ball with herbs. The piece of wood was carved into a peg with a notch around the center. One end of a ribbon, string or wire was tied around the notch, and the peg was inserted into the ball and placed horizontally across the hole. The ball could then be hung in any location.

Local tradition may have determined the purpose of the various types of witch balls. In the Cape Cod area, decorative witch balls made by the Boston and Sandwich Glass Company were meant to be hung in houses — on porches, in windows, and even in bedrooms to protect children. Some were made of spatter glass, but most were a marbrie design of four loopings. Four types of marbrie fragments known to be from witch balls were dug at the factory site — clear with white loopings, clear with pink loopings, white with pink loopings, and clear with alternating pink and white loopings. The loopings divide the ball into four parts. Witch balls blown in a single color were meant to be hung in barns to protect livestock. They can be found in amber, amethyst, blue, green, even white, and are quite heavy.

Single color witch balls blown in South Jersey that had matching stands were obviously made to be used in houses. It certainly would not have been practical to use a ball on a stand in an outbuilding. But these were made in areas with different traditions from Sandwich.

A fifth type of marbrie design fragment dug at the site was made from a gather of opaque white glass with red and blue loopings. Many of the red, white and blue balls were *militia balls*. They were an outgrowth of the tampion,

173

a wood plug or stopper put in the muzzle of a gun not in use. After the Civil War, it was the custom for men who were in the militia to march in holiday parades. They were in uniform and carried muskets in an upright position alongside their leg. The bayonet was reversed on the musket. If the men were glassworkers or were escorting glassworkers, they placed a red, white and blue glass ball on the muzzle end of the musket. The balls were up to five inches in diameter and had a long glass rod-like extension that was inserted into the barrel. This was done at Sandwich for several years on the Fourth of July, and the *Crockery Journal* dated June 24, 1875, provides us with a colorful description of New England Glass Company workers marching in the Bunker Hill celebration parade on June 17.

> In the procession there appeared a creditable display of glass companies and kindred establishments, foremost among which was the New England Glass Company. First came as escort the "Coventry Cadets" of Cambridge—45 men headed by a drum corps, each soldier carrying in the muzzle of his musket a glass globe, the three colors, red, white and blue, being so distributed as to produce a pleasing effect.

If you find what you believe to be a red, white and blue witch ball with the remains of a glass plug extension, you very likely have found a militia ball. The workmanship is not good. No time was taken to make even loopings.

Similar balls, made with a tapered extension and in a single color, were made by the Boston and Sandwich Glass Company and the New England Glass Company. The January 20, 1855, issue of *Ballou's Pictorial* illustrates several of them in the New England Glass Company showroom. Mounted on tall standards, they could be used as single-unit apothecary show globes. The Boston and Sandwich Glass Company made them to use at trade exhibitions. To delineate the perimeter of the space allotted the glass company, and to keep the public a safe distance from the glass-laden tables, a curb was nailed together out of wood. The top boards had evenly spaced large holes to accept the extensions of the balls. The side boards were high enough to cover the lower half of each ball. After the balls were inserted, the space between each ball and the side boards was filled with confetti. At one particular exhibition, green balls alternated with white ones, and green and white confetti filled the spaces. The judges were impressed by how much the colorful curb added to the decor of the booth.

After the trade show was over, the decoration balls were piled in the Boston showroom and soon were being used as handled cover balls for wide-mouthed store jars. Today, all of our candy and over-the-counter medicine is sealed against contamination. In the Nineteenth Century, bacteria and viruses were not understood, and a storekeeper handled everything with his bare hands. Extremely large jars that could hold two or three gallons were used for dispensing pills, liquid medicines and candy. The mouth of the jars was wide enough for a man's arm, so that he could twist his elbow inside the jar to scoop or ladle from the very bottom.

When the jars were originally purchased from the glass companies, they had a glass cover with a knob-like finial. The cover had an inside flange that was machined to fit tightly against the inside of the neck of the jar, like the plug of a stopper. This original cover did not lend itself to rapid, constant use. The tight fit prevented evaporation, but the cover chipped when it was hurriedly replaced, causing slivers of glass to fall into the jar. The leftover

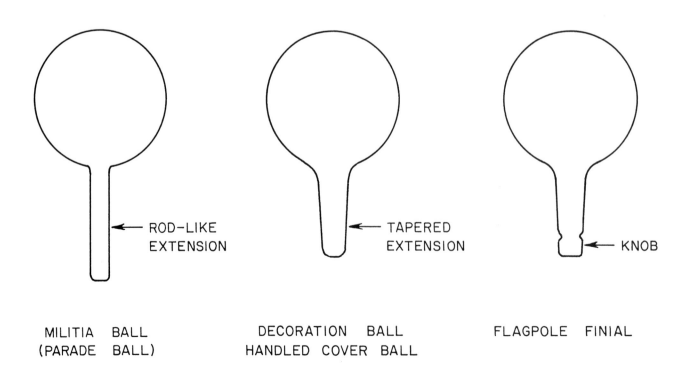

MILITIA BALL   DECORATION BALL   FLAGPOLE FINIAL
(PARADE BALL)   HANDLED COVER BALL

rade show decoration balls with their easy-to-grasp ta-
ered extensions made perfect handled cover balls. A busy
merchant could remove and replace them rapidly, and the
ound balls did not chip.

It was a custom in Sandwich to mount ruby glass balls
n the tops of flagpoles, where their reflection on a sunny
ay could be seen some distance away. Balls that were in-
nded for flagpole finials had a knob on the end of the ex-
nsion so that they could be set in plaster without pulling
ut, either directly into a hole drilled into the end of the
ole or into a metal fitting that was mounted on the pole.
Ve do not know whether this custom was only a local one
r if it extended to other glass factory villages.

Lastly, our discussion of balls with extensions should in-
lude the ball that was the uppermost unit of a Sandwich
pothecary show globe. Show globes are large jars that
ere placed in store windows to indicate the presence of
druggist. Many people could not read. They depended
n figural symbols, such as the spiral striped pole of a
arber. Show globes were made up of several jar units,
ne above the other, each with a plug extension that was
iserted into the neck of the unit directly below it. Part of
e extension rested flatly on the lip of the lower unit, as
een in the illustration. This provided stability for each
nit, necessary because most show globes were made from
lear glass and were filled with colored water.

Any of these balls could be mistaken for a witch ball if
ie extension was broken off, and several of these forms—
specially in smaller sizes—could be mistaken for a darn-
ig ball.

Balls with an opening were also used for target shooting,
uch as the clay pigeon is used today. The balls were
lled with anything that would be visible when they were
iattered by a bullet, such as feathers, confetti, or cotton.

No time was spent in their manufacture because they were
for one-time use only. The opening is generally jagged,
and the glass from which they were produced was made
primarily from cullet. This accounts for their great variety
of colors—apple green, light blue, and several shades of
amber. Fragments that we have been able to identify as
target balls were blown into a mold that is dated October
23, 1877, and carries the name of its patentee, Ira Paine,
in a band circling the center. Paine's target ball was also
found in excavations at a New York glass house, indicating that the mold was a private one sent to any house
that gave a low bid. Fragments dug at Sandwich indicate
that the Boston and Sandwich Glass Company must have
been low bidder at least once.

Two types of *closed* balls without extensions were made
at the Boston and Sandwich Glass Company. First, thick-
walled blown balls were used as covers on pitchers, bowls
and store jars. They were weighted at the pontil end to
keep them from rolling and were annealed for strength.
Second, free-blown balls with thin walls were produced not
as a saleable item but for packing. They were placed upon
vases as a support for the rims during shipment. This important factory practice was discovered at the dig site. The
remains of a wooden case were uncovered with twelve
blown trumpet vases inside, all damaged. Six vases were
canary in color, six were amethyst. Two of the canary
vases had canary balls still in perfect condition placed on
the vase openings, showing how the vases had been packed
in the case.

Author Ray Barlow and fellow Sandwich historian
Francis (Bill) Wynn experimented with this technique in
1968, using Tappan vases from the Late Blown Period.
They placed twelve vases in a wooden box and packed salt
marsh hay around them just as the factory did. Packing

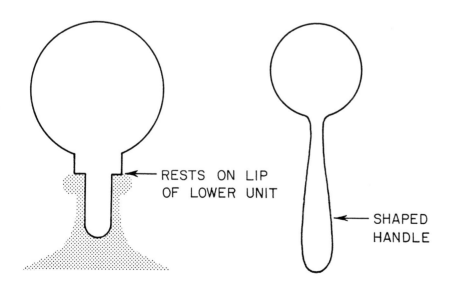

RESTS ON LIP
OF LOWER UNIT

SHAPED
HANDLE

TOP UNIT OF
SHOW GLOBE

DARNING BALL

Fig. 12 Identifying features of blown
balls with extensions. Militia balls are
multi-colored, with a rod-like extension
that fits into the muzzle of a musket.
Decoration balls left over from trade
exhibitions were used as jar covers. The
tapered extension made a comfortable
handle. Balls used on the tops of flagpoles were blown with a knob on the
end, not unlike early holy water bottles.
Apothecary globe units have extensions
that fit into the neck of a lower unit, but
are shaped to rest flatly on top of the
lower unit. Some of these forms resemble darning balls, but a darning ball has
a shaped handle.

balls were placed on six of the vases, while six other vases were left with their rims uncovered. The packed case was placed in the back of a station wagon and left there for two weeks, assuming that two weeks of normal driving would equal one trip from Sandwich to Boston in an 1850 horse-drawn wagon. When the box was opened, the salt marsh hay had settled into and around the vases without the balls, exposing the rims. The hay had not moved around the vases with the balls. Any rough treatment to the box would have rendered the vases without packing balls vulnerable to damage. The vases with balls would have been able to sustain abusive treatment and still would have arrived at their destination intact.

When looking for such balls to add to your collection, understand that they were meant to last only until the vases were unpacked. They are paper-thin and were not annealed. As long as pressure was maintained evenly on all areas of their surface, they had strength. When separated from the vase they were blown to fit, their strength was lost and they shattered more easily than an eggshell, particularly if the air inside expanded from the heat of your hand. Because they were blown bubble-thin, their pigment is barely visible, even though the balls and the vases were made from the same color glass.

There are available on the antiques market large quantities of glass balls made in Japan. Some are used for decorative purposes, others were made to be used as floats for fishing nets. The openings of these balls are closed with a separate glob of glass that is forced into the opening while the ball is still hot. This permanently seals the opening, making the ball airtight. This method of closing the ball was not used at Sandwich. Sandwich glass balls used as covers and for packing were closed as they were broken from the blowpipe.

THESE SIMPLE HINTS WILL HELP YOU IDENTIFY SANDWICH GLASS BALLS.

Glass balls made in Sandwich do not have their openings plugged with a separate glob of glass.

Marbrie witch ball fragments dug at the factory site are clear with white loopings, clear with pink loopings, white with pink loopings, and clear with alternating white and pink loopings. The loopings divide the ball into quarters.

Witch balls used to protect animals in outbuildings are of one color and very heavy.

Militia balls are similar to marbrie witch balls, but have a long glass plug extension that is the same diameter its entire length. If you find a red, white and blue ball with an exceptionally rough opening, with the remains of a glass rod-like extension, you have a militia ball.

Balls used for decoration and as handled covers are a single color, are heavy and have a tapered extension.

Balls mounted on flagpoles are heavy and have a knob on the end of the extension.

Apothecary show globe units have an extension that partly rests on a lower unit. The remainder of the extension is a plug that fits into the neck of a lower unit.

Balls without extensions used as covers are heavy, are weighted on the pontil end to prevent rolling and have no opening.

Packing balls were blown very thin, are of one color and were not annealed. They have no opening.

Target balls marked "IRA PAINE" and dated October 23, 1877, were made at Sandwich, and also at other factories. They are one color.

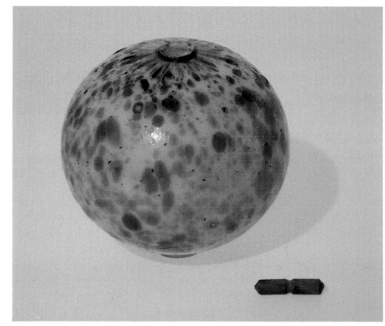

225 WITCH BALL
½" Dia. 1830–1840

This witch ball may be the earliest one shown in this chapter. It was blown using opaque white glass as the basic color, and, while molten, was rolled over fragments of red and blue glass. The ball cooled so rapidly that the colored pieces did not melt into the white. The surface, therefore, remained rough and jagged. This ball is one of four in the collection of a Cape Cod family descended from a Sandwich worker. The four original wood peg hangers accompanying the balls are ¾" to 1¼" long. Their diameter varies depending on the diameter of the hole into which they were inserted. "Art glass" type witch balls were meant for household use.

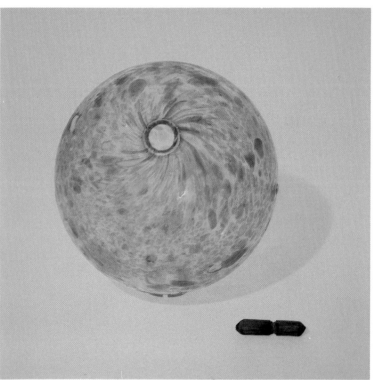

226 WITCH BALL
½" Dia. 1840–1850

This ball was found on Cape Cod with its original hanger. It has family ties to a Sandwich worker and was used in a house. There is no question about how this spatter glass piece was made. The clear glass ball was started on the end of a blowpipe. Pieces of broken red and white glass were spread on the marver. While the clear glass was still hot, it was rolled over the colored pieces. They melted into the clear glass and became a part of the ball. Some of the red pieces did not adhere properly, and can be picked out, leaving a clear indentation such as can be seen on the upper left edge.

227 WITCH BALLS
" Dia. 1850–1870

All of the marbrie witch ball fragments dug at the site of the Boston and Sandwich Glass Company have a four-loop configuration. The ends of all of the loops are at the opening of the ball. The loops are well defined, but vary in size. Multi-colored (called *parti-colored* in the 1800's) witch balls were used in dwellings. It was believed that hanging them over the entrance door stopped evil spirits at the threshold, and they would enter the ball instead of the house.

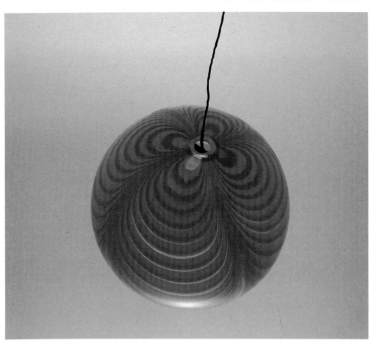

3228 WITCH BALL

5½" Dia. 1850–1870

This is as excellent an example of marbrie, four-loop con struction as you will find in Sandwich glass. Note the clea glass in one of the loops, showing that Sandwich work manship was not up to the industry's standards for th type of glass. The original hanging wire has a wood pe fastened to the end of it. It was inserted into the openin of the ball, and positioned across the opening. Many con panies made witch balls. It is extremely difficult, if n impossible, to attribute them to a particular glass hou without documentation.

3229 WITCH BALL

4" Dia. 1860–1880

In addition to documentation, two clues will help attribu witch balls to Sandwich. First, there are four loops in th marbrie design. Second, to make the loop design, th threads of glass were dragged from the bottom of the ba all the way up to the top, so that the lower loops as we as the smaller loops begin and end at the opening. Th opening is large enough to easily accept herbs and wooden peg hanger. Not every marbrie ball is a witch bal Red, white and blue ones are likely to be militia balls.

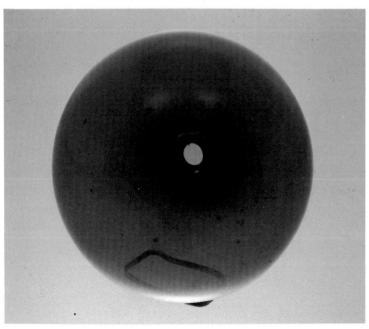

3230 WITCH BALL

4¼" Dia. 1850–1870

Witch balls of one color were hung in barns and sheds t protect animals, particularly cows. It was believed that ev spirits had the power to reduce the production of milk an could deform newborn animals. This ball was found in th cupola of a barn in East Sandwich. All Sandwich witc balls made for barn use were heavy and thick walle Herbs could be placed inside the opening before the woo peg hanger was inserted.

3231 WITCH BALL
8" Dia. 1840-1850
This witch ball was one of four found on Cape Cod, still belonging to descendants of a Sandwich glassworker. All four have their original wood peg hangers. Each peg was hand carved and varied in diameter according to the size of the opening in the ball. A string of ribbon was tied around the notch in the peg, which was inserted into the ball. It could then be hung from a rafter.

3232 WITCH BALL
5⅛" Dia. 1840-1850
This ball has a very small opening and is very heavy. It was an extremely difficult ball to hang because the diameter of the wood peg is too narrow for the weight of the ball. It is difficult to remove an original peg released inside a ball because the ribbon or string frayed and rotted. Rather than remove the peg, other makeshift methods of hanging were devised, such as inserting a stick or a nail. This is why several hangers are occasionally found inside the ball, sometimes with their strings attached. This one has an extremely high-gloss finish. It was used in an outbuilding on Cape Cod.

3233 WITCH BALL
a) Ball 7" Dia. 1850-1870
b) Holder 1¾" H. x 2¾" Dia. 1835-1845
This plain witch ball was originally made for barn use. It is placed on what we now refer to as a Lacy pressed salt. Its owner has identical witch balls in blue and green, placed on identical matching blue and green Lacy holders. The Lacy pieces are well documented Sandwich patterns. The question is whether they are indeed salts, or were they made as matching stands for witch balls? We believe the Lacy holder was combined with the witch ball at a later time.

3234 MILITIA BALL (PARADE BALL)
5" Dia. 1860–1880
Glassmaking was a proud industry. In its earliest days glassworkers set themselves apart by adopting certain cus toms that would differentiate them from workers in othe trades. When glassworkers marched in parades, they ofte covered themselves with sparkling glass dust, or hung glas stars and crescents from their clothing. Sometimes the were escorted by the Militia. Each soldier carried in th muzzle of his musket a red, white and blue glass globe Each globe had a long glass plug extension that fit into th barrel. The extension is .65 mm. or less in diameter an is the same diameter all along its length. When militi balls are found today, the plug is usually broken off, so i is incorrectly assumed that they are witch balls. Parade and ceremonies were an important part of life in the lat 1800's.

3235 MILITIA BALL (PARADE BALL)
5¼" Dia. 1860–1880
Collectors of balls believe it is impossible to tell which glas company made a particular one. All of the balls in thi chapter have matching dug fragments and/or family tie to Sandwich workers. A careful study of this ball show that the workmanship at Sandwich in ornamental glas was not up to the standards set by English glass factorie or by the New England Glass Company in East Cam bridge, Massachusetts. This piece should not have hanger. Small militia balls may find their way into collec tions of darning balls.

3236 DECORATION BALL, ALSO USED AS A HANDLED COVER BALL
6" Dia. ball with 3" L. extension 1850–1887
Decoration balls were used by the Boston and Sandwic Glass Company at trade shows. They were placed atop wooden curb to delineate the perimeter of the booth an keep the public away from the glass-laden tables. They sa secondary use as handled cover balls for busy storekeeper who kept pills, medicine and candy in extremely large jars The merchant could easily grasp the tapered extension hold the cover in one hand while he reached into the ja to dispense its contents, then replace the cover, all in on fluid motion. This practice was simply a more sophisti cated application of the much earlier ball covers withou handles. Unlike militia balls, these were made in singl colors and the "handles" are tapered.

3237 COVER BALLS
(a) Amber 2½" Dia.
(b) Blue 3" Dia.
(c) Red 3" Dia. 1825–1850

A glass ball with the end closed was used as a cover on food containers and store jars. They are heavy because they were made to withstand rough, daily use. Flies and insects were a major problem in the 1800's. This ingenious method of protecting food was common. The balls could be tossed into a basket when they were not needed with less fear of breakage than when a cover with a finial was used, although they were weighted on the pontil end to keep them from rolling. They were gradually superseded by covers, usually with a rim and finial. Bear in mind that we are discussing tableware used in the homes of mechanics and laborers, not of the people who would have used pewter or silver on their dining table. In recent years, a decorative ball, lighter in weight, has been produced and can easily be mistaken for a Nineteenth Century cover ball. The new balls are bright and show no wear.

3238 PACKING BALLS
3" Dia. 1840–1870

When you find a free-blown ball with the end closed, and it weighs no more than a gram, it is *not* a witch ball. It is a cover to be placed on Sandwich blown vases to protect their rims during shipment. They were blown in the same color as the vase they were to be placed upon. Their primary purpose was to insure delivery of undamaged vases. Very little labor or material was invested in them.

3239 PACKING BALLS IN USE
(a) Packing Balls 2¾" Dia. 1830–1887
(b) Vase 10" H. x 3" Dia. 1840–1860

Blown vases are difficult to attribute unless they have family ties to men who worked at the factory. This vase, with its original packing ball, came from the Tobey family in Sandwich. Mrs. Tobey used the ball as a dust cover when the vase was not being used for flowers.

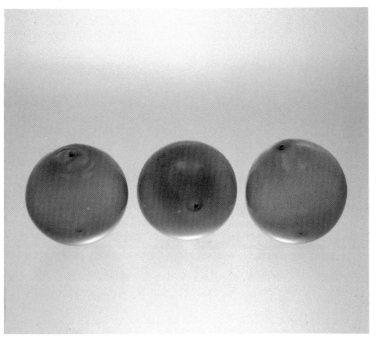

3240 PACKING BALLS
2¾" Dia. 1840–1870

These three packing balls were found at the site of the Boston and Sandwich Glass Company. They were still in position on their vases in the remains of the original shipping box. The box had been dropped and discarded. They were used, in an experimental duplication of the company's shipping methods, by Francis (Bill) Wynn of Sandwich and Ray Barlow.

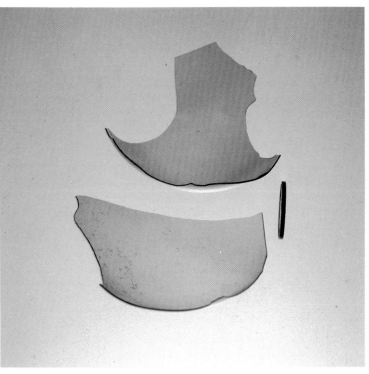

3241 PACKING BALL FRAGMENTS

These fragments, dug at the Sandwich site, have a penny standing beside them to show how thin they are. Do not hold a packing ball in your hand if it is cold. The rapid temperature change will cause the air inside the ball to expand, breaking it like an eggshell.

3242 TARGET BALLS (PRACTICE BALLS)
3" Dia. 1877–1887

Target balls were filled with feathers, cotton, or confetti. They were thrown into the air for target practice in the same way that clay pigeons are used today. They are approximately the same size as packing balls, but are not free-blown. They were blown into a mold and their tops left open. This ball was patented by Ira Paine, whose name is molded into the ball around the center. It is dated October 23, 1877. Many matching fragments were dug at the Boston and Sandwich Glass Company site, although Paine's ball was also made by other glass factories from the same mold. This was a private mold that was sent to the company that quoted the lowest price.

CHAPTER 9

COVERED CONTAINERS FOR SPECIALIZED USE

1830–1908

Most glass companies derived a large part of their income from the manufacture of containers that were designed for a particular use. Some had commercial use to hold hair pomade and medicinal or perfumed ointment. They were wholesaled to business firms distributing pomade or ointment or were manufactured using private molds that were owned by the distributor. Some covered pieces were not intended for commercial use and could be rightly included with pressed pattern and Lacy tableware, but their specialized use justifies their separation from those categories for detailed study. Finally, there are the one-of-a-kind patterned and figural pieces that were purchased for specialized use in the home, such as melon dishes, soap boxes, and puff jars.

The use of many of these pieces has long been open to debate, largely because some pieces made in the 1840–1870 period were designed for multiple uses. If a customer came to the Boston and Sandwich Glass Company showroom to purchase a *butter*, the salesman would likely sell him a 6" nappie (shallow bowl) with a cover. A piece listed as a *pomade* by one glass company might be listed as a

horseradish by another company. The famous figural bear produced by the Boston and Sandwich Glass Company was made for several pharmaceutical houses to hold bear grease for hair. The names of the bear grease distributors can be found molded into the bottom of the containers. But in a magazine article written by Amanda Harris in 1887, the bears are called "match safes for the five-cent stores". The bears that were sold as match holders did not have a distributor's name molded into them. However, the marked bears would also have been used for matches after the hair grease was gone.

Several footed pomade jars were manufactured in patterns that matched pressed pattern tableware. Their lower units were made in the shape of an egg cup, and a matching cover was added. Some of the lower units were the same height as an egg cup in the same pattern; others were pressed in a mold that was slightly shorter than an egg cup in the same pattern. Based on writings of glass authority Ruth Webb Lee, these pomade jars became known as "covered egg cups". Lacking documentation from an illustrated catalog, this could be a logical conclusion. However,

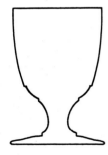

EGG CUP IF CLEAR

POMADE IF COLORED AND/OR COVERED

POMADE

HORSERADISH

SALT

Fig. 13   Because pressed pattern pomade and horseradish jars are not recognized as such, they have been assimilated into collections of egg cups and salts. The general proportion of most egg cups is shown in the illustration on the left. If you find a colored piece proportioned like an egg cup, you have found the lower unit of a pomade jar. The illustration in the center shows the shape most often mistaken for an egg cup. Whether clear or colored, it should have a cover and was marketed for pomade and horseradish. It is taller than a salt, shown on the right.

since we find more of them in colored opaque and translucent glass than in clear glass, this cannot be considered a justifiable conclusion today, because some of them have the same names molded into them as the figural bears. Moreover, colored glass was used to hide the color of the pomade.

We cannot find "covered egg cups" listed in bills of lading, order sheets, or catalogs from *any* glass company, either in the East or Midwest. This includes the Boston and Sandwich Glass Company, New England Glass Company, Union Glass Company, McKee and Brothers, and Bakewell, Pears and Company. Nor are "covered egg cups" mentioned in correspondence to glass factory personnel. It can be argued that, in a listing for a sugar bowl, a cover would be implied and not mentioned. Similarly, a cover for an egg cup would not be mentioned. However, careful study of factory sloar books and work sheets show that egg cups were made, *but not covers for egg cups*. So we must conclude that, after the retail customer emptied the pretty pomade jar, he very likely used the lower unit for eggs. A large family could accumulate enough pomade jars to make a set of "egg cups". Since styles did not change rapidly, the pomade distributor used the same pattern container for many years.

Unlike egg cups, covers *were* made for containers that stored condiments that were shared at the table, such as mustard and horseradish. The lower unit of a horseradish jar can also be mistaken for an egg cup or an open salt because the jar may not have an inside ridge to indicate that there should be a cover. So it becomes important to distinguish between egg cups and open salts that did not have covers, and horseradish jars that did. If the piece you are buying is an egg cup or an open salt, you are buying a complete piece. If the piece you are buying turns out to be the lower unit of a horseradish jar, you are buying only half the piece and should pay accordingly.

Conversely, if you are searching for pomades and horseradishes, you may find these jars among other types of glass utensils. If they have a stem, they may be mistakenly included in egg cup collections. If they have a short, stubby base, they could be mixed with salt collections. It is helpful to think of pomade and horseradish lower units in relation to egg cups and salts in *order of height*, as you would think of stemmed drinking vessels. When we see a champagne, we automatically think, "Goblet, champagne, wine, cordial". In the same manner, think, "Egg cup, pomade/horseradish, salt". Buy it inexpensively—then keep it in mind as you search for the cover. *The value of covered pieces is in the cover.*

An added note—a condiment container with a cover that has a cutout for a spoon handle in a *mustard*. If there is no cutout, the jar was not originally intended to be for mustard.

THESE SIMPLE HINTS WILL HELP YOU IDENTIFY SANDWICH COVERED CONTAINERS.

If you find a footed piece that is shorter than an egg cup and taller than a salt, consider the possibility that it may be the lower unit of a pomade or horseradish.

Mustards have a cutout in the cover to accept the handle of a mustard spoon.

If you find a cover that matches any of the covers in this study, buy it. The lower unit will eventually surface.

3243 LACY PEACOCK EYE (PEACOCK FEATHER) AND SHIELD RECTANGULAR DISH

a) Dish 5⅛" H. x 6⅜" L. x 3⅞" W.
b) Cover 2¾" H. x 5½" L. x 3⅛" W.
c) Combined size 5⅛" H. x 6⅜" L. x 3⅞" W.
   1835–1845

All of the pieces that are designated as *Lacy* were made by pressing glass into a mold. Because pressing was a new technique that required experimentation, and because the best quality sand was not readily available to make the glass, the piece was completely covered with intricate patterns and stippling to hide defects. The double Peacock Eye on each side of the shield can be seen on other Lacy pieces. This variation of Peacock Eye has a cable pattern surrounding the "eyes" and a fine diamond pattern. The shape of the dish closely resembles covered salts made during the same period. Note the pine cone finial on the cover. *Courtesy, Sandwich Glass Museum, Sandwich Historical Society*

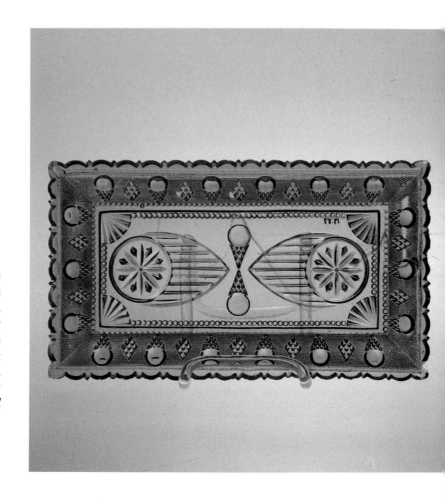

3244 LACY PEACOCK EYE (PEACOCK FEATHER) AND SHIELD TRAY FROM ABOVE DISH

" H. x 8⅜" L. x 4⅝" W. 1835–1845

This tray in clear glass is the underplate for the above dish. The shields match the shield in the dish and the cover. The tray is often found in clear glass, separated from the other units. It can be identified as Sandwich by the pattern of alternating "eyes" and diamonds on the sides. There is no cable pattern surrounding the "eyes", but this combination of "eyes" and half-diamonds is repeated on the ends of the dish. A complete three-unit set is very rare. *Courtesy, Sandwich Glass Museum, Sandwich Historical Society*

3245 LACY GOTHIC ARCH AND HEART RECTANGULAR DISH WITH DOMED COVER AND TRAY

(a) Dish 2¾" H. x 6¼" L. x 4" W.
(b) Cover 2⅜" H. x 5⅞" L. x 3⅜" W.
(c) Tray 1" H. x 7¼" L. x 4½" W.
(d) Combined size 5⅜" H. x 7¼" L. x 4½" W.
 1835–1845

Many seemingly unrelated patterns were combined on Lacy pieces. On three-unit combinations, not every pattern appears on each of the units. There are gothic arches and hearts on the sides of the dish. The arches are repeated on the cover, but the hearts are not. The hearts are repeated on the tray, but the arches are not. This set is very seldom found complete. Watch for the units separately, in clear and color. They will often be in box lots at auctions. *Courtesy, Sandwich Glass Museum, Sandwich Historical Society*

3246 LACY GOTHIC ARCH DOMED COVER FROM ABOVE DISH

Note the pattern of thistles on the cover—completely foreign to the dish itself. The pattern is on the inside of the cover, but on the outside of the dish. The value of rare covered pieces is in the cover. If you see a cover for sale don't pass it up. The lower unit will eventually be found.

3247 LACY GOTHIC ARCH AND HEART RECTANGULAR DISH WITH STEPPED COVER AND TRAY

(a) Dish 2¾" H. x 6¼" L. x 4" W.
(b) Cover 2½" H. x 5¾" L. x 3⅜" W.
(c) Tray 1" H. x 7¼" L. x 4½" W.
(d) Combined size 5⅜" H. x 7¼" L. x 4½" W.
 1835–1845

This three-piece assembly has the same dish and tray, but the cover is completely different. The cover is stepped instead of domed. The arches on the cover were lengthened to cover the top of the step. This gives the complete set a different look. The tray with its Heart border is shown on the following page. *Courtesy, Sandwich Glass Museum, Sandwich Historical Society*

248 LACY GOTHIC ARCH STEPPED COVER FROM ABOVE DISH

Compare this stepped cover to the domed cover. Instead of thistles, there are two quatrefoils on each side of the finial. The Toledo Museum of Art has a beautiful deep blue complete set in their collection. The pattern on the cover of the Toledo piece can barely be seen because it is on the inside. It may have been easier to make the mold for the cover with the pattern on the inside, but our photo of this piece in color would not have shown the detail of the pattern.

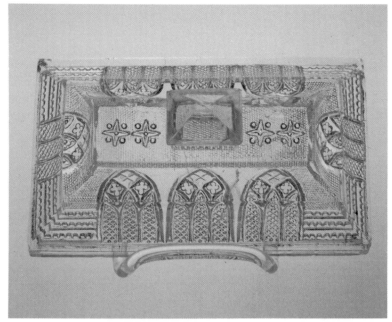

249 LACY HEART TRAY FROM GOTHIC ARCH AND HEART DISH

⅛" H. x 7" L. x 4⅝" W. 1835-1845

The only resemblance to the dish is the pattern of hearts and the scallop and point rim that matches the rim of the dish. Note the tiny flowers in the center, a pattern used in toy dishes. Fragments also show this tray with a waffle center. Another variation has the *U.S.F. Constitution* in the center. The *Constitution* tray is a rare historical piece and very likely was not meant to be used with the dish and cover. Trays that match Lacy rectangular dishes have a scallop and point rim. *Courtesy, Sandwich Glass Museum, Sandwich Historical Society*

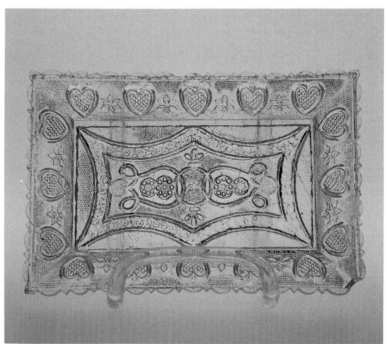

250 PRESSED HORN OF PLENTY (COMET) RECTANGULAR DISH

a) Dish 2⅞" H. x 6½" L. x 4" W.
b) Cover 2¾" H. x 5⅞" L. x 3⅜" W.
c) Combined size 5¼" H. x 6½" L. x 4" W.
   1845-1855

The pattern, called *Horn of Plenty* today, was called *Comet* by the factories that made it. It was made over a long period of time, but the shape of this piece indicates early vintage. Rectangular covered dishes were not practical because the corners of the cover struck the rim of the dish, easily damaging both. Therefore, this form was discontinued early. Although the pattern is a carry-over from the Lacy Period, the background is not stippled. With the beginning of complete lines of pressed pattern tableware, all of the elements that make up the pattern are on both units. If a rectangular tray was part of the set, the Comet pattern should be on the rim. *Courtesy, Sandwich Glass Museum, Sandwich Historical Society*

3251 BLOWN MOLDED SANDWICH MELON DISH
(a) Dish 2⅝" H. x 5⅜" L. x 4" W.
(b) Cover 3⅛" H. x 5½" L. x 4" W.
(c) Pressed underplate 1⅛" H. x 7⅜" L. x 6" W.
(d) Combined size 5⅞" H. x 7⅜" L. x 6" W.
    1850–1870

The Sandwich Melon is one of the rarest pieces manufac
tured by the Boston and Sandwich Glass Company. We
believe it was made in other colors. The stem finial can
be seen on other pieces made in Sandwich, such as the
Overshot covered bowl shown on page 121 in Volume 4.
One of the ways to identify an original Sandwich melon
is to look inside the cover, and you will see a rough ponti
mark under the stem finial. According to the Sandwich
Glass Museum, there are only two known examples of this
truly unique dish and underplate. *Courtesy, Sandwich Glas.
Museum, Sandwich Historical Society*

3252 UNITS OF ABOVE DISH
The melon is split horizontally in the center, and the cove
will go on only one way. The cover has nine ribs, and no
rim. The bottom of the melon has eleven ribs, and a rim
over which the cover fits. The underplate was pressed into
the form of a melon leaf with an irregular outer edge. I
also has a stem, and a center deep enough to accept the
base of the melon.

253 PRESSED HEN DISH
a) Dish 1⅞" H. x 7⅜" L. x 5¼" W.
b) Cover 4" H. x 8" L. x 5¾" W.
c) Combined size 5¾" H. x 8" L. x 5¾" W.
   1850–1870

The construction of the Sandwich hen is unique in several ways. The cover consists of the hen sitting in the center surrounded by a wide rim of straw. The side of the oval dish has a drape pattern that alternates with two vertical lines, while the base has a completely unrelated block pattern. Neither pattern relates to the hen. It is difficult to find the hen without damage to the beak and comb. We have seen this piece in clear, canary, green, and several shades of blue. If each unit is a different color, use caution — the units may be married.

254 UNITS OF ABOVE HEN DISH
This photo shows the unusual turn of the hen's head. The tail is hollow, with the opening beneath the cover. Some hens made in the Pittsburgh area have hollow tails that open to the back of the tail. Note the pattern on the oval dish. If found alone at an antiques show, it could easily be overlooked or thought to be French.

3255 PRESSED SPANIEL DISH
(a) Dish 1⅞" H. x 4⅝" L. x 3¼" W.
(b) Cover 2¼" H. x 4¼" L. x 2¾" W.
(c) Combined size 3⅜" H. x 4⅝" L. x 3¼" W.
1895–1908

Ruth Webb Lee, in her book *Victorian Glass*, states that th
dog can positively be attributed to Sandwich. Othe
authorities believe the green cast to the glass make it a
unlikely candidate for Boston and Sandwich Glass Com
pany manufacture. Actually, the spaniel, with this base
was probably made by one of the short-lived companie
that attempted production at the Boston and Sandwic
site. This accounts for the scarcity of the spaniel. Som
fragments were found at the site, but very few, indicatin
an extremely short production period. A 1906 newspape
reported that the Sandwich Glass Company was makin
novelties. The Alton Manufacturing Company also pro
duced small amounts of novelties until 1908. The lattic
pattern is only on the two long sides. The ends are stipple
and the rim is beaded. An oval dish with a similar spani
was made by McKee. The Sandwich dish is rectangula

3256 PRESSED TURTLE SOAP DISH
(a) Base 1¼" H. x 5¼" L. x 2¾" W.
(b) Shell cover 1" H. x 4⅜" L. x 3¼" W.
(c) Combined size 2¼" H. x 5⅜" L. x 3¼" W.
1907–1908

The turtle's shell is the cover of the soap dish. The dee
grooves separating the segments of the shell are gilded
There are no shell markings under the bottom unit. Th
mouth and eyes are very distinct. A mold mark can b
seen running down the center of the head, between th
eyes, bisecting the mouth, and continuing down the cente
of the neck to the base. This was a product of the Alto
Manufacturing Company. It can be found in opaqu
white without the gilding and brown color. *Courtesy, Sand
wich Glass Museum, Sandwich Historical Society*

3257 PRESSED HORSESHOE BOX
1¾" H. x 3½" L. x 3⅛" W. 1907–1908

This masculine box was made to hold collar buttons an
similar accessories on a man's chest-of-drawers. The hea
of a horse is on the cover, surrounded by a horseshoe
Two horseshoes are molded into the end panel. A whi
and bugle can be seen on each side. *Courtesy, Sandwich Gla
Museum, Sandwich Historical Society*

3258 PRESSED HORSESHOE BOX
1½" H. x 3½" L. x 3" W. May 1907

Here is absolute proof of Sandwich manufacture—the same box as shown above, signed and dated by the Alton Manufacturing Company. It is easy to differentiate between pieces decorated by the original Boston and Sandwich Glass Company and pieces inexpensively decorated by the several companies that later occupied the same buildings. Study this piece and the pressed turtle soap dish and the pressed Great Blue Heron vase attributed to the Alton Manufacturing Company in Chapter 2. You will find that the high standards set by the Boston and Sandwich Glass Company were not maintained by those who attempted to re-open the factory. *Courtesy, Sandwich Glass Museum, Sandwich Historical Society*

3259 PRESSED DRUM POMADE
3¾" H. x 2½" Dia. 1850–1870

This is the only figural drum known to have been manufactured in Sandwich. It was made in two sizes, the tall one shown here and a shorter one that is 2½" high. The cover is nothing more than a thin disk that rests on a recessed ridge. The drumstick, intended to be used as a hand hold, protrudes only 3/16" above the rim of the drum, so it is virtually impossible to remove the cover without turning the drum over and dropping the cover in your hand. As a result of this design, the covers were easily broken. A shield can be seen lying on its side under the ropes of the drum. An amethyst drum in our collection is marked "PHALON & SON" on the shield. The blue drum in this photo is not marked. It may have had a paper label. Other companies made smaller drums as parts of a child's set of tableware and large ones for an adult-size set. Made primarily in clear glass, they do not have the shield.

3260 PRESSED CAVALIER POMADE
3¾" H. 1850–1870

This gay, sprightly fellow is unique to Sandwich. His sitting position allows the jar to hold the same amount of pomade as the same size bear would hold and gives stability. The ones we have examined are marked "E. T. S. & Co NY." underneath. Two types of hats were made: the short plumed one shown here, fragments of which were dug at the Boston and Sandwich site, and a tall top hat patterned after the Prism Panel toy tumbler made by the Cape Cod Glass Company and shown in Chapter 10. A photo of the tall version can be seen in the booklet *Sandwich Glass*, published by the Sandwich Historical Society. *The brim of the hat is part of the lower unit. The crown and plume form the cover, and must match in color.* If the cover is a different color or a different shade, the units are married and the value is significantly decreased.

3261 PRESSED BEAR JARS
(a) Large, "R. & G. A. WRIGHT" on base 5⅛" H.
(b) Medium, "J. HAUEL & CO. PHILADA." on base
    4½" H.
(c) Small, no mark on base 3¾" H. 1850–1887

Figural bears were originally designed to hold bear grease which, according to a label at the Sandwich Glass Museum, was for "promoting the growth and luxuriance of hair". As the bear population decreased, an odorless pomade took the place of the grease. Bear A is the largest size normally found, but the rarest was at least 8" high and held a quart or more. It was sometimes placed at the back of the kitchen stove and used as a receptacle for waste fat. The names on the base are those of the retail distributor of the contents. Other bears are marked "X BAZIN PHILA", "PHALON & SON NY", "F. B. STROUSE NY", and "EUGENE BIZE & FRICKE SUCCESSOR TO J. HAUEL & C". A narrow paper label surrounded the neck sealing the head to the body. Some bears are not marked and were sold by the Boston and Sandwich Glass Company directly to the retail customer to be used as match boxes.

3262 PRESSED BEAR JARS
(a) Clambroth
(b) Black amethyst fragment
(c) Black amethyst
(d) Opaque white 3¾" H. 1850–1887

These are the smallest size. The black amethyst was made over a long period of time and is the most common. It was listed in 1883 union records, but no other color was given as a regular line item. In order of scarcity, clambroth is second, followed by white and blue. Diggings at the factory show colors that have never been found—opaque green, opaque lilac, and soft pink. The color we call *clambroth* was known as *alabaster*.

3263 PRESSED BEAR JAR
(a) Blue, "X BAZIN PHILADA" on base 4⅝" H.
(b) Wooden bear contemporary to above 4⅞" H.
    1850–1870

Xavier Bazin founded his perfumery and toilet soap laboratory in 1850. This style of bear is very difficult to find. He sits back on his haunches, his front paws are crossed and there is a chain around his neck. He does not have a muzzle. The bear on the right is made of wood and is almost identical except for the collar around his neck. The more common glass bear was also made in pottery and had an English registry mark. This raises the eternal question—which one is a copy? The answer—probably neither. The bear was a piece that took the buying public's fancy and was manufactured by several different companies in several mediums. In the same way, Tulip vases were made in both glass and pottery, while Lacy glass pieces were duplicated in Meissen porcelain.

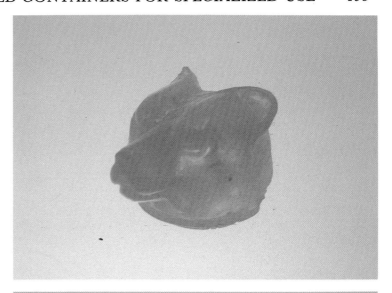

264 PRESSED WOLF JAR COVER

¼" H. 1850–1870

The wolf head has been dug in sufficient quantities to establish its origin as the Boston and Sandwich Glass Company, but we have found neither the body alone nor a complete jar. The wolf can be differentiated from the bear by examining the ears. They are hollowed out and are positioned differently. The eyes are lower, slanted, and not as widely opened. The snout is shorter and is not muzzled. We have seen the wolf head used with a bear body, but we do not believe the jar was shipped from the factory this way.

265 PRESSED CABLE POMADE

" H. x 2⅝" Dia. 1840–1870

The bottom unit of this pomade was marketed as the egg cup in Cable pressed pattern tableware. Adding a cover turned it into a pomade, so the Boston and Sandwich Glass Company used the same mold for several purposes. This piece has also been found in opaque green. Most of the pieces originally designed for pomade have a small unpatterned area where a tiny paper label was applied—such as the panel between the Cable pattern, the "eye" in Bull's Eye and Bar, and the band above Diamond Point. In clear glass, this covered piece could also be used for horseradish. *Courtesy, Sandwich Glass Museum, Sandwich Historical Society*

266 PRESSED FLAT DIAMOND AND PANEL POMADE

⅝" H. X 2½" Dia. 1850–1870

Pomade was a perfumed ointment, used primarily for the hair. Sometimes an egg cup mold was used to make the bottom unit of the pomade. Many collectors, therefore, mistakenly believe that these pomade jars are covered egg cups, but that was not the intent. Most pomades that are egg cup-shaped were produced in translucent and opaque colors because the color of the ointment was not attractive. This pomade is taller than most, but the height is in the cover. The cover appears to be darker than the bottom unit, which could suggest that the cover was replaced. However, the cover is darker only because it is thicker. When considering a purchase, hold each unit up to a bright light and look through the glass. If each unit is a different *hue*, they were combined at a later time. *Courtesy of the Toledo Museum of Art (Acc. No. 65.16)*

3268 PRESSED BULL'S EYE (LAWRENCE) POMADES

(a) Complete with cover 5⅜" H. x 2⅝" Dia.
(b) Lower unit only 3⅞" H. x 2⅝" Dia. 1850–1870
Our acquisition of the Wennerstrom fragment collection resulted in a wealth of new information. Frank and June Wennerstrom dug only at the site of the Cape Cod Glass Works, so the collection is not contaminated by fragments from the Boston and Sandwich Glass Company site. Fragments of this pomade were found in the Wennerstrom diggings, so the piece can be attributed to the Cape Cod Glass Works and the Cape Cod Glass Company, as well as to the Boston and Sandwich Glass Company. It was made in several other translucent pastel colors. The formulas for these colors are in James D. Lloyd's formula book, written in 1868, when Lloyd was working at the Cape Cod Glass Company. Full sets of tableware were made in this pattern, which can be seen in a New England Glass Company catalog. The original pattern name was *Lawrence. The Bennington Museum, Bennington, Vermont*

3267 PRESSED BULL'S EYE AND BAR

(a) Wooden pattern
(b) Pressed pomade 1850–1870
Before a mold was made, the pattern was first carved i wood. The wooden pattern shown here is the bottom pai of the pomade. Pomades were shipped out of the factor to wholesale houses that filled them with the ointment. I most cases, after the container was empty, the bottom un was used for an egg cup. We cannot find in the recorc of any glass company an indication that *covered* egg cup were sold as part of a tableware pattern. We suggest tha you not buy a *colored* jar, hoping to locate a matchin cover, unless it is reasonably priced. It is virtually imposs ble to find one made from the same batch of glass, so th color will not be an exact match. *Courtesy, Sandwich Gla. Museum, Sandwich Historical Society*

3269 PRESSED DIAMOND POINT (SHARP DIAMOND) POMADE

5⅝" H. x 2⅝" Dia. 1850–1870
This pattern was made under the name *Sharp Diamon* The bottom unit was pressed in a mold that was mor complicated than most. Four seams run vertically throug the diamond pattern, but only two opposite ones continu straight down the stem and across the foot. The other tw make a right angle below the pattern, then angle again continued down the stem. We have no idea why the pa tern could not have been made in a mold with the usu: three seams, as was done for the cover. Note the pro trusion below the diamonds that makes up the upper pa of the stem. It is not on the mold used to make the Di: mond Point egg cup. The pomade's close resemblance the egg cup made it an excellent substitute. Note the di coloration along the mold mark. Pieces in this clambrot (alabaster) color often have black spots. While we wis they were not present, they do not detract from value.

3270 PRESSED FINE RIB (REEDED) WITH SHIELD POMADE

5½" H. x 2⅝" Dia. 1850–1870

Fine Rib tableware pieces were made by several factories in New England and Pennsylvania. The catalog name was *Reeded*. The pomade is attributed to Sandwich. Only the pomade always has a shield. The shield may have the name of the distributor molded into it, such as "Phalon & Son". Some shields are smooth to take a paper label. The pomades were made in several colors and also in clear. If you find a Fine Rib pomade without the shield, you have two married pieces—a pomade cover on an egg cup.

3271 PRESSED FINE RIB (REEDED)

(a) Pomade, with shield 3½" H. x 2⅝" Dia.
(b) Egg cup, no shield 4" H. x 2⅝" Dia. 1850–1870

Dug fragments show that both pieces were made by the Boston and Sandwich Glass Company. There can be no argument about the difference when they are placed side by side. Note the height of the egg cup. It is approximately the size of most egg cups made during this time period. The green pomade is shorter than the egg cup, but taller than a salt. The pomade was made in a three-piece mold, the egg cup in a two-piece mold. This can be seen by holding each one up to the light and looking down from the top onto the upper surface of the foot. The pomade has three mold marks that extend to the outer edge of the foot, which was not reworked after removal from the mold. The foot of the egg cup has the remains of two mold marks near the stem. The foot was expanded and fire polished, obliterating the marks. The lack of finish work on the pomade is another indication that it was meant for one-time use as a container for a commercial product.

3272 PRESSED NEW YORK HONEYCOMB (NEW YORK, UTICA) POMADE

4¼" H. x 2½" Dia., without cover 1850–1870

At the time this pomade jar was made, the term *Honeycomb* was not used. Pieces with the pattern half way up the sides were called *New York* by the New England Glass Company and *New York Honeycomb* by collectors. The pattern is illustrated in the Cape Cod Glass Company list of glassware, reprinted in Chapter 4 of this book, where it is called *Utica*. Large quantities of fragments were found at the Boston and Sandwich Glass Company site, and it was made by many other factories as well. In her book *Glass Tableware, Bowls & Vases*, Jane S. Spillman notes that this shape is confusing because it is large for an egg cup, but has a stem too short for a wine. It is neither an egg cup nor a wine, but is the lower unit of a pomade jar. We have seen it with the pomade distributor's name molded into the upper surface of the base in a circle. To be complete, it must have a matching cover.

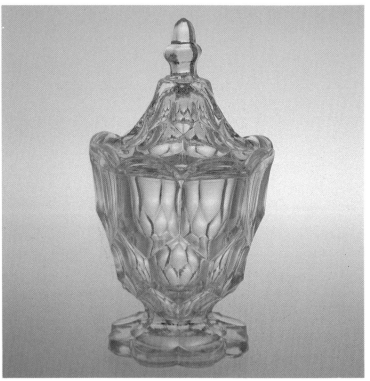

3273 PRESSED VERNON HONEYCOMB (VERNON) POMADE

4¾" H. x 2¼" Dia. 1850–1870

The present-day collector calls this pattern *Honeycomb*, sometimes preceded by the original name of the pattern—in this instance, *Vernon*. On Vernon pieces, the honeycomb pattern extends almost to the rim of the lower unit. Fragments show that it was made in quantity at the Boston and Sandwich Glass Company. This piece is also illustrated in a New England Glass Company catalog, where it is listed as a pomade. It is shown in the New England catalog with a complete line of Vernon tableware, so it may not have been a commercial piece. Except for the octagonal finial and the ten-sided short stem, it is a miniature version of the Vernon sugar bowl. A different mold was used for Vernon egg cups. An 1861 catalog from James B. Lyon and Company, a Pittsburgh manufacturer, shows a similar piece in Cincinnati, the pattern name for another Honeycomb variant. It is listed as a horseradish.

3274 PRESSED GIANT HONEYCOMB HORSERADISH

4¾" H. x 2¾" Dia. 1845–1860

This is a variant of the Honeycomb pattern made by several companies in both New England and Pittsburgh. The pattern is so large that three rows complete the lower unit from the scallops on the rim to the scallops on the base. Two rows of pattern are on the cover. The finial is a common one found on other Sandwich items. Note again the proportions of the lower unit. Careful study of factory catalogs reveals that horseradish containers were made in a number of patterns. However, they are largely ignored as such by collectors because they are bought without their covers. If they have a stem, they find their way into egg cup collections. If they have a short stubby base, they are included in salt collections. *Courtesy, Sandwich Glass Museum, Sandwich Historical Society*

3275 PRESSED SAWTOOTH (MITRE DIAMOND) POMADE

3" H. x 2¾" Dia. 1850–1870

Because of an early lack of original documentation, this pattern became known as *Sawtooth*. A New England Glass Company catalog lists it as *Mitre Diamond*, and pieces by that name can be found on Boston and Sandwich Glass Company invoices. Several Midwest factories produced it also, so there are many variants that differ only slightly from one another. This Sandwich pomade has a cover that one usually associates with spice jars and wide-mouthed apothecary jars. Even though the cover is hollow with a rayed pattern beneath the finial, the pomade was called *stoppered* because the cover was ground to fit the inside of the jar in the same manner as the plug of a stopper. This mold was also used to make an oil bottle by drawing the top of the jar into a long neck, then forming a spout and applying a handle. *Courtesy, Sandwich Glass Museum, Sandwich Historical Society*

3276 PRESSED SAWTOOTH (MITRE DIAMOND) HORSERADISH OR SALT

(a) Small finial, ridged foot 5⅜" H. x 2½" Dia.
(b) Faceted finial, smooth base 5¼" H. x 2¼" Dia.
   1850–1870

This container is more easily found than any other. Note the variations in the finial and foot. Fragments of all four units were dug in quantity at the Boston and Sandwich site, and they are interchangeable. A canary one in our collection has the ridged foot on A and the faceted finial of B. Usually considered to be a salt, it may originally have been designed for horseradish. The mold's versatility resulted in additional use when it was made in non-lead glass at a later time by Bryce Brothers of Pittsburgh. They manufactured a toy tableware set and used this piece as the sugar. The cover of the toy sugar has the small finial.

3277 PRESSED SAWTOOTH (MITRE DIAMOND)

(a) Wooden pattern for cover with faceted finial
(b) Pressed horseradish or salt

The wooden pattern was the first step in making the mold for the cover. In this photo, it has been placed on an opal lower unit to show how the diamonds interlock, obviating the need for an inner rim. The diamonds increase in size from the finial to the rim, then decrease in size from the rim to the hexagonal stem. There are the same number of diamonds in each horizontal row. Not all pieces of Mitre Diamond have a sawtooth edge. Most pieces do, but an open salt has a plain rim. Note the plain foot on this variant. *Courtesy, Sandwich Glass Museum, Sandwich Historical Society*

3278 LACY PEACOCK EYE (PEACOCK FEATHER) MUSTARD

2½" H. x 2¾" Dia. 1830–1845

Without its cover, this piece could be mistaken by a novice collector for a child's mug. It is often shown with an underplate, but there is nothing in the records to prove that an underplate is correct. The underplates we have studied do not fit the base of the container. The pattern more closely resembles peacock feathers than a peacock's eye, but we will not change the name established by Ruth Webb Lee. The pattern is on the outside of the container, but is on the inside of the cover. This was common at Sandwich and works well with clear glass. When this mustard was made in a deep color, the pattern cannot be seen through the cover. The cover is cut out to accept a mustard spoon, which was usually made of bone or olive wood. The handle was molded as part of the container. Note the fine diamond point pattern alternating with stippling, one of many variations of the Peacock Eye pattern. *Courtesy of The Toledo Museum of Art (Acc. No. 68.20)*

3279 PRESSED OPAL LUNCH CASTER

(a) Complete caster 5¼" H.; 4⅜" across
(b) Mustard cover 1½" H. x 2⅛" Dia. 1870–1887
We have shown you a very early mustard and now a very late one. During the middle years, a mustard bottle was included in four and five-bottle caster sets and very few individual ones were made. Containers that were designed for mustard always have a cutout in the cover for the spoon. This piece is pictured in the 1874 Boston and Sandwich Glass Company catalog and belonged to the family of glassworker Joseph Henry Lapham. Note the detail on the finial of the cover. The pattern of ribs is similar to the blown molded cologne in Chapter 5. If you find this set without its cover, you only have half of the piece. The plain rim on the mustard compartment would make the lack of a cover obvious. *Courtesy, Sandwich Glass Museum, Sandwich Historical Society*

3280 PRESSED COVERED BASKETS

(a) Match holder 4¾" H. x 2¾" Dia.
(b) Toothpick holder 4" H. x 2½" Dia. 1850–1870
This matched set of baskets still had their original contents when we photographed them in the home of descendants of Sandwich glassworkers. Basket A held long matches that had to be struck on a flint. Basket B held the first of the wooden toothpicks. The knopped finial made the cover easy to grasp and simple to remove without chipping or breaking. They are, in the opinion of the authors, examples of Sandwich at its finest. Note the handles on the side of the baskets. Study the weave of the basket—three horizontal rods woven over and under a single vertical rod. The difference between the Sandwich weave and a similar weave made in Baccarat, France, is shown in the illustration.

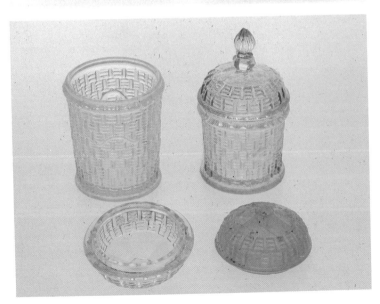

3281 PRESSED COVERED BASKETS

(a) Bottom unit of match holder
(b) Complete toothpick holder
The bottom unit of the match holder and toothpick holder has a plain rim above the weave pattern. A flange on the cover fits inside the rim. If you buy a Sandwich basket with a plain rim, remember that you are buying only half the piece. The bottom unit alone is worth less than half the value of the complete covered piece. The canary and green covers without their finials were dug at the Boston and Sandwich Glass Company site.

3282 PRESSED BASKETS
(a) 1½" H.
(b) 2" H. 1850–1870
Here are Sandwich baskets with the same weave pattern, but they were not designed to have covers. The rims are patterned as they would have been finished on real Nineteenth Century woven wicker baskets. Note that basket B is approximately the same size as the bottom unit of the covered basket match holder, shown in photo 3281. There can be handles on the sides. If you find a Sandwich basket with the patterned rim, you have a complete piece. Its value is greater than the value of the bottom unit alone of the covered basket. Several Pennsylvania glass factories produced figural basket items during the 1870's and 1880's. The Pennsylvania patterns do not stand out in deep relief and the glass is of lesser quality. We are grateful for the help of the Sandwich glassmakers' descendants who have so willingly allowed us to photograph their heirlooms.

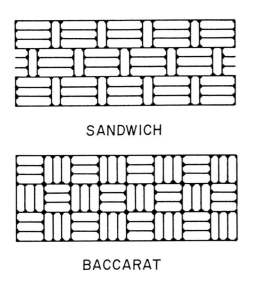

SANDWICH

BACCARAT

Fig. 14   The basket pattern used on Sandwich toothpick holders and match holders is a wicker weave composed of three pliable horizontal rods woven over and under widely spaced, single, rigid vertical rods. The Baccarat weave of three horizontal rods woven over and under three closely spaced vertical rods gives the effect of a splint basket.

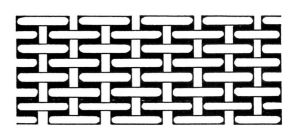

Fig. 15   **BASKET PATTERN ON OVAL COVER FRAGMENT** 5" L. x 3" W. approximate size of cover 1850–1870
Fragments of this basket pattern were dug in Sandwich. The largest fragment we have seen is on display at the Sandwich Glass Museum. It is a piece of a translucent blue oval cover, the type that could have been used on a large oval top hat. Many covered hats were made by Compagnie des Cristalleries de Baccarat, but they have the weave pattern of three vertical rods shown previously. To date, we have not located a complete cover with its bottom unit.

3283 PRESSED DENTIFRICE JAR
3½" H. with metal cover; 2" Dia. 1840–1860
Although our forefathers might not have admonished their children to brush their teeth three times a day, tooth powder and toothbrushes were a part of their toilet. The *Yarmouth Register*, a Cape Cod newspaper, advertised domestic and British tooth powder, compound chlorine tooth wash, and toothbrushes as early as 1837. This jar held tooth powder. A small amount of the powder was coaxed into the bowl-shaped metal cover and mixed with water to form a paste. The jar, metal cover, and melted fragments were dug at the Boston and Sandwich site.

3284 PRESSED DENTIFRICE JAR
3⅛" H. x 2¾" Dia. 1840-1860
This jar was manufactured by the Boston and Sandwich Glass Company and was wholesaled to the company that made the tooth powder. The piece is octagonal, with an oval in each of the eight panels. There is no pattern on the octagonal cover. It is perfectly flat so that a paper label could be pasted on it. A similar jar was made in France in the 1840's. The French jar is hexagonal and its six panels extend to a ridge just below the rim. *The Bennington Museum, Bennington, Vermont*

3285 PRESSED ACORN WITH BEADING SOAP BOX
(a) Box 2½" H. x 3½" Dia.
(b) Cover 1" H. x 3¾" Dia.
(c) Combined size 3½" H. x 3¾" Dia. 1850-1870
Many fragments of this box have been recovered from the Boston and Sandwich Glass Company site, in a variety of colors. The use of this piece was determined from a description of a like item illustrated in a French catalog. The acorns and oak leaves on the box and cover are in deep relief not often associated with American pressed glass. The bottom is stippled, and there is stippling on the surface where there is no design. The cover fits snugly.

3286 UNITS OF ABOVE SOAP BOX
The dug fragments were found in the portion of the dump known to have been used in 1850. The Sandwich Glass Museum has a canary soap box on display. A reproduction was made by the Wheaton Glass Company. It is the same diameter, but is shorter and there is no stippling. The reproduction is signed.

3287 BLOWN MOLDED ROSETTE PUFF BOX

(a) Box (Jar) 2⅝" H. x 4⅛" Dia.
(b) Pressed Cover 1" H. x 4⅛" Dia.
(c) Combined size 3⅜" H. x 4⅛" Dia. 1850–1870

Today we would call this piece a *powder jar*. It originally held a puff used to powder hair. The six-petaled rosettes at the base of the jar are considerably smaller than the ones near the top. Six rows of evenly spaced rosettes make up the jar, which was blown into a mold and weighs less than half the weight of the cover. The cover is thick and heavy because it was pressed into a mold. *Courtesy, Sandwich Glass Museum, Sandwich Historical Society*

3288 UNITS OF ABOVE PUFF BOX

The cover has a rim, which fits inside the box. A single row of rosettes surrounds the large dahlia-like rosette that makes up the center. The cover does not have a finial, making the box difficult to open. In order to open it, one must grasp the whole cover.

3289 PRESSED OVAL HOBNAIL PUFF BOX

a) Box 3¼" H. x 4½" Dia.
b) Cover 3" H. x 3½" Dia.
c) Combined size 5¾" H. x 4½" Dia. 1850–1870

This puff box was made to be combined with a pair of the Oval Hobnail colognes shown in the cologne chapter. It was also made in France. The Sandwich one can be identified by looking inside the cover. A heavy, rough pontil mark is directly under the finial, where the cover was held while the finial was reheated and bent. The French box is lighter in weight, and the underside of the cover is smoothly molded. This stem finial was also used on the melon dish. The number of dug fragments indicate that it was made in many colors.

3290 CUT OVERLAY PANEL AND STAR PUFF BOX

(a) Box 3" H. x 2⅞" Dia.
(b) Cover 2¼" H. x 2⅞" Dia.
(c) Combined size 4¾" H. x 2⅞" Dia. 1850–1870

This puff box was blown into a mold and then cut to match the Panel and Star cologne. Concentric rings on the cover match rings on the shoulder of the cologne. This piece was difficult to use without damaging it. The upper row of stars is on the side of the cover, not the jar. The cover must be removed by lifting it vertically. Otherwise, the rim of the cover will catch the inner rim of the jar and chip it. Like a stopper, the cover is fitted to this particular jar. There is a number inscribed inside the cover, beneath the finial. It matches the number on the base of the jar. A star is cut into the top of the finial. The base also has a star.

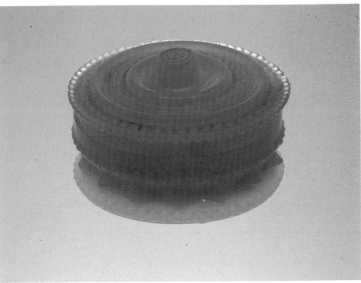

3291 PRESSED MITRE DIAMOND WITH BEADING OINTMENT BOX

1½" H. x 2¾" Dia. 1840–1845

These small containers held salves that were the consistency of vaseline. The earliest of them had glass covers. There are two rings of beads on the upper surface of the cover, alternating with plain concentric rings. Concentric rings are repeated on the finial. A third ring of beads surrounds the cover, just underneath the very edge. The height of this box indicates large capacity, but the base is ½" thick and is only slightly recessed. When emptied, this piece may have seen double duty as a patch box.

3292 PRESSED OINTMENT BOXES

(a) Mitre Diamond with Beading
(b) Diamond Panel 1⅛" H. x 2¾" Dia. 1840–1860

Each of the ointment boxes shown here matches fragments dug in quantity at the Boston and Sandwich Glass Company site, but they were not produced exclusively at Sandwich. They were also produced by the New England Glass Company, so they are not difficult to find. Ointments were applied topically to burns and skin disorders. Before Federal control of food and drug advertising, a purchased remedy was expected to cure everything. Box A has the same pattern as the box with the glass cover. It is not as high, but holds the same amount. It has a thin base, so the rim begins just above the beading. It holds the same amount of ointment as a box with a thicker base, but many more could be made from the same amount of glass. Box B has a raised diamond in each of twelve panels.

3293 PRESSED OINTMENT BOXES
(a) Outlined Diamond with Beading 1" H. x 2⅝" Dia.
(b) Concave Panels, standing on its side 1⅛" H. x
    2¾" Dia. 1840–1860

Ointment boxes were made in clear glass as well as fiery opalescent. There are degrees of opalescence. Some boxes barely have color, and others that are very fiery have bases that are almost transparent. Covers in good condition are difficult to locate because the salve ate into the soft metal and dissolved it. Note how shallow the boxes are compared to the penny in the foreground.

3294 PRESSED OINTMENT BOXES
(a) Concave Panels 1⅛" H. x 2¾" Dia.
(b) Diamond, Fleur-de-lis and Oval in Panels
    1⅛" H. x 2⅝" Dia. 1840–1860

Some covers are pewter, some are white metal, and some are tin. They do not fit tightly. The boxes could be turned upside down without spilling the contents. We have seen an ointment box with an original paper label affixed to the top of the cover, but the words were illegible. Box A has twelve concave panels. A blue box in our collection has straight sides with sixteen panels. The base is marked "DR. L. C. DALE'S PATENT 1850". Box B has nine panels, with each motif repeated three times.

3295 PRESSED OINTMENT BOX
⅞" H. x 2" Dia. 1850–1873

Inexpensive commercial containers were made by many glass factories, including the Boston and Sandwich Glass Company. Inside the cover is the mark "J. P. PRAY'S ROSALINE NEW YORK". *Rosaline* was a face cream or ointment made from crushed rose hips. The recessed base is marked "½ oz". This indicates the capacity of the box, not necessarily the weight of the contents. The same box without the lettering inside the cover might contain patches, which weighed practically nothing. This piece is fiery opalescent, which helps us to date it. It, and many like it, were dug at the factory site. The 1887 sloar book notes that Edward Brady's shop made 498 ¾ oz. rosaline boxes for Pray the week of August 1.

3296 PRESSED OPAL POMADE BOXES
(a) Large 1¼" H. x 2½" Dia.
(b) Small 1⅛" H. x 1¾" Dia. 1873–1887
A list of pressed ware recorded by Sandwich union members in 1883 includes two-ounce pomades. A trade catalog from a Pittsburgh firm indicates that these small round containers were also sold as patch boxes. The tiny silk patches were used by Nineteenth Century women as "beauty spots" to hide defects and smallpox scars. These boxes were dug at the Boston and Sandwich Glass Company site. The glass is poor quality because they were made for one-time use only. A circle about the size of a penny is in the inside center of the cover and base of the larger box. Numbers or letters molded into the recessed base do not always indicate capacity. The smaller box is marked "700¼". The style or stock number is 700 and the capacity is ¼ ounce. If there were several identical molds for the same container, a small letter or number identified each mold in case there was a problem in the pressing. Box A is marked "2" on the base and box B is marked "C".

3297 PRESSED OPAL PATCH BOX DECORATED WITH LADY TRANSFER PRINT
1½" H. x 3¼" Dia. 1873–1887
This 1½ ounce patch box was meant to be used on dressing table. To make the piece more decorative, a decal was transferred to the cover. A gilded ring surrounds the cover and the base of the box. Do not overlook a good Sandwich decorated piece because the transfer faces in the opposite direction. Decals were purchased by the sheet from outside sources and were changed from time to time. It in no way affects value. *Courtesy, Sandwich Glass Museum, Sandwich Historical Society*

3298 PRESSED OPAL OVAL BOX
1⅝" H. x 4" L. x 2½" W. 1873–1887
The meanings of words change over the years, so we must consider these changes in our study. The 1847 edition of Webster's dictionary describes *box* as "a case of any size and of any material". In 1872, *rectangular* was still not a prerequisite. American Flint Glass Workers Union records from Sandwich list several types of boxes: Quinlan, white boxes, new white boxes. Without catalogs, we cannot relate their listing to known sizes and shapes. The Boston and Sandwich Glass Company sloar book in 1887 listed Quinlan boxes as small as ¼ ounce. Many types of ointments and salves were marketed as well as patches used for "beauty spots" to hide facial scars of smallpox. Many containers found general secondary use after they were emptied. The base of this oval box is recessed ¼". Oval boxes also came with metal covers. *Courtesy, Sandwich Glass Museum, Sandwich Historical Society*

3299 PRESSED ROUGE BOXES

1¼" H. x 1¼" Dia. 1850–1887

These tiny pieces are sometimes sold as pill boxes or ring holders. We purchased one that had rouge in it. It would be difficult to transfer rouge from one container to another, so we believe this was the original use.

3300 PRESSED ROUGE BOX FRAGMENTS

a) Blue green, chip on base
b) Green, perfect
c) Blue, destroyed rim
d) Light blue cover

All of these pieces are dug fragments. The great assortment of colors is an indication of their popularity. They were made at very little cost because they were made from the puddles of good glass left toward the bottom of the batch after the bulk of the glass was used up. This was called "finishing out the pot". Some have a satin finish.

INVENTORY OF SANDWICH GLASS

No.	Description	Condition	Date Purchased	Amount	Date Sold	Amount

CHAPTER 10

TOYS

1825–1897

The earliest glass houses in the United States devoted some part of their production to satisfying the needs of children. Glassworkers took home for their own children free-blown toys made during the idle time between batches. The toys were so loved that they soon became a regular part of a glassmaking day, and special child and doll-size molds were made so that toys could be commercially marketed. It was necessary for every glass house to include tiny items in their inventory. As each shop neared the bottom of a batch of glass, all of the glass was not usable. Pools of good glass remained that could be used for pieces such as eye cups or individual salts and toys. This was called "finishing out the batch".

On July 9, 1825, the first day that the Sandwich Glass Manufactory produced glass commercially, fifteen toy decanters were listed in the company record book. On July 10, 220 blown molded toy wines were produced at a cost of four cents each. Over one thousand toy articles were manufactured during July in the first three weeks of production. Included were tumblers and *jugs*, which was the term for pitchers. By August 1825, toy hats and toy patty-pans were added to the production line. A *patty* was a small pie—we would call it a tart. On June 23, 1827, Michael Doyle's shop made 166 blown molded, footed, toy lamps. Three styles of toy lamps were listed in July, and style number three was made with and without a handle. Heavy production of toys continued throughout the life of all four major companies—Sandwich Glass Manufactory, Boston and Sandwich Glass Company, Cape Cod Glass Works, and Cape Cod Glass Company—and the minor companies that attempted to reestablish the glass industry in the 1890's.

The first of the toys made at the Sandwich Glass Manufactory were free-blown and blown molded. Although we have fragments of this type of glass, it is virtually impossible to identify them as having been intended for a toy. However, by the second half of 1827, the pressing of glass became established, beginning with a thick cup-plate-like toy plate and advancing to a variety of doll-size tableware. Once pressing began at Sandwich, the manufacture of toys increased substantially, so that, today, large quantities of

pressed toy items are available to the collector.

By 1830, a large percentage of adult glassware was being pressed in intricate patterns that had a stippled background. These ornate patterns, called *Lacy*, were duplicated in the pressing of toys. Floral motifs used on adult Lacy salts lent themselves to tiny dishes. Toy plates, vegetable dishes, bowls, and tureens were made in clear glass and several colors. A limited number of patterns predominated: diamonds, scrolls, leaves, lilies, roses, rosettes and fans. Several of these motifs were combined on one piece, such as diamonds and scrolls or diamonds, scrolls and lilies. Although the same pattern or combination of patterns might not appear on every piece, the various table pieces combined nicely to make a set of doll-size dishes that brought happiness to the little girl who was fortunate to own it.

During this period, the same shape used in Lacy toy dishes was also pressed in a pattern of simple panels. Variety was created by combining the panels with rayed bases or concentric rings. As the Lacy era came to an end in the 1850's, the style and character of toys kept pace with changes in the style of their adult-size counterparts. The patterns with stippled backgrounds were discontinued and replaced with a larger assortment of paneled pieces. Finally, even the patterned bases disappeared, giving way to plain ones. The simplest possible forms were used to mass produce large quantities of toys for the ever expanding American market.

As stated earlier, glass factories in Sandwich were not the only ones that devoted part of production to children's articles. The book *M'Kee Victorian Glass*, published by The Corning Museum of Glass, reproduces five catalogs of glassware manufactured by McKee and Brothers, a Pittsburgh company, between 1859 and 1871. Toy candlesticks and flat irons scaled for doll houses, identical to the Sandwich products, are illustrated, proving that identical molds were purchased from commercial mold makers and were filled with glass by different companies. This makes attribution of a random piece to a particular factory impossible unless its history can be traced and documented by family records, in lieu of glass company records. Experts who use catalogs as the only source of proof for origin are limiting their attribution to only one company, when other companies frequently made the same pieces.

Glass toys came in several sizes. Some were scaled for small dolls and doll houses, others for large dolls and play houses large enough for a child to enter and set up housekeeping. Still others were sized to a child's hands, such as lamps with working burners, and fair sized tumblers. The McKee catalogs show a fluted toy tumbler that holds ½ gill (four tablespoons or ¼ cup). This is twice the capacity of the tumbler we usually think of as a toy—the size often referred to as a "whiskey taster" that holds two tablespoons of liquid. Both of these tumblers are larger in scale than the Lacy cup and saucer. Yet all are listed as toys in the records, making it difficult for us to differentiate between pieces meant to be used by a child in play or at the dinner table and pieces intended as doll dishes.

In his book *The Romance of Old Sandwich Glass*, author Frank W. Chipman lists an inventory of molds belonging to the Boston and Sandwich Glass Company. The list was taken from original factory records. It is undated, but the mold for a General Grant cigar holder is included. Ulysses S. Grant was a General of the Union Army in the Civil War. He was elected President in 1868, so we conclude that the list is an inventory taken in the mid-1860's. The factory owned the following toy molds:

Centre bowl (Ed. note: a compote)
Pitcher
Decanter
Dish & cover
Nappie & top
Basin
Tureen
Sugar
Cream
Cup & saucer
Tumbler
Lemonade
Salt
Mustard

A Cape Cod Glass Company list of glass (reproduced in its entirety in Chapter 4) includes the following selection of toys. The list dates from 1864 to 1869, so it is not likely that any of the pieces would be Lacy.

Tumblers
Lemonades
Cups and Saucers
Sugars
Creams
Butters
Salts
Nappies, (3 in.)
Ewers and Basins
Decanters
Flat Irons
Oval Dishes
Candlesticks
Castor Bottles
Castors, (4 bottles)

The Cape Cod Glass Company was primarily a wholesale operation and sold most of its inventory in bulk. Toys were shipped by the box lot, not by the set. Catalogs from several glass companies indicate that, in the 1860's, the four-piece table set so important to collectors of adult tableware had not come into being. Sugars, creams, spoon holders, and butters (covered nappies) were sold individually and were not necessarily shown on the same page in the catalogs. The Cape Cod Glass Company did not list a toy spoon holder at all.

Note the listing of a 3" nappie. A *nappie* is a shallow bowl normally listed with full-size pressed pattern glass. The 3" nappie would be considered a scarce piece by a pattern glass collector and would not be considered at all by a toy collector. The Cape Cod list proves that the same piece had several uses. There are no illustrations, but this example raises another problem. Elsewhere in the Cape Cod document are listed 3" individual butters and 3" plates, in addition to 3" nappies. Were these pieces interchangeable with toys? Whatever the answer, it is clear that some pieces originally intended as toys have found their way into other categories and are now being admired as free-blown "courting lamps", blown molded "whiskey tasters", pressed cup plates, pressed Lacy salts, and pressed pattern honey dishes.

By the time the Boston and Sandwich Glass Company closed, the smallest scale toys were no longer in style. Toy four-piece table sets were marketed by Pittsburgh houses, but we find no evidence of Sandwich manufacture. Pressed toy tumblers are listed in a record book kept by member of the American Flint Glass Workers Union Local No. 16 that is dated 1879–1883. Manufacture of these tumblers and some larger scale toy caster bottles were continued by several glass companies that occupied the Boston and Sandwich Glass Company site, judging by the many poor quality fragments that were found near the surface in the factory yard.

THESE SIMPLE HINTS WILL HELP YOU IDENTIFY SANDWICH TOYS.

Study the simple diamonds, lilies, roses, rosettes, leaves, scrolls and fans that are used on Lacy pieces and accept any combination of these patterns as a product of the Boston and Sandwich Glass Company.

Scallops on the rims and bases of Lacy pieces are all the same size.

If a tiny handle makes adult use awkward, the piece was intended to be a toy.

To identify use based on form, compare toys with their adult counterparts.

At antiques shows and flea markets, expect Sandwich toys to be mixed in with salts, shot glasses, penny candy scoops, cup plates, individual butter plates, nut dishes, and other similar small pieces—antique and contemporary.

On toy Sandwich candlesticks, the inside diameter of the socket is approximately ¼", much larger than the ³⁄₁₆ diameter of a present-day birthday candle. If the hole in the socket is small, the piece was not made at Sandwich.

301 FREE-BLOWN TOY HAND LAMP

½" H. to top of neck 1825–1835

The dimensions of the font, the little handle and the size of the cork tube burner tell us that this lamp was meant for a child. Ignore the crimped trailing end of the applied handle and study just the portion that is held. The handle that would easily slip out of an adult hand would be comfortable between the thumb and fingers of a child. The tube is only ¹³⁄₁₆" long with an outside diameter of ³⁄₃₂". The tube has the tiniest slot for the needle-like pickwick used to raise the wick. Original factory documents prove that toy lamps were made in abundance and sold readily. Larger handled lamps for adults were called *chamber lamps*. We have no evidence in factory records of lamps specifically designed to be "courting" or "sparking" lamps. *The Bennington Museum, Bennington, Vermont*

302 BLOWN MOLDED RIBBED TOY HAND LAMP *McKearin GI-7*

⅛" H. to top of font; 2¼" Dia. 1825–1835

Early hand lamps made for children can be distinguished from small "courting" or night lamps by the size of the handle. If the hole will not take an adult finger, the lamp was made for a child. The amount of whale oil that this lamp would hold is limited. The glass was blown into a ribbed ball stopper mold, and reworked to form a melon font. The single tube burner is the earliest type used at Sandwich. It is held in place by the pressure of a cork stopper against the rim. According to writings of C. C. P. Waterman dated April 27, 1865, "Mr. Jarves invented the cork tubes for lamps which he sold to William Carleton (owner of a Boston lamp manufacturing business and a director of the Boston and Sandwich Glass Company) for $100." The tin plate through which the tube passes is marked "PATENT". *Courtesy, Sandwich Glass Museum, Sandwich Historical Society*

303 BLOWN MOLDED TOY HAND LAMP

a) Matching stopper 3⅜" H. x 2½" Dia.

b) Toy hand lamp 2" H. 1828–1835

Toy lamps were often made from the same molds that were used to make decanter stoppers. The rayed pattern that is on the top of this stopper became the rayed base of the lamp. The glass that would have formed the plug of the stopper was sheared off, leaving a rim that was the right diameter for a tiny whale oil burner. The Bennington Museum also has a candlestick made from a stopper mold, which can be seen in photo 4001. *The Bennington Museum, Bennington, Vermont*

3304 BLOWN MOLDED DIAMOND DIAPER TOY LAMP

McKearin GII-18 2" H. x 1⅞" Dia. 1825–1826
This tiny lamp originated in a mold that had a band c
diamond diapering around the center with bands of vert
cal ribs above and below. After the glass was remove
from the mold, the piece was crimped below the diapere
band to form the ribbed foot and drawn in at the top t
form a rim to fit the tin whale oil burner. Subsequen
photos show similar pieces that, when removed from th
mold, were formed into a footed jug and a footed handle
custard. Sixteen diamonds in a circle form the base pa
tern. Blown molded pieces that can be identified as to
from factory records command higher prices than the
adult-size counterparts. *The Bennington Museum, Benningtor
Vermont*

3305 FREE-BLOWN TOY LAMP WITH DIAMOND CHECK TOY PLATE BASE

4⅛" H. to top of font; 2⅜" Dia. 1828–1835
This is the child's version of the adult cup plate lamp. Th
base of this lamp was pressed in the 2⅛" Dia. Diamon
Check toy plate mold. Note its thickness, indicating earl
manufacture. The solid knopped standard was free-blow
as part of the font and applied to the center of the botton
of the plate. All early lamps with plate bases have a roug
pontil mark underneath, on what would be the smoot
upper surface of the plate. Cork tube whale oil burners ar
still often found on their lamps. *The Bennington Museun
Bennington, Vermont*

3306 FREE-BLOWN TOY LAMP WITH DIAMOND CHECK TOY PLATE BASE AND MALLORY LAMP GLASS

(a) Lamp 3⅞" H. x 2¼" Dia.
(b) Mallory lamp glass (chimney) 2½" H. x 1⅛" Dia.
    at bottom flare
(c) Combined size 6¼" H. x 2¼" Dia. 1828–1835
Here is the same lamp with the addition of an applie
handle. The ridged collar, called a *cap* by the industry, wa
permanently fastened to the rim of the font. This was th
earliest threaded collar used at Sandwich. A threade
whale oil burner was fitted to it, providing more stabilit
than a cork tube burner. The blown cylindrical chimne
was illustrated by Deming Jarves in a letter dated Noven
ber 23, 1825. It was called a *Mallory lamp glass*. Today w
would not allow a child to play with fire, but if childre
did not learn to handle open flame, they would be left wit
no light at all. They learned to respect fire at an early ag
but reports of death due to accidents when handling lamp
were common. *Courtesy, Sandwich Glass Museum, Sandwi
Historical Society*

3307 BLOWN MOLDED RIBBED TOY TUMBLER

McKearin GI-6 1⅞" H. x 1¾" Dia. 1830–1835
The pattern of vertical ribs is the simplest of the blown molded geometric patterns. This makes attribution to the Boston and Sandwich Glass Company extremely difficult unless the piece is accompanied by documentation. The rim was reworked, wiping out the already shallow pattern. Often called a "whiskey taster" because of its present-day usage, it was listed as a toy tumbler in the company sloar book. *Courtesy, Sandwich Glass Museum, Sandwich Historical Society*

3308 BLOWN MOLDED DIAMOND DIAPER

McKearin GII-16
(a) Toy tumbler 1¾" H. x 1⅝" Dia.
(b) Toy hat salt 1¾" H. x 2" Dia. 1825–1830
Note that both pieces were blown in the same pattern. The bands of ribbing and diamond diapering are identical on the tumbler and the hat. The tumbler has a plain base with an open pontil mark, and the hat has concentric circles on the base. Both blown molded toy hats and hat salts are listed in company records. The Sandwich Glass Manufactory sloar book shows that 250 toy hats and 600 toy decanters were made from the same batch of glass. *Courtesy, Sandwich Glass Museum, Sandwich Historical Society*

3309 BLOWN MOLDED DIAMOND DIAPER TOY TAPER TUMBLER

McKearin GII-19 2½" H. x 1⅞" Dia. 1830–1835
If a piece was blown into a mold, the pattern can be felt on the inside of the piece because the hot glass conformed to the contours in the mold. This pattern was identified from fragments dug at the site of the Boston and Sandwich Glass Company. The bands of vertical ribbing and diamond diapering are similar to the tumbler shown previously, but a narrow band of diagonal ribbing was added. Blown molded pieces are generally named for the pattern in the widest band or the motif that is most dominant. Study this piece carefully—it has been reproduced.

3310 BLOWN MOLDED DIAMOND DIAPER TOY HANDLED CUSTARD

McKearin GII-19 1¾" H. x 1½" Dia. 1825–1826
There is no question that these small items were for children. The strap handle and the size of the bowl do not lend themselves to adult use. The bowl holds slightly over one tablespoon of liquid. The handle is attached to the bowl with such delicacy that it would be an easy matter to snap it off. Fragments in large quantities have been found matching the base and the rim in an area of the dump site at the factory that indicates very early production. If this piece had been made in 1900, it would be called a "punch cup". In earlier years, handled pieces shaped like egg cups were used for custard.

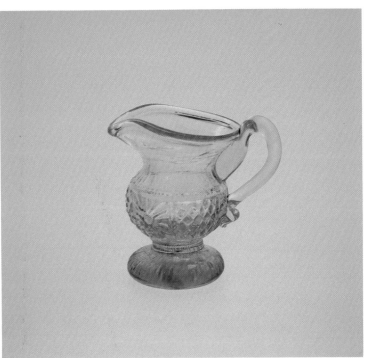

3311 BLOWN MOLDED SUNBURST TOY JUG

McKearin GIII-12 2¼" H. x 1¾" Dia. 1825–1826
This jug is about the same size as the handled custard. The base is similar to the fragments that accompany the custard. The wide band of pattern has two blocks of the sunburst motif and two blocks of diamond diapering. The rim was reworked to make a spout and the handle was applied. Note how much of the length of the handle was applied to the body. Reproductions of creamers made in the 1900's for *decorative* purposes have handles lightly attached to the body. *Courtesy of The Toledo Museum of Art (Acc. No. 71.23)*

3312 BLOWN MOLDED SUNBURST TOY JUG

McKearin GIII-12 2⅛" H. 1825–1835
It is difficult for us today to visualize these beautiful pieces in the hands of playful children. Keeping small children entertained until they were old enough to take on chores was a major part of a mother's day. Only the tiniest fingers could grasp this handle and make use of the jug's contents. This is a piece that was meant to be used—note how firmly the handle is attached. Blown molded toy jugs were listed in the company sloar book during the first month of glass production, July 1825. By the end of 1825, toys blown molded from blue glass were being made. *Courtesy Sandwich Glass Museum, Sandwich Historical Society*

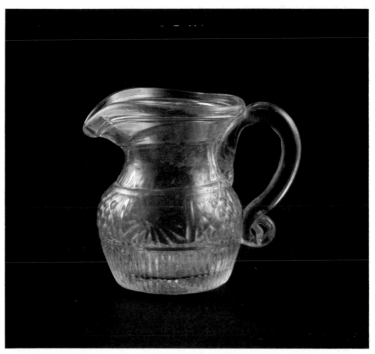

3313 BLOWN MOLDED SUNBURST TOY JUG
McKearin GIII-12 2⅛" H. 1825–1835
The earliest pieces were first crudely blown into a mold, then removed from the mold and finished by hand. How a piece was finished was left to the discretion of the worker. The blue Sunburst jug has a plain rim, but this clear jug has a rim folded to the inside. The blue piece shown above has a crimp above the curl at the bottom of the handle; this piece has only the curl. There are concentric circles on the base of the jug, but another otherwise identical jug may have a plain base. Minor differences in the patterned mold or in the hand finishing have little effect on value. However, with each passing year, the difference in value between clear and colored pieces becomes greater. *The Bennington Museum, Bennington, Vermont*

3314 BLOWN MOLDED DIAMOND SUNBURST TOY JUG
McKearin GIII-21 2¾" H. 1825–1835
Study the widest horizontal band of the pattern. It is divided into six panels. Three panels of tiny diamonds, called *diamond diapering*, alternate with three panels of a sunburst pattern. A diamond, divided into nine parts, is in the center of the sunburst. This diamond-centered sunburst indentifies the jug as *Diamond Sunburst*. It is always combined with bands of diagonal ribbing. This piece has a rayed base, but other pieces in the Diamond Sunburst pattern could have concentric circles on the base, a circle of diamonds, or no pattern at all. *The Bennington Museum, Bennington, Vermont*

3315 BLOWN MOLDED SUNBURST TOY DECANTER WITH HAND-FORMED SUNBURST STOPPER
McKearin GIII-12 3½" H. x 1⅝" Dia. 1825–1835
Deming Jarves' Sandwich Glass Manufactory opened its doors on July 4, 1825. The records show that toy decanters were made on the first full day of glassmaking, July 9. Note how the left side of the decanter is different from the right side. The mold slipped during production, causing the glass to seep into the seam and make a rounded rib the full length of the decanter. This gives the piece character and is not a defect. Articles that were blown into these early molds have soft mold marks, unlike the thin, sharp mold marks of pressed items. These early pieces have pontil marks.

3316 LACY TOY EWER AND BASIN
(a) Ewer 2½" H.
(b) Basin 1" H. x 3¼" Dia. 1835–1850
All of the pieces we call *Lacy* are pressed with a stippled background. Note the unique handle on the ewer with its three thorn-like protrusions. Note, too, the manner in which the forward part of the top of the handle is molded into the body. The mold mark can be seen on the side of the handle and across the thorn at the highest point of the handle. This is important, because it is a characteristic of the earliest pressed ewers. The body is circular, with a six-petaled rosette on each side. A basket of flowers is on each side of the lower part, and a band of flowers encircles the basin. When buying two-unit sets, make sure the color of each unit is an exact match. *Courtesy, Sandwich Glass Museum, Sandwich Historical Society*

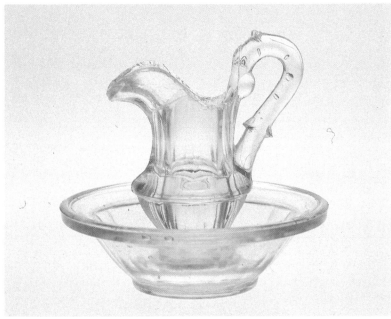

3317 PRESSED PANELED TOY EWER AND BASIN
(a) Ewer 2½" H.
(b) Basin 1" H. x 3⅛" Dia. 1840–1855
The Lacy Period came to an end after an excellent grade of glass sand was discovered in Western Massachusetts. It was no longer necessary to hide defects with a stippled background. The intricate floral pattern was replaced by simple panels, although the shape of the ewer remained the same, even to the thorns on the handle.

3318 PRESSED PANELED TOY EWERS
(a) Amethyst
(b) Green 2⅜" H. 1845–1870
Where both handles reach their highest point there appears to be a chip. However, this is deliberate delineation in the mold seam just forward of the thorn. This mold seam, which, on the Lacy ewer, crossed the handle on the thorn, has been brought forward. This change in mold design caused the hot glass to seep into the juncture where all three mold pieces met, creating a roughness that looks like a chip. A mold mark continues down the outside of the handle to the base of the ewer. Another mold mark is directly opposite, from the center under the spout to the base. This tells us that the body was molded in two pieces. A third piece formed the upper surface of the spout and the forward part of the handle. The next step in the evolution of the ewer was to eliminate the thorns entirely. The Corning Museum of Glass has such a ewer in its collection. *Courtesy, Sandwich Glass Museum, Sandwich Historical Society*

319 PRESSED PANELED TOY PITCHER AND BASIN

a) Pitcher 2¼" H.
b) Basin ⅞" H. x 3⅛" Dia. 1855–1870

Simplification continued as the ewer form was replaced by the pitcher, mirroring the style changes of adult porcelain and ironstone sets. The ornate handle was replaced by a simple one, and the spout was shortened. The panels begin at the base and continue to the rim without the interruption of the exaggerated horizontal convex band halfway down the ewer. This simple form increased productivity of the shops and kept the Sandwich glass industry competitive. *Courtesy, Sandwich Glass Museum, Sandwich Historical Society*

320 LACY POINTED OVAL TOY TUMBLERS WITH CIRCULAR BASE

a) Fiery opalescent
b) Canary 1¾" H. x 1¾" Dia. 1830–1850

Toy tumblers in this pattern were quite popular. Many have survived and are still available in several colors. Pressed patterns with stippled backgrounds are called *Lacy* today. The base is smooth underneath and flares out to give the impression of a foot. The stippling begins above this flared base. Much thought was given to the making of this tumbler. The Pointed Oval pattern is repeated five times around the body, which was pressed in a three-part mold. All three mold marks can be seen in tumbler A. The pattern was repeated twice on two sections of the mold, while the third section of the mold repeated the pattern only once and was only half the width of the other sections. If you hold tumbler A up to the light, it resembles the red and yellow color that reflects from a fire opal gemstone.

321 LACY POINTED OVAL TOY TUMBLERS

a) Fiery opalescent, circular base 1¾" H. x 1¾" Dia.
b) Blue-green, scalloped base 1¾" H. x 1⅝" Dia.
c) Clear, circular base, bottom view 1¾" H. x 1¾" Dia. 1830–1850

Lacy Pointed Oval tumblers were also produced with a scallop on a slightly raised foot. This is the rarest of the child's tumblers. Despite years of searching, each scalloped foot tumbler we have seen has been found only in the beautiful blue-green shown in the center. The upper surface of the scallops are plain, but the concave base is rayed underneath to the outer edge of each scallop. The effect is that of a footed tumbler. All Sandwich lacy pieces were made by the Boston and Sandwich Glass Company. By the time the Cape Cod Glass Works was founded, lacy glass was out of favor.

3322 LACY HEART CHILDREN'S LEMONADE
2" H. x 2" Dia. 1830-1835
On May 28, 1830, Deming Jarves was issued a patent for an improvement in glassmakers' molds. "The improvement claimed is for the joining of a handle, or handles, or other similar projections, on glass cups, by pressure, at one operation, instead of attaching them to the cup after it has been blown, in the way heretofore practiced." This piece is the earliest known example of use of the 1830 patent. Only two Lacy Heart lemonades are recorded as being in existence at this time. Three hearts alternate with three fleur-de-lys variants. This production method was used to make the Lacy Peacock Eye mustard, an item not as rare as this Heart piece. *The Bennington Museum, Bennington Vermont*

3323 PRESSED PANELED TOY TUMBLERS
1⅝" H. x 1⅝" Dia. 1845-1870
Because the use of a piece can change over the years, we may assign it to the wrong category. Today, for example, most toy tumblers would be called "whiskey tasters" by collectors because they are the size of the small shot glasses we use now to measure liquor. Many items originally listed as toys have taken on different identification. The 3" nappie that was a part of adult tableware was also included in toy listings but are not seen in glass toy collections now. When you are at a flea market or antiques show, look for toy tumblers mixed in with contemporary shot glasses, especially in clear glass.

3324 PRESSED PANELED TOY TUMBLER FRAGMENTS
(a) Whole tumbler fragment
(b) Assembled from three fragments 1⅝" H. x 1⅝" Dia. 1845-1870
Both tumblers were dug at the Boston and Sandwich Glass Company site. Tumbler A had been discarded because it had an underfill at the base. Tumbler B had an underfill on the rim. Sufficient fragments were found to prove without a doubt that they were made in Sandwich. Underfill resulting from not enough glass pressed into the mold does not detract from value today. We think of underfill and overfill as something that gives our glass character.

3325 PRESSED PRISM PANEL

(a) Blue opalescent toy tumbler
(b) Amethyst toy lemonade 1¾" H. x 1¾" Dia.
 1859–1869

Fragments of these pieces in these colors were found at the Cape Cod Glass Company site. Unfortunately, that Company's list of glassware does not identify toys by pattern name, but a King Glass Company catalog shows tumbler A as *Prism*. We are adding the word *Panel* to differentiate it from Prism pattern adult tableware, which is not paneled. In the East, small tumblers with handles were known as *lemonades*. They were not mugs. Mugs were handled pieces that are smaller in diameter at the top than at the base. The pattern and color of tumbler A (not the size) was used to make the hat cover for the Cavalier pomade shown in Chapter 9. *Courtesy, Sandwich Glass Museum, Sandwich Historical Society*

3326 PRESSED FLUTE TOY LEMONADE

1⅝" H. x 1⅝" Dia. 1840–1870

This lemonade is divided into nine flutes that come only half way up the side. The handle was pressed in one piece with the body and is in the middle of a flute. Note the excess glass inside the handle, called overfill. It may appear at any point along a seam where the mold is worn. Overfill does not change the value. *Courtesy, Sandwich Glass Museum, Sandwich Historical Society*

3327 PRESSED FLUTE TOY LEMONADE

1⅝" H. x 1⅝" Dia. 1840–1870

Here is the nine-flute lemonade accompanied by fragments dug at the Boston and Sandwich Glass Company. This is the only configuration of pressed lemonade handle that we can document as Sandwich. Clear glass lemonades are sometimes sold as penny candy scoops, and find their way into collections of store and advertising items.

3328 PRESSED FINE RIB (REEDED)
(a) Toy tumbler
(b) Toy lemonade 1¾" H. x 1¾" Dia. 1850–1870

The pattern we call Fine Rib was listed as Reeded by the companies that made it. A New England Glass Company catalog illustrates many patterns, including Reeded, that were also made at Sandwich. The smallest tumblers and lemonades shown in full-size tableware hold ⅓ pint (⅔ cup). The smallest in the Cape Cod Glass Company list is ½ gill (¼ cup). These pieces hold half that. "Whiskey tasters" are not listed, nor are they listed in the Pittsburgh area catalogs we have studied. Note how the ribs come almost to the rim, matching the rim of the fragment dug at the Boston and Sandwich Glass Company. The handle on the lemonade was applied after the piece was removed from a toy tumbler mold. Note the size of the opening, which only a child's hand could use.

3329 PRESSED FINE RIB WITH BAND TOY TUMBLERS
(a) Transparent blue-green
(b) Translucent blue 1¾" H. x 1⅝" Dia. 1850–1870

This pattern is the same shown previously with a 3⁄16" band surrounding the rim. The fragment is one of many dug at the Boston and Sandwich Glass Company site that matches the band and reeding of the whole tumbler. This tumbler is more likely to be found in a variety of colors than in clear, unlike the plain Fine Rib without the band. Toy pieces in color are considerably more valuable than clear.

3330 BLOWN CHILDREN'S MUG ENGRAVED "WARREN"
3" H. x 2¼" Dia. January 14, 1863

Henry F. Spurr, general manager of the Boston and Sandwich Glass Company in the 1880's, had a son Warren, who was born January 14, 1861. Warren was given this piece on his second birthday. The design engraved around the rim, the wreath and the eight-pointed stars can be seen on a Late Blown goblet in photo 4245 in Volume 4. Without the engraving, this piece would have been sold as an adult lemonade.

331 BLOWN CHILDREN'S MUG ENGRAVED "BABY"

" H. x 2½" Dia. 1860-1870

Descendants of the Lapham family have many pieces made at the Boston and Sandwich Glass Company for the Lapham children. Sometimes the children watched the engraver, who then presented the piece to the child as a memento of his visit. Sandwich engravers used six-pointed and eight-pointed stars to fill in the background after the border design, lettering, and wreath had been completed. The stars were quickly made by striking the side of the piece either three or four times. These copper wheel engraved designs were used until the company closed, but later pieces were blown much thinner than the one shown here.

332 LATE BLOWN CHILDREN'S MUG ENGRAVED "BABY"

⅛" H. x 2⅛" Dia. February 17, 1883

According to Sandwich Glass Museum records, this piece was made by Nathaniel Ham(b)len. The lettering and date are surrounded by a copper wheel engraved wreath of rosettes and ferns. It is interesting to study the use of various sizes of drinking vessels during different time periods. If this piece were not engraved, most experts would identify it as a "handled whiskey taster". But a study of the Boston and Sandwich Glass Company 1874 catalog shows a similar piece listed as a *children's mug*. Rays cut into the base were called *star bottom* in the catalog. *Courtesy, Sandwich Glass Museum, Sandwich Historical Society*

333 FREE-BLOWN TOY PATTY-PAN

⅜" H. x 3" Dia. 1825-1835

Whether glass or tin, a pan has sloping sides and a flat bottom. They ranged in size from large adult utility milk pans to this toy version that was in production by August 1825. The rim is folded to the outside, away from the surface that would be in contact with food. *Patties* were small pies, called tarts today. Were the toy pans for real food or mud pies? *The Bennington Museum, Bennington, Vermont*

3334 PRESSED HEXAGONAL TOY SPOON HOLDERS
(a) Translucent green
(b) Clear 1¾" H. x 1½" Dia. 1850–1870
These spoon holders have found their way into collection of "whiskey tasters" and even salts. When recognized a children's pieces, however, they are usually identified a tumblers, even though the proportions more closely re semble an adult spoon holder. Many toy spoon holder have survived. The clear one is the most common of al toy pieces. Keep in mind they have more value as to pieces than as adult pieces. When searching for this piece look for the two rows of horizontal ribbing and the roun base.

3335 PRESSED HEXAGONAL TOY SPOON HOLDER
1¾" H. x 1¼" Dia. 1850–1870
This spoon holder has six panels that extend onto the foot Note the roughness of the inside edge of the rim, indi cating rapid release from the mold. Toys were produced in great quantity, and were not fire polished or reworked in any way. Rough mold seams are not chips and do no reduce value.

3336 LACY TOY JUGS
(a) Opaque blue, scalloped base 1¾" H.
(b) Clear, circular base 1⅝" H. 1835–1850
Pitchers were called *jugs* in the early 1800's. Toy jugs were used by children to serve milk. Jug B is the most common of the Lacy pattern toys and is easily recognized by the shape of the spout and the unusually large flanged rim The handle was molded with the body. A mold mark runs up the outside of the handle and another divides the spout To minimize the seam under the spout, corrugations were put along the edge of each mold piece, resulting in a zipper-like effect. A third piece of the mold formed the top of the spout and the flanged rim. The pattern combine a diamond and scroll motif with a lily. A variation of jug A has a smaller spout with a scalloped rim. *Courtesy, Sand wich Glass Museum, Sandwich Historical Society*

337 LACY TOY CUP AND SAUCER
a) Cup 1" H. x 1⅛" Dia.
b) Saucer ⅜" H. x 1⅞" Dia. 1835-1850
This cup matches the toy jug shown previously and was molded in the same manner, even to the "zipper" that minimizes the mold mark. The diamond and scroll with lily pattern is on each side of the cup. This cup was also made with a solid, small, five-lobed handle. The saucer that always accompanies the cup does not match in pattern. Diamonds and roses are in the center, surrounded by a band of roses and rosettes. The same shape of cup and saucer was also made in a plain paneled pattern.

338 LACY TOY BOWL ON LOW FOOT
" H. x 1⅝" Dia. 1835-1850
The bowl in the photo is fiery opalescent, but it can be found in clear and a variety of colors. As with most glass toys, it is difficult to find this piece without damage because it had hard use as a plaything. The pattern of diamond and scroll with lily is repeated three times around the bowl, on each of three mold pieces. There is no pattern on the foot.

339 LACY TOY OVAL BOWL
¾" H. x 1⅞" L. x 1¼" W. 1835-1850
The lily motif is well known on adult Sandwich Lacy pieces and is repeated on many toy pieces, combined with a diamond and scroll. There is a single row of beading around the scalloped rim and no design on the base. Lacy toys tend to be thicker than the later paneled pieces, and while minor flakes are acceptable, major chipping takes away value. Keep in mind that toys are often mistaken for adult salts and nut dishes, so they have been assimilated into those categories. This bowl in particular is included in salt collections. When large salt collections come up for sale, check them for children's glass. *Courtesy, Sandwich Glass Museum, Sandwich Historical Society*

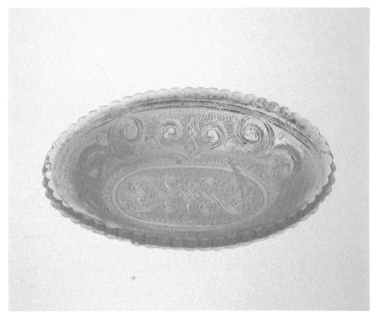

3340 LACY TOY OVAL DISH
½" H. x 3" L. x 2" W. 1835-1850
The ½" height of this dish did not allow the use of the lily
so it was eliminated from the diamond and scroll pattern
Tiny rose leaves were placed between the scrolls, and
rosettes inside the curl of the scrolls. This piece is fier
opalescent and dates from the late 1830's. The coloring re
sembles an opal gemstone and was accomplished by usin
a special formula that reacted to the reheating of clear glas
after it was taken out of the mold. Do not look for mol
marks running up the sides through the stippling. Shallow
pieces were made by using a one piece mold and
plunger. Scallops on the rims of Sandwich toys are all th
same size.

3341 LACY TOY OVAL DISHES
(a) Amethyst ½" H. x 3" L. x 2" W.
(b) Amber ⅝" H. x 3" L. x 2" W. 1835-1850
These oval dishes are the same as the fiery opalescent dish
shown previously. Note the diamond and scroll pattern o
the base. A row of beading is around the base. Rose leave
can be seen between the scrolls above the base. Chips a
large as the ones on dish B seriously hurt the value. Som
of the toy dishes are too large in scale to be used in dol
houses, but they were the correct size for the larger pla
houses. Play houses were high enough for small childre
to stand up in. None of these dishes were "miniatures"
They were produced for children's use, not display
Courtesy, Sandwich Glass Museum, Sandwich Historical Societ

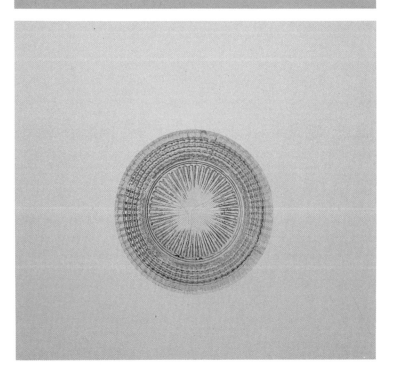

3342 PRESSED TOY PLATE
⅝" H. x 2¾" Dia. 1827-1835
The first of the pressed toy plates were thick and ver
crude. There are two such pressed patterns that can b
attributed to the Boston and Sandwich Glass Compan
without question—this piece and the Diamond Check to
plate that was sometimes used as a foot for a toy lamp
The base is rayed. There is a pattern of concentric ring
on the underside of the rim. A pattern of prisms is presse
into the upper surface of the rim. The lines of the prism
crossing the concentric rings give a diamond effect. Be
cause a pattern was pressed into the upper surface all th
way to the outer edge, they were easily damaged. Note th
diameter of the plate. If you find a larger version, it is
cup plate. Later toy plates and cup plates were smooth o
the upper surface. *Courtesy, Sandwich Glass Museum, San
wich Historical Society*

3343 PRESSED DIAMOND CHECK TOY PLATE
¼" H. x 2⅛" Dia. 1828-1835
This toy plate is often used as a base for a toy lamp. The lamp is not too difficult to find, but the plate alone is rare. When this plate was used for a lamp base, it was turned upside down, and, while hot, the stem of the lamp was applied into the Diamond Check pattern on the bottom of the plate. Look at the plate in the photo. The upper surface is smooth and the pattern shows through. There are two concentric rows of pattern on the rim. *The Bennington Museum, Bennington, Vermont*

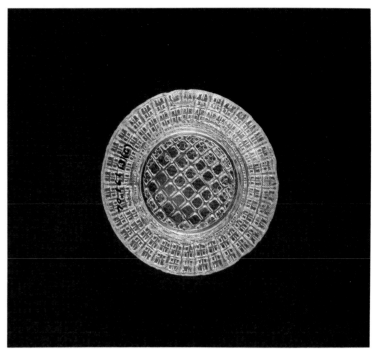

3344 LACY TOY PLATES
(a) Canary, concentric rings
(b) Clear, band of rosettes ¼" H. x 2¼" Dia.
    1835-1850
Although plate A is slightly more than 2" across, it carries all the features of adult pieces—concentric rings, Lacy pattern with stippling, and a ridged bottom. The ridge, which is the part that rests on the table, has tiny diagonal cuts that make a cable (rope) pattern. Note that the scallops on the rim are not damaged. This is unusual because they were commonly chipped when the plate was removed from the mold. Slight chipping that does not penetrate beyond the scallops should not deter from the value. Plate B has the same diamond and scroll center, surrounded by a sophisticated band of leaves and rosettes. *Courtesy, Sandwich Glass Museum, Sandwich Historical Society*

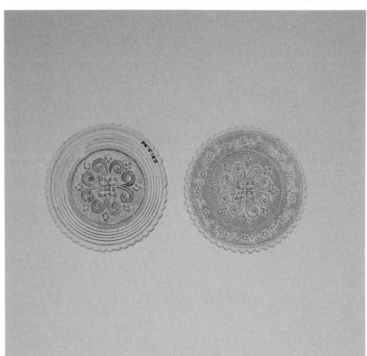

3345 LACY TOY NAPPIES ON HIGH FOOT
(a) Correct base with mold properly filled
(b) Small base from underfilled mold 2" H. x 1⅞"
    Dia. 1835-1850
A *nappie* was a shallow bowl with a flat base. If a nappie was put on a high or a low standard, the result was a piece we would call a "compote" today. Lacy pieces are pressed and usually quite thick, which allows them to withstand much abuse. The footed nappie on the left has the proper base. The small base of the nappie on the right was caused by underfilling the mold. Not enough glass was used at the time of pressing. Underfill does not change the value of a piece. Note the knop in the center of the standard. *Courtesy, Sandwich Glass Museum, Sandwich Historical Society*

3346 LACY TOY VEGETABLE DISHES ON FOOT
(a) Large, scalloped rim, ribbed foot
   1⅜" H. x 2¾" L. x 1⅞" W.
(b) Small, plain rim, scalloped foot
   1" H. x 1⅞" L. x 1¼" W. 1835–1850

The pattern on dish A consists of several elements. Scrolls surrounded the sidewalls below the scalloped rim, interrupted on each of the four sides by a three-leaved motif that resembles a fleur-de-lys. A beaded swag loops from corner to corner on the two long sides. A tiny lily and diamond covers the narrow panels making up the four corners. This piece is in scale with the largest of the Lacy toy dishes, but may have seen double duty as an adult salt. The scallops on the rim are the same width as the scallops on the base of dish B. The dimensions of the base of dish A approximate the rim of dish B. There is no doubt that both were the product of the same mold maker. Lilies cover the corner and end panels of dish B. All of the pieces we have studied are rough on the plain rim where the mold was opened. It, too, may have had another function as a toy salt.

3347 LACY TOY TUREEN
(a) Tureen 1¼" H. x 3" L. x 1⅞" W.
(b) Cover ¾" H. x 2¾" L. x 2" W.
(c) Combined size 2" H. x 3" L. x 2" W. 1835–1850

At first glance, Sandwich Lacy toy pieces seem to have varied patterns that do not match each other. It is true that there are several motifs, but they are combined so that each motif becomes an element in an overall pattern. The tureen is the only Lacy piece with a fan, but to the fan are added all the other elements. Each side of the fan extends into a scroll. A lily is at the end of each scroll and a rosette is centered in the curl of each scroll. There are two rosettes on the base. Their six petals are the same as that on the ewer in photo 3316. Here they are surrounded by a cable. Fans and scrolls are on the cover, and a row of beading surrounds a quatrefoil finial. This tureen should have a tray that matches in color. There is also a larger size toy tureen. *Courtesy, Sandwich Glass Museum, Sandwich Historical Society*

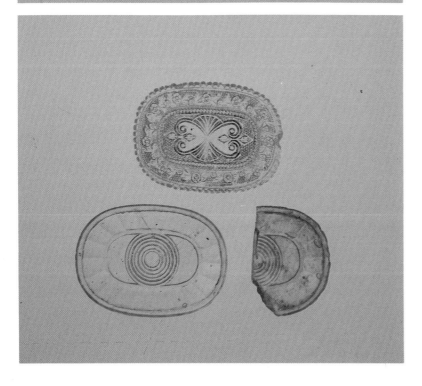

3348 PRESSED TOY TRAYS FOR TUREENS
(a) Lacy ⅜" H. x 2¾" L. x 1⅞" W.
(b) Paneled ⅜" H. x 2¾" L. x 2" W. 1835–1850

Tray A was made to be used with the Lacy tureen. Fans and scrolls are in the center, and diamonds have been added. The ridge that rests on the table has a cable pattern. There is a band of leaves with large and small rosettes—no roses. Even scallops make up the edge. We believe tray B was meant to be combined with a pressed paneled tureen. We have never located one, but it could very well be in a salt collection without its cover and tray. For a tureen, the distinguishing feature is two curled handles. We have seen the paneled tray combined with the Lacy tureen, but if you find such a mixture, you can be sure the pieces were combined at a later date. A married set does not have the value of a set that was assembled at the time of its manufacture. The fragment was dug at the Boston and Sandwich Glass Company site and is one of many found.

349 PRESSED PANELED

A) Toy plate, concentric circles ¼" H. x 2¼" Dia.
   1835–1850
B) Toy nappie, rayed base ½" H. x 2" Dia.
   1850–1870

Plate A is flat with eighteen panels and concentric circles on the base. The two marks on the left are airtrapped bubbles. They do not deter from the value of the plate unless the bubble breaks out. B is a nappie, or shallow bowl. Note its rayed center. It is not a star—the rays extend to the edge of the bottom. The nappie has fourteen panels. The panels on both pieces are approximately the same width. In larger sizes, the center dimension was changed and the number of panels increased. The tureen tray has twenty panels.

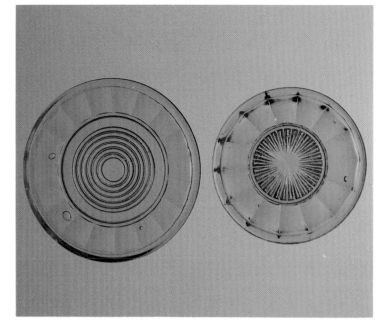

350 PRESSED TOY BOWLS

A) Large paneled, on foot 1⅜" H. x 2" Dia.
B) Small fluted ¾" H. x 1¼" Dia. 1850–1870

The simple lines of the paneled and fluted pieces were used throughout this period. The Lacy Period had come to an end, and the pressed floral and geometric patterns that were fashionable during the last quarter of the century were not made in Sandwich. Note the lack of pattern on the foot of bowl A, which has fourteen panels. The base of B is also plain. This twelve-flute piece is usually combined with the paneled nappie in photo 3349 to make a handleless cup and deep saucer. Even though paneled dishes were produced after Lacy ones, there are less of them now. Look for bowl A in salt collections. *Courtesy, Sandwich Glass Museum, Sandwich Historical Society*

351 PRESSED PANELED TOY SUGAR BOWL

A) Bowl 1⅛" H. x 1⅜" Dia.
B) Cover 1" H. x 1½" Dia.
C) Combined size 2" H. x 1½" Dia. 1850–1870

Panels are simply and quickly pressed, yet give a piece some design quality. Twelve panels are on the bowl and there is no pattern on the foot. The cover has twelve matching panels that stop short of the circular nippled finial. Although these details are obvious in the photo, either unit separately could easily be overlooked in an antiques shop. Paneled pieces are often thought to be of twentieth century manufacture. The bowl alone might be considered a Midwest salt or nut dish. The cover might find its way into a box of odd parts or stoppers. The rule for quality stoppers holds true for toy covers—do not be afraid to purchase the cover alone. The bottom unit will eventually surface, and most of the value of the complete piece is in the cover. *Courtesy, Sandwich Glass Museum, Sandwich Historical Society*

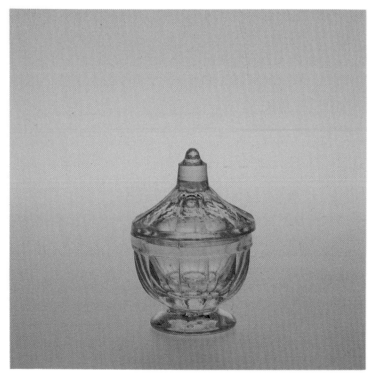

3352 PRESSED PANELED TOY NAPPIE
(a) Nappie bottom unit ⅞" H. x 1¾" Dia.
(b) Cover 1⅛" H. x 1¾" Dia.
(c) Combined size 1¾" H. x 1¾" Dia. 1850–1870
The raised base gives the impression of a deep bowl, bu
this piece may have been the paneled version of a shallo
nappie. With a cover, it may have been used for butte
but we are speculating. There are eleven panels on th
nappie and cover. The panels on the cover are steppe
down from the smooth center, which has a plain finial.
band around the cover matches the band on the nappi
Courtesy, Sandwich Glass Museum, Sandwich Historical Socie

3353 PRESSED PRISM PANEL
(a) Sugar bowl without cover 1⅜" H. x 1⅜" Dia.
(b) Salt 1" H. x 1" Dia. 1860–1875
These two pieces are interesting to study. There is
doubt that they are toys. The larger piece has the form
a sugar bowl. If that was its intent, then the small pie
must be a salt. Salts were listed in the Cape Cod Gla
Company inventory, but we do not know of any actual s
identified as such by any authority on children's glass. Th
"salt" was dug from the Boston and Sandwich Glass Con
pany site. It has a high lead content and was made in th
same manner as a flat iron and candlestick. The botto
was ground flat to take away excess glass by which it w
attached to a center fountain. The larger piece was press
by a more sophisticated method and is concave under th
foot.

3354 PRESSED PRISM PANEL TOY BUTTER
(a) Nappie bottom unit ½" H. x 2⅛" Dia.
(b) Cover ⅞" H. x 1¾" Dia.
(c) Combined size 1½" H. x 2⅛" Dia. 1860–1875
These pieces were made later than the paneled pieces tha
follow the lines of Lacy toys. Like the paneled dishes with
out prisms, the panels remain the same width on a larg
piece, but the number of panels increases. There are te
plain panels alternating with ten prism panels on the bo
tom unit and the cover, yet it is obvious that the butte
matches the footed pieces that have six plain panels alte
nating with six prism panels. It would be easy to miss th
nappie bottom unit if it were on a sale table with inexpe
sive, pressed, adult, individual salts. *Courtesy, Sandwi
Glass Museum, Sandwich Historical Society*

355 BLOWN MOLDED PANELED TOY CASTER BOTTLES

a) Pepper (perforated metal shaker cap)
   3" H. x 1" Dia.
b) Mustard (pressed cover) 3" H. x 1" Dia.
c) Bitter (metal tube with screw cap)
   3⅜" H. x 1" Dia.
d) Cruet (pressed stopper) 3¾" H. x 1" Dia.
   1870–1887

These bottles were blown into a three-piece mold. Each bottle has nine panels, with three panels between each mold mark. The metal bitter bottle top is marked "LARKIN CO. BUFFALO N. Y." The Larkin Company manufactured soap and promoted its sale through the use of premiums such as this caster set. Many other glass factories in the East and Midwest produced identical toy caster bottles during this period, but the bottles dug at the Sandwich site that were damaged during manufacture prove their Sandwich origin.

356 BLOWN MOLDED TOY CASTER BOTTLES

a) Pepper (perforated metal shaker cap)
   3⅛" H. x 1" Dia.
b) Mustard (pressed cover) 3" H. x 1" Dia.
c) Cruet (pressed stopper) 3¾" H. x 1" Dia.
   1870–1897

Here is "SHERWOOD'S SQUARE TOY Caster" set exactly as pictured on the label of its original box. The mustard has a pressed glass cover, but the set is sometimes found with a metal cover with a finial. The pepper and mustard on the right were two of many bottles dug at the site of the Boston and Sandwich Glass Company. A variation of the stoppered cruet was dug that has a wide lip pulled down on opposite sides. The pressed cruet stopper in the foreground was also dug at the site. Because these caster bottles and the following ones are large in scale, and some were made from glass with no lead content, we are assigning them to the Boston and Sandwich Glass Company and one of the several glass companies that occupied the site after the Boston and Sandwich Glass Company closed.

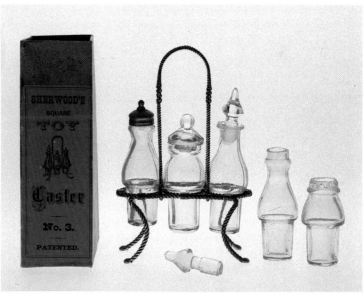

357 BLOWN MOLDED TOY CASTER BOTTLES

a) Pepper (perforated metal shaker cap)
   3⅜" H. x 1" Dia.
b) Mustard (pressed cover) 3⅛" H. x 1" Dia.
c) Cruets (pressed stoppers) 3¾" H. x 1" Dia.
   1870–1897

Doris Anderson Lechler in her book *Children's Glass Dishes, China, and Furniture* shows the box to this set. It is labeled "SHERWOOD'S PATENT TOY Caster. Four Bottles". To determine the use of toy pieces, remember that they are the same as their counterparts in adult tableware. *Peppers, mustards,* and *cruets* are the terms used on a Cape Cod Glass Company list under "Common Castor Bottles". A Pittsburgh glass company lists *vinegars* rather than *cruets*. Salt shakers were not part of a caster set. Most glass companies sold toy caster bottles, both in sets with the stand and in bulk to manufacturers like Sherwood, who would put them in their stands and box them for retail sale.

3358 BLOWN MOLDED RIBBON BAND TOY CASTER BOTTLES
(a) Pepper 3¾" H. x 1¼" Dia.
(b) Mustard 3½" H. before finishing 3¼" H. x 1¼" Dia. final size
(c) Cruet 3¾" H. x 1¼" Dia. 1880–1897

These caster bottles are never thought of as having bee made in Sandwich. If only the three pieces shown here this pattern had been dug at the factory site, we wou concur, but many more were found. Bottle B is exactly it came out of the mold. It was discarded before it w. completed. Note the ridge around the neck ¼" down fro the rim. The top of the bottle should have been sheare off at this point to accept a metal or pressed glass musta cover. Bottle A has been sheared and should have a pe forated metal shaker cap. Bottle C should have a press stopper.

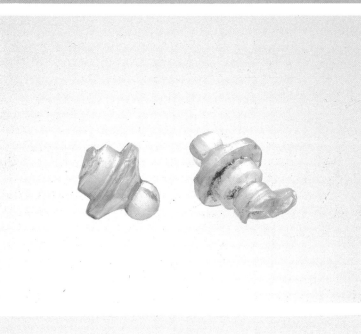

3359 PRESSED TOY MUSTARD COVERS
(a) Paneled
(b) Round with paneled finial ⅞" H. x ⅞" Dia. 1870–1897

Many covers that were made to fit the toy mustard bottl from the caster sets were dug at the site of the Boston ar Sandwich Glass Company. Cover A was probably droppe while it was being machined. It must have been very diff cult to hold. A slight gouging by the cutter's wheel can l seen on the plug. Cover B still has a large part of tl wheel mold fountain still attached, which proves that it ha to have been made at the Boston and Sandwich Gla Company site.

3360 PRESSED TOY CANDLESTICKS
1½" H. x 1" Dia. 1850–1870

Candlesticks for dollhouse tables were very popular. T date, this is the only one that can be documented, from fragments, as having been made unquestionably at Sand wich, although it was also made by McKee and Brothe in Pittsburgh. Six panels begin at the hexagonal base an end with six flutes on the socket, which has a round rin If the candlestick is an old one, the hole in the socket wi be the depth and diameter of an eraser on a commo pencil. If the socket is small enough to hold a moder birthday candle, the candlestick was not made in Sand wich. The Cape Cod Glass Company included toy candl sticks in a list of glassware, and the fragments shown he were dug at the site of the Boston and Sandwich Gla Company. Candlesticks were pressed in a wheel mol The bases were attached to a center "hub" from which tl hot metal was forced into each candlestick mold. In tl pair shown here, not enough glass went into each mol The holes in the sockets extend down through the kno and into the bases.

3361 PRESSED TOY FLAT IRONS

(a) Blue-violet, side view
(b) Green, bottom view ⅞" H. x 1⅜" L. 1850–1870

This iron was the only toy utensil produced commercially at Sandwich that was not meant to be placed on a table. Irons were made in a mold in a manner similar to the pressing of stoppers on a stopper wheel. They were attached to the fountain (hub) of the wheel at their back end. When they were broken away from the fountain, a rough extension of glass was left on the back of the iron. This excess glass was machined away and polished. Sometimes the mold mark that runs through the center of the bottom was polished, but not much time was spent on this procedure. The Boston and Sandwich Glass Company and the Cape Cod Glass Company both made flat irons. Irons were also manufactured by McKee and Brothers in Pittsburgh, Pennsylvania, where they were called *toy sad irons*.

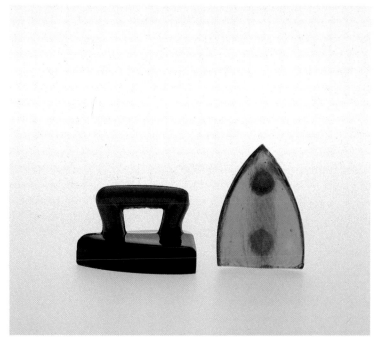

3362 SOUVENIR BRACELETS

(a) Blue and white 2¼" Dia.
(b) Red, green, white and goldstone 2½" Dia.
(c) Red, green, blue, white and goldstone 2½" Dia.
   1876

When Sandwich celebrated the Fourth of July, its glass companies entered a float in the parade. On the float was a replica of a glass furnace. Wood was aboard to stoke a fire, and gaffers and their helpers simulated the making of glass. Boxes of ready-made trinkets were hidden on the wagon and warmed up, then passed out to children. Bracelets made from imported glass rods were given to little girls. The three shown here were recovered from the 1876 Centennial parade. They were picked from the ground together with some souvenir roosters.

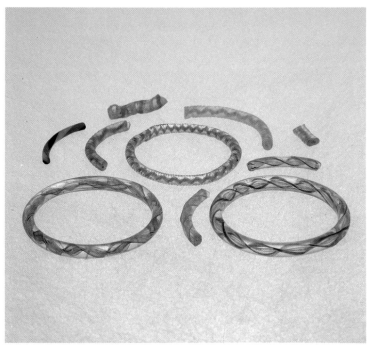

3363 FREE-FORMED SOUVENIR HEN

2½" H. 1876

A parade in a glassmaking town must have been a beautiful sight. Glassworkers hung glass ornaments from their clothing and sprinkled themselves with ground glass particles. Colorful glass balls were inserted into the muzzles of the rifles carried by the militia who accompanied the parade. Smoke pouring out of the simulated furnace chimney made many a boy believe that his souvenir hen had been made before his very eyes. A boxful of souvenirs picked up after the 1876 Centennial parade in Sandwich and hidden away for one hundred years revealed these delightful bird and bracelet trinkets.

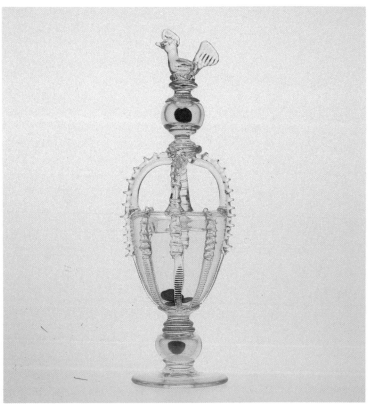

3364 FREE-FORMED BIRD WHIMSEY
6½" H. x 3⅛" Dia. 1840–1887

Odd pieces that were not made for commercial purposes are called *whimsies* because they are thought to have been made by a gaffer in his spare time. Many of them were, but many others were made to be given to children at holiday parades. Some were simple bird-forms with only the semblance of a head and tail. Others were sophisticated ornaments made up of a swan or rooster on a three to seven-knopped standard which could be used for a paperweight. This piece belongs to the family of James Lloyd and Hiram Dillaway. Similar birds were used as finials on glass banks.

3365 MONEY BOX WITH ROOSTER FINIAL
11¼" H. x 3" Dia. 1845

Banks were called *money boxes* in factory records. They are very rare today because their coins cannot be removed without breaking the glass. The bank has the form of a hollow-knopped goblet. A glass plate with a slot covers the bowl section. It is easy to drop coins into the slot, but an inside flange makes it impossible to slide them back out. The bank was assembled from five units. The base was made, then a hollow knop was blown, enclosing an 1844 half dime that moves freely inside the knop. The money box unit consists of the bowl with its slotted plate and the rods with rigaree arched over the top. Two units make up the finial, another hollow knop encloses an 1845 half dime, all surmounted with a free-form rooster. The units are held to each other with wafers. Inside the bank are ten 1853 three-cent pieces and one 1863 Indian head penny. This particular piece can be traced back to the family of James Lloyd.

3366 CUT TOY BOOKS
(a) Green canary from the family of Hiram Dillaway
    1⅛" H. x ⅞" W. 1840–1860
(b) Vasa Murrhina from the family of Charles W.
    Spurr 1" H. x ½" W. 1883–1884
(c) Dark ruby fragment dug at the Boston and
    Sandwich Glass company site. ¾" H. x ½" W.
    1850–1860

Unlike the larger cut book paperweights, little books were not a commercial product. Glass cutters used pieces of broken annealed glass, cut them into rectangular blanks, and then made the cuts that would turn them into little books. Some were presented to their loved ones as a token of affection. Others were given to their children to use as playthings. Books fashioned from beautiful glass are likely to have simple cuttings. All three have straight cuts on the covers and spine, and serrated edges called *beading*. Book B is exquisite. It has three layers of glass: Vasa Murrhina front cover, clear pages, and a blue back cover. Three edges of the book are concave to represent the pages.

3367 VASA MURRHINA CUT TOY BOOK FRAGMENT

1¼" H. x 1" W. 1883–1884

This book was dug at the site of Nehemiah Packwood's cutting shop on Willow Street, across the street from the site of the Vasa Murrhina Art Glass Company. The cutting shop was in operation from 1900 to 1922. At that time it was possible to pick up large fragments of beautiful glass simply by walking around any of the factory sites, so the date of the cutting may not coincide with the date of production of the glass. This holds true for all of the little books. The study of the Vasa Murrhina Art Glass Company and the Packwood cutting shops are in Volume 4 of this series.

3368 CUT OVERLAY TOY BOOK

1¼" H. x ⅞" W. 1874–1887

This book is from the John B. Vodon family collection and is believed to have belonged to one of his children. Vodon was an engraver who came to work for the Boston and Sandwich Glass Company in the early 1870's. The red overlay glass is good quality, but the cutting isn't. Vodon's three sons all became glass cutters, so it is possible that this piece was a first attempt by one of them. If so, the cutting could date from after the closing of the Boston and Sandwich Glass Company. Understand that, if you were to find this piece at an antiques show or flea market, there would be no way to attribute it to a particular glass factory. Only documented family pieces from family collections can be attributed with certainty. Vodon went on to establish his own cutting and engraving shop at Spring Hill in Sandwich. For information on glass cut and engraved by J. B. Vodon and Son, see Volume 4.

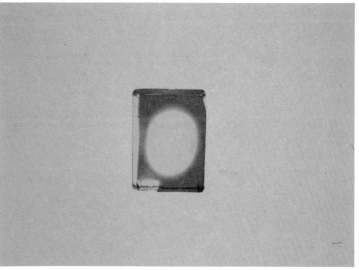

3369 CUT TOY BOOK FRAGMENT

2" H. x 1½" W. 1900–1922

It is thought that simple books with scant detail were meant to be used as the "family Bible" in a little girl's doll house. Fragments cut into book shapes were dug in areas known to have been used as a dump by the Boston and Sandwich Glass Company in the 1830's, showing that books for toys and larger book paperweights were made over the entire period that glass was cut in Sandwich. This book fragment was excavated from the Willow Street site of Nehemiah Packwood's cutting shop.

3370 CUT TOY BOOKS
(a) Octagon Diamond 1½" H. x 1¼" W. 1870–1887
(b) Checkered Diamond fragment 1" H. x ¾" W. 1870–1887
(c) Alternate Block Diamond 1" H. x ¾" W. 1888–1891
(d) Nailhead Diamond fragment ⅝" H. x ½" W. 1890–1900

Book A is a beautifully executed piece in a design frequently used by the Boston and Sandwich Glass Company. Three edges are concave to form pages. Book B was dug at the Boston and Sandwich site. Book C is from the family of James Lloyd. The glass lacks brilliance and does not fluoresce under a black light. It has the same color of documented glass from the Sandwich Co-operative Glass Company, in which Lloyd figured prominently. The design was cut with little skill and is similar to other pieces attributed to this company. Book D was also dug at the Boston and Sandwich site. Its design was in vogue after the close of the Boston and Sandwich Glass Company, so we attribute it to N. Packwood and Company. They rented the cutting shop until 1900.

3371 CUT OVERLAY TOY BOOK FRAGMENTS
(a) Alternate Block Diamond ⅝" H. x ½" W.
(b) Octagon Diamond 1" H. x ¾" W. 1870–1887

The penny clearly shows the size of such books. Book A would be completely covered if the penny were placed on top. Watch for toy books in display cases at antiques shows. They are often marked "samples", although we have not been able to document their commercial sale in any of the catalogs we have studied from cutting shops in the East or Midwest. The books are intricately cut on one cover. The other cover is cut in a simple design like photo 3366. Note the single diagonal lines cut through every other Block Diamond in Book A. When two parallel diagonal lines are made, they cut through the corners of the Block Diamonds, resulting in the Octagon Diamonds of Book B. Both were dug at the Boston and Sandwich Glass Company site.

CHAPTER 11

THE CREATIONS OF NICHOLAS LUTZ DURING HIS YEARS AT SANDWICH

1870–1892

Nicholas J. Lutz stands high among the names of those who helped make Sandwich glass famous. He was responsible for bringing to the American glass industry several techniques that originated in Europe. Using skills he had acquired in France, he led the way in the design and manufacture of paperweights, striped glass and threaded glass. He encased ribbons of colored glass in clear glass rods and found ways to assemble them into lamps and tableware. He combined small amounts of colored glass with large amounts of clear glass in ingenious ways, and thus made it possible for the Boston and Sandwich Glass Company to compete inexpensively and profitably in the art glass market. He also developed methods for mass producing his work, making it possible for today's collector to find excellent examples of Sandwich glass made by Lutz and the men he trained.

Lutz was born to Nicholas and Ursula Lutz in Munzthal-Saint Louis, France, on February 21, 1835. His father was a skilled glass blower, like many of his relatives. Young Nicholas was apprenticed in 1845, at the age of ten, to the Cristalleries de Saint-Louis. Seven years later, he completed his apprenticeship and served the four years in military service required by the French government. At the age of twenty-one he returned to Saint Louis to improve his skills in making blown tableware and paperweights. Toward the end of 1860, production of paperweights had peaked in Europe. Now twenty-five, Lutz and six other glassworkers immigrated to New York City. Early in 1861 he began to work for Christian Dorflinger in Brooklyn.

Dorflinger had left the Saint Louis factory in 1846. After working in Philadelphia, Pennsylvania, and Camden, New Jersey, he established the Long Island Flint Glass Works in Brooklyn in 1852. He went on to establish two more factories in Brooklyn, one on Plymouth Street in 1858, and a third on Commercial Street in 1860. This last venture was the Greenpoint glassworks, noted for making Dorflinger's finest glass, and this is where Lutz was employed. Dorflinger himself left Brooklyn in 1863, planning to retire near White Mills, Pennsylvania. But by late 1865, he was hard at work in a new facility in White Mills. He moved experienced workers, including Nicholas Lutz, to

White Mills from his Brooklyn plants. By this time Lutz had expanded his area of expertise and was making other types of glass, such as stemware, finger bowls and inkwells. In the spring of 1867, he completed his employment with Christian Dorflinger and moved to the Boston area to work at the New England Glass Company in Cambridge.

Lutz brought with him the skills that allowed the New England Glass Company to engage successfully in the

Nicholas Lutz, head gaffer. *Courtesy, Sandwich Glass Museum, Sandwich Historical Society*

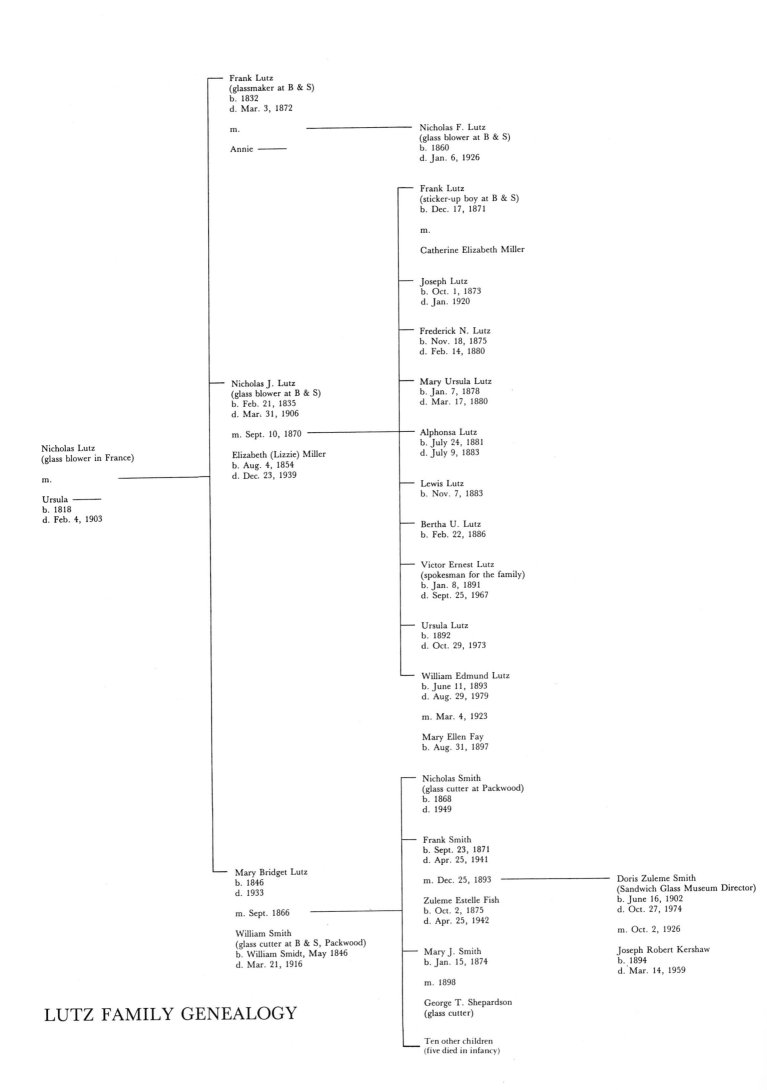

Frank Lutz
(glassmaker at B & S)
b. 1832
d. Mar. 3, 1872

m.

Annie ———

Nicholas F. Lutz
(glass blower at B & S)
b. 1860
d. Jan. 6, 1926

Frank Lutz
(sticker-up boy at B & S)
b. Dec. 17, 1871

m.

Catherine Elizabeth Miller

Joseph Lutz
b. Oct. 1, 1873
d. Jan. 1920

Frederick N. Lutz
b. Nov. 18, 1875
d. Feb. 14, 1880

Mary Ursula Lutz
b. Jan. 7, 1878
d. Mar. 17, 1880

Nicholas J. Lutz
(glass blower at B & S)
b. Feb. 21, 1835
d. Mar. 31, 1906

m. Sept. 10, 1870

Elizabeth (Lizzie) Miller
b. Aug. 4, 1854
d. Dec. 23, 1939

Alphonsa Lutz
b. July 24, 1881
d. July 9, 1883

Lewis Lutz
b. Nov. 7, 1883

Bertha U. Lutz
b. Feb. 22, 1886

Victor Ernest Lutz
(spokesman for the family)
b. Jan. 8, 1891
d. Sept. 25, 1967

Ursula Lutz
b. 1892
d. Oct. 29, 1973

William Edmund Lutz
b. June 11, 1893
d. Aug. 29, 1979

m. Mar. 4, 1923

Mary Ellen Fay
b. Aug. 31, 1897

Nicholas Lutz
(glass blower in France)

m.

Ursula ———
b. 1818
d. Feb. 4, 1903

Nicholas Smith
(glass cutter at Packwood)
b. 1868
d. 1949

Frank Smith
b. Sept. 23, 1871
d. Apr. 25, 1941

m. Dec. 25, 1893

Zuleme Estelle Fish
b. Oct. 2, 1875
d. Apr. 25, 1942

Mary Bridget Lutz
b. 1846
d. 1933

m. Sept. 1866

William Smith
(glass cutter at B & S, Packwood)
b. William Smidt, May 1846
d. Mar. 21, 1916

Doris Zuleme Smith
(Sandwich Glass Museum Director)
b. June 16, 1902
d. Oct. 27, 1974

m. Oct. 2, 1926

Joseph Robert Kershaw
b. 1894
d. Mar. 14, 1959

Mary J. Smith
b. Jan. 15, 1874

m. 1898

George T. Shepardson
(glass cutter)

Ten other children
(five died in infancy)

LUTZ FAMILY GENEALOGY

paperweight market. When the need for weights slackened, he made other articles that were part of the regular production run. During this time, he met Elizabeth (Lizzie) Miller, who later became his wife. His drive, however, to use his other glassmaking talents compelled him to leave the New England Glass Company in 1869.

Lutz spent the winter of 1869–1870 in Pittsburgh. While he was there, he wrote to the Phoenix Glass Works in South Boston to apply for a position. Phoenix made plans to hire him, but backed out of their agreement, citing a change of plans. In a letter dated March 29, 1870, the Phoenix Glass Works agent informed Lutz that if he came to Phoenix, they could use him only until the 16th of May.[1] If Lutz did indeed work at Phoenix (and there is no sure evidence he did), it was only for this short period of time. He married Lizzie Miller on September 10, 1870, and moved to Sandwich shortly thereafter to become a head gaffer at the Boston and Sandwich Glass Company.

Glassmaker families were closely-knit, and often went to great lengths to stay together. Nicholas' brother Frank was a glassmaker in Sandwich at the time of his death at the age of thirty-nine on March 3, 1872. Frank's teenage son, Nicholas F. Lutz, moved in with his Uncle Nicholas and Aunt Lizzie, who by this time had a son Frank, who

was born in Sandwich on December 17, 1871. Young Nicholas also became a glassblower at the Boston and Sandwich Glass Company. From time to time, he was listed in newspapers and union records as "Nicholas Lutz II" and "Nicholas Lutz, the younger of that name". To further complicate matters, young Frank became a sticker-up boy in the shop where his father was the gaffer, James Grady was the servitor, and William McQue[2] was assistant to the servitor. The children's grandmother, Ursula Lutz, also emigrated from Saint Louis and lived in the household. A sister, Mary Bridget, also came from France, and in September 1866, had married William Smith (William Smidt), a Sandwich glass cutter.

The birth of Nicholas and Lizzie's second son Joseph, on October 1, 1873, prompted the Lutz family to buy a house on State Street.[3] Nicholas was now employed by a company that allowed him the freedom to work at his trade as he saw fit. He could try new things in glassmaking, experiment with different colors, fabricate new molds for making more complex rods, and improve his skills to heights he had not reached before. By the 1870's, the company had grown to six hundred men and boys. As head gaffer, Lutz at last found complete happiness and a place to call "home".

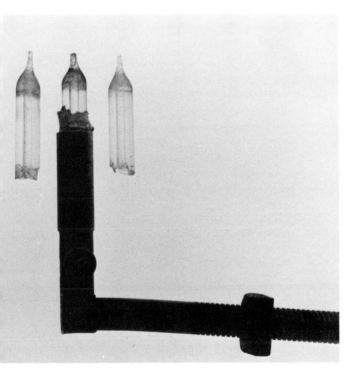

Gas burners used by Lutz in his Sandwich home for lampwork. The little glass tubes are each little burners that were fired by gas piped to his workbench. They were used to heat the glass rods to make flowers for paperweights. The ends of the tubes are seared as a result of the flame and the heat that the work generated. The burner on the left has a valve to control the flow of gas. The nut threaded onto the pipe was used to fasten the burner to the bench. The Y-shaped burner on the right carried two flames. All three flames burned at the same time. A jet of compressed air stretched the flame so that it burned a maximum amount of oxygen, giving an excellent heat source for working the glass. These burners were salvaged from Lutz's workbench and are now in the collection of the authors.

The house on State Street had gas piped into it, so Lutz made a work area in his cellar so that he could do *lampwork* during the hours he was not at the factory. Two small gas burners were attached to his workbench, supplying the heat he needed to make fruit, petals and leaves for paperweights by melting small amounts of glass taken from rods he had made at the factory. The petals and leaves were painstakingly assembled into flowers. Sometimes they did not meet the industry's standards, so Lutz discarded them. His bench had a hole in the center, large enough to take a completed weight. When an item he was working on did not come out the way he liked, down the hole it went into a drawer below. When the drawer was full, Lutz threw away its contents.

In addition to set-ups for paperweights, Lutz made writing pens from glass rods. These, too, were fabricated at home and then taken to the factory to add to his daily production. His reasons for conducting a "cottage industry" at home are not clear. Did he make flowers in the cellar because he enjoyed making them, or was he paid extra by the company? He often had fellow workers with him, teaching them how to make little glass finials, ducks, footballs. If the results were satisfactory, the pieces were retained by their makers, but if they were bad, they were thrown into the discard drawer.

It can be concluded, from an examination of Lutz's paperweight components and rods, that he worked mainly in red and blue combined with clear glass or opaque white. Perhaps his choice of color was influenced by love of country during the period of his becoming a citizen in 1876, which was also the year of America's Centennial.

A third son, Frederick N., was born on November 18, 1875, and a daughter, Mary Ursula, on January 7, 1878. They died within a month of each other in the spring of 1880.

In the late 1870's, a special machine was invented in England that could extrude a hot glob of glass into a thin continuous thread. The Boston and Sandwich Glass Company took immediate interest, and, toward the end of 1880, the factory was producing threaded glass in several colors (see Chapter 13, Volume 4). Pages from the 1887 factory sloar book, two of which appear at the end of the history portion of this chapter, show that much of the threading was done by Lutz's group.

He also made chandelier parts out of glass. The gaslight era created a need for elaborate lighting devices and gas shades. The company expanded its lighting operation in this field, so there was plenty of work for a highly skilled gaffer.

Lutz's young son, Frank, worked in his father's shop, and, after school on Saturdays, he and some of the other boys would return to the factory to pick up glass that had broken during manufacture. They sorted it into boxes according to color and were paid ten cents a box by the company.

The Lutz family was growing. A little girl, Alphonsa, was born on July 24, 1881. She lived less than two years, but was followed by Lewis, born November 7, 1883, and Bertha U., born February 22, 1886. Lutz sang tenor with a musical group in town. He also played a large part in the growth of the American Flint Glass Workers Union Local No. 16, to which his nephew, Nicholas F. Lutz, also belonged. The union, however, was prepared, perhaps unwittingly, to destroy everything Lutz had worked for. On November 27, 1887, it gave the glass company an ultimatum: improve working conditions and increase salaries or the union men would not return to work in the New Year (see Chapter 1 in Volume 4). On January 2, 1888, after the normal Christmas shutdown, the union lived up to its word. The fires remained blocked while workers and management waited out the stalemate in contract negotiations.

Lutz was sure the strike would not last, but he was able, at least, to supplement his income with outside work. Late in February, for example, he received a letter from a Pennsylvania glass house asking him to decorate ten thousand blown, opaque white, cigar holders. He agreed, and eleven thousand holders were sent to him to allow for error. They also sent matching boutonniere holders for men's lapels. With this volume of business conducted from his home, his family was able to remain in Sandwich and await the time when he would once again be employed at the factory. The younger Nicholas left Sandwich by June, but he was to return at a later time.

However, the Boston and Sandwich Glass Company did not reopen. The buildings were offered for sale in October 1888. Lutz's bench at home became a full-time operation. By the end of the year, he added the making of glass writing pens to his little cottage industry. He could no longer make rods at the factory, so he made arrangements with his relatives in France who were still employed at Cristalleries de Saint-Louis to export a quantity to Boston. The three-foot-long latticinio rods were shipped in bundles that were twelve to fourteen inches in diameter. The bundles were packaged in cylinders that were each placed in a box. Six boxes constituted one order. Lutz traveled to Boston to get them, and accompanied them on the train to Sandwich to make sure they did not break. The straight middle section of each rod was cut into pen handle lengths. The ends of each rod that were tapered (deliberately made this way to avoid breakage in shipping) were thrown down the discard slot in the workbench and into the drawer below. By adding a decorative finial to the handle, and a writing point fashioned from a slender reeded rod, Lutz had a salable item requiring minimal labor. He sold them through Jones, McDuffee and Stratton, a wholesale house in Boston.

The Boston and Sandwich Glass Company also sold its inventory to Jones, McDuffee and Stratton in the spring of 1889 (see page 19 in Volume 4). This inventory included all of the finished glass stored in the Boston warehouse and all glass, finished and unfinished, that was left in the still unsold factory in Sandwich. There were threaded wines and champagnes with no stems, and boxes of feet not yet attached. Jones, McDuffee and Stratton asked Lutz to complete the wines and champagnes by using the pen handle rods for stems. For the next several months, the Lutz boys carted boxes and barrels of glass from the factory to the house.

Lutz got other jobs from the wholesale house. He made

This photo was taken in Sandwich early in 1892, just before the Lutz family moved to New Bedford. From left to right are Nicholas, six-year-old Bertha, eighteen-year-old Joseph, eight-year-old Lewis, nephew Nicholas Lutz (also a glassworker), Elizabeth (Lizzie) holding one-year-old Victor, who was the last child to be born in Sandwich, twenty-year-old Frank, who was the oldest, and Ursula Lutz, the children's grandmother.

little glass hands that were wired to the arms of leather dolls and clock faces that were glued to toy grandfather clocks. Like so many of his co-workers, he found a way to make a living and stay in Sandwich for a while.

But financial needs became more and more demanding. He and Lizzie now had five children. Victor Ernest was born on January 8, 1891. Nicholas watched as the factory was sold to the Electrical Glass Corporation, which failed. He waited again as George B. Jones attempted to make glass — and failed. He finished decorating the last of the cigar holders, his inventory of stemware was depleted and the sale of writing pens became limited. In the spring of 1892, he decided to close down his business and take a position offered to him at the Mount Washington Glass Company in New Bedford.[4] He packed his belongings, including his workbench, his gas burners, and the one thousand extra cigar holders, decorated with little dots, that were in excess of the ten thousand needed by the Pennsylvania manufacturer.

The Lutz family settled down to life in New Bedford, where two more children were born, Ursula in 1892 and their last child, William Edmund, in 1893. But two years

after Nicholas started working in his new position, changes began to take place. On July 14, 1894, the Mount Washington Glass Company became part of the Pairpoint Manufacturing Company. Frederick Stacey Shirley, the guiding force behind Mount Washington's success, decided to try to revive the glass industry in Sandwich. He became part of a group associated with Albert V. Johnston that invested heavily in the Boston and Sandwich Glass Company II (see page 80 in Volume 4). Still owning his State Street house in Sandwich, Lutz invested his savings in the project[5] and put his Mount Washington job on the line. He was informed in no uncertain terms that if he left his position to return to Sandwich, his job would not be waiting for him if the Sandwich factory failed. The Boston and Sandwich Glass Company II began making glass in mid-1895, but by the end of 1896, the people of Sandwich witnessed another failure that brought financial disaster to many people, including the Lutz family.

By this time, Lutz had moved his family of seven children to Somerville, Massachusetts, and was working as a head gaffer at the Union Glass Company. He took the tools he needed at the factory, but left his home workbench

From time to time, Lutz's relatives sent examples of the work they did in France. The pieces were incorporated into the Lutz family collection. When these pieces entered the antiques market, the legend that every one was made by Nicholas Lutz became well established.

with its contents in the cellar at New Bedford. He had not used it because there was no gas piped into his New Bedford home. When lampwork was needed during the three years he was at Mount Washington, he did it at the factory. Lutz remained at the Union works until his death on March 31, 1906.[6] The small bench was forgotten, left to rot in the cellar.

HISTORY STORED IN A WORKBENCH

Our research into the work of Nicholas Lutz extended over a long period, from the time Doris (Smith) Kershaw, a granddaughter of Lutz's sister Mary, became the director of the Sandwich Historical Society in the 1940's, and Victor Ernest Lutz, son of Nicholas and spokesman for the family, disposed of the Lutz family's glass. We examined documents from many sources: Sandwich Archives and Historical Center, Sandwich Historical Society, Henry Ford Museum, and scrapbooks and records still in the care of Lutz family descendants. We were faced with the difficulty of segregating the glass made by Nicholas Lutz while he worked in Sandwich from the glass he made when he worked in France, Brooklyn, Pennsylvania, and other parts of Massachusetts. We had to evaluate his singular talent in order to be able to differentiate between Lutz family pieces that were made by Nicholas and pieces that were made by relatives in France. We had to deal with the "Lutz-type" glass made in Europe during the late 1800's,

as well as the never-ending problem of reproductions. A more and more factual information emerged, we were ab to reach many conclusions. These were substantiated whe the contents of Lutz's workbench became part of th Barlow collection in 1984.

As previously described, the bench was moved from Lutz's house in Sandwich to his home in New Bedford Because gas was not available to him in New Bedford, h did not work at home. He lost interest in the bench. Whe he relocated again, the bench, with its drawer-full of re jected paperweight setups and tapered rod ends, was lef in the New Bedford cellar. It remained there for ove seventy-five years, until dampness took its toll. The leg rotted, the bench fell over and the drawer spilled out frag ments that had been thrown into it *when Lutz was still i Sandwich.*

The drawer contained over five hundred sections o rods. There were over one thousand leaves, petals an fruit for paperweights. There were completed paperweight with defects that made them unsalable. There were writin pens, cigar holders, hands for leather dolls. There wer birds, footballs and crosses that could be used in paper weights or as finials on pens. The list is long, and we mus emphasize that these were not first-line items. They wer all seconds (or worse) that were discarded by Lutz and th glassworkers that were tutored by him.

Lutz brought to Sandwich the techniques, but not th

ills, of the French masters. He left France when he was
twenty-five years old. He gained experience over the next
ten years, but at no time in his glassmaking career did he
equal or surpass his French contemporaries. One need
only to see a French paperweight side by side with an
American one to know that the fledgling glass industry in
the United States had a long way to go to equal work done
in France. Lutz did not make great quantities of filigree
(twisted) rods and ribbon rods that he fused together to
make finger bowls, underplates, vases and pitchers.
According to Victor Lutz, these very well made rods were
sent to him from France. Nicholas incorporated them into
writing pens and stemware. From time to time, family
members sent examples of finished articles made from the
same rods. These articles became Lutz family heirlooms,
so over the years, as they were sold out of the family
collection, the facts regarding their origin faded. Descendants living today have not retained pieces made from
used rods. Fragments have not been found at the Boston
and Sandwich Glass Company dig site, and the 1887 sloar
book pages preserved at the Sandwich Archives show that
Lutz's workload consisted of a daily routine similar to other
gaffers at the factory.

Nicholas Lutz excelled at combining a minimal amount
of colored glass with a larger amount of clear glass to give
the appearance of colored art glass.

He did this in one of four ways. The first was by en-
casing colored glass lampwork in clear glass to make
paperweights. Most of the paperweights were flowers that
resembled poinsettias. Some were pansies and other recog-
nizable flowers, others were composed of imaginatively
arranged petals having no botanical origin. The 1874 Boston and Sandwich Glass Company catalog simply lists
flower paperweights and the 1887 sloar book lists *fancy weights*.
It is the paperweight collector who gives them fanciful
names. It is our opinion that the single complex cane in
the center of the flowers was cut from imported rods that
Nicholas rationed out very carefully. There are fruit
weights, and some with colored leaves arranged into a
flower form. Victor Lutz delighted in telling about his
father working at home on the setups.

Secondly, threaded glass was made by him and/or under
his direction. Most threaded glass was made by winding
colored threads around the outside of thinly blown clear
glass. Other gaffers to whom this work can be attributed
worked in Lutz's shop. But there is, in our opinion, no difference between his work and the work of his assistants.
Threaded glass should be attributed to Lutz's hand only
with the strongest documentation.

Thirdly, Lutz made clear glass hollow ware, such as
lamp fonts and wafer trays, with colored threads incorporated into the clear glass in a swirl configuration.

His fourth technique was similar, combining ribbons of
colored glass in clear glass hollow ware to make swirled
stripes. Striped glass has a larger proportion of color.
Pieces made by Lutz that are all color were largely in the
form of red, white and blue off-hand pieces such as
epergnes, flasks or pipes. They were not part of the regular
production line of the company.

Art glass that can be positively attributed to him was
made when he was at the Mount Washington Glass Company and the Union Glass Company. According to Victor
Lutz, in a letter dated January 31, 1955, Nicholas made
a set of Burmese children's dishes for one of his daughters
while he was still at Sandwich. He would only have been
legally allowed to do this when he was helping Frederick
S. Shirley establish the Boston and Sandwich Glass Company II in 1895.

The finding of Lutz's workbench should put to rest the
use of the term *Lutz-type*, generally applied to glass made
by fusing twisted filigree and ribbon canes side to side.
Since there is no evidence that Nicholas Lutz made this
type of glass, we do not have to deal with it at all, whether
it be foreign or domestic, original or reproduction. In an
article written for the Spring 1981 issue of *The Acorn*, Sandwich Glass Museum Director Barbara Bishop stated,
" . . . there is no factual basis on which to say that any of
the glass now called "Lutz-type" was made by Nicholas
Lutz or under his direction." Regardless, Lutz has secured
his place in history as a dedicated glassworker who devoted
many hours to the service of his employer. His name will
always be linked with Sandwich glass.

The paperweights and lampwork setups for paperweights that are shown in the following photos are those

Nicholas Lutz in his later years.

that we have traced back to Nicholas Lutz and can document without question. The Boston and Sandwich Glass Company made other paperweights, many "built" by the method employed by Lutz, some pressed and some cut. They are treated in a chapter devoted to Sandwich paperweights, and related items elsewhere in this series.

THESE SIMPLE HINTS WILL HELP YOU IDENTIFY SANDWICH GLASS MADE BY LUTZ.

Lutz used a small percentage of colored glass, predominantly red, white and blue, with a large percentage of clear glass.
Look for:

- Clear glass paperweights with colored lampwork.
- Threaded glass (threads applied after the piece was made).
- Colored threads incorporated into clear glass, swirled when the piece was being made.

- Striped glass (colored ribbons, sometimes alternating with threads, swirled when the piece was being made)

Learn the basic configuration of Lutz paperweight, i.e., a single flower with a complex cane center, a stem with two leaves, and an extra leaf or bud. You must have irrefutable documentation to attribute a particular weight to his years at Sandwich, because he used the same configuration at the New England Glass Company from 1867 to 1869.

All Lutz writing pens have slender reeded nibs. Lutz used only two types of rods—single color rods made the Boston and Sandwich Glass Company before 1888 and imported latticinio rods. Both types of rods have smooth surface.

Venetian-type tableware, made by fusing filigree and ribbon rods side to side, was not made by Lutz. This type of art glass was not made at Sandwich by anyone.

NOTES TO CHAPTER 11

1. Letter from the Phoenix Glass Works, addressed to Mr. Nicholas Lutz, Care F. T. South, Esq., Cor. 37th & Buttler Sts., Pittsburgh, Penn. It begins, "Since last we wrote you . . ." (Courtesy, Sandwich Glass Museum, Sandwich Historical Society).

2. As written in Lutz family documents. A William McHugh is listed as a glassworker in the 1880 Census.

3. Barnstable County (Massachusetts) Registry of Deeds, book 171, pages 72–73, dated October 9, 1873.
   According to *The Seaside Press*, a Sandwich newspaper dated October 25, 1873, Lutz purchased the homestead on State Street from the estate of Joseph Hobson. Hobson had been a glassworker.

4. *The Sandwich Observer* of July 19, 1892, stated that Mr. and Mrs. Nicholas Lutz of New Bedford were guests of William Smith. William Smith was a Sandwich glass cutter married to Nicholas' sister Mary.

5. Several original Boston and Sandwich Glass Company II documents were given to the Sandwich Glass Museum by the Lutz family. A list of Sandwich men on the payroll, dated after Frederick S. Shirley became general manager in 1896, does not include Lutz himself. It should not, because Lutz was an investor. (Courtesy, Sandwich Glass Museum, Sandwich Historical Society).

6. The death of Nicholas J. Lutz is recorded in the April 10, 1906 issue of *The Bourne Pioneer*.

372 LAMPWORK FOR PAPERWEIGHTS

a) Blue flower 1¼" across

b) Blue and white striped flower 1¼" across

c) Fruit forms ¼" Dia.

d) Leaves ⅝"-¾" L.

e) Flower buds and vegetable forms ½" L.

f) Two red flowers 1¼"-1½" across 1870-1887

Realizing the historical value of their father's work, Lutz's descendants saw to it that the best of his effort was permanently preserved. These pieces may be seen at The Bennington Museum. Others are at the Sandwich Glass Museum. The leaves were shaped like petals. While each piece was still hot, Lutz placed it into a leaf-shaped squeeze mold. The two parts of the mold were in the jaws of pliers. The pattern of veins is only on the upper surface of each leaf; the back is flat. Some of Lutz's stems have red thorns applied to them. When the work on each tiny piece was completed, the leaves were attached to stems, the stems to flower petals, and the complete assembly was ready to be "built" into a paperweight. Once the setup was encapsulated by clear glass, it was a permanent part of the finished product. *The Bennington Museum, Bennington, Vermont*

373 LAMPWORK FLOWERS FOR PAPERWEIGHTS

a) Blue "weedflower" 1¼" across

b) Red flower 1½" to bottom of stem 1870-1887

These intricate examples of Lutz's work clearly show his skill as a glassworker. The flowers are all made of glass. When placed in a weight, the curved surface magnifies the lampwork, making it look much larger. The blue flower is made up of eight parts: a cane center, five petals and two leaves. Flowers with striped petals are called *weedflowers* by collectors. The red flower is made up of nine parts: a center, five petals, a stem and two leaves, one of which has been broken off. Three of the petals and the center were made from a white rod that was cased with red. The rod was cut into thin slices, which were assembled as petals. Lutz was capable of making two-color rods, but not the complex cane used in the center of the blue flower. *Courtesy, Sandwich Glass Museum, Sandwich Historical Society*

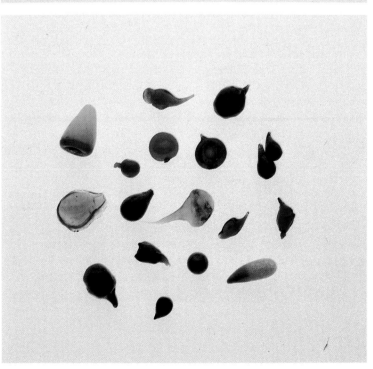

374 LAMPWORK FRUIT FOR PAPERWEIGHTS

¼"-⅞" L. 1870-1887

Fruit was used by Lutz at the New England Glass Company as well as at the Boston and Sandwich Glass Company. He made some of the fruit forms by pressing small globs of glass in a little mold, then reworking each molded piece into its final shape. Stems were hand formed and applied to the fruit by hand. The fruit was assembled, leaves were added, and the completed setup became the center of a paperweight.

3375 RODS FROM LUTZ'S WORKBENCH
4"–9" L. 1870–1887
Every glass factory that made tableware was capable o
producing simple rods. Thick ones were reheated to for
handles that were applied to creamers, custards an
molasses cans. Lutz made the thin rods shown here at th
factory in Sandwich. He took them home to use for h
lampwork. These pieces from the discard drawer in hi
bench are the tapered ends of the rods, left over after th
straight usable portions were cut out. Some of the rod
have white centers. They were cut into short segments an
flattened out to form round flower petals with white cen
ters, as shown in photo 3373. The rods when made wer
pulled like taffy until they were the required thickness
then cut into three foot lengths.

3376 LAMPWORK PETALS FOR FLOWERS
(a) Petals divided lengthwise
(b) Rod from which they were made 1870–1887
The rod is 50 percent red and 50 percent white. The peta
were made by heating the end of the rod. When the ro
softened, a small amount of glass was taken from the en
of the rod, and was shaped into a petal. Lutz made sur
each petal was divided by color lengthwise. If each peta
was divided horizontally, only the color at the top of eac
petal would show in the finished assembly. The rod wa
made at the Boston and Sandwich Glass Company. Glas
could not be made at Lutz's home, only reheated and re
shaped.

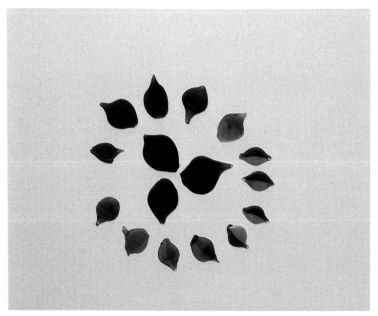

3377 LAMPWORK PETALS FOR FLOWERS
1870–1887
We have shown you how the four red and white petals a
the top of the photo were fashioned from a two-color rod
The single-color petals were made in the same manne
from single-color rods. The larger petals were used i
flowers that had only five or six petals. Lutz used smalle
petals for flowers that had ten or more petals surrounde
by leaves.

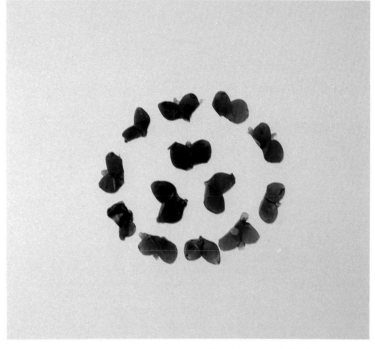

HOW LUTZ ASSEMBLED A SETUP FOR A FLOWER PAPERWEIGHT

378

When we studied Nicholas Lutz's rejects, we realized that broken assemblies that were in the discard drawer could be reassembled to show you how a paperweight setup was made. The first step, after the individual units were formed, was to heat two petals and join them, using little dots of green glass, in the same manner that the Boston and Sandwich Glass Company used wafers of glass to join large units of tableware. Lutz's little "wafers" cannot be seen in the finished product.

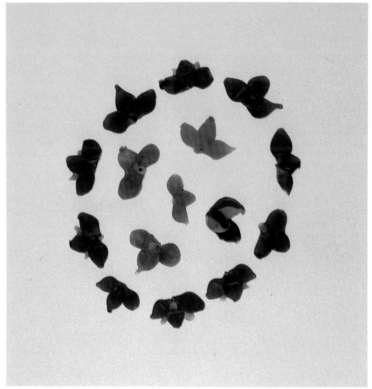

379

Here are assemblies to which Lutz added a third petal. Great care had to be taken in heating so that the shape of each petal would not be distorted. By applying a petal onto the little "wafer" rather than directly onto another petal, there was less chance of cracking the petals already assembled.

380

Here are four-petal and five-petal assemblies. The flower is beginning to take shape. Lutz used the large flowers in ½" Dia. weights and the small flowers in 2" Dia. weights. We seldom see a large weight made by Lutz that has several small flowers in it, although he often added a bud. Lutz reheated the dot in the center and applied a tiny section of cane.

HOW LUTZ ASSEMBLED A SETUP FOR A FLOWER PAPERWEIGHT (CONTINUED)

3381
Lutz completed these simple flowers, then added th
leaves. At this point, they broke. They have been put bac
together, leaving the breaks visible so that you can see wh
he threw them away. It took a patient individual to mak
enough setups so that the company could include flowe
weights in their catalog as part of their regular production
One can be seen on page 42 of the 1874 catalog.

3382
Stem and leaf assemblies, made beforehand, were attache
to the flower assemblies. An assortment of canes, bough
by the Boston and Sandwich Glass Company from outsid
sources, were cut into thin segments and were applied t
the center dot. The completed setup on the left has a cen
ter that was cut from a white over red hexagonal cane
The flower on the right has a white star-shaped cane wit
a red center. *The Bennington Museum, Bennington, Vermon*

3383
On the day when paperweights were to be made, Nichol
Lutz reportedly left his State Street home carrying doze
of setups ready to be encapsulated into "fancy weights
The center of the flower in this weight has eight point
The center canes in this weight and in the setups abov
are simple, and may have been supplied by another glas
house in the United States. *The Bennington Museur
Bennington, Vermont*

3384 FLOWER PAPERWEIGHT
1¾" H. after polishing; 2¾" Dia. 1870–1887
Although color variation can be seen in this grouping, sameness of form is apparent. A motif of two leaves on a flower with a cane center was repeated extensively, showing the mass production atmosphere prevalent at the Boston and Sandwich Glass Company during this period. Records show that on November 7, 1887, Lutz's shop made 150 such weights. There is some variation in the center cane, but these canes were made elsewhere. This weight has a complex cane made up of a predominantly white cane center surrounded by white and blue-green canes, most likely imported by the company from a French glass house. *Do not attempt to identify a Lutz weight by the center cane.* This weight was dug at the factory site, then polished so that we could study the flower, which had slipped to the side.

3385 FLOWER PAPERWEIGHT
1¾" H. x 2¾" Dia. 1870–1887
Lutz's paperweights are simple, straightforward and well-made, but lack imagination. Some of them have controlled bubbles strategically placed to look like dew drops. This flower is well-centered in the weight, but others are not. If they slipped slightly, they still maintained their salability. If they slipped badly, they were discarded. This flower has a cane with a rosette center surrounded by white and red. We describe the imported canes only to show their variety, not for identification. Our research places Lutz high on the "skilled" roster at Sandwich, but he was no competition to the French masters who made the complex center canes.

3386 FLOWER PAPERWEIGHT
1⅞" H. x 3¼" Dia. 1870–1887
Here is the same flower, the one most often referred to by collectors as a *poinsettia*. Its sameness is relieved only by a very complex center cane, made by surrounding a light blue and white cane with four red, white and blue canes that alternate with four white ones. The 1874 catalog lists *flower paperweights* without regard to their botanical name. The 1887 sloar book refers to *fancy weights*. What is a six-petalled flower? How many petals must it have to be called a clematis? At what point does a many-petalled clematis become a dahlia? Lutz didn't care—his shop mass produced pretty pieces to brighten a desk and hold down papers.

3387 FLOWER PAPERWEIGHT WITH LATTICINIO GROUND

2" H. x 2¾" Dia. 1870–1887

Lutz did not deviate much from his "basic model" con-figuration. Here is the familiar poinsettia varied by the placement of three large leaves behind it. But note its similarity to the paperweight below—the identical two-leaved stem on a latticinio ground. The flower center was made by surrounding a red, white and blue cane with alternating white and blue canes, bonded together by dark blue. Lutz must have regarded lampwork as a hobby in order to be able to devote to it so many hours.

3388 FLOWER PAPERWEIGHT WITH LATTICINIO GROUND

1¾" H. x 2⅝" Dia. 1870–1887

The petals on this flower were made by pressing yellow, pink, blue and green glass into the little mold that Lutz used to form leaves. A red and white star-shaped cane forms the center. This weight was among the contents of Lutz's workbench. It was unsalable because, when the clear glass cap was put over the flower, a streak of milky-colored gall (residue on the surface of hot glass in the pot) was deposited over the yellow petal. It would have been a beautiful weight. Unfortunately, weights could easily be spoiled. This particular paperweight was made in Sand-wich, but Lutz also made them when he was at the New England Glass Company from 1867 to 1869. Any of the weights shown in this chapter may be found either with a latticinio or colored ground.

3389 FLOWER PAPERWEIGHT WITH SEPARATED SETUP

1½" H. x 2⅜" Dia. 1870–1887

Not every weight came out the way its maker wanted it to. This is what happened when the gaffer hesitated as he was positioning the hot cap of glass over the setup. The hot glass must completely surround the setup instantly. If there is hesitation for even a fraction of a second, the setup will break apart and the separated units will slide around. The red glass is the center of the flower. The striped petals were originally placed around the center to make a clematis-like flower, called a *striped flower* by collectors. It has also been found with a center that looks like a tiny rose.

3390 FLOWER PAPERWEIGHT
1¾" H. x 2⅞" Dia. 1870–1887

Here is a perfect paperweight that Nicholas Lutz was undoubtedly proud of. The petals were individually placed in perfect position, and the leaves were positioned properly on the stem. The complex cane was applied in the exact center of the flower. It was made by fusing together a red, white and blue cane surrounded by two concentric rings of blue and amber canes. A bud can be seen peeking out from behind the striped flower, replacing the third leaf in the weight shown previously.

3391 FLOWER PAPERWEIGHT
1¼" H. x 2⅞" Dia. 1870–1887

This pansy-like flower slid to the left. Study the flower and you will see that the red glass in the top petals overheated and ran as a result of the movement of the setup. This type of flower, with several striped petals, is called a *weed-flower* by some collectors. It has been found in other color combinations and may be on a latticinio ground. The center of this flower is made from a complex cane purchased elsewhere. Many white canes are encased in red, and there is a goldstone center. Lutz added a third leaf behind the flower and controlled "dew drop" bubbles. *The Bennington Museum, Bennington, Vermont*

3392 FRUIT PAPERWEIGHT WITH LATTICINIO GROUND
1⅝" H. x 2⅜" Dia. 1870–1887

Setups for fruit and vegetable paperweights were assembled in the same manner as petals for flowers. Each fruit or vegetable unit radiated from the center. This weight has four pears alternating with four small cherries or radishes. Another large pear is in the center. The same leaves that were used on flowers protrude from beneath the fruit. This weight was also made by Lutz when he was at the New England Glass Company, where it continued to be made after Lutz left. The New England version has more fruit, brighter colored glass and more clarity to the transparent glass. No Sandwich fruit weight has been found that contains more than five large fruit units.

3393 LATE-BLOWN VASES WITH PAPERWEIGHT BASE
(a) 7¾" H. x 4" Dia.
(b) 7⅞" H. x 4⅛" Dia. 1870–1887
Documentation from the Lutz family and The Bennington Museum reveals that Nicholas made this pair of vases for his wife, Lizzie. The workmanship lacks the detail and exactness of French pieces, yet the vases were made many years after Lutz's apprenticeship. From a Sandwich standpoint, they are more than acceptable, but below the standards set by the glass industry for this time period. Pink, blue and yellow bits of glass were formed into apples, pears and vegetables. Green leaves were added, and the base was "built up" into a paperweight. A spool stem and blown upper unit completed each vase. Museum records state that they were intended for cutting. There were several glass cutters in the Lutz family. *The Bennington Museum, Bennington, Vermont*

3394 BLOWN LAMP WITH TWISTED RIBBON STANDARD
9½" H. x 4½" Dia. 1876
Once again we see Nicholas Lutz's application of red, white and blue in the twisted ribbon rod that he used for the standard of this kerosene lamp. Just above the rod, a wafer holds the standard to the knop that forms the font extension. A second wafer below the rod holds the standard to the knop that is part of the base. The lamp was one of the pieces made for Elizabeth (Lizzie) Lutz both to commemorate Lutz's citizenship and the country's centennial. This piece is documented beyond doubt, but do not make the mistake of believing that every Lutz piece using these colors was made for the Centennial. Lutz produced many pieces with twisted ribbon standards when he worked at the Union Glass Company in Somerville. *The Bennington Museum, Bennington, Vermont*

3395 LETTER SEAL HANDLE WITH PAPERWEIGHT KNOB AND TWISTED RIBBON SHANK
2⅞" H. x 1⅛" Dia. 1870–1887
This piece is from the family of glass engraver John B. Vodon. Vodon worked at the Boston and Sandwich Glass Company and later established his own cutting and engraving shop, where in 1895 he was polishing out pontil marks for the Boston and Sandwich Glass Company II. An initialled metal piece was slipped onto the square end of the shank and was used to impress sealing wax. We understand that, in later years, similar handles were made with a complete set of interchangeable initials. Lutz was capable of making the twisted ribbon rod used for the shank, but not the complex quatrefoil canes that are arranged in two concentric circles in the knob. The authors are not the first to speculate that the Boston and Sandwich Glass Company imported canes from Cristalleries de Baccarat.

3396 BLOWN PIPE
12¼" L. to broken mouthpiece; 2⅝" Dia. bowl
1870-1887
Pipes had no practical purpose. They were carried in parades and hung above fireplaces. Although they were not part of a company's regular production, we have seen an invoice for one, so not only glassworkers owned them. Without documentation, there is no way to tell where simple blown pieces were made. This pipe is in a Sandwich home. The design made by trailing threads into loops is called *marbrie*. For more information on this technique, see the marbrie witch balls in Chapter 8.

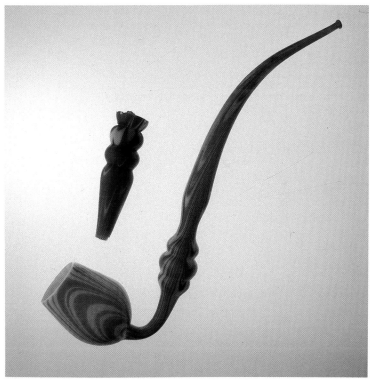

3397 BLOWN PIPE
19½" L.; 3⅛" Dia. bowl 1870-1887
Fragments of pipes dug at the factory site are red and white, blue and white, and red, white and blue. In her booklet *History of Sandwich Glass* published in 1925, Bangs Burgess stated that gaffer Lutz made her a pipe that held a pound of tobacco. The red and white fragment matches the red and white pipe in photo 3396.

3398 BLOWN FLASK
7" H. x 4¼" W. x 1¾" D. 1876
This flask was made by Nicholas Lutz, who used it at a celebration when he became an American citizen on October 13, 1876. Lutz's daughter Ursula remembered seeing it being used on several other special occasions. It was sold to the author by son Victor. This piece has enough documentation behind it so there is no doubt of its origin.

3399 BLOWN EPERGNE
20" H. x 10¼" Dia. 1876
This epergne again shows Lutz's use of red, white and
blue. He made it for his family as a constant reminder that
he became a citizen in the year of his adopted country's
Centennial. The loops are similar to the loops on witch
balls. The underside of the base and the inside of the
trumpet and center bowl are cased in white. The bowl has
a ruby rim. The base is held to the bottom of the bowl
with a wafer. The trumpet is attached to the bowl with the
same threaded fittings that the Boston and Sandwich Glass
Company used on Onion lamps. Fruit was placed in the
center bowl, and flowers were placed in the trumpet. *The
Bennington Museum, Bennington, Vermont*

3400 BLOWN STRIPED CREAMER
4¼" H. 1870–1887
Striped glass is rarely found on the open market, so little
is known about it. The fragments in the foreground are
an exact match. Many fragments were dug at the Boston
and Sandwich Glass Company in clear with blue and
white, clear with pink and white, and clear with white.
Matching rods that were used to make the handle were
found in Lutz's workbench. The creamer was blown, then
held by a pontil rod while the handle was attached. Study
the way the gaffer applied the top of the handle to the
body of the creamer. The upper end of the striped rod was
flattened and spread out to give the handle strength. Then
the rod was bent close to the body and was firmly attached
at its lower end. This creamer was made for table use, not
as a decorative "shelf piece". Do not buy a piece of hollow
ware that has a crack radiating from the spot where the
handle was applied. Unscrupulous dealers often try to sell
broken pieces by saying that it cracked in the making.
Glass factories did not sell broken dishes.

3401 BLOWN STRIPED TUMBLER
3⅛" H. x 2⅜" Dia. 1870–1887
Glassworkers often brought home "seconds". When we
evaluate a worker's talent by examining his own collection
we must keep this constantly in mind. This tumbler has
a pink stripe missing, with an extra white stripe in its
place. Ruth Webb Lee shows another "second" from the
Lutz collection on plate 23 in her book *Sandwich Glass*.
Study the tumbler on the right of plate 23 and count the
stripes from the bottom up. The first stripe is white, the
second is colored, the third is white, the fourth is colored,
the fifth is white, and the sixth *should be colored*, but it is
not. We consider "seconds" more desirable because they
have characteristics that make them one-of-a-kind. There
is no question that striped glass was made in the shop
headed by Lutz.

3402 BLOWN STRIPED WAFER TRAYS

a) Red, white and clear 2¼" H. x 3⅛" Dia.
b) Blue, white and clear 2" H. x 2½" Dia. 1870-1887

Nicholas Lutz, as head of a shop, worked in many ways. These beautiful, delicate pieces are not toy compotes. They are wafer trays, to hold the wafers that were used to seal letters before the advent of envelopes. The letters were folded, sealed, and the address was written on the back. The Boston and Sandwich Glass Company also produced striped inkwells. A matching wafer tray and inkwell made a lovely set for a lady's desk. This type of glass is often mistaken for Venetian work. Three of these were purchased from the Lutz family and are now in the authors' collection. Over a dozen were available at the time. The penny gives you an idea of their size.

3403 THREE-DOLPHIN LAMP WITH CIRCULAR BASE AND BLOWN STRIPED FONT

11½" H. 1870-1887

The three-dolphin standard was made over a long period of time. The brass fitting connecting the standard to the font dates back to the beginning of the kerosene era. But it is unlikely that striped glass was produced at the Boston and Sandwich Glass Company before Lutz came in 1870. This blown kerosene font is a combination of a blue stripe alternating with white threads. Striped fonts are more attractive when they are filled with kerosene because the stripes do not reflect through from the opposite side. The type of work shown in this chapter is as close as the Boston and Sandwich Glass Company ever came to producing "art glass".

3404 THREADED CREAMERS

a) Plain 4" H. x 2½" Dia.
b) Rigaree and needle etching 4" H. x 3¼" Dia.
   1880-1887

Threaded glass did not come to Sandwich until 1880, but for seven years after it was heavily produced. It was well liked by factory personnel and can be found in many family collections. Pieces matching creamer A are in the family collection of Henry F. Spurr, general manager of the company. Creamer B is the same straight-sided shape (called a *can*), but rigaree was applied over the threading. The rigaree made it difficult to apply the handle, so it lacks the pleasing form of the handle in A. The piece is clumsy to handle and hard to store. Needle etching in the plain area resembles Craquelle glass. See Chapter 13 in Volume for more information about machine threading.

3405 THREADED DOUBLE-HANDLED TANKARD
10⅛" H. x 4⅝" Dia. 1880–1887

After Nicholas Lutz died, the bulk of the glass he had made for his family was left for Victor E. Lutz to dispose of, with the family's permission. Victor became the spokesman for the family, and helped to spread his father's fame throughout the collecting world. Victor made sure that the highest quality articles were made available to museums. According to Richard Carter Barret, former director-curator of The Bennington Museum, there are only two known examples of this tall double-handled tankard. Boston and Sandwich Glass Company pieces were machine threaded, using a method that originated in England in the late 1870's. *The Bennington Museum, Bennington, Vermont*

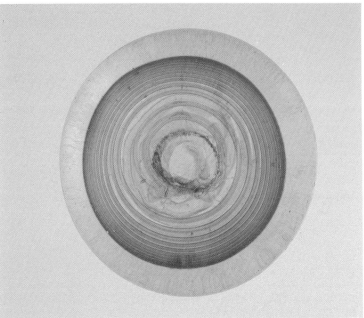

3406 THREADED PAPERWEIGHT
1¾" H. x 3⅛" Dia. 1880–1887

Here we see the use of threading that did not work. Ruby threads were arranged on the surface of a dome-shaped core of clear glass. To complete the weight, a clear glass cap was placed over the threads. The result was a disaster, so Lutz took it home. Families were often the recipients of failures. After all, this weight held down paper even if it did little to add to the decor of the desk. Some threaded weights did reach the market, but have more value as threaded curiosities than as paperweights. The black discoloration is the rough pontil mark on the base reflecting through the glass.

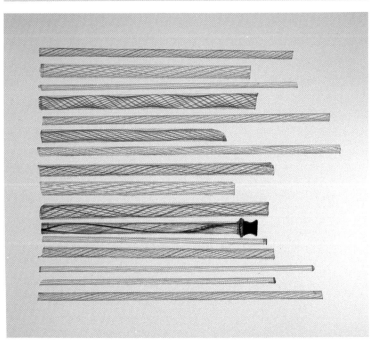

3407 LATTICINIO RODS FROM LUTZ'S WORKBENCH
¼"–⅝" Dia. 1888–1892

Rods with delicate threads running through them, either parallel o twisted, were not made in Sandwich. Nicholas Lutz did no have this talent. They were shipped from France by hi glassworker relatives to aid him in the making of pens afte the Boston and Sandwich Glass Company closed. Note the limited use of color, and the predominance of red and blue. Records show that the rods were 36" long. Lutz cu the straightest parts into pen-length sections. The piece in this photo are the short tapered sections that were lef over. Look at the sixth rod from the bottom. Lutz had be gun the assembly and it broke. Keep in mind that all o the fragments left in his bench were accumulated durin his Sandwich years.

3408, 3409, 3410 WRITING PENS MADE BY LUTZ

7½"–9⅝" L. 1870–1890

This fine collection of pens was assembled by Victor E. Lutz. They were purchased from him by The Bennington Museum, where they are on display, mounted to avoid breakage. The best, straightest pens were made when Lutz was at the factory, where he had better control of the gas burners for more accurate work. Most of the pens that were sold by the Boston and Sandwich Glass Company were made from solid color rods. After the factory closed, Lutz continued to make the same pens at home, but his supply of Sandwich rods ran short, so 1890 is a realistic approximation of the end of their production. All of the pens known to have been made by Lutz himself have long clear glass writing points. These nibs were made from the same type of reeded rods that were used to make reeded handles and claw feet on tableware, but were more slender. The reeds formed long grooves that held a surprisingly good supply of ink, allowing for continuous writing for several minutes. *The Bennington Museum, Bennington, Vermont*

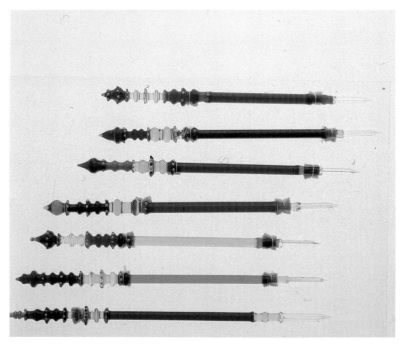

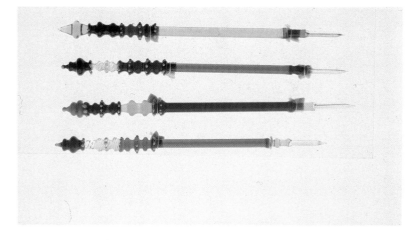

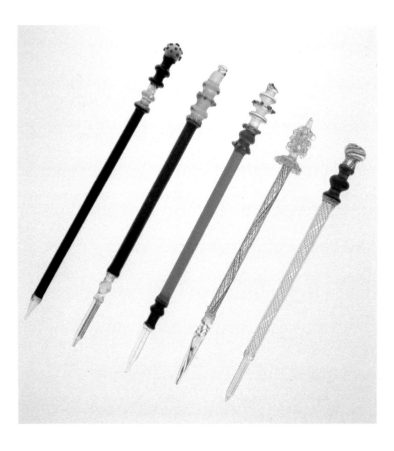

3411 WRITING PENS
(a) Short nib 1849–1855
(b) Slender reeded nib made by Lutz 1870–1890
(c) Slender reeded nib made by Lutz 1870–1890
(d) Twisted nib 1865–1870
(e) Slender reeded nib made by Lutz 1888–1892
    5¾"–6½" L.

The easiest way to date Sandwich pens is to examine the nibs (writing points). Pen A, at top, a perfect pen with red dots on the finial, has a short, smooth nib. This nib is the earliest, most primitive writing point that can be attributed to the Boston and Sandwich Glass Company. The short nib was improved by making grooves to hold the ink just above the taper, as shown in Fig. 16B below. Pens B and C were in Lutz's bench, discarded because the tops of the finials had broken. They have the slender reeded nibs perfected by Lutz, and were assembled from single-color rods produced by the Boston and Sandwich Glass Company. Pen D with the curly finial, broken at the top, has a long twisted nib that was used at the factory after the Civil War and before Lutz was employed there. The latticinio rod was purchased from an outside source. This twisted nib was a refinement over the earlier grooved nib, but it did not write as well as pen E, a perfect pen with a slender reeded nib, assembled by Lutz from a French latticinio rod.

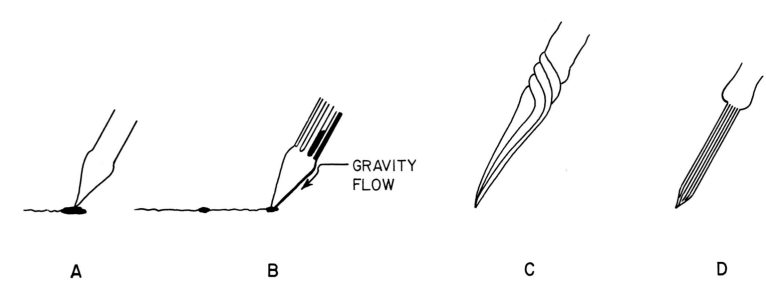

Fig. 16   Nibs on Sandwich pens. Nib A is found on the earliest pens, made at the Boston and Sandwich Glass Company between 1849 and 1855. The nib is short, with no grooves to hold a supply of ink. It did not write well. The ink did not flow evenly and left large ink blobs on the paper. Only a word or two could be written. The short nib was improved in 1855 by adding grooves *above* the taper, shown on nib B. Writing time was increased, but the nib still left small blobs. Gravity released ink from one groove at a time, so the pen had to be rotated each time a groove was empty. This nib was employed until 1860. The Civil War temporarily halted the production of non-essential items. After the Civil War, reeded handles and claw feet came into style on Late Blown Ware. The reeded rods used to make the handles and claw feet were twisted to make nib C with its rounded ribs on a lengthened taper. When Lutz came to Sandwich in 1870, he pulled the reeded rods until they were thin, and did not twist them. This turned out to be the perfect solution. If you want pens assembled by Lutz, look for nib D with its straight reeded shaft ending in a fine tapered point.

412 WRITING PEN FRAGMENTS FROM LUTZ'S WORKBENCH
1870-1892

Broken pen parts are a great help in identifying Lutz pens. The latticinio rods shown in photo 3407 can be seen in some of the partial assemblies. Lutz's slender reeded nib is in the center of the top row. Study the way it is fastened to the blue rod, a characteristic of Nicholas' work. Finials with latticinio canes were assembled after 1888. The red, white and clear striped glass finial on the right of the second row was made by Lutz at the factory prior to 1888. Red, white and blue are the dominant colors, even in assemblies that date into the 1890's. If you study the two types of rods used by Lutz, you will not make an error in identifying his work. The making of glass pens was revived in the 1920's, for use by savings banks as premiums when a new account was opened. Some are exquisite—birds with finely detailed eyes, beaks and wings.

413 THREADED CHAMPAGNE WITH LAMPWORK STEM
5⅝" H. x 3½" Dia. with damaged stem
6⅜" H. x 3½" Dia. if perfect 1889

Jones, McDuffee and Stratton bought all of the leftover stock after the Boston and Sandwich Glass Company closed. There were boxes of champagnes and wines that were not complete. The tops were threaded and the feet were made, but there were no stems. Nicholas Lutz was asked to assemble them at home. He made the stems the same way he built up his pens. Jones, McDuffee and Stratton sold them from their Boston showroom. This piece is broken just below the threading. The Bennington Museum believes there should be another ¾" to balance that length at the bottom of the stem. *The Bennington Museum, Bennington, Vermont*

414 BLOWN CIGAR HOLDERS DECORATED BY LUTZ
3"-3¼" L. 1888-1892

These cigar holders were not made in Sandwich. Eleven thousand of them were sent to Lutz to be *decorated* at his home. He was to complete an order for ten thousand and was allowed the extra ones for breakage. Lutz's only overhead for this job was labor. Leftover tapered ends of rods could be melted down to make designs out of dots. The holders were to be given away by cigar stores, along with boutonniere holders. The affidavit signed by Nicholas' son Victor indicates that Lutz made them for cigarettes. Victor, born in Sandwich in 1891, had no way of knowing that his father did not *make* them. A letter from Alice Montague Kelleher, sister-in-law of Sandwich glassworker Thomas Kelleher, states that Thomas told her the holders were for small *cigars*. The rims were crimped to prevent the holders from rolling off the table. Look for them at flea markets. Some have deer on them, and some have evergreen trees, made from little dots.

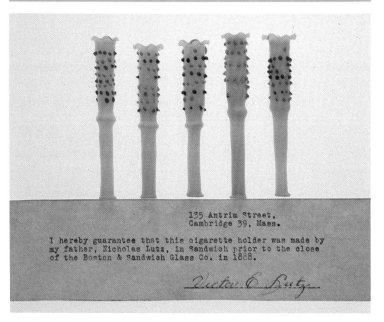

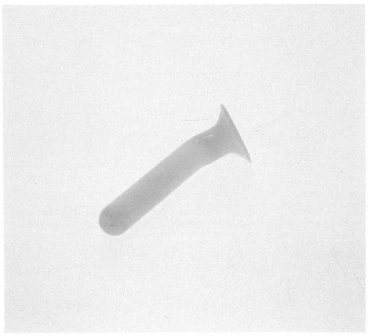

3415 BLOWN BOUTONNIERE HOLDER

2¼" L. x ¾" Dia. at rim; ⅜" Dia. of tube 1888-1892
Not made in Sandwich, this flower holder for a man's lape
was produced by a Pennsylvania glass house to match th
cigar holder. The Lutz family remembers that Nichola
often used one in his lapel for flowers that he grew in h
garden. A small amount of water placed in the holder ke
the boutonniere fresh. This holder is still in the Lu
family collection.

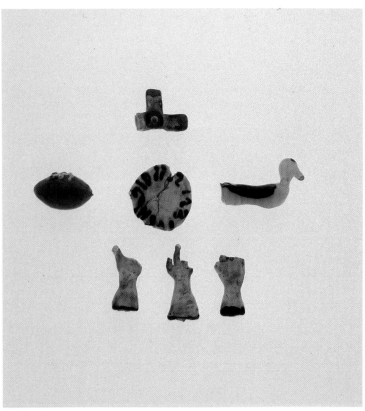

3416 LAMPWORK FROM LUTZ'S WORKBENCH

1870-1892
Nicholas Lutz's bench had some interesting things in i
At the top of this photo is part of a cross, used in pape
weights dating back to 1870, and as the finial for writin
pens. A football, the face of a toy clock and a bird are i
the center row. The bird has blue eyes and a yellow bea
The hands were made for the arms of leather dolls. If the
weren't formed correctly so they could be wired onto th
doll, they were discarded. The left one has only a thumb
Lutz made the clock faces and hands for Jones, McDuffe
and Stratton, a wholesale house that distributed the fin
ished toys. These artifacts do not represent Lutz's talen
Remember that they were discards, and some of the
may have been made by glassworkers he was teaching

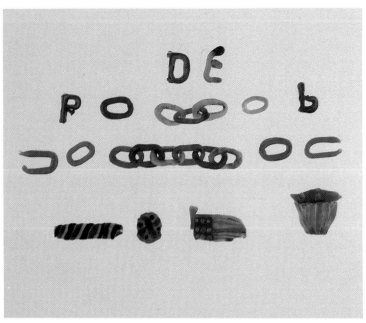

3417 LAMPWORK FROM LUTZ'S WORKBENCH

1870-1892
Many of the pieces were poorly made. We learned tha
Lutz taught young men who visited his home. This wou
explain the lack of quality. Most of the letters were to
large to become part of a Sandwich paperweight, bu
might have been the forerunners for the larger weigh
made at the Union Glass Company in Somerville, Massa
chusetts. Chains were a challenging exercise because it wa
difficult to keep the links from adhering to each other. Th
military bars, flags, and shields reflect Lutz's passion fo
red, white and blue. We may never know what many
the items in his bench were intended for.

57

1887   *Nicholas Lutz*

N: move	articles	N° made	Loss	packed	
7	Ink wells for Stand	4	made wrong		
	bruet rd to patt	2+2		1	1 in hand
8	F/Bowls to patt RC	103	3 broken	100	
9	Sm F/Bds offr	155	2 "	153	
10	Cor'd F/B to patt S/t	73	3 " 1 had	16—15—3 / 5—3	
	" " " S/t	20		3—m 2 / 27	
			Aug 29th		
1	Star B Bottl	138	3 crooked 2 chipp	133	
2	Mustds + Cor	20+21	1 broken 1 bad	20. 20	2 on hand
	Tmbs to patt	44		44	
	F/B "	16		16	
3	1 cor for Box	1		1	
	Laps to patt	154			
4	Inks "	115	} 8 broken	287	
5	" "	180	}		
6	Glo Mustds	78		78	
	st "	67		67	
7	Lmng to for frame	3		2	1 "
	Ink wells 2 sizes	4		2	2 "
	Sms to patt	2		1	1 "
	" "	12	1 broke	11	
	F/B pr Lgr S to patt	17		17	
	Inks to patt blue	57	2 bad	55	
	Lmng to for frame	4	2 broken	2	
	Shade to patt	6		6	
8	F/2 pr Catsup Bottl	125	} 2 bad	141	
9	"	18	}		
	3 Life Glo hand oil	129	1 crooked		
10	Clarets to patt	79	3 broke 1 bad	76	
	Sm F/Glo offr	28	1 flew	27	
			Sept 5th		
1	Goblets to patt	126	2 bad chipp 1 bro	123	
2	Lgr Spice Bn r	159+1	4 " "		
	Tmbls to patt	20	1 "	19	
3	F/2 pr Oyr h Oils	127	6 crooked in W		
4	" Catsup Bottl	123	3 bad made		
5	Mustard Lin	84		84	
	Senl S to patt	14		14	
	Cover "	2			
	Rods 35 in Long 3/4 dia	5		2	3 on hand
	Fessenden Goblt	36	1 crooked 2 cord	33	
6	Clarets to patt	142	5 broken 1 "	136	
7	F/2 Glo st Oils	152	8 crooked		
8	F/3 " S to patt m	188	1 Bad	183	

Page 57 of the Boston and Sandwich Glass Company sloar book. Nicholas Lutz's shop was required to make ten moves each week. The top of the page is a continuation of the week of August 22, 1887. For the eighth move, the shop made 103 finger bowls with ruby threads. Three were broken and one hundred were packed. For move ten, Lutz made seventy-three covers for 5" Dia. finger bowls with green threads and thirty covers with blue threads. Today a covered piece would not be recognized as a finger bowl. Part of move five for the week of September 5 was five 35" L. x 3/4" Dia. rods. Two were packed and three were kept for their own use. Seventeen pages record Lutz's work from May 31, 1887, to the end of the year. *Sandwich Archives and Historical Center*

Nicholas Lutz

1887

M. M.	Articles	No. Made	Loss	Packed	
6	Stoppr to patt	2		1	1 on hand
	F/f " "	2		1	1 "
	Sml Alr Cork'd patt	33		33	
7	" " "	1116	11 specky	95	
8	Bottles to patt	83	2 broken	81	
	Rml Alr Corks	21	2 " 5 specks	13	
	Deep Custards	26	1 broken hand	25	
9	Gill hand Oils	291	4 "	287	
10	Lowfr finger bowls purple	24	1 bad	23	
	6in Fish offr	107	(3 flew)	104	

Oct 31st

1	Insults to patt	81	2 bad 2 bro	77	
	Biskr " "	4		4	
	Linings to for metal	10	1 broken	9	
2	Oval Bot Mustards	2		1	1 on hand
	Inks 2 size	61		61	
	Vinegars fct Stuart 28-29			28-29	
	4½ Mar'l Mustd copy	18		18	
3	" " "	13	2 broke	11	
	Gill Grape Glass top	30		30	
	Vacuum Glass	1		1	
	Jr Can to samples	2	1 bro	1	
	Linings to for frames	8		6	2 on hand
	" " " "				
	Box to for Cov	2		1	1 "
	Lining to for frames blue	2	will not fit		
4	Lowfr finger bowls purple	136		136	
5	" "	142	11 broken		
6	Saucer Champ to patt	137	1 bad 3 broken	133	
7	U.C. F Bowls to patt	114	1 " 3 "	110	
	Blue lining for pure	2		2	
	Flint " "	2		2	
8	100/3 Hot Whiskies	140	4 crooked 1 broken	135	
9	4½ inks 1 s	no 6 c		no c 110 9	
	5 " Mustds	40-9			
	1 btl "	48-9	1 broke 1 bad	46-9	

Nov 7th

1	Fancy P Weights	150	2 broke	148	
2	" "	44	1 "	43	
	for S to patt ncks	42		42	
	Stoffr "	2		1	1 on hand
	Lifys	92		92	

Page 61 of the Boston and Sandwich Glass Company sloar book. The notations can be deciphered with careful study. Move ten for the week of October 24, 1887, consisted of twenty-four purple low foot finger bowls and 107 6" Dia. fish globes "off feet". One finger bowl was bad, leaving twenty-three to be packed. Three fish globes flew (shattered in the annealing leer) and 104 were packed. The shop began the week of November 7 by making 150 fancy paperweights, two of which broke. Note the number of plain linings that were made to fit metal frames. Because they have no pattern, they cannot be identified as Sandwich glass today unless you know the company that made the frame and have invoices showing the linings were ordered from the Boston and Sandwich Glass Company. *Sandwich Archives and Historical Center*

APPENDIX

Deming Jarves maintained a very complicated business relationship with several partners. During the time he was active in Sandwich's glass industry, he also owned the Mount Washington Glass Works in South Boston and a retail store in Boston that dealt in imported and domestic glass. The store's domestic glass was manufactured at Mount Washington. This time chart will help you understand the inner workings of these relationships. Keep in mind that these business ventures were all active simultaneously, sometimes complementing and often conflicting with each other.

825   George Deming Jarves, son of Deming, was born in February.

837   The glass factory that would later be known as the Mount Washington Glass Works was established by Deming Jarves. It was located in South Boston, between First Street and Second Street, near Dorchester Street. It was not called by that name in the Boston City Directory. Documents from the family of mold maker/machinist Hiram Dillaway refer to the "Mount Washington Glass Manufactory".

839   Mount Washington Glass Works reportedly reverted to Labree and Jarves, a partnership between Deming Jarves and John D. Labree.

840's   Minutes of the Board of Directors meetings held in the early 1840's indicate that Deming Jarves bought glass privately from the Boston and Sandwich Glass Company and sold it through his private business enterprise in Boston.

843   January 24: Records show that John D. Labree and Henry Cormerais were employed by the Boston and Sandwich Glass Company. They worked in the company counting house located at 137 Milk Street in Boston.

844   January 11: Deming Jarves, on a personal basis, was planning to erect a store or stores in Boston for the use of the Boston and Sandwich Glass Company. They were to be built to the specifications of the company and rented to it by Jarves. January 12: The Boston and Sandwich Glass Company planned to pay rent and taxes for two stores to be built on Federal Street in Boston. October 18: Deming Jarves notified the Board of Directors that he would remain in the employ of the Boston and Sandwich Glass Company if, among other things, it would rent one of the stores on Federal Street and consider the possibility of renting the adjoining one. Jarves felt that they needed better facilities. The company's address in the Boston City Directory was still 137 Milk Street.

1845   George D. Jarves, twenty years old, is listed as a clerk in the Boston City Directory. The Boston and Sandwich Glass Company address has been changed to 51 Federal Street, on the corner of Franklin.
December 7: Boston and Sandwich Glass Company consigned a large amount of glass to Deming Jarves, at a discount.

1846   February 4: A legal partnership was formed under the name of Labree and Jarves. John D. Labree and George D. Jarves (age 21) were listed as general partners, and Deming Jarves was listed as a special partner.
Labree (John D.) and Jarves (George D.) are listed in the directory as having a glass factory on First Street (Mount Washington Glass Works) and also as a firm dealing in lamps and chandeliers with an office at 71 Summer Street. This was the location of Deming Jarves' home, where George Jarves also lived.
September 26: John D. Labree died.

1847   G. D. Jarves and Cormerais was established. This was a partnership between George D. Jarves, then twenty-two years old, and Henry Cormerais.

1850   March 5: George D. Jarves, son of Deming, died of consumption. He was twenty-five years and twenty-four days old, according to records at Mount Auburn Cemetery in Cambridge, Massachusetts. The firm of G. D. Jarves and Cormerais was continued by partners Deming Jarves and Henry Cormerais.

1851   William L. Libbey was employed as a bookkeeper by G. D. Jarves and Cormerais at 45 Federal Street.

1852   In April, the firm of G. D. Jarves and Cormerais leased the Mount Washington Glass Works (still not called by that name), located in South Boston, from Deming Jarves.

1853   December 17: Records show that the Boston and Sandwich Glass Company and G. D. Jarves and Cormerais planned to share a store at 51 Federal Street, next to the present office of the Boston and Sandwich Glass Company on Federal Street. Each firm was to share equally the rent, taxes, and expense of fitting the new store.

1856   Mount Washington Glass Works was first listed as such in the Boston City Directory.

1858   June 9: Deming Jarves severed his relationship with the Boston and Sandwich Glass Company.

1859   April 1: John W. Jarves and Company was established for the running of the Cape Cod Glass Works in Sandwich, with an office at 51 Federal Street.

         G. D. Jarves and Cormerais are also at 51 Federal Street in 1859.

1860   Mount Washington Glass Works closed, then was leased by Timothy Howe, who had been employed there as a clerk since 1856.

1861   G. D. Jarves and Cormerais went into receivership. An invoice dated November 1861, shows that John Lowell was the receiver. After 1861, the firm was no longer listed in the Boston City Directory. Henry Cormerais became the agent of the Union Glass Company, located in Somerville, Massachusetts.

         On November 1, 1883, the *Crockery and Glass Journal* printed an article that had been written by one "Uncle Tobey", and published in *The Boston Herald*. Facts were related regarding the breakup of Deming Jarves' business relationship with Henry Cormerais:

> Mr. Jarves was a rather peculiar, positive man, with a high and ungovernable temper, and his partner was a good deal like him in many respects. Both obstinate as mules and once they took a position would not give away though the heavens should fail. There are a lot of foolish people in the world just like them, who will allow their tempers to make fools of them, and lead them to say and do things which no sane person under the circumstances should be guilty of. As the story goes: One day a messenger came in with a bank notice for Mr. Cormerais and laid it upon Mr. Jarves' desk. Mr. Cormerais, noticing the action of the messenger, very quickly picked up the paper and put it in his pocket. It was a notification that a certain note would fall due on a certain date, and in a hasty glance Mr. Jarves mastered its contents. He did not believe in making or giving notes and asked his partner what it meant. Mr. Cormerais said it was a private transaction and he would attend to it. Mr. Jarves pressed further, and Mr. Cormerais said it was none of his business. Mr. Jarves

> was determined to find out what it meant, and proceeded to follow up the inquiry in a way that angered Mr. Cormerais and led to a bitter quarrel between the partners. The result was a determination of both to wind up the business, and a receiver was appointed to that end. The receiver proceeded to do his work and sold by auction a very valuable stock of goods for a mere song. Probably not 25 cents on a dollar were realized on the goods at the sale. Thus, this foolish quarrel which had no real foundation to start on, beyond high temper and hasty action resulted in breaking up one of the most prosperous businesses of its kind in the country, and left the partners comparatively poor men. Within a year or two of this breakup, the war of the rebellion broke out, and, if the partners had got along together and were in business, and had such a stock on hand as they had when they dissolved, it would have more than doubled in their hands within a year after hostilities commenced.

Mount Washington Glass Works was taken over by William L. Libbey and Timothy Howe.

1863   May 21: John W. Jarves, son of Deming, died of tuberculosis. He was twenty-eight years and five months old, according to records at Mount Auburn Cemetery in Cambridge, Massachusetts.

         May 22: The firm of John W. Jarves and Company was dissolved.

1864   February 8: Cape Cod Glass Works was reorganized as the Cape Cod Glass Company. Deming Jarves was one of five directors.

1866   In September, Deming Jarves sent James D. Lloyd to the Mount Washington Glass Works. Lloyd's task was to determine the cost of fuel and the amount of glass that could be melted each week, so that Jarves would know the cost of running the factory. According to Lloyd family documents, Jarves was planning on running the South Boston factory which was making samples using some of the same patterns as the Cape Cod Glass Company.

1867   October 10: William L. Libbey leased the Mount Washington Glass Works in South Boston after the death of Timothy Howe.

1869   April 15: Deming Jarves died, and the Cape Cod Glass Company closed the same day.

1870   January 4: William L. Libbey purchased the New Bedford Glass Company, located on Prospect Street in New Bedford, Massachusetts. This company had been founded in 1866 by Theodore Kern and others. Libbey terminated his lease in South Boston, and moved the Mount Washington Glass Works from South Boston to the New Bedford site.

GLOSSARY

ADVENTURINE See *goldstone*.

ANNEAL The gradual reheating and slow cooling of an article in a leer—an oven built for the purpose. This procedure removes any stress that may have built up in the glass during its manufacture.

APPLIED The fastening of a separate piece of glass, such as a base, handle, prunt, or stem, to an article already formed.

BATCH Mixture of sand, cullet, and various raw materials that are placed in the pot to be heated into metal, or molten glass.

BLANK A finished piece of glass requiring additional work, such as decorating or engraving.

BLOWN GLASS Glass made by the use of a blowpipe and air pressure sufficient to give it form.

BLOWN MOLDED GLASS Glass made by blowing hot glass into a plain or patterned mold, and forcing it with air pressure to conform to the shape of the mold.

BOX A container of any shape and any size. It can be square, rectangular, circular or oval.

BUTTON STEM A connector between the base and the body of any article, with a button-shaped extrusion in its center.

CANE In *paperweight making*, a bundle of various colored rods that are arranged into a design, fused by reheating, pulled until it is long and thin, cooled and then cut into segments.

CASING A different colored layer of glass, either on the inside or outside of the main body of a piece.

CASTOR PLACE The location in the factory where glass was cast (pressed) into molds.

CLAW FOOT An applied reeded foot resembling a scallop shell.

CLUSTER On *cut glass*, a grouping of similar designs in close proximity.

CRAQUELLE Glass that has been deliberately fractured after it has been formed, and reheated to seal the fractures, leaving the scars as a permanent design.

CROSSCUT DIAMOND On *cut glass*, a diamond that is divided into quarters.

CULLET Glass made in the factory and saved from a pot to be used in making future batches. Also, glass items already annealed; either produced in the factory or purchased, and broken to be included in future batches.

CUTTING The grinding away of a portion of the surface of a blank, using wheels and wet sand, to produce a design.

DECORATING The ornamenting of a blank by painting or staining it with a non-glass substance.

DESIGN The ornamentation of glass after it has been annealed, by cutting, engraving, etching or decorating.

DONUT On *Trevaise*, the wafer-size glob of glass applied to the base. In most cases, the center of the wafer is dished out, leaving the shape of a donut.

ENGRAVING The process of cutting shallow designs and letters into a blank using copper wheels and an abrasive.

ETCHING An inexpensive method of producing a design by using hydrofluoric acid to eat into the surface of a blank.

FILIGREE ROD A rod that has spiral or straight threads running through it. Also called *latticinio*.

FINIAL The decorative, terminal part of a newel post, writing pen, etc. The part of a cover used as a handle.

FIRE POLISHING Reheating a finished piece to remove marks left by tools or molds, leaving the article with a smooth surface.

FLASHED On *cut glass*, a fan-like design located between the points of a fan, hobstar, or star.

FLINT GLASS Glass made from metal containing lead. In the 1800's, the factory term for clear glass.

FLOATED In *decorated opal glass*, the method used to apply a solid color background.

FLUTE The hand-crimping of a rim. On *pressed* or *cut glass*, a panel rounded at the top.

FOLDED RIM A rim on either the body or base of a piece, the edge of which is doubled back onto itself, resulting in greater strength.

FRAGMENTS Broken pieces of finished glass, discarded at the time of production.

FREE-BLOWN GLASS Glass made by blowing hot glass and shaping it into its final form by the use of hand tools.

GAFFER   In a group of glassworkers, called a *shop*, the most skilled artisan; the master glass blower.

GATHER   The mass of hot metal that has been gathered on the end of a blowpipe.

GATHERER   The assistant to the master glass blower, who gathers the hot metal on the end of the blowpipe.

GAUFFER   To crimp or flute.

GILDING   The application of gold for decorative purposes.

GLASS GALL   Impurities skimmed from the surface of melted glass. Also called *sandever, sandiver*.

GOLDSTONE   Glass combined with copper filings.

HOBSTAR   On *cut glass*, a many-pointed geometrically cut star.

KNOP   A round knob, either hollow or solid, in the center of a stem.

LAMPWORK   The making and assembly of leaves, petals, stems, fruit and other small parts from rods of glass that have been softened by heating them over a gas burner. Originally, oil lamps produced the open flame.

LAPIDARY STOPPER   A cut, faceted stopper.

LATTICINIO   A rod of glass or a paperweight background composed of threads arranged in lattice, spiral or swirl configurations. The threads are usually white.

LEER   A tunnel-shaped oven through which glass articles are drawn after formation for the purpose of annealing. Also spelled *lear, lehr*.

MAKE-DO   A damaged item that has been repaired to "make it do" what was originally intended.

MARBRIE   In *blown glass*, a loop design made by looping and trailing threads of glass through another color, such as in paperweights and witch balls.

MARVER   Iron plate on which hot glass is first shaped by rolling, in preparation for blowing into its final form.

MERESE   A wafer-shaped piece of hot glass, used to connect individual units to make a complete piece, such as the base and socket of a candlestick or the bowl and standard of a footed nappie.

METAL   Glass either in a molten condition in the pot, or in a cold, hardened state.

MOLD   A form into which glass is blown or pressed to give it shape and pattern. Also spelled *mould*.

MOLD MARKS   On glass that has been blown or pressed into a mold, the marks or seam lines left by the edges of the units of the mold.

MOVE   A period of time during which a shop makes glass continuously. A glass blower is expected to make ten *moves* each week.

NAPPIE   A shallow bowl of any size, whether round bottomed or flat bottomed, which can be on a standard. Also spelled *nappy*.

NEEDLE ETCHING   Done by coating a blank with an acid-resisting substance, then inscribing a design into the resist with a sharp needle. The blank is then dipped into hydrofluoric acid, which etches the glass where the design was inscribed.

NIB   The writing point of a pen.

OVERFILL   On pieces that have been blown or pressed into a mold, the excess hot glass that seeps into the seams of the mold.

PANEL   A section with raised margins and square corners.

PATTERN (ON GLASS)   The specific ornamentation into which *hot* glass is formed.

PATTERN (WOODEN)   Wooden model carved in detail that is sent to the foundry, used as a guide to shape a mold.

PEG   On a *lamp*, the unit that holds the oil and is attached to the base with a metal connector.

PICKWICK   A pointed instrument for picking up the wick of a whale oil or fluid lamp.

PILLAR-MOLDED GLASS   Glass made by first blowing a hot gather of glass into a mold with vertical ridges (pillars). A second cooler gather is blown into the first. The hot outer layer conforms to the shape of the mold while the cooler inner layer remains smooth.

PINWHEEL   On *cut glass*, a design resembling a hobstar in motion; its points angled in a clockwise or counterclockwise position.

PONTIL MARK   Rough spot caused by breaking away the pontil rod.

PONTIL ROD   A rod or iron used by glassworkers to hold the glass while it is being formed.

POT   A one-piece container in which glass is melted, usually made of clay and able to withstand extreme heat.

PLINTH   A square block forming the base for a standard. Also, a base and standard molded in one piece used as the lower unit of a lamp.

PRESSED GLASS   Glass made by placing hot glass into a mold and forcing it with a plunger to conform to the shape of the mold.

PRISM   A pattern or design of deep parallel V-grooves that reflect the light.

PRUNT   A blob of glass applied to the surface of a vessel, for the purpose of decorating or hiding a defect.

PUNTING   The process of dishing out a circle with a cutting wheel, usually to remove the mark left by the pontil rod.

PUNTY   A concave circle made by dishing out the glass with a cutting wheel.

QUILTING   In *art glass*, an all-over diamond design, permanently molded into the piece as it was being blown.

RIBBON ROD   A rod that has twisted flat ribbons of glass running through it.

RIGAREE   A heavy thread of glass applied to the surface of a piece, giving a decorative rippled or fluted effect.

ROD   A straight shaft of glass that will be reheated to form other things. Thin rods are fused together to make canes, and are also softened to supply glass for lampwork. Thick rods are formed into chandelier arms and epergne units. Reeded rods are used to form handles and claw feet on Late Blown Ware, as well as nibs for glass writing pens.

SERVITOR   The first assistant to the gaffer in a group of glassworkers called a *shop*.

SHEDDING   The flaking of the surface of finished glass exposed to the air, cause by minute particles of fire clay in the sand. According to C. C. P. Waterman, writing in 1875, " . . . small specks of fire clay which shed themselves very much to their annoyance throughout the melted glass."

SHELL FOOT See *claw foot*.

SHOP A group of workmen producing glass at the furnace, consisting of a master glass blower and his help.

SICK GLASS Discoloration of the surface of an article.

SLOAR BOOK The book in which an accounting was kept of the output of glass produced by each shop at the furnace.

SLOAR MAN The glassworker who entered the output of each shop in the sloar book.

SOCKET EXTENSION On a *candlestick*, the section between the socket and the wafer, molded in one piece with the socket.

SPIDER PONTIL An iron unit placed on the end of the pontil rod, consisting of several finger-like rods. The fingers gave support to items that could not be held by a single rod in the center.

STAINED GLASS A finished piece of clear glass that is colored wholly or in part by the application of a chemical dye—most commonly ruby. The article is re-fired, making the dye a permanent finish.

STICKER-UP BOY The boy who carries hot glass on a V-shaped stick in a group of glassworkers called a *shop*.

STRAWBERRY DIAMOND On *cut glass*, a diamond which is crosshatched. Also the name of a cut glass design that utilizes crosscut diamonds.

TAKER-IN BOY The boy who carries the hot finished product to the leer in a group of glassworkers called a *shop*. During slow periods, he assists in the removal of glass from the cold end of the leer.

TALE Articles sold by count rather than by weight. In the words of Deming Jarves, "Tale was derived from the mode of selling, the best glass being sold only by weight, while light articles were sold tale."

UNDERFILL An insufficient amount of glass blown or pressed into a mold, resulting in an incomplete product. This is a characteristic, not a defect.

VESICA On *cut glass*, a pointed oval.

WAFER A flattened piece of hot glass, sometimes called a merese, used to join separately made units into a complete piece, such as the base and socket of a candlestick or the bowl and standard of a footed nappie.

WHIMSEY Unusual, one-of-a-kind item made of glass by a worker in his spare time.

Gaffer Bob Matthews shaping the foot of a wine glass.

BIBLIOGRAPHY

UNPUBLISHED SOURCES

Account book of various activities of the Boston and Sandwich Glass Company, such as the company store, seagoing vessels, wages, and wood for construction and fuel. April 17, 1826, to July 1830. Ms. collection in the Tannahill Research Library, Henry Ford Museum, Edison Institute, Dearborn, Michigan.

Burbank, George E. *History of the Sandwich Glass Works.* Ms. in the Barlow collection.

Corporate records. Office of the Secretary of State, The Commonwealth of Massachusetts, Boston, Massachusetts.

Correspondence pertaining to the management of the Boston and Sandwich Glass Company and the Cape Cod Glass Company, such as glass formulas, letters, special notices and transfers. Ms. collection in the Tannahill Research Library, Henry Ford Museum, Edison Institute, Dearborn, Michigan.

Correspondence pertaining to the management of the Boston and Sandwich Glass Company, the Boston and Sandwich Glass Company II and the Cape Cod Glass Company, such as glass formulas, letters, statements, etc. Ms. collection in the Rakow Library, The Corning Museum of Glass, Corning, New York.

Correspondence to and from glass authorities and writers on the subject of glass, pertaining to the excavation of the Boston and Sandwich Glass Company site and the discussion of fragments. Ms. consisting of the Francis (Bill) Wynn papers, now in the Barlow collection.

Documentation in the form of fragments dug from factory and cutting shop sites. Private collections and the extensive Barlow collection, which includes the former Francis (Bill) Wynn collection.

Documentation of Sandwich glass items and Sandwich glassworkers, such as hand-written notebooks, letters, billheads, contracts, pictures, and oral history of Sandwich families recorded on tape by descendants. Ms. in the Barlow collection, Kaiser collection and private collections.

Documents pertaining to the genealogy of the family of Deming Jarves. Mount Auburn Cemetery, Cambridge, Massachusetts.

Documents pertaining to the Sandwich glass industry and other related industries, such as statistics from Sandwich Vital Records, information from property tax records, maps, photographs, family papers and genealogy. Ms. in the care of the Town of Sandwich Massachusetts Archives and Historical Center, Sandwich, Massachusetts.

Documents relating to the North Sandwich industrial area, such as photographs, account books and handwritten scrapbooks. Ms. in the private collection of Mrs. Edward "Ned" Nickerson and the Bourne Historical Society, Bourne, Massachusetts.

Documents relating to the Sandwich Co-operative Glass Company, such as account books, correspondence and glass formulas. Ms. in the private collection of Murray family descendants.

Glass formula book. "Sandwich Aug. 7, 1868, James D. Lloyd." Ms. collection in the Tannahill Research Library, Henry Ford Museum, Edison Institute, Dearborn, Michigan.

Lapham family documents, such as pictures and genealogy. Ms. in the private collections of Lapham family descendants.

Lutz family documents, such as pictures, handwritten biographies and genealogy. Ms. in the private collections of Lutz family descendants.

Mary Gregory documents, such as diaries, letters and pictures. Ms. in the Barlow collection, Kaiser collection, other private collections, and included in the private papers of her family.

Minutes of annual meetings, Board of Directors meetings, special meetings and stockholders meetings of the Boston and Sandwich Glass Company. Ms. collection in the Tannahill Research Library, Henry Ford Museum, Edison Institute, Dearborn, Michigan.

Minutes of meetings of the American Flint Glass Workers Union, Local No. 16. Ms. in the Sandwich Glass Museum, Sandwich Historical Society, Sandwich, Massachusetts.

Nye family documents relating to the North Sandwich industrial area and the Electrical Glass Corporation. Ms. in the Barlow-Kaiser collection.

Oral history recorded on tape. Tales of Cape Cod, Inc. collection in the Cape Cod Community College Library, Hyannis, Massachusetts.

Patents relating to the invention of new techniques in glassmaking, improved equipment for glassmaking, new designs and styles of glass, and the invention of other items relating to the glass industry. United States Department of Commerce, Patent and Trademark Office, Washington, D. C.

Population Schedule of the Census of the United States. Ms. from National Archives Microfilm Publications, National Archives and Records Service, Washington, D. C.

Property deeds and other proofs of ownership, such as surveys, mortagage deeds, and last will and testaments. Ms. in the Barnstable County Registry of Deeds and Barnstable County Registry of Probate, Barnstable, Massachusetts.

Sloar book, a weekly accounting of glass produced at the Sandwich Glass Manufactory and the Boston and Sandwich Glass Company, and the workers who produced it. July 9, 1825, to March 29, 1828. Ms. collection in the Tannahill Research Library, Henry Ford Museum, Edison Institute, Dearborn, Michigan.

Spurr family documents, such as pictures, handwritten autobiographies, glass formulas and genealogy. Ms. in the private collections of Spurr family descendants.

Vodon family documents, such as pictures and genealogy. Ms. in the private collection of Vodon family descendants.

Waterman, Charles Cotesworth Pinckney. Notes on the Boston and Sandwich Glass Company, dated November 1876, and deposited in the Sandwich Centennial Box. Ms. in the care of the Town of Sandwich Massachusetts Archives and Historical Center, Sandwich, Massachusetts.

PRINTED SOURCES

Amic, Yolande. *L'Opaline Francaise au XIXᵉ Siecle.* Paris, France: Library Gründ, 1952.

Anthony, T. Robert. *19th Century Fairy Lamps.* Manchester, Vermont: Forward's Color Productions, Inc., 1969.

Avila, George C. *The Pairpoint Glass Story.* New Bedford, Massachusetts: Reynolds-DeWalt Printing, Inc., 1968.

Barbour, Harriot Buxton. *Sandwich The Town That Glass Built.* Boston, Massachusetts: Houghton Mifflin Company, 1948.

Barret, Richard Carter. *A Collectors Handbook of American Art Glass.* Manchester, Vermont: Forward's Color Productions, Inc., 1971.

_____. *A Collectors Handbook of Blown and Pressed American Glass.* Manchester, Vermont: Forward's Color Productions, Inc., 1971.

_____. *Popular American Ruby-Stained Pattern Glass.* Manchester, Vermont: Forward's Color Productions, Inc., 1968.

Belknap, E. McCamly. *Milk Glass.* New York, New York: Crown Publishers, Inc., 1949.

Bishop, Barbara. "Deming Jarves and His Glass Factories," *The Glass Club Bulletin,* Spring 1983, pp. 3-5.

Bishop, Barbara and Martha Hassell. *Your Obdᵗ. Servᵗ., Deming Jarves.* Sandwich, Massachusetts: The Sand-

wich Historical Society, 1984.

Brown, Clark W. *Salt Dishes.* Leon, Iowa: Mid-America Book Company, reprinted in 1968.

_____. *A Supplement to Salt Dishes.* Leon, Iowa: Prairie Winds Press, reprinted in 1970.

Burbank, George E. *A Bit of Sandwich History.* Sandwich, Massachusetts: 1939.

Burgess, Bangs. *History of Sandwich Glass.* Yarmouth, Massachusetts: The Register Press, 1925.

Butterfield, Oliver. "Bewitching Witchballs," *Yankee,* July 1978, pp. 97, 172-175.

Cataldo, Louis and Dorothy Worrell. *Pictorial Tales of Cape Cod.* (Vol. I) Hyannis, Massachusetts: Tales of Cape Cod, Inc., 1956.

Cataldo, Louis and Dorothy Worrell. *Pictorial Tales of Cape Cod.* (Vol. II) Hyannis, Massachusetts: Tales of Cape Cod, Inc., 1961.

Childs, David B. "If It's Threaded . . . ," *Yankee,* June 1960, pp. 86-89.

Chipman, Frank W. *The Romance of Old Sandwich Glass.* Sandwich, Massachusetts: Sandwich Publishing Company Inc., 1932.

Cloak, Evelyn Campbell. *Glass Paperweights of the Bergstrom Art Center.* New York, New York: Crown Publishers, Inc., 1969.

Covill, William E., Jr. *Ink Bottles and Inkwells.* Taunton, Massachusetts: William S. Sullwold Publishing, 1971.

Culver, Willard R. "From Sand to Seer and Servant of Man," *The National Geographic Magazine,* January 1943, pp. 17-24, 41-48.

Deyo, Simeon L. *History of Barnstable County, Massachusetts.* New York, New York: H. W. Blake & Co., 1890.

DiBartolomeo, Robert E. *American Glass from the Pages of Antiques; Pressed and Cut.* (Vol. II) Princeton, New Jersey: The Pyne Press, 1974.

Dooley, William Germain. *Old Sandwich Glass.* Pasadena, California: Esto Publishing Company, n.d.

_____. "Recollections of Sandwich Glass by a Veteran Who Worked on It," *Hobbies,* June 1951, p. 96.

Drepperd, Carl W. *The ABC's of Old Glass.* Garden City, New York: Doubleday & Company, Inc., 1949.

Fauster, Carl U. *Libbey Glass Since 1818.* Toledo, Ohio: Len Beach Press, 1979.

Freeman, Frederick. *History of Cape Cod: Annals of the Thirteen Towns of Barnstable County.* Boston, Massachusetts: George C. Rand & Avery, 1862.

Freeman, Dr. Larry. *New Light on Old Lamps.* Watkins Glen, New York: American Life Foundation, reprinted in 1984.

Gaines, Edith. "Woman's Day Dictionary of American Glass," *Woman's Day,* August 1961, pp. 19-34.

_____. "Woman's Day Dictionary of Sandwich Glass," *Woman's Day,* August 1963, pp. 21-32.

_____. "Woman's Day Dictionary of Victorian Glass," *Woman's Day,* August 1964, pp. 23-34.

Gores, Stan. *1876 Centennial Collectibles and Price Guide.* Fond du Lac, Wisconsin: The Haber Printing Co., 1974.

Grover, Ray and Lee Grover. *Art Glass Nouveau.* Rutland, Vermont: Charles E. Tuttle Company, Inc., 1967.

Grover, Ray and Lee Grover. *Carved & Decorated European Art Glass*. Rutland, Vermont: Charles E. Tuttle Company, Inc., 1970.

Grow, Lawrence. *The Warner Collector's Guide to Pressed Glass*. New York, New York: Warner Books, Inc., 1982.

Hammond, Dorothy. *Confusing Collectibles*. Des Moines, Iowa: Wallace-Homestead Book Company, 1969.

_____. *More Confusing Collectibles*. Wichita, Kansas: C. B. P. Publishing Company, 1972.

Harris, Amanda B. "Down in Sandwich Town," *Wide Awake* 1, 1887, pp. 19–27.

Harris, John. *The Great Boston Fire, 1872*. Boston, Massachusetts: Boston Globe, 1972.

Hartung, Marion T. and Ione E. Hinshaw. *Patterns and Pinafores*. Des Moines, Iowa: Wallace-Homestead Book Company, 1971.

Haynes, E. Barrington. *Glass Through the Ages*. Baltimore, Maryland: Penguin Books, 1969.

Hayward, Arthur H. *Colonial and Early American Lighting*. New York, New York: Dover Publications, Inc., reprinted in 1962.

Heacock, William. *Encyclopedia of Victorian Colored Pattern Glass; Book 1 Toothpick Holders from A to Z*. Jonesville, Michigan: Antique Publications, 1974.

_____. *Encyclopedia of Victorian Colored Pattern Glass; Book 2 Opalescent Glass from A to Z*. Jonesville, Michigan: Antique Publications, 1975.

_____. *Encyclopedia of Victorian Colored Pattern Glass; Book 3 Syrups, Sugar Shakers & Cruets from A to Z*. Jonesville, Michigan: Antique Publications, 1976.

_____. *Encyclopedia of Victorian Colored Pattern Glass; Book 4 Custard Glass from A to Z*. Marietta, Ohio: Antique Publications, 1976.

_____. *Encyclopedia of Victorian Colored Pattern Glass; Book 5 U. S. Glass from A to Z*. Marietta, Ohio: Antique Publications, 1978.

_____. *Encyclopedia of Victorian Colored Pattern Glass; Book 6 Oil Cruets from A to Z*. Marietta, Ohio: Antique Publications, 1981.

_____. *1000 Toothpick Holders; A Collector's Guide*. Marietta, Ohio: Antique Publications, 1977.

Heacock, William and Patricia Johnson. *5000 Open Salts; A Collector's Guide*. Marietta, Ohio: Richardson Printing Corporation, 1982.

Heckler, Norman. *American Bottles in the Charles B. Gardner Collection*. Bolton, Massachusetts: Robert W. Skinner, Inc., 1975.

Hildebrand, J. R. "Glass Goes To Town," *The National Geographic Magazine*, January 1943, pp. 1–16, 25–40.

Hollister, Paul, Jr. *The Encyclopedia of Glass Paperweights*. New York, New York: Clarkson N. Potter, Inc., 1969.

Ingold, Gérard. *The Art of the Paperweight; Saint Louis*. Santa Cruz, California: Paperweight Press, 1981.

Innes, Lowell. *Pittsburgh Glass 1797–1891*. Boston, Massachusetts: Houghton Mifflin Company, 1976.

Irwin, Frederick T. *The Story of Sandwich Glass*. Manchester, New Hampshire: Granite State Press, 1926.

Jarves, Deming. *Reminiscences of Glass-making*. Great Neck, New York: Beatrice C. Weinstock, reprinted in 1968.

Kamm, Minnie W. and Serry Wood. *The Kamm-Wood Encyclopedia of Pattern Glass*. (II vols.) Watkins Glen, New York: Century House, 1961.

Keene, Betsey D. *History of Bourne 1622–1937*. Yarmouthport, Massachusetts: Charles W. Swift, 1937.

Knittle, Rhea Mansfield. *Early American Glass*. New York, New York: The Century Co., 1927.

Lane, Lyman and Sally Lane, and Joan Pappas. *A Rare Collection of Keene & Stoddard Glass*. Manchester, Vermont: Forward's Color Productions, Inc., 1970.

Lanmon, Dwight P. "Russian Paperweights and Letter Seals?" *The Magazine Antiques*, October 1984, pp. 900–903.

_____. "Unmasking an American Glass Fraud," *The Magazine Antiques*, January 1983, pp. 226–236.

Lechler, Doris Anderson. *Children's Glass Dishes, China, and Furniture*. Paducah, Kentucky: Collector Books, 1983.

Lechler, Doris and Virginia O'Neill. *Children's Glass Dishes*. Nashville, Tennessee, 1976.

Lee, Ruth Webb. *Antique Fakes & Reproductions*. Wellesley Hills, Massachusetts: Lee Publications, 1966.

_____. *Early American Pressed Glass*. Wellesley Hills, Massachusetts: Lee Publications, 1960.

_____. *Nineteenth-Century Art Glass*. New York, New York: M. Barrows & Company, Inc., 1952.

_____. *Sandwich Glass*. Wellesley Hills, Massachusetts: Lee Publications, 1939.

_____. *Victorian Glass*. Wellesley Hills, Massachusetts: Lee Publications, 1944.

Lee, Ruth Webb and James H. Rose. *American Glass Cup Plates*. Wellesley Hills, Massachusetts: Lee Publications, 1948.

Lindsey, Bessie M. *American Historical Glass*. Rutland, Vermont: Charles E. Tuttle Co., 1967.

Lovell, Russell A., Jr. *The Cape Cod Story of Thornton W. Burgess*. Taunton, Massachusetts: Thornton W. Burgess Society, Inc., and William S. Sullwold Publishing, 1974.

_____. *Sandwich; A Cape Cod Town*. Sandwich, Massachusetts: Town of Sandwich Massachusetts Archives and Historical Center, 1984.

Mackay, James. *Glass Paperweights*. New York, New York: The Viking Press, Inc., 1973.

Manheim, Frank J. *A Garland of Weights*. New York, New York: Farrar, Straus and Giroux, 1967.

Manley, C. C. *British Glass*. Des Moines, Iowa: Wallace-Homestead Book Co., 1968.

Manley, Cyril. *Decorative Victorian Glass*. New York, New York: Van Nostrand Reinhold Company, 1981.

Mannoni, Edith. *Opalines*. Paris, France: Éditions Ch. Massin, n.d.

McKearin, George S. and Helen McKearin. *American Glass*. New York, New York: Crown Publishers, Inc., 1941.

McKearin, Helen and George S. McKearin. *Two Hundred Years of American Blown Glass*. New York, New York: Bonanza Books, 1949.

McKearin, Helen and Kenneth M. Wilson. *American Bottles & Flasks and Their Ancestry*. New York, New York: Crown Publishers, Inc., 1978.

Measell, James. *Greentown Glass; The Indiana Tumbler and Goblet Company*. Grand Rapids, Michigan: The Grand Rapids Public Museum with the Grand Rapids Museum Association, 1979.

Metz, Alice Hulett. *Early American Pattern Glass*. Columbus, Ohio: Spencer-Walker Press, 1965.

_____. *Much More Early American Pattern Glass*. Columbus, Ohio: Spencer-Walker Press, 1970.

Millard, S. T. *Goblets II*. Holton, Kansas: Gossip Printers and Publishers, 1940.

Miller, Robert W. *Mary Gregory and Her Glass*. Des Moines, Iowa: Wallace-Homestead Book Co., 1972.

Moore, N. Hudson. *Old Glass*. New York, New York: Tudor Publishing Co., 1924.

Mulch, Dwight. "John D. Larkin and Company: From Factory to Family," *The Antique Trader Weekly*, June 24, 1984, pp. 92–94.

Neal, L. W. and D. B. Neal. *Pressed Glass Salt Dishes of the Lacy Period 1825-1850*. Philadelphia, Pennsylvania: L. W. and D. B. Neal, 1962.

Pearson, J. Michael and Dorothy T. Pearson. *American Cut Glass Collections*. Miami, Florida: The Franklin Press, Inc., 1969.

Pearson, J. Michael and Dorothy T. Pearson. *American Cut Glass for the Discriminating Collector*. Miami, Florida: The Franklin Press, Inc., 1965.

Pepper, Adeline. *The Glass Gaffers of New Jersey*. New York, New York: Charles Scribner's Sons, 1971.

Peterson, Arthur G. *Glass Patents and Patterns*. Sanford, Florida: Celery City Printing Co., 1973.

_____. *Glass Salt Shakers: 1,000 Patterns*. Des Moines, Iowa: Wallace-Homestead Book Co., 1960.

Raycraft, Don and Carol Raycraft. *Early American Lighting*. Des Moines, Iowa: Wallace-Homestead Book Co., n.d.

Revi, Albert Christian. *American Art Nouveau Glass*. Exton, Pennsylvania: Schiffer Publishing, Ltd., 1981.

_____. *American Cut and Engraved Glass*. Nashville, Tennessee: Thomas Nelson Inc., 1972.

_____. *American Pressed Glass and Figure Bottles*. Nashville, Tennessee: Thomas Nelson Inc., 1972.

_____. *Nineteenth Century Glass*. Exton, Pennsylvania: Schiffer Publishing, Ltd., 1967.

Righter, Miriam. *Iowa City Glass*. Des Moines, Iowa: Wallace-Homestead Book Co., 1966.

Robertson, Frank E. "New Evidence from Sandwich Glass Fragments," *The Magazine Antiques*, October 1982, pp. 818–823.

Robertson, R. A. *Chats on Old Glass*. New York, New York: Dover Publications, Inc., 1969. Revised and enlarged by Kenneth M. Wilson.

Rose, James H. *The Story of American Pressed Glass of the Lacy Period 1825-1850*. Corning, New York: The Corning Museum of Glass, 1954.

Rushlight Club. *Early Lighting; A Pictorial Guide*. Talcottville, Connecticut: 1972.

Sandwich Glass Museum. *The Sandwich Glass Museum Collection*. Sandwich, Massachusetts: Sandwich Glass Museum, 1969.

Sauzay, A. *Wonders of Art and Archaeology; Wonders of Glass Making*. New York, New York: Charles Scribner's Sons, 1885.

Schwartz, Marvin D. *American Glass from the Pages of Antiques; Blown and Moulded*. (Vol. I) Princeton, New Jersey: The Pyne Press, 1974.

Smith, Allan B. and Helen B. Smith. *One Thousand Individual Open Salts Illustrated*. Litchfield, Maine: The Country House, 1972.

Smith, Allan B. and Helen B. Smith. *650 More Individual Open Salts Illustrated*. Litchfield, Maine: The Country House, 1973.

Smith, Allan B. and Helen B. Smith. *The Third Book of Individual Open Salts Illustrated*. Litchfield, Maine: The Country House, 1976.

Smith, Allan B. and Helen B. Smith. *Individual Open Salts Illustrated*. Litchfield, Maine: The Country House, n.d.

Smith, Allan B. and Helen B. Smith. *Individual Open Salts Illustrated; 1977 Annual*. Litchfield, Maine: The Country House, 1977.

Smith, Frank R. and Ruth E. Smith. *Miniature Lamps*. New York, New York: Thomas Nelson Inc., 1968.

Spillman, Jane Shadel. *American and European Pressed Glass in The Corning Museum of Glass*. Corning, New York: The Corning Museum of Glass, 1981.

_____. *Glass Bottles, Lamps & Other Objects*. New York, New York: Alfred A. Knopf, Inc., 1983.

_____. *Glass Tableware, Bowls & Vases*. New York, New York: Alfred A. Knopf, Inc., 1982.

_____. "Pressed-Glass Designs in the United States and Europe," *The Magazine Antiques*, July 1983, pp. 130–139.

Stanley, Mary Louise. *A Century of Glass Toys*. Manchester, Vermont: Forward's Color Productions, Inc., n.d.

Stetson, Nelson M. *Booklet No. 6; Stetson Kindred of America*. Campbello, Massachusetts: 1923.

Stow, Charles Messer. *The Deming Jarves Book of Designs*. Yarmouth, Massachusetts: The Register Press, 1925.

Swan, Frank H. *Portland Glass*. Des Moines, Iowa: Wallace-Homestead Book Company, 1949. Revised and enlarged by Marion Dana.

_____. *Portland Glass Company*. Providence, Rhode Island: The Roger Williams Press, 1939.

Taylor, Katrina V. H. "Russian Glass in the Hillwood Museum." *The Magazine Antiques*, July 1983, pp. 140–145.

Teleki, Gloria Roth. *The Baskets of Rural America*. New York, New York: E. P. Dutton & Co., Inc., 1975.

The Toledo Museum of Art. *Art in Glass*. Toledo, Ohio: The Toledo Museum of Art, 1969.

_____. *The New England Glass Company 1818-1888*. Toledo, Ohio: The Toledo Museum of Art, 1963.

Thuro, Catherine M. V. *Oil Lamps; The Kerosene Era in North America*. Des Moines, Iowa: Wallace-Homestead Book Co., 1976.

_____. *Oil Lamps II; Glass Kerosene Lamps*. Paducah, Kentucky and Des Moines, Iowa: Collector Books and Wallace-Homestead Book Co., 1983.

Thwing, Leroy. *Flickering Flames*. Rutland, Vermont: Charles E. Tuttle Company, 1974.

Towne, Sumner. "Mike Grady's Last Pot," *Yankee*, March 1968, pp. 84, 85, 136–139.

VanRensselaer, Stephen. *Early American Bottles & Flasks*.

Stratford, Connecticut: J. Edmund Edwards, 1971.

Vuilleumier, Marion. *Cape Cod; a Pictorial History*. Norfolk, Virginia, 1982.

Walsh, Lavinia. "The Romance of Sandwich Glass," *The Cape Cod Magazine*, July 1926, pp. 9, 26.

_____. "Old Boston and Sandwich Glassworks . . . .," *Ceramic Age*, December 1950, pp. 16, 17, 34.

Watkins, Lura Woodside. *American Glass and Glassmaking*. New York, New York: Chanticleer Press, 1950.

_____. *Cambridge Glass 1818 to 1888*. New York, New York: Bramhall House, 1930.

Webber, Norman W. *Collecting Glass*. New York, New York: Arco Publishing Company, Inc., 1973.

Webster, Noah. *An American Dictionary of the English Language*. Springfield, Massachusetts: George and Charles Merriam, 1847. Revised.

_____. *An American Dictionary of the English Language*. Springfield, Massachusetts: George and Charles Merriam, 1859. Revised and enlarged by Chauncey A. Goodrich.

_____. *An American Dictionary of the English Language*. Springfield, Massachusetts: G. & C. Merriam, 1872. Revised and enlarged by Chauncey A. Goodrich and Noah Porter.

Wetz, Jon and Jacqueline Wetz. *The Co-operative Glass Company Sandwich, Massachusetts: 1888–1891*. Sandwich, Massachusetts: Barn Lantern Publishing, 1976.

Williams, Lenore Wheeler. *Sandwich Glass*. Bridgeport, Connecticut: The Park City Eng. Co., 1922.

Wilson, Kenneth M. *New England Glass & Glassmaking*. New York, New York: Thomas Y. Crowell Company, 1972.

CATALOGS

A. L. Blackmer Co. Rich Cut Glass 1906–1907. Shreveport, Louisiana: The American Cut Glass Association, reprinted in 1982.

Amberina; 1884 New England Glass Works; 1917 Libbey Glass Company. Toledo, Ohio: Antique & Historical Glass Foundation, reprinted in 1970.

Averbeck Rich Cut Glass Catalog No. 104, The. Berkeley, California: Cembura & Avery Publishers, reprinted in 1973.

Boston & Sandwich Glass Co., Boston. Wellesley Hills, Massachusetts: Lee Publications, reprinted in 1968.

Boston & Sandwich Glass Co. Price List. Collection of the Sandwich Glass Museum, Sandwich Historical Society, Sandwich, Massachusetts, n.d.

Catalog of 700 Packages Flint Glass Ware Manufactured by the Cape Cod Glass Works, to be Sold at the New England Trade Sale, Wednesday, July 14, 1859 at 9½ O'clock. Collection of The Corning Museum of Glass Library, Corning, New York, 1859.

C. Dorflinger & Sons Cut Glass Catalog. Silver Spring, Maryland: Christian Dorflinger Glass Study Group, reprinted in 1981.

Collector's Paperweights; Price Guide and Catalog. Santa Cruz, California: Paperweight Press, 1983.

Cut Glass Produced by the Laurel Cut Glass Company. Shreveport, Louisiana: The American Cut Glass Associ-ation, reprinted, n.d.

Egginton's Celebrated Cut Glass. Shreveport, Louisiana: The American Cut Glass Association, reprinted in 1982.

Empire Cut Glass Company, The. Shreveport, Louisiana: American Cut Glass Association, reprinted in 1980.

F. X. Parsche & Son Co. Shreveport, Louisiana: American Cut Glass Association, reprinted in 1981.

Glassware Catalogue No. 25 Gillinder & Sons, Inc. Spring City, Tennessee: Hillcrest Books, reprinted in 1974.

Higgins and Seiter Fine China and Cut Glass Catalog No. 13. New York, New York: Higgins and Seiter, n.d.

Illustrated Catalog of American Hardware of the Russell and Erwin Manufacturing Company 1865. Association for Preservation Technology, reprinted in 1980.

J. D. Bergen Co., The; Manufacturers of Rich Cut Glassware 1904–1905. Berkeley, California: Cembura & Avery Publishers, reprinted in 1973.

Lackawanna Cut Glass Co. Shreveport, Louisiana: The American Cut Glass Association, reprinted, n.d.

Launay Hautin & Cie. Collection de dessins representant . . . Collection of The Corning Museum of Glass Library, Corning, New York, n.d.

Launay Hautin & Cie. Des Fabriques de Baccarat, St. Louis, Choisey et Bercy. Collection of The Corning Museum of Glass Library, Corning, New York, n.d.

Launay Hautin & Cie. Repertoire des Articles compris dans la Collection . . . Collection of The Corning Museum of Glass Library, Corning, New York, 1844.

Launay Hautin & Cie. Usages principaux pour services de table . . . Collection of The Corning Museum of Glass Library, Corning, New York, n.d.

Libbey Glass Co., The; Cut Glass June 1st, 1896. Toledo, Ohio: Antique & Historical Glass Foundation, reprinted in 1968.

List of Glass Ware Manufactured by Cape Cod Glass Company. Collection of the Sandwich Glass Museum, Sandwich Historical Society, Sandwich, Massachusetts, n.d.

M'Kee Victorial Glass; Five Complete Glass Catalogs from 1859/60 to 1871. New York, New York: Dover Publications, Inc., reprinted in 1981.

Monroe Cut Glass. Shreveport, Louisiana: American Cut Glass Association, reprinted, n.d.

Morey, Churchill & Morey Pocket Guide to 1880 Table Settings. Watkins Glen, New York: Century House, reprinted, n.d.

Mt. Washington Glass Co. Clinton, Maryland: Leonard E. Padgett, reprinted in 1976.

Mt. Washington Glass Company (cut glassware). Collection of The Corning Museum of Glass Library, Corning, New York, n.d.

Mt. Washington Glass Company; Crystal Gas Fixtures. Collection of The Corning Museum of Glass Library, Corning, New York, n.d.

Mt. Washington Glass Works (glass prisms and beads). Collection of The Corning Museum of Glass Library, Corning, New York, n.d.

Mt. Washington Glass Works Price List. Collection of The Corning Museum of Glass Library, Corning, New York, n.d.

New England Glass Company. Collection of The Corning Museum of Glass Library, Corning, New York, n.d.

New England Glass Company (list of glassware). Collection of The Corning Museum of Glass Library, Corning, New York, n.d.

Picture Book of Authentic Mid-Victorian Gas Lighting Fixtures; A Reprint of the Historic Mitchell, Vance & Co. Catalog, ca. 1876, with Over 1000 Illustrations. Mineola, New York: Dover Publications, Inc., reprinted in 1984.

Public Auction Richard A. Bourne Company, Inc. Boston, Massachusetts: The Nimrod Press, Inc., 1970–1985.

Quaker City Cut Glass Co. Shreveport, Louisiana: American Cut Glass Association, n.d.

Rich Cut Glass Pitkin & Brooks. Berkeley, California: Cembura & Avery Publishers, reprinted in 1973.

Sandwich Glass Patterns. West Englewood, New Jersey: Bernadine Forgett, n.d.

Taylor Bros. & Company, Inc., Manufacturers of Cut Glass. Shreveport, Louisiana: American Cut Glass Association, n.d.

BUSINESS DIRECTORIES

Boston City Directories. 1789–1891.

Resident and Business Directory of Bourne, Falmouth and Sandwich, Massachusetts. Hopkinton, Massachusetts: A. E. Foss & Co., 1900

NEWSPAPERS AND TRADE PAPERS

Academy Breezes. 1884–1886.

Acorn, The. Sandwich, Massachusetts: The Sandwich Historical Society, 1967–1985.

American Collector. New York, New York: Educational Publishing Corporation, 1933–1946.

Barnstable Patriot. 1830–1869.

Barnstable Patriot, The. 1869–1905, 1912–1916, 1918–1923

Bourne Pioneer, The. 1906–1907.

Brockton Searchlight, The. 1909.

Cape Cod Advocate, and Nautical Intelligencer. 1851–1864.

Cape Cod Gazette. 1870–1872.

Casino Bulletin. 1884–1885.

Chronicle of the Early American Industries Association, The. Flushing, New York: Leon S. Case, January 1938.

Crockery & Glass Journal. New York, New York: George Whittemore & Company, 1885–1890.

Crockery Journal. New York, New York: George Whittemore & Company, 1874–1884.

Glass Club Bulletin, The. The National Early American Glass Club, 1938–1985.

Hyannis Patriot, The. 1908–1909, 1916–1918, 1923–1925.

Independent, The. 1895–1908.

Sandwich Collector, The. East Sandwich, Massachusetts: McCue Publications, 1984–1985.

Sandwich Independent. 1920–1921.

Sandwich Independent, The. 1908–1909.

Sandwich Mechanic and Family Visitor. 1851.

Sandwich Observer. 1846–1851.

Sandwich Observer, The. 1884–1895, 1910–1911.

Sandwich Review, The. 1889–1890.

Seaside Press, The. 1873–1880.

Village Broadsider, The. 1978–1985.

Weekly Review, The. 1881–1882.

Yarmouth Register and Barnstable County Advertiser. 1836–1839.

Yarmouth Register and Barnstable County Weekly Advertiser. 1839–1846.

Yarmouth Register. 1849–1906.

INDEX

Bold type denotes pages with photographs and illustrations